Gone to Texas

Genealogical Abstracts from
The Telegraph and Texas Register
1835-1841

Compiled by
Kevin Ladd

HERITAGE BOOKS
2008

HERITAGE BOOKS
AN IMPRINT OF HERITAGE BOOKS, INC.

Books, CDs, and more—Worldwide

For our listing of thousands of titles see our website
at
www.HeritageBooks.com

Published 2008 by
HERITAGE BOOKS, INC.
Publishing Division
100 Railroad Ave. #104
Westminster, Maryland 21157

Copyright © 1994 Kevin Ladd

All rights reserved. No part of this book may be reproduced or transmitted in any form or by any means, electronic or mechanical, including photocopying, recording or by any information storage and retrieval system without written permission from the author, except for the inclusion of brief quotations in a review.

International Standard Book Numbers
Paperbound: 978-0-7884-0005-6
Clothbound: 978-0-7884-7724-9

This Volume
Dedicated to the Memory Of

JOHN V. CLAY
(1912 - 1986)

MISS JOYCE CALHOON
(1923 - 1982)

WILEY SMITH, JR.
(1924 - 1993)

Contents

Introduction..............................vii
Abstracts...................................1
Surname Index............................285
Place Index..............................315
Slave Name Index.........................321

INTRODUCTION

The Telegraph and Texas Register was born on October 10, 1835, in the midst of the developing Texas Revolution. It was the first Texas newspaper to achieve any measure of success and quickly became the official journal of the new Republic of Texas. Founded in San Felipe de Austin, its first editors were Gail Borden Jr., Thomas H. Borden, and Joseph Baker. The advance of Mexican soldiers under the command of Antonio Lopez de Santa Anna prompted the editors to flee after publication of their March 24, 1836 issue, and Baker left the firm to join the army. The editors next moved to Harrisburg in April, when it was seized by the Mexican forces. The printing press was tossed into Buffalo Bayou. Another press was obtained and publication was resumed at Columbia on August 2, 1836. So long as the government remained in Columbia, the Telegraph remained there as well. It moved to the new capital, Houston, in April 1837.

The newspaper changed owners, with Thomas H. Borden selling his interest to Francis Moore, Jr. on March 9, 1837. Gail Borden Jr. sold his interest to Jacob W. Cruger on June 9. Moore operated the editorial end, while Cruger took the financial management side of it. The paper operated under this format until 1851, at which time Cruger sold all of his interst to Moore.

The Telegraph eventually had any number of competitors, but no one quite challenged it as the national paper of the Republic of Texas.

The pages from which these genealogical abstracts have been gleaned are rife with error and mangled spellings. I have not attempted to correct such mistakes, save for a few instances where correct names are added in brackets.

Kevin Ladd, Director
Wallisville Heritage Park
P. O. Box 16
Wallisville TX 77597

Saturday, October 10, 1835
[Published at San Felipe de Austin]

Adv. dated Oct. 10 announces Wm. SIMPSON, a watch and clock maker, is located at San Felipe and will pursue above named business.

Saturday, October 17, 1835

A woman by name of McLELLAN and her children escaped from their Indian captors while they were sleeping. They report cruel treatment.

Monday, October 26, 1835

Died in this town on Sat. last, John JAMES.
Died on Sunday morning, Pedro SALINAS.

Saturday, November 7, 1835

The volunteer Grays from New Orleans arrived at Velasco on 25th ult. under direction of Edw. HALL. They have since elected officers: Capt. Robert L. MORRIS, 1st Lt. Wm. G. COOKE, 2nd Lt. Chas. R. BANNISTER, 1st Sgt. Nathaniel R. BRISTER, 2nd Sgt. H. S. SMITH, 3rd Sgt. Edw. WRENTMORE, Surgeon Albert M. LEVEY, and Commissary & Quartermaster Mandred WOOD.

Letter from Stephen F. AUSTIN, HQ, Mission Conception, dated Oct. 28: 300 Mexican Cavalry and 100 Infantry attacked at sunrise this morning a detachment of our Army under command of Col. James BOWIE and Capt. J. W. FANNIN. I regret to say one of our men, Richard ANDREWS of Mina, was seriously wounded and may die.

Stray horse came up to this plantation last spring. Will return to rightful owner if they apply to: Rebecca CUMMINGS, Cummings Creek, seven miles above San Felipe. Nov. 7 adv.

Saturday, November 14, 1835

D. C. COLLINSWORTH was killed by Indians 12 miles from Goliad while leading four or five of his men to Bejar. Others escaped. All of the men are from "Bay Prairie" and Nueces River and were commanded by Capt. P. B. DEMMIT.

Letter from New Orleans warns residents to be on guard against W. B. GRIFFIN, who has been purchasing goods in there and forging the signatures of Chas. S. LEE and Lewis F. NORRIS, two wealthy planters of Rodney, Miss. GRIFFIN is tall, slim, 5'10", 25 years old, dark comp.

Official acct. of action on 28th ult. at the Conception mission notes that forementioned Richard ANDREWS has died.

Miss McHENRY announces plans to open Montville Boarding School for Ladies on Feb. 1, '36 at residence of David AYERS, Montville.

Wednesday, November 21, 1835

A Mr. HOUSE from Spring Creek fell from his horse and broke his neck on 8th inst. during an engagement between Texas volunteers and Mexican soldiers. Engagement took place 30-40 miles beyond San Antonio.

Mr. and Mrs. TAYLOR's home on "Little river" was attacked on 1st inst. by party of Waco or Caddo Indians. Both husband and wife bravely fought off Indians, who slaughtered livestock.

Wednesday, December 2, 1835

Wm. J. HEARD is my agent during my absence from Texas. Thos. J. WINSTON, San Felipe.

Lt. Marcelino GARCIA killed during recent battle of Lepantitlan near San Patricio.

Will he hired at the store of the subscriber on 1st. day of Jan. next to the highest bidder, a Negro man belonging to Esther JACKSON, for 12 mos. on approved security. James COCHRANE, San Felipe, Nov. 28.

Will be sold at public auction on Dec. 10 at my store in San Felipe, about 100 head of cattle and league of land granted to Ignacio SARTUCHE. Sold as prop. of est. of Jose C. SARTUCHE. James COCHRANE, adm., Nov. 28.

Saturday, December 12, 1835

Jas. TYLEE not responsible for debts of his wife Matilda, who his bed and board on or about May 20th.

Saturday, December 26, 1835

Col. Benjamin R. MILAM, gallant leader of the storming party of Texas volunteers, fell at 3:30 on 3rd day of Siege of Bexar (Dec. 7). I have apptd. my bro-in-law James F. PERRY as my sole agent to attend to all my business during my absence from TX. S. F. AUSTIN.

Saturday, January 9, 1836

Appts. made by General Council in Legion of Cavalry: William B. TRAVIS, Lt. Col. W. P. MILLER, Major. Capts.: John N. SEGUIN, Robert WILSON, John H. FORSYTH, B. J. WHITE, Haden EDWARDS, & John YORK. 1st Lt's: Wm. G. HILL, Meriwether W. SMITH, Allen LARISON, Jonathon BURLESON, Placido BENAVIDES & Wm. BRACKEN. 2nd Lt's: Jos. E. SCOTT, Jas. B. BONHAM, John M. THRUSTON, Manuel CARVAJAL, Jas. DRAKE & John Bevil Jr. Cornetts: E. Y. Barbot, J. V. Morton, Prospect McKAY, W. O. LLEWELYN, John C. GOODRICH, & Darwin M. STAPP. Commissary general Thos. F. McKINNEY. Quarter Master Thos. R. JACKSON. Pay Master McHenry WINBURN.

Saturday, January 16, 1836

At meeting held on board schooner Santiago, which embarked from New Orleans to Brazoria on Dec. 9, 1835, we hereby declare that we have left our respective places of abode to relieve our oppressed brethern in Texas: Geo. P. DIGGES, New Orleans; J. M. WOLFE, Benton, Miss.; Edward B. WOOD, Versailles, Ky.; C. S. THROCKMORTON, Louisville, Ky.; Jos. CALLAGHAN, ditto; Dr. J. J. DAVIS, Quincy, Tenn.; Dr. S. B. DICKINSON, Fayette, Miss.; R. W. BALLENTINE, Alabama; W. A. ABERCROMBIE, Ga.; C. H. SIMMONS, Charleston, SC; J. N. MAXWELL, Ark.; Samuel WALLACE, Lexington, Va.; J. M. CHADWICK, Mo.; W. J. COWAN, Ga.; Amos KENYON, Miss.

Proclamation by Gov. Henry SMITH of Tx. calling for arrest of Jos. P. LOLLER, who severly beat Matthew CALDERELL of Gonzales on Dec. 9. LOLLER is ab. 25, 5'8", dark hair and eyes.

The Georgia Battalion, lately arrived in Texas, tenders its thanks to Col. J. W. FANNIN, for kindness and cordiality with which they have been greeted since arriving in Texas. Signed by Maj. Wm. WARD, Reg. Surg. Warren J. MITCHELL, Capt. W. A. O. WADSWORTH, Quartermaster David L. HOLT, Adj. Henderson COJART, Capt. James E. WYNN, and Capt. V. J. BULLOCK.
Henry JONES appt. adm. in Wm. STYLES succ.

Saturday, January 30, 1836

Abner DOWNING of "Cane Break" publishes open letter dated Jan. 22 to his cousin, Major Jack DOWNING, editor of Downingville (Maine) <u>Gazette</u> and informing him of conditions in Texas.
Thos. BARNETT named adm. of est. of John BROWN, dec., dated Jan. 30.

Saturday, February 20, 1836

Mr. WARD, one of the New Orleans Grays, who lost a leg in storming of Bexar, is now here.
We the undersigned prisoners of war are condemned to be shot on Monday, Dec. 14, 1835 at 7 p.m. in Tampico, Mexico. These men were found guilty by military tribunal for an attack upon Tampico on Nov. 15. Those named are: Arthur N. CLEMENT, 40, native of Penn, no parents; Thos. WHITAKER, 30, nat. of Penn., father in Penn.; Wm. C. BARCLAY, 20, native of NY, parents in NY; Jacob MORISON, 21, native of NY, parents in KY; Edward MOUNT, 23, native of NY, mother in NY; Chas. GROSS, 23, native of Penn., mother in Penn.; Isaac E. LEEDS, 30, native of NJ, no parents; Mordecai GIST, 53, native of MD, father in MD, his own last res. in Indiana; David LONG, 25, native of Ohio, mother in Ohio; Jonas STUART, 33, native of VT, mother in VT; Wm. H. MACKAY, 20, native of VA, mother in VA; Daniel HOLT, 18, native of Canada, parents in Canada; James CRAMP, 22, native of Eng., parents in Lake Oswego, NY; Lewis JACOBS, 21, native of Eng., mother in Lower Canada; Thos. H. ROGERS, 23, native of Ireland, parents in Ireland; Daniel DONNELLY, 20, native of Eng., parents in

St. John's, N. B.; James FARRELL, 25, native of Ireland, father in Greene Co., N.Y.; John M. IVES, 35, native of England, no parents, 2 brothers in New Orleans; August SAINT CYR, 22, native of France, parents in France; Auguste DEMOUSSENT, 25, native of and parents in France; Fred. DELBOY, 24, native of and parents in Dantzie; Fred. Wm. MAUER, 22, native of Germany, parents in Saxony; Henry WAGNER, 24, native of Germany, no parents, last res. in Philadelphia; John IVISH, 24, native of Germany, no parents; Andreas HELM, 50, native of Germ., no parents; George J. SELIN, 27, native of Germany, father in Germany; Wm. H. MORRIS, 28, native of New Providence, no parents; L. M. BELLEPONT, 26, native of Hanover, no parents. Three prisoners died in the hospital, viz: FLEMING, aged about 25, native of Pittsburg, PA; Harris BLOOD, 40, native of England; and James McCORMICK, 30, a native of Kentucky.

Saturday, February 27, 1836

Elizabeth HEADY named adm. of est. of Samuel HEADY, San Felipe, February 23.

Saturday, March 12, 1836

John P. HOIT named adm. of Saml. HOIT est., thereby annulling powers granted unto J. W. E. WALLACE. Hoit names Seth INGRAM as his agent during his absence from state, dated Feb. 26.

Thursday, March 24, 1836

The following named men fell on March 6, at the battle of the Alamo: Colonels W. B. TRAVIS (commandant), James BOWIE, and David CROCKETT, of Tenn.; Capt's. FORSYTH & HARRISON of Tenn., Wm. BLAZEBY (of N.O. Grays), BAKER (Miss. volunteers), EVANS & CAREY (TX militia), S. C. BLAIR (vol. militia); Lt's. John JONES (N.O. Grays), J. G. Baugh (of N.O.); Robert EVANS (mast. ord., Ireland), WILLIAMSON (sgt. major), Dr. MICHISON & Dr. POLLARD (surgeons), Dr.

THOMPSON (Tenn.), Chas. DESPALIER, Eliel MELTON (qtr. master), ANDERSON (asst. QM), and BURNELL (asst. QM); Privates: NELSON, NELSON (clerk of Austin), Wm. SMITH (Nacogdoches), Lewis ----? (Trinity), E. P. MITCHELL (GA.), F. DESANQUE (Philadelphia), John (a clerk in Desanque's store), THURSTON, MOORE, Christopher PARKER (Natchez), HEISKELL, ROSE (Nacogdoches), BLAIR, David WILSON, John M. HAYS (Tenn.), STUART, SIMPSON, W. D. SUTHERLAND (Navidad, Texas), Dr. HOWELL (N.O.), BUTLER, Chas. SMITH, McGREGOR (Scotland), RUSK, HAWKINS (Ireland), HOLLOWAY, BROWNE, SMITH, BROWNE (Philadephia), KEDESON, Wm. WELLS (Tenn.), Wm. CUMMINGS (Penn.), VOLUNTINE, COCKRUN, R. W. VALENTINE, S. HOLLOWAY, Isaac WHITE, DAY, Robt. MUSELMAN (N.O.), Robt. CROSSMAN (N.O.), Richard STARR (England), J. G. GANETT (N.O.), Jas. DINKIN (England), Robt. B. MOORE (N.O.), Wm. LINN (Boston), HUTCHINSON, Wm. JOHNSON (Philadelphia), NELSON (Charleston, SC), Geo. TUMLINSON, Wm. DEARDUFF, Daniel BOURNE (England), INGRAM (England), LEWIS (Wales), Chas. ZANCO, Jas. EWING, Robt. CUNNINGHAM, BURNS (Ireland), Geo. NEGGAN, Maj. G. B. JAMIESON, Col. J. B. BONHAM (Ala.), Capt. WHITE, ROBINSON (Scotland), SEWELL (shoemaker), HARRIS (Ky.), DEVAULT (plasterer, Mo.), Jonathon LINDLEY (Ill.), Tapley HOLLAND, DEWELL (blacksmith, NY), James KINNEY, CANE, WARNER, John GARVIN (Mo.), WORNEL, ROBBINS (Ky.), John FLANDERS, Isaac RYAN (Opelousas), JACKSON (Ireland). The following men were from Gonzales: Capt. A. DICKINSON, Geo. C. KIMBALL, Jas. GEORGE, Dolphin FLOYD, Thos. JACKSON, Jacob DURST, Geo. W. COTTLE, Andrew KENT, Thos. R. MILLER, Isaac BAKER, Wm. KING, Jesse McCOY, Claiborn WRIGHT, Wm. FISHBACK, MILLSAP, Galby FUGUN, John DAVIS, and Albert MARTIN. "Our dead were denied the right of Christian burial; being stripped and thrown into a pile and burned. Would that we could gather up their ashes and place in urns?"

NOTE: At this point publication in interrupted and the paper eventually relocates in Columbia.

Tuesday, August 2, 1836 [Columbia, TX]

Letter from New Haven, CT, Apr. 28, 1836: "I had a brother by the name of Wm. D. LEWIS, who was in in San Antonio on the 2d of last May, nearly a year ago, since which time I have not had a line or heard any thing from him. . . Yesterday, we beheld the name of LEWIS among the murdered ones at San Antonio. The first name was not mentioned; only "Lewis, of Wales. My brother was a Philadelphia, but his father was from Wales; he was nearly six feet high, his complexion ruddy, and he was 24 years of age." Signed CORNELIA VANCLEVE BARNES. Please direct any info. to Mrs. Daniel Barnes, New Haven, Conn.

Tuesday, August 9, 1836

Info. sought on Wm. HEMPHILL, 19, who landed at mouth of Brazos on Jan. 3 in a vessel from New Orleans and in company of several men from Kentucky, all of whom were passengers on steamboat Madison. Please send info to: John HEMPHILL, Philadelphia; SLOO & BYRNE, New Orleans; or Wm. M. WALKER, Cincinnati, Ohio. Bill this adv. to the New Orleans <u>Bulletin</u>.

Edmund ANDREWS named adm. to succ. of Theodore LENTNER, Brazoria, July 23.

The 14 prisoners listed below were tried at Matamoros, Mexico and sentenced to die Apr. 20. FERNANDEZ, the Mexican commander there, has delayed their execution and will accept $30,000 for their ransom. They are: Thos. S. MITCHELL, 24, born in Caswell, Milton Co., NC; S. S. CURTIS, 23, born in Madison Co., NY; S. W. McKINLEY, 17, born in Jacksontown, East Feliciana, La.; Lewis H. KERR, 33, born in Pa.; P. S. MAHAN, 22, born in Philadelphia; Reuben R. BROWN, 25, born in Greene Co., Ga.; James WILSON, 23, born at corner of Spring & Sullivan streets, New York; Wm. B. BENSON, 20, born in Cincinnati, Ohio; Sebastian FRANCIS, 20, native of France; Geo. COPELAND, 16, born in Philadelphia; Wm. LAUGHEEN, 20, born in Germany; W. HALL, 24, born in England; and Hutchings M. PITTMAN, 26, born in Wilson, Tenn., son of Wm.

Tuesday, August 16, 1836

Died at Velasco, on the 10th inst., Lieut. STOUFFER, Texian Army, of Baltimore, and one of the heroes of San Jacinto.

Died, Mrs. BALLOU, at Brazoria.

Married, Major D. J. WOODLIEF, Texian Army, to Miss Harriet J. REYNOLDS of Brazoria.

For Sale. A negro woman, age 22, first rate cook, washer, ironer, and good house servant, also a good hand in the field; has been in this country 10-12 years. She would not be parted with but her owner is going to the U.S. for his health. Apply to Mrs. FEARIS at Columbia.

Tuesday, August 23, 1836

Died at Brazoria last week, Dr. Ira JONES.

Died, Isaac JAQUES, on 6th ult., of Lynchburg, whose family is expected to arrive shortly from the United States.

Died July 1st, while on his way to the army, Jacob A. LAURTON, 42, a printer, of Capt. GRAHAM's company of New Orleans Volunteers; originally from Baltimore, but has resided in New Orleans for many years.

On Capt. SPLANE's planation, a Negro boy by name of NELSON, aged 18, on the 15th inst. picked 155 lbs. of cotton in one day's time.

Tuesday, August 30, 1836

Married, John BEGLEY to Miss Eliza NEWMAN, both of Colorado.

Married, at Velasco, John M. SHREVE to Miss Sarah BAILEY, both of that place.

Died at Columbia, Thursday, 25th inst., James L. THACKSTER, a baker and native of Eng.

Died at Nacogdoches on 1st inst., Wm. FITZMORRIS, of England.

Died at "LaBaca," on July 10, Augustus QUIGLEY, OF Capt. Graham's co., New Orleans Volunteers, a native of Washington, D. C.

Samuel KEESECKER, a volunteer, was shot here on 25th inst., but is likely to recover.

Tuesday, September 6, 1836

Born to Mrs. Erastus SMITH, a son, Aug. 31.
Died in this place on Friday evening last, Capt. LOGAN, one of the heroes of San Jacinto, formerly of Mississippi.
List of Mexican officers killed on April 21, at the battle of San Jacinto: Gen. Manuel CASTRILLON; Colonels Jose BATRES, Antonio TREVINO, Augustin PERALTA, Jose ARENAS, & Esteban MORA; Lt. Col's. Mariel AGUIRRE, Dionosio COS, Santiago LUELMO, Carile LARUMBO, Manuel VALDEZ, Mariano OLAZARAN, Francisco AGUADO, Miguel VELASQUEZ; Captains Nestor GUZMAN, Benito RODRIGUEZ, Ygnacio BERRA, Ramon HERRARA, Alonzo GONZALES, Antonio FRIAS, Juan MONJARRA, Ramon ROCHA; Lts. Jose Ma PUELLES, Luis VALLEJO, Trinidad SANTIESTABAN, Juan SANTA CRUZ, Pedro GONZALES ("We understand that this individual is still in existence at La Bahia, as a prisoner of war.") Antonio CASTRO, Jose SOUZA, Ygnacio BRASAIL, Antonio NAVARRO, Francisco MOLINA; Sub. Lts. Joaquim PERALTA, Basilio ESPINO, Juan MONTANA, Jose Maria TORRICES, Victoriano MARTINEZ and Secundio ROSAS. Total 38 officers. The names of several Sgts. were omitted, not being known.

Tuesday, September 13, 1836

Died at Quintana, 5th inst., Capt. William SERGEANT, of the steamboat Yellow Stone.
Died, at [David Levi] KOKERNOT's on San Jacinto Bay, 11th ult., Col. Edward HARCOURT, of Texian Army and native of Germany, who commanded the Artillery of the Zacatecas when Santa Anna invaded Texas-Coahuila.
At Coleto, 18th ult., Erasha DANIEL, of Wayne Co., Tenn., and a vol. in Capt. REED's Co., Gen. GREEN's Brigade.
Died at Velasco, 31st ult., L. T. PEASE of Connecticut.
Died at Velasco, 22d ult., Dr. Johnson HOLCOMB, of Lambertville, or Allentown, N. J.
Died at Columbia, 10th inst., Geo. HAMILTON, printer and vol., with friends in west. Penn.
Died on 17th ult., Alexander HODGE, aged 70.

Tuesday, September 20, 1836

Died at Columbia, on 15th inst., Mrs. T. H. BORDEN.
Died, at Nacogdoches, on 12th ult., Don Francisco ROXO.
Died at Nacogdoches, on 18th ult., Don Juan Angel SEGUIN.
Wm. G. HILL named adm. of est. of Zeno PHILLIPS, decd., Columbia, Sept. 19.
W. SCOTT named adm. of est. of Jas. BRADLEY by Judge of Harrisburg Jurisdiction: when SCOTT applied to owner of home where BRADLEY died for his possessions, he was told 2 men from the Brazos had already appeared. They had shown authorization from President David G. BURNET and had taken possession of BRADLEY's estate. SCOTT serves notice that he will be pursuing the case through the courts.
"The Subscriber having been appointed adm. of the est. of James BRADLEY, dec., hereby notifies all persons indebted to said est. to make payment, and all those having claims against said est., will present the same within the time prescribed by law. Alex. RUSSELL, Adm'r." Brazoria, Sept. 16.
For sale. A likely negro fellow, 20 years of age of unique good character. E. M. CHAMBERS, Columbia, Sept. 19.

Tuesday, September 27, 1836

A GROGGY MARRIAGE. At Towanda, Penn., Mr. Junius WATERS, 16, and Mrs. Rosina WHISKEY, 84. The very best recipe for grog---fresh water and old whiskey.---Petersburg <u>Constellation</u>.
Died in Gen. GREEN's Brigade, Army of Texas, on Sept. 11, W. FITSHUGH, surgeon dentist and vol., from Prince William's Co., Va., a young man of promising talents.
Died on Aug. 26 at Quintana, Thos. PARAMORE, of Washington Co., NC.
Died Friday, 28th, at Orozimbo, Joshua BARSTOW, native of Boston and hero of San Jacinto.

"TO THE PUBLIC. I observed in the last 'Telegraph" a notice signed by Mr. Wm. SCOTT, describing himself as adm. of the est. of James BRADLEY, dec., containing a threat 'so soon as there are courts in which redress can be had for such lawless proceedings, to proceed forthwith against all persons who have meddled with the est.' Jas. BRADLEY, lately of Columbia, died while attached to the army, in a 'tent' at Harrisburg, about the 15th May, 1836. Knowing that BRADLEY neither had heirs or relations in this country. . .I applied to the judge, in and for the district of Brazos, for authority to collect and administer the effects of the decd. It was in executing the order granted, that the two persons from the Brazos, Capt. R. J. CALDER (sheriff of the dist.) and myself took possession of the effects of the deceased. David G. BURNET had nothing to do with the matter directly or indirectly. . ." Alexander RUSSELL, Adm'r of James BRADLEY, decd.

Died on 1st inst. at Victoria, John MATCHITT (native of England), New York city papers please copy.

Died here yesterday, John CLARK, late of Baltimore, Maryland.

A stout, full-made negro man, of medium age, calling himself John VOSE, has been passing as a free man in New Orleans for the past 3 years, and is now in prison on charge of talking a boy into running away from his owner, a Mr. WALKER. VOSE has a woman with him by name of Rebecca ELLIS, who says his real name is Sawney THOMPSON and that he formerly belonged to Nicholas ELLIS of Hopkinsville, Ky. and was sold by ELLIS to a gentlman named SMEDIE, who lives near or with a Mr. SMELSER on the Brazos River.

Tuesday, October 4, 1836

Died at Velasco on Sept. 23, at 2 a.m., of the whooping cough, Jacob George, infant son of his Excellency David G. BURNET, President of this Republic.

On the 21st ult., as Leander and Collin BEASON and Maxwell STEEL were searching for runaway slaves belonging to the Beason's, they were attacked by a party of Indians, possibly Caddo. The attack took place while they were crossing the Guadalupe River just below Gonzales. The men were compelled to abandon their horses and save themselves by swimming to the opposite side. Leander BEASON survived. Body of Collin BEASON has been found. STEEL has not been found, but is presumed to be dead.

Tuesday, October 11, 1836

Died on Caney Creek, of congestive fever, the Hon. Bailey HARDEMAN, late Secy. of Treasury, leaving a wife and three children.

Died at Columbia, of congestive fever, Mary Elizabeth, age 9, dtr. of Lewis AYRES.

Died on Monday night, 19th ult., at Camp Johnson near Dimmit's Landing on the "La Bacca" River, Wm. H. BOOMER, a member of the Zavala Volunteers, under command of Lt. W. B. SMITH. Mobile, N. O. and Phila. papers please copy.

Mansen McCORMICK named adm. of est. of late David McCORMICK.

J. M. LYONS named adm. of est. of Jas. WEST, decd., Brazoria, October 5.

Tuesday, October 18, 1836

Died on the Brazos on 8th inst., William R. ROYALL, of Virginia.

Died at Camp LaBacca on Thursday, Sept. 6, John WILLIAMS of Nashville, Tenn.

Died on Sept. 26, at residence of Geo. HUFF, Don Gaspar FLORES, 55, the former commandant of Austin's colony and citizen of San Antonio.

H. L. COOK named adm. of est. of Jas. COOK.

Thos. BARNETT named adm. of est. of John DZSANSKI, decd., San Felipe, Sept. 21.

I hereby authorize my wife, Martha STAFFORD, as my lawful agent and attorney to take possession of all my property in Texas and transact business thereupon concerning. Wm. STAFFORD, Orleans, September 27.

Tuesday, October 25, 1836

Died at Velasco on Sept. 27, John Duncan SOMERVILLE, a member of Capt. ELLIOTT's company and late of New Orleans.
Died, Henry HARCOURT, colonel in chief of engineers, Army of Texas, at KOKERNOT's grove, San Jacinto Bay, on Aug. 11, native of Prussia.
Died in this place on 19th inst., Charlotte Sophia AYRES, 3 years, dtr. of David AYRES.
Died on 22nd, Thos. TODD, formerly of Phila.
Died at Lynchburg on Wed., Oct. 19, Mary TIFFIN, dtr. of late gov. of Ohio, WORTHINGTON, and consort of Col. David B. MACOMB of TX army.
Died at Camp Johnson on LaBacca River on 3rd inst., Robt. J. FRIEND, native of Williamsport, Md., in 37th year of his age.
Notice. J. S. D. BYROM, agent and atty. in fact for heirs of Jos. H. HAWKINS, decd., has been informed "that there are certain persons settling on and commiting waste on the lands of the heirs." Legal proceedings will be started if they do not leave. Brazoria, Oct. 8.
Robt. SCOBEY named adm. of est of Jesse STROTHER, decd., Bailey's Prairie, Oct. 20.

Tuesday, November 2, 1836

Married on 25th inst., John SHARPE of Brazoria to Miss Sarah J. W. CALVIT.
Died on 1st inst. at Velasco, Wm. L. SARGENT of Texian Army, son of Dr. SARGENT of Phila. His remains were interred at burial ground at Velasco with the honors of war by Capt. SNELL's company and attracted a large crowd.
James MURPHY named adm. of est. of Thomas TODD, decd., at Columbia, Oct. 23.

Tuesday, November 9, 1836

Among those under the command of Col. FANNIN and massacred at Goliad: In Capt. DUVALL's Co.: Pvts. John G. DUVAL, John HOLLIDAY, ----- SHARPE, C. B. SHAINE, John VAN BIBBER; from Capt. PETTUS' Co. "San Antonio Grays": Sgt. Wm. L. HUNTER, and Pvts. ---- HOLLAND, David J. JONES, Wm. BRENAN, John REESE, Milton IRISH; from Capt. BULLOCK's Co.: 1st Sgt. F. M. HUNT, 3rd Corp. S. T. BROWN; from Capt. WADSWORTH's Co.: 3rd Sgt. Saml. WALLACE; from Capt. BURKE's Co.: Pvts. Thos. KEMP, Herman EHRENBERG, and N. J. DWENNY; from Capt. Jack SHACKLEFORD's Co.: Z. S. BROOKS and D. COOPER; from Capt. HORTON's Co.: Daniel MARTINDALE, Wm. HADDON, and Chas. SMITH; others with FANNIN included: Nat. HAZEN, Wm. MURPHY, and John WILLIAMS.

Married last evening by Judge B. C. FRANKLIN were Col. J. EBERLY & Mrs. A. B. AEYTON, both of this town.

Married on 18th Oct., John F. MARTIN to Miss Caroline HADLEY, both of Washington Co., TX.

Died here on Oct. 26, John H. SCAGGS.

Died at Camp Johnson, Oct. 6th, John S. WILLIAMS, vol. in Texian Army, late of Nashville. His heirs will be entitled to 1476 acres.

Died in this place on 26th ult., Delia Caroline AYRES, dtr. of Lewis AYRES, aged 5 mos.

Died Sept. 16 at Dimmit's Landing on the Labacca, Blueford GARRETT of Spencer Co., Ky., a private in co. of Capt. James P. PRICE.

Shot near Camp Johnson on 4th inst., Elijah L. GARRETT, in the act of preventing a rencounter, belonging to same company as above.

Drowned on 5th inst., in crossing the Brazos at Point Bolivar, David L. FORD, of Oxford Co., Upper Canada.

L. KELCEY named adm. of est. of Dr. Amos POLLARD, decd. Notice of public sale on 20th inst. in town of Columbia, a house and lot now occupied by Mrs. FARNES and belonging to est.

Hiram THOMPSON named exr. of est. of Jesse THORN, San Felipe de Austin, Oct. 22.

For rent until Jan. 1, 1838, the well known stand our house of entertainment on Colorado River formerly occupied by late Robert J. MOSELY, including 60 acres under fence and comfortable dwellings; for particulars, apply to Robt. STEVENSON at Cole's settlement.
$30 Reward. Deserted from this infantry co. on morning of 7th inst., Pierre QUELIN, Frenchman, age 18, small in stature, 5'3", dark complexion, dark brown hair, black eyes. Signed Capt. R. B. IRVINE, 1st Inf. Regt., Texas Army, Columbia, Nov. 7.
Walter C. WHITE named adm. for estates of Jas. THAXTER and Pelatiah W. GORDON, deceased, Columbia, Nov. 1.

Wednesday, November 16, 1836

Wm. ECKEL named adm. of est of Ephraim ANDERSON, Brazoria, Nov. 6.
Select Committee of TX House of Rep. recommends against a $500 donation for relief for Mrs. Susannah DICKINSON and her child by late Lt. DICKINSON who fell at the Alamo, Nov. 7.

Saturday, November 19, 1836

Married at Matagorda, Wed. evening, Nov. 6, Lewis GOODWIN and Miss Ellen HARRIS, both of that place.
C. CAMPBELL named adm. of est. of John H. SCAGGS, decd., Nov. 16.

Wednesday, November 23, 1836

Rep. BUNTON presents a pet. to House of Rep. on Nov. 11 from Capt. Wm. OLDHAM, adm. of James BOWIE estate for claims.
Jas. MURPHY named adm. of Hugh FRAZIER est., Columbia, Nov. 2.

Saturday, November 26, 1836

Claims from Capt. OLDHAM on Jas. BOWIE est. are sent to committee for an audit.

Col. Lorenzo DE ZAVALA, our distinguished and talented fellow citizen, died on 15th inst. at his residence on San Jacinto Bay.

Married last evening, Mr. McDERMITT to Mrs. THAXTER, both of this place.

Died here sometime in Sept., John W. MOORE, a native of Tennessee.

Died Oct. 21, at residence of Col. W. D. C. HALL, Geo. W. PEEK, native of Ga., formerly of Montgomery Co., Ala., and hero of San Jacinto.

Died here 24th inst., John James OGSBURY, a native of New York City.

Died at Camp Johnson on 20th ult., Charles MURHARD, 25, native of Hesse in Germany, member of Capt. FRAILEY's co. of Baltimore Texian Guards.

Notice. Will be hired to highest bidder in San Felipe on Jan. 1st, the negro man JIM, belonging to Esther JACKSON, for term of 12 mos. James COCHRAN, Guardian.

Tuesday, November 30, 1836

Wm. J. EATON of this town was walking in dark on night of 28th, fell and struck his chest against a stump, which caused his death eight hours later.

I offer for sale my place on the Colorado River, known as Cayce's ferry, too well known to require description, as it is on the great national road. Terms: cash and ready money. Apply to Thos. CAYCE.

To rent. My farm on Caney Creek, consisting of 40 acres cleared land, under good cultivation and good fence, and all necessary bldgs. attached to it. For terms, apply to prop. now living in Matagorda. Thos. M. DUKE, Nov. 25.

Tuesday, December 6, 1836

Married Thursday, 1st inst., at res. of Dan. ELAM, A. B. FLEURY and Miss Louisa HANNUM.

Thos. DAVIS named adm. of Henry BURT est., Marion, Dec. 5.

Friday, December 9, 1836

Our valued friend and citizen Deaf SMITH has left this place on the 6th for the west and may likely settle in San Antonio de Bexar.

Tuesday, December 13, 1836

Joint Resolution adopted by House & Senate, Dec. 9, calling for president to issue scrip to amount of 500,000 acres of land to Thos. TOBY of New Orleans for his service to Texas.
Died on 20th ult., at Groce's Retreat, Col. Jared E. GROCE, 53, one of the first pioneers of Texas, having emigrated here in 1822.
Wm. ECKEL named adm. of Dr. Jesse COUNSEL est., Brazoria, Dec. 10.
J. H. CARTWRIGHT and I. M. PENNINGTON named adm's. of late Wm. McFARLAND, Columbia.
C. B. STEWART, adm. of S. YOUNG est., plans estate sale at Brazoria on 2nd Monday in Jan.; also announces public sale of lands a Columbia on 1st Monday in Feb. for lands from estates of J. WHITE & Zeno PHILLIPS, Columbia, Dec. 8.
Mrs. Ann D. W. SPLANE plans to est. a Female Academy on Chocolate Bayou, Brazoria Co., at late res. of Wm. HARRIS.
Report from Zanesville, Ohio *Courier* dated Oct. 15 says comp. of Texas emigrants raised at Zanesville by Col. Geo. H. BURROUGH together with Col. COLERICK's co. of Mt. Vernon embarked for Texas on Monday last.

Saturday, December 17, 1836

Died Nov. 29, on Lake Creek settlement, Ann Rebecca, 1, youngest dtr. of Wm. & Ann MOCK.
Ellen CASH named adm. of Geo. W. CASH est., Brazoria.

Thursday, December 22, 1836

I. C. HOSKINS named adm. of Wm. S. BROWN estate by Hon. B. C. FRANKLIN.

Depositions dated Dec. 3, 1836 and signed by several soldiers in the Texian Army at Camp Johnson on the "LaBacca." These include James WHITE, Elisha J. W. LORORY, Chas. S. ALEXANDER, Jas. H. ASHBY, David H. WAGGONER, and Matthew KELLEY, stating that they were members of Col. E. J. WILSON's expedition from KY. and were present in Col WILSON's tent when Capt. G. L. POSTLEWAITE returned from Velasco and proposed plundering Texas. They were stationed at Galveston at time, and POSTLEWAITE offered them $500 to join. Other names listed in a similar document are: Lt. J. W. MURRAY, Archibald DUNLAP, Jas. ROSE, Thos. ALLEN, Chas. S. BROWN and G. S. SMITH. The depositions refer to WILSON's expedition as "The Ladies Legion."

Francis J. HASKINS named adm. of estates of Robt. W. P. CARTER and Samuel MAY, Velasco.

Friday, December 30, 1836

We perform a most painful duty in reporting that Gen. Stephen F. AUSTIN departed this life on 27th inst at 12:30 p.m. at home of Judge McKINSTRY. His remains left Columbia at 9 a.m. yesterday and were conveyed to the landing and placed on board the steamboat Yellow Stone. He was buried at Peach Point with full honors.

Died on 26th inst., Zillah, dtr. of Arthur BACON, aged 20 years and 6 months.

C. B. STEWART named adm. of Saml. YOUNG est. in Brazoria County.

We are just informed that Mr. HERVEY, his wife and son, of Robertson's Colony, were found dead and scalped at their home 25 miles above Tenoxtitlan on east side of Brazos. Their 8 or 9 year old dtr., and negro girl are missing.

Letter from Sam HOUSTON, signed Dec. 13 at Columbia, recommends highly Judge John WOODWARD of New York, lately arrived in this country and planning to bring emigrants here shortly.

Tuesday, January 3, 1837

C. B. STEWART, adm. for Jos. WHITE est., is offering for sale at Feb. 1 public auction a quarter of a league on west side of San Bernard River, being upper quarter of a league granted to late WHITE. Will also offer for sale a lot and 2 houses belonging to Saml. YOUNG est., Brazoria, Dec. 24.

Res. of respect adopted by officers of the Army of Texas at Camp Johnson, La Baca River, on Dec. 15, 1836, noting the death of Major James L. HOLMES of KY. Volunteers, who "yesterday we consigned to the grave."

Friday, January 6, 1837

Married on Tues. last in Brazoria, R. J. CALDER to Miss Mary W. DOUGLASS.

Wednesday, January 11, 1837

Notice. I have seen in your Nov. 16th paper remarks by Wm. H. WHARTON in the Senate in which he claims my family was not represented in the late revolution. My son Moses A. BRYAN and Mr. John W. HASSEL were both active in the battle of San Jacinto as private soldiers. My son Wm. J. BRYAN returned from the Army whilst on its retreat from the Colorado. I took four Negro men to Galveston Island and assisted in fortifying the Island. James F. PERRY, Peach Point, December 10.

Married 3rd inst., Davis D. BAKER to Miss Mary Ann CAYCE, both of Matagorda.

Died at Quintana on Dec. 16, Wm. M. CATS of Alabama.

Died on 27th ult., Nathaniel HAZEN at this place, who fought with Col. Fannin and was marched out on 27th of the same to be shot, but survived to fight at San Jacinto.

Died at Columbia on 8th inst., A. LESASSIER of New Orleans; dec. was Texas Army volunteer, a hero of Bexar and San Jacinto and buried with full military honors.

Wednesday, January 18, 1837

Brazoria County probate court announces that following individuals are seeking letters of adm. for following estates: John CHAFFIN, for S. M. HALE; Wm. T. AUSTIN, for A. G. REYNOLDS; Nathaniel TOWNSEND, for Wm. ATTWELL; Amanda BOSTWICK (widow of late Wm. H. EATON) and W. H. SECREST, for Wm. H. EATON est.; A. UNDERWOOD, for Robt. COCHRAN and Henry J. HOWELL estates; show cause hearings for these cases set at Courthouse in Brazoria for Monday, 23rd inst.

Married on 29th ult., John PETTUS and Sarah YORK, both of Austin County.

Wm. W. THOMPSON selling ¼ league of land on est bank of Colorado a few miles above Attuscacito or Alley's crossing, sd. land being upper part of league granted to Jas. TUMLINSON in 1824, Columbia, Jan. 17.

Saturday, January 21, 1837

Maj. Wm. HEMPHILL, from Alabama, who emigrated to the this country last spring with his family, was accidentally shot on 12th inst. with his own pistol when it fell from his belt and discharged. At time of his death, he was on his way to Milam's Colony on west side of Colorado.

Married on 16th inst., Col. E. G. HEAD and Miss Harriet HUNTER.

Pres. Sam HOUSTON has directed Col. John N. SEGUIN to San Antonio for collection and interment of the "ashes and bones" of the immortal heroes who fell at the Alamo.

Express from the corps of rangers of Robertson's Colony has just arrived and informs that a skirmish between a body of 100 Indians and 14 rangers took place on 7th inst., in which two of our men, David CLARK and Francis CHILDRESS, were killed. The company had to retreat before the overwhelming forces.

Friday, January 27, 1837

Md. Sunday evening last, in this town, John BUCHANAN, chief clerk of Navy Dept., to Miss Emily BURNS.
Md. 15th inst., Fort Bend, Gustavus A. PARKER to Mrs. Susan RANDON.
Md. yest. evening, John G. WELSCHMEYER, the secy. of Texas RR, Navigation & Banking Co., to Mary ANDREWS, widow of late R. ANDREWS, who was killed at battle of Conception.

Friday, February 3, 1837

Md., 19th ult., Wm. FREAM to Miss Eunice W. WOODWARD, both of Matagorda County.
Md. 18th ult., Thos. J. ALLCORN to Miss Emma CAPLES.
Md. 11th ult., Joseph FESSENDEN to Miss Mary BOWLS.
Md. 26th ult., John PICKETT to Miss Mary ROBERTS, both of this county.
Died at res. of Col. W. G. HILL on 2nd inst. Stephen F. AUSTIN, 8 year old son of James B. AUSTIN, decd.
Died in this place on 2nd inst., Christopher, son of Widow JACKSON, aged 3 years.
Died on 20th ult. on Caney, Daniel DECKROE, a native of Maine.

Friday, February 10, 1837

Undersigned passengers have left Velasco on board the schooner Julius Caesar bound for New Orleans. Most of them are volunteers from the U.S. who have completed their tours in the army of Texas: Wm. BRATTON, W. F. HUBBARD, C. LUDWICK, Isaac TINDALL, Saml. CAVETT, John H. YERBY, H. COPENDOLPHER, J. H. ASHBAUGH, J. M. ALEXANDER, Joel HUTCHINSON, John GALLARICK, W. B. CUNNINGHAM, D. H. WEIGART, W. C. RAMY, V. CARR, John CASH, I. D. WATKINS, C. B. McUNE, Rich. BURKITT, Abijah I. McGEE, James F. WHITE, W. C. COCHRAN, Jas. CAPAL, Wm. W. NICHOLLS, N. MURPHREA, B. M. HAWKINS, C. G. FERMID, Francis

FRO, Henry SMOCK, Thos. CURTIS, Robt. STEWART, Henry BOONE, A. VAUGHAN, and C. H. RIDDLE.
We have lately received a group of Mexican newspapers dated up to Dec. 7, one of which includes an obituary published by order of French embassy that Eugene ROBERTSON died in Mexico City. Cause of his death is not known.

Tuesday, February 14, 1837

Hiram GRIGGS named adm. of John GORDON est., Brazoria, February 3.

Tuesday, February 21, 1837

Col. John T. COLLINSWORTH, about 27, died at Camp Independence on 29th ult.; dec. served as Inspector Gen. of Army of TX; entered West Point as a cadet from Tenn. in June 1826; and served in U.S. Army until 1836, when he emigrated to Texas.

Following individuals are seeking letters of adm. from Brazoria Co. Probate Ct. in following estates: Abner HARRIS, for Wm. HARRIS est.; Jos. FESSENDEN, for Benj. BOWLES; Henry AUSTIN, for Green B. JAMIESON; Edmund ANDREWS, for Wm. CATE. Show cause hearings set for Feb. 27.

"This is to inform my brother and relations that I am at present settled in town of Liberty on the Trinity river, at which place I intend to remain two to three months. Should they see this, I wish to hear from them." February 20, Thos. J. JORDAN.

W. C. JENKS has established a school for the instruction of youths at Columbia; during the past 15 years has been employed as superintendent of some large schools in the north that follow the Lancasterian model.

Tuesday, March 7, 1837

Jesse BARTLETT named adm. of Joshua G. SNELL est., New Years Creek, Washington Co., Feb. 15.

Notice. This is to forewarn all persons from trading for one treasury draft No. 2115 in amount of $234.60 drawn in favor of B. F. MIMS, and believed to have been taken from a trunk in the residence of Jos. MIMS on or about Jan. 15. I suspect a man by name of DOUGLASS who was employed at that time making clothes for Negroes. DOUGLASS is of fair complexion, 5'6" or 5'7", light hair, well-made, 140 lbs., large grey eyes, and has an eagle printed on his left arm, put on with India ink. He is believed to be headed for Matagorda. B. F. MIMS.

Resignation. "Lt. Owen H. STOUT begs leave to inform his fellow citizens that having been for some time chin deep in authority, as a officer of the Patrol Guard, he wishes now without any longer jaw upon the subject, to resign. Columbia, March 5th, 1837."

Tuesday, March 28, 1837

Col. Juan SEGUIN paid final honors of war to the remains of the Alamo heroes; ashes were found in three separate places, after which the remains were collected and placed in a single black coffin; names of TRAVIS, CROCKETT and BOWIE were inscribed on the inside lid; a procession began at 3 o'clock on Feb. 25 at parish church, marched to the Alamo for final ceremonies, with the procession stopping at each of the three spots where ashes were found.

Wm. OLDHAM, adm. for James BOWIE, notifies all persons with claims to present them to said est., Washington, March 10.

A. BRIGHAM named adm. of Edward ROBERTSON, Brazoria Co., April 24.

If Wm. TAYLOR of Henry Co., Tenn., is living in Texas, he will find a communication left for him with Messrs. WHITE & KNIGHT, in Marion, signed by J. B. LYNCH.

Notice. Sale set for Sat., April 8, at home of A. E. WESTALL in Gulf Prairie for 200 head of cattle belonging to est. of Thos. & Sarah WESTALL, decd. James F. PERRY, adm. Peach Point, March 23, 1837.

Robt. STEVENSON named adm. of estates of Robt. J. MOSELY and David CROCKETT, Cole's Settlement, Washington Co., March 26.

James D. OWEN named adm. of Thos. J. ROBINSON est., Texana, Jackson Co., March 3.

Wm. B. DEWES and Leander BEESON named adm's. of Collin BEESON est., Feb. 28.

John REED named adm. of Wm. WAGGONER est.

John R. JONES named adm. of Wm. B. TRAVIS est., Marion, March 12.

Wm. B. DEWES, Abel BEESON & Leander BEESON have obtained letters of adm. in est. of Benjamin BEESON, Columbia, March 9.

Individuals seeking letters of adm. in Brazoria County are: Thos. F. McKINNEY, for est. of Francis ADAMS; Francis J. HASKINS, for Saml. MAY and Robert J. W. CARTER estates; Cyrus CAMPBELL, for John H. SCAGGS; and Jos. McCORMIC, for David McCORMICK, March 20.

Tuesday, April 4, 1837

New Orleans Picayune reports that Mr. B. H. SMITH died "yesterday" at New Orleans charity hospital, and that SMITH was lately returned from Texas and a brother to Gen. SMITH of Texas Army. Editor of Telegraph adds: "Charity requires us to state that Texas has never had a Gen. Smith in her service. . ."

Unfortunate incident took place at Velasco on evening of 24th ult., between Lt. J. T. SPROWL and his comm. officer Capt. SNELL. The latter went with 2 or 3 soldiers to arrest the former. SPROWL resisted violently, striking SNELL to ground and wrestling his sword from him. Capt. SNELL instantly drew a pistol and shot SPROWL in the head. He has since died.

Information wanted on a youngster by name of Geo. L. RAMESDALE, who left his family at Matagorda in Aug. 1835. He may be in New Orleans or in Texas Army. Anyone with info. should contact F. RAMESDALE at Shreve's Port, Red River, La.

John ANDREWS and Robt. MILBY named adm's of H. H HUNT est., April 1.

A. UNDERWOOD named adm. of Henry J. HOWARD and Robt. COCHRANE, Marion, April 2.
Warning. A fellow styling himself as Robert WYERS, of the Red Lands, a brick maker, contracted with this subscriber and several other gentlemen here in Richmond to make a quantity of brick and has refused to fulfill his obligations. R. E. HANDEY, March 30.
W. P. BENSON, one of the prisoners captured at San Patricio by the Mexicans in Feb. 1836, has just arrived from Matamoros via New Orleans and gives us the names of other American prisoners recently arrived at New Orleans from that place: S. S. CORTES, of Phila.; BRYANT, of TX; H. CRAIG, of N.J.; G. SMITH, of N.Y.; BENSON, of Ohio; PITTMAN, of Ky.; FRANCIS, of Ohio; and LANGAMAN, of Holland. The remainder of the prisoners will probably arrive on the Comanche. Their names are: JONES, KER, HALL, COPELAND.

Tuesday, April 11, 1837

Died March 14, Allen REYNOLDS, a citizen of TX. and former resident of New York.
D. J. WOODLIEF and Lewis A. REYNOLDS named adm's. of Allen REYNOLDS est., Washington, March 27.
James COCHRANE named adm. of Jas. DARWIN est. in Austin County.
Henry AUSTIN named adm. of G. B. JAMIESON est., February 27.
James F. PERRY named executor of last will & testament of Stephen F. AUSTIN, April 5.

Tuesday, May 2, 1837 [Houston, TX]

An elderly man by the name of PARKER, who came to Columbia with Capt. COLE's wagon train, died on the night of the 12th inst., at George BROWN's. The relatives and friends of dec. are requested to apply to BROWN for full info.
A. J.. HARRIS named adm. of GOWIN HARRIS est.
A free Negro, Thos. BEALE, who enlisted as a seaman on schooner of war Brutus, ranaway last night. A. HURD, Commander of the Brutus, Houston, May 3(?), 1837.

Tuesday, May 9, 1837

Tabathy IIAMES, alias Tabitha HARRIS, prays to Probate Court, Harrisburg Co., for a final settlement of est. of John IIAMES, decd. April Term, 1837. [IIAMES also appears as IJAMS in other records. - Compiler]

Md. Apr. 21st, R. M. WILLIAMSON, judge of 2nd district, to Miss Mary Jane, dtr. of Col. Gustavus E. EDWARDS, all of Austin County.

Died at Nacogdoches on April 14, Dr. John S. WINSTON, 37, native of Louisa Co., Va.; entered Army of Texas on Feb. 9, 1836, asst. surgeon at San Jacinto, and continued to serve under Col. MILLARD until ill health forced him to leave.

James S. HOLMAN named adm. of H. H. LEAGUE, est., May 8.

Edmund ANDREWS named adm. of estates of Theodore LENTER and Wm. M. CATO, Brazoria Co., May 1.

J. S. MENEFEE named adm. of John HINKSON est., Texana, May 2.

Proclamation by War Dept., Houston, Apr. 22: This is to certify that B. L. WADDELL and John ROGAN have been dishonorably discharged for desertion from the Army of Texas.

Tuesday, May 16, 1837

Died about middle of last November, Henry HARRISON, res. in Austin's colony for 11 years, living most of that time at or near Attuscacito or Tuscaceet, on Colorado River; dec. was a former resident of Ohio.

Geo. RAMESDALE hereby notifies his parents at Shrieve's Port, Red River, or wherever else they may be, that he is alive and well and living in city of Houston, May 15.

Abraham ALLEY named adm. of est of Henry HARRISON, Colorado Co., April 12.

Wm. J. E. HEARD named adm. of est. of LeRoy WILKINSON, decd. (who was mortally wounded at San Jacinto), Colorado Co., April 12.

Abraham ALLEY named adm. of Eliz. BETTS est.

League of land granted to John BLAIR as a citizen of TX. in 1835, by order of Dist. Court in San Augustine, will be sold in Liberty on June 1. This land is situated at Wolf's Point on the road leading from Liberty to Beaumont. Wm. M. LOGAN, sheriff of Liberty Co., Apr. 28.
According to previous appt., a meeting was held at office of Dr. MARSH in Houston on May 8 at 3 o'clock P.M. at which were present the following resident ministers of the Gospel in TX.: W. W. HALL, M.D., of Houston, Presbyterian, from Ky.; W. P. SMITH, M.D., of Washington, Methodist, from Tenn.; L. L. ALLEN, of Washington co., Methodist, from N.Y.; Dr. H. MATTHEWS, of Houston, Methodist, from La.; Dr. R. MARSH, of Houston, Baptist, from Ala.; Z. MORRELL, of Milam, Baptist, from Tenn.

Friday, May 26, 1837

An Indian was murdered a few miles from this place on 23rd by a man named RICHARDS from the Red Lands; the suspect has since been arrested and is awaiting trial at Sept. term of court.
Abner HARRIS, adm. of Wm. HARRIS est., will sell at public auction on June 13 all that land lying on Chocolate Bayou and belonging to said succ. as well as undivided half int. in grist mill, oxen, wagon, etc. Brazoria, May 9.
C. B. BANNISTER named adm. of Wm. ATTWELL est., Brazoria Co., May 9.
Petition of Elizabeth Ann PRICE for divorce presented to Tx. House and sent to judiciary committe
Pet. submitted by Mr. McKINNEY in behalf of orphan child at Red River praying for appt. of John STYLES as her guardian, May 18.
$50 reward will be given for delivering to me on Bailey's Prairie, 7 miles from Columbia, a Negro man named JOE, belonging to succ. of the late Wm. Barret TRAVIS, who ranaway and took with him a Mexican, two horses, saddles and Bridles. This Negro was in the Alamo with his master when it was taken, and was the only

man from the colonies not put to death; he is about 25, 5'10" or 11", very black and has good countenance; when he left on April 21st, he was wearing a dark mixed sattinet round jacket and new white cotton pantaloons. If the runaways are taken more than 100 miles from my home, I will pay all reasonable expenses in addition to reward. Bailey's Prairie, May 21. John R. JONES, Ex'r of W. B. Travis.

Notice from Geo. N. HAWKINS, adm., that he will prosecute anyone trespassing on land belonging to estates of late Edward St. John HAWKINS or late Joseph H. HAWKINS.

Saturday, June 3, 1837

Petition of Mrs. Ellen McGARY praying for a divorce, presented to Tx. House, May 26.

Md. in Milam Co., Henry P. WEBB to Miss Frances GRIGGS.

Md., Thos. A. GRAVES, sheriff of said co., to Miss C------ BAILEY.

Md., Andrew Jackson POWERS to Mrs. Annette CHILDERS(?), dtr. of Col. E. L. R. WHEELOCK.

Died at Marion, May 5th, Capt. John HARDIN?.

Martin ALLEN seeking letters of adm. on est. of Patrick DUNN, Houston, May 30.

Thos. EARLE, adm. of Luke MOORE, decd., to conduct a public auction of all personal property from the est., at my house on July 11; published at Harrisburg.

J. H. POLLEY named adm. of Gaines BAILEY, est., Brazoria, May 13.

Frederick NIEBLING named adm. of Ebenezer R. HALL est., Tenoxtitlan, May 13.

Thursday, June 8, 1837

Petition of Robt. STEPHENSON, praying for a divorce, presented to Tx. House, May 31.

Edw. WRAY petitions Probate Ct., Houston, on 29th inst. to be named adm. of Hugh KILGORE est. and as curator to minor Sarah Ann KILGORE, heiress of Hugh, Houston, May 30.

Petition of John KELLEY to be named guardian of minors Louisa, Lucinda, Andrew and Mary ROARK, heirs and children of Elijah ROARK, decd., Houston, May 30.

Darwin M. STAPP named adm. of John M. HEARD est., Texana, May 30.

$50 Reward. Ranaway from my plantation on Oyster Creek, 2 Negro men, one by name of GUMBY (who is about 5'10" and has a remarkably well look) and TOM (about 6'1"); both were dressed in blue cotton clothing and red caps when they left. Edwin WALLER.

Wanted. A negro woman between ages of 15-30 who understands cooking and washing; for such a fair price will be paid. Robt. Eden HANDY, Richmond, June 6.

Statement by Lt. J. W. TAYLOR regarding a recent engagement between Texas government vessel Independence and 2 enemy brigs of war. Our vessel was captured by Capt. DAVIS of the Libertador and Commodore LOPEZ of the Vincendor. From "Brazos de St. Iago," Taylor writes on April 21, they will be leaving this place tommorrow for Matamoros as prisoners of war. Capt. WHEELWRIGHT was very dangerously wounded in the engagement. In addition to officers and crew of our vessel ("our crew consists of 31 men and boys"), we had on board as passengers: the Hon. Wm. H. WHARTON; Mr. Levy, Surgeon, Texas Navy; Capt. DUROCHER, Tx. Army; Mr. THAYER of Boston; Mr. WOOSTER, an English subject; Acting Lt. Geo. ETESS, Tx. Navy; and Henry CHILDS.

Tuesday, June 13, 1837

Deserted from Post Galveston on night of June 8th, Corp. Thos. BLACKSTOCK of Co. A, 1st Infantry Regt.; native of Scotland, 24 years old, 5'6", fair complex., grey eyes, fine hair, by occupation a butcher. R. D. McCASKEY, Comm. Officer.

Died at Houston on 14th inst., Wm. S. HULL, son of the late Rev. Wm. HULL of New Orleans.

Died at Houston on 15th inst., Lt. David GRIEVES, of Tx. Army, a native of Scotland.

Drowned on the 18th inst., in Buffalo Bayou, E. J. W. LOWERY, nat. of Lexington, Ky.

James A. YORK and Noah SCOTT named adm's. of Thos. YORK est., San Felipe de Austin, June 6.

Nancy MATHER and John W. CLOUD named adm's. of Elisha MATHER, est., Brazoria Co., April 14.

The capt., crew and passengers of American schooner Julius Caesar, citizens of U.S., embarked at New Orleans on evening of April 8th for port of Brazoria, Tx. We were overtaken by the Mexican brig-of-war Gen. Teran on the 12th. The following crew members were on board: Andrew MOORE, master of the Julius Caesar, Bedford, N.H.; S. M. KNIGHT, 1st mate, Portland, Maine; Chas. FOSTER, 2nd mate, Winthrop, Maine; Wm. QUINDLEN, Phila.; Geo. BROCKWAY, Saybrook, Ct.; Jos. C. BECKFORD, Del.; John STEPHENS, N.Y. Passengers on board: Jas. M. GATEWOOD, Page Co., Va.; Harrison S. ALLENWOOD?, Shenandoah Co., Va.; Andrew J. BRUME, West Feliciana, La.; Dr. WATSON and John SHARP, N.Y.; B. B. BOLLING, Ala.; G. W. HATHAWAY, Mass.; Daniel SLACK, Hunterdon Co., N.J.; Alex. C. DOUGALL, Phila.; Moses NOLAN, Ross Co., Ohio; Nathan BARKLEY, N.Y.; Francis P. WEBSTER, Erie Co., Pa.; Volney O'STRANDER, West Feliciana, La.; S. BOOKER, S.C.; M. P. DUVAL, Tenn.; Deshay BUNTON & lady, Tenn.; James KENDALL & lady, Tenn.; John W. BUNTON & lady, Tenn.; Capt. LOVE, Ky.; and F. C. GRAY & son.

Saturday, June 24, 1837

Tribute of respect to late Col. Henry TEAL adopted at San Augustine, noting that TEAL was murdered by unknown assailants while in service of his country.

Mary KINCHELOE named curatrix of vacant succ. of Jacob BETT and the succ. of Wm. KINCHLOE, Matagorda Co., June 1.

$30 reward for delivery of Pvt. Simon HOLMES who deserted Post Galveston on night of June 8. He is 28 yoa, native of England, 5'7", brown hair, grey eyes. Pvt. in Co. A, 1st Infantry.

Hon. John W. BUNTON and lady, passengers on the Julius Caesar, have recently arrived from Matamoros via N.O. They report Capt. WHEELWRIGHT is recovering from his wounds.

Saturday, July 1, 1837

Capt. Jos. POWELL of Columbia assassinated by Dr. T. HUMPHRIES while on his way to dinner with friends on 26th. POWELL was shot through the heart and died instantly. HUMPHRIES was seized immediately and imprisoned.
Died in this city on Tues. last, Levi L. LAURENS, aged about 21 years, late reporter for the House of Rep. and recently located here from New York. LAURENS died of wounds received in a duel at the hands of Dr. Chauncey GOODRICH, recently from Vicksburg, Miss. The entire capital was thrown into shock and mourns his untimely demise.
Two runaway Negroes have been taken into custody by the subscriber. One, who calls himself ITALIA, is about 5'7" and was wearing casinett pants, no coat or jacket. The other, who calls himself WILL, is 5'5" and was wearing coarse white duck pants. Both speak intelligent English and appear to be brothers. Spring Creek, June 27, Jacob DUCKWORTH.
Died in this city, Robt. T. WALKER of Nashville, Tennessee.
In this city, on Thurs. last, Wm. FACETT, a German, committed suicide by drowning. Supposed to have been insane.
Geo. DUTY named adm. of Matthew DUTY est., Mina, Tx., May 30.

Saturday, July 8, 1837

Died in this city on 7th inst., Miss Mary McELROY, aged 18.
Capt. THOMPSON, formerly comm. of the Montezuma, has left the Mexican service, and is now at Brazoria on his way to Houston. He intends to engage in the services of Texas.
We have just learned that Col. R. M. COLEMAN was drowned a few days since at Velasco.

Saturday, July 15, 1837

Drowned in Buffalo Bayou on 12th inst., John Francis WARD, 23, formerly of Washington, D.C.

Capt. WHEELWRIGHT and Dr. LEVY have escaped from Matamoros. They came in a small boat to Matagorda and report that Hon. Wm. H. WHARTON is being held in close confinement.

Public auction to be held Sept. 11 at Mina, on one fourth of league belonging to A. DUNN est., also one fourth a league belonging to Chas. S. SMITH est., along with block of bldgs. in town of Mina; and also 2 bldg. lots in Mina belonging to est. of Levi JOHNSON. Mina, June 30, T. KENNEY, Adm'r.

Saturday, July 29, 1837

Geo. N. HAWKINS, aged 26 or 27, died on 8th inst. at Brazoria.

E. MARKHAM died at Fort Bend on 19th inst.

Died at Harrisburg on 26th inst., Merriwether M. SMITH.

Died at his res. on Gal. Bay, 19th inst., James ROUTH, an old and respected citizen.

$100 reward offered for delivery of 2 African Negro men who ranaway from my farm on Oyster Creek near Brazoria last March. Both men are about 5'10" and between 20-25 years of age. Edward WALLER.

Saturday, August 5, 1837

Elias C. EVERT died in this city on July 31.

Benj. F. DEY, formerly of Penn Yan, NY, died in Harrisburg on July 24.

Died near Washington, July 14, Sgt. Jas. J. WILLIAM, of the Army of Texas.

Thos. J. ALLCORN named adm. of Elijah CAPLE est., August 1.

Both Archibald WYNN and Wm. M. BIRCH have filed letters of adm. for est. of John MERRY, decd.; a hearing on this case set for August term by Probate Ct., Harrisburg Co.

Probate Ct., Harrisburg Co., at July Term approved appts. of following administrators: John WOODRUFF (Chas. THOM est.), Wm. B. GOODMAN (Giles A. GIDDINGS est.), and A. M. TOMKINS (Geo. W. KIMBELL est.).

Runaway from me 3 mos. ago, an African Negro man named ARCH, about 25, tall slender fellow, very black, some scars on forehead, neck and both sides of his face. He escaped from me 5 or 6 times, twice breaking off the irons. He is a very bad rascal, speaks little English. My brother P. D. McNEEL has an African Negro man named IONA that ran off with ARCH. He is about 28 years old, has scars on face and both cheeks, yellow complexion, and stout build. He ran off last year and was taken up in Robertson's Colony. I will pay a liberal reward for ARCH, and my brother for IONA. They should be delivered to my place 8 miles below Brazoria, Gulf Prairie, July 24. Leander H. McNEEL.

Saturday, August 12, 1837

Proclamation by President Sam HOUSTON offers $200 reward for arrest of J. H. NASH, who is belived to have stabbed a Mexican youth aged 16 or 17, on 20th ult. in San Antonio. NASH is 5'8", with black hair and eyes, stout build, ruddy complexion, about 28 years old. Dated at Houston on Aug. 8.

Jas. QUIGLEY named adm. of Augustine QUIGLEY est., Houston, Aug. 8.

John FISHER named adm. of John Francis WARD est., Houston, August 12.

Nathaniel LEWIS named adm. of Jesse FERNANDEZ est., San Antonio de Bexar, July 26.

List of passengers who arrived at Galveston on the Crusader from N.O.: A. C. ALLEN & lady, Miss LOVE, Mrs. HOLBROOK, D. J. PARK & lady, G. F. LANGFORD, John S. GAITHER, Jacques BLANDIN, P. PAQUIRT, Wm. BAKER, Gen. Leigh REED, Dr. S. WALLACE, J.A. NEWLAND, T. J. PIPER, J. L. McALISTER, Mr. BACHE, W. MALCOLM, H. G. EDDY, Thos. BAILEY, W. B. MARTIN, Wm. MARLEY, Jas. W. JOHNSON, John COUGHLIN, B. H. EASTON, James

FLOYD, T. W. BENNETT, J. KAMMAC, Wm. ROULSTONE, A. F. BURCHARD & lady, Miss F. BURCHARD, P. BURCHARD, A. BURCHARD, James TIVY, Mrs. M. TAYLOR, Mary TAYLOR, Emeline TAYLOR, W. TAYLOR, John TAYLOR, Joash TAYLOR, Chas. TAYLOR, Rachel TAYLOR, F. LUNDT, Wm. OLDMANN, C. KELLY & lady, Jane McDONALD. Date of arrival was 3rd inst.

Saturday, August 19, 1837

Died at this city on 12th inst., David Porter RICHARDSON.
Died at Columbia on morning of 13th inst., in his 71st year of age, Wm. SMEATHERS, one of the earliest pioneers of this country, having resided here nearly 17 years.
Michael YOUNG named adm. of A. J. JAMES est. by order of Austin Co. Probate Ct., Fort Bend Settlement, July 30.
Two men, named ROSS and STEVENS, have been found murdered and scalped near Goliad. Lipan Apaches are believed to be the guilty parties.
Report from Santa Fe indicates that a party of traders led by a Mr. WHITE from Fayette were waylaid and robbed by Apaches at a narrow pass on the road from Chihuahua to Santa Fe. A man, by name of KUYKENDALL, was shot and left for dead but will likely recover.

Tuesday, August 22, 1837

A young man named Jackson M. PARKER killed recently near the Nueces by Tonkawa Indians. While gathering cattle for the army, PARKER and a companion went after 3 or 4 oxen that strayed from the drove and entered into a mesquite thicket. One of the Indians was in hiding and instantly killed the young man.
Henry Percy BREWSTER named adm. of est of John S. D. BYROM, August 5.
Caty McCOY named adm. of Jos. McCOY est., Washington Co., August 12.
Mr. BUCHANAN, of firm of Hensley & Buchanan, was reportedly killed near the "Sevilla" by a Indian party; HENSLEY, his partner, escaped.

Saturday, August 26, 1837

Died on the Brazos, Harrisburg Co., Mary BATTLE, consort of M. M. BATTLE, after a short illness of bilious fever. Should Sarah and M. DERRET, who are on a visit to U.S., learn of this, they are requested to return to Tx. to inherit their estate. Editors for St. Louis, N.O. and Richmond, Va. papers please note.

Report in last issue of BUCHANAN's death is thankfully incorrect. He and Mr. HENSLEY have just returned here. We would not have printed it except for fact that info. came from his own family and was corroborated by several gentlemen from the vicinity of the Cibolo.

Achilles McFARLAND named adm. of est. of Wm. McFARLAND, San Felipe de Austin, Aug. 23.

John W. MOORE and Leo A. E. ROARK, adm's. of Mrs. Cynthia ROARK, decd., to hold public auction of her property on Sept. 16 in Houston.

Robt. P. CROCKETT named adm. of succ. "of my father David CROCKETT, decd.," Bexar County, August 22.

Susannah DENTON seeking info. on her husband, John, who left her home on June 12 to join a comp. of Rangers forming at Houston. He may have been murdered. August 22.

Thos. BLACKWELL named adm. of Saml. MAY and Ephraim ANDERSON est's., Brazoria Co., Aug. 12.

Basil G. IJAMS named adm. of John CHAFFIN est., Marion, August 18.

Saturday, September 2, 1837

Hon. Wm. H. WHARTON has escaped from Matamoros and is safely at his home on the Brazos. His journey home took 18 days.

A message from Bexar states that Gen. GREEN was shot down by Indians and scalped, but not killed! He has been taken to Bexar and is recovering slowly.

Died in this city on 20th inst., the 1 year old son of Mr. C. KELLY. His 18 year old wife died here on the 21st inst.

Public notice. C. KELLY offers for sale at the City Recess these articles, low for cash: coffee, spice, liquors (all kinds), spectacles, calicoes, all kinds of thread; shoes, hats and ready made clothing; carpenter tools. I'm compelled to sell on acct. of losing my wife and child, and due to my own bad health. Houston, August 21.

Letters of adm. granted to Albert GALLATIN at Feb. term of this Ct., on est. of Abraham GALLATIN, have been revoked and new adm. shall be apptd. at Sept. term. D. W. C. HARRIS, Clk. of Probate, Harrisburg County.

Additional filings with Probate Ct., Harrisburg Co.: Saml. WOOD, for adm. of John ROBERTSON, est.; James SPILLMAN seeking guardianship of John and George OWEN, minors of Conrad OWEN; Danl. S. HARBERT seeking ltrs. of adm. in est's of Jos. F.A. SCOTT, Wm. JOHNSON, Wm. N. FRENCH, Wm. WINFIELD & Wm. DUMPSEY; Jas. PERRY seeking ltrs. of adm. for Alex McCOY est. Show cause hearings set for Sept. term.

Littleberry HAWKINS named adm. of Edmund St. Johns HAWKINS, Geo. N. HAWKINS & Norborne HAWKINS, by Brazoria Co. Prob. Ct. on Aug. 1.

Saturday, September 9, 1837

Notice to the public that Cornelius KELLY has been judged insane and incapable of managing his own affairs. Samuel H. BANCROFT named curator by Probate Ct. of Harrisburg Co.

Late rumor respecting Gen. GREEN is incorrect. He arrived at Bexar safe and healthy.

Saturday, September 16, 1837

Dr. Chauncey GOODRICH recently killed at Bexar by a young man named ALLEN. GOODRICH was in an affray and had tried to kill ALLEN. He was found dead later in his chamber.

Runaways. BEN, about 25, dark mulatto, took with him rifle, pistol & good supply of half used clothing. Also accompanied by JESSE, an African born Negro, about 50, well set, & very

black; they left together on the 28th inst.; a liberal reward on their del. to me on Galveston Bay six miles below Cedar Bayou. Wm. RICHARDS, Houston, Sept. 7.
M. EDWARDS named adm. of John FLANDERS est., Brazoria, Sept. 12.
Public sale of land, Negroes &c. Whereas on Sept. 12, 1836, the subscriber sold to Monroe EDWARDS, of Brazoria Co., certain property as described below; on which prop. with the consent of said EDWARDS, a certain pledge, mortgage and hypothecation was retained, with full power to sell the same whenever any of the payments became due and were not paid; and whereas the last payment of $18,000, due on the 10th of last month, is now due; I will sell the following property on Oct 16th: All that parcel of land on which the subscriber formerly lived, and on which now Wm. J. RUSSELL now lives, east of Oyster Creek, supposed to contain 1300 acres more or less, with all of the improvements and being the same land purchased by me from Aarchy HODGE, Jared E. GROCE jr., and A. HODGE. Also, the following Negroes: HARRY, CATO, GEORGE, DICK, TONEY, PETER, WILLOWE, ADILEGNA, QUACCO, ADO, SIMON, DANIEL, CUDJO, ITALA, ANTHONY, ELI, and BARCOLA. Terms of sale, Cash. And should any one bid off the property, or any part of it, and make payment when required, the property will be immediately resold. Title made on the premises. Houston, Sept. 15, Benj. F. SMITH
"As my name is necessarily used in the foregoing adv., and as the conclusion would naturally be that I am embarrassed or unable to pay my debts, in explanation. . .I will remark that in the purchase of the above named property I acted merely as the nominal purchaser for the benefit of one Warren D. C. HALL; the personage and the property itself being bound for the amount due thereon. Columbia, Sept. 12, 1837." M. EDWARDS.
Edward BAILEY named adm. of est. of Merriwether Woodson SMITH, Harrisburg Co., Sept. 16.
Died at Quintana, about midnight on the 2nd inst., of congestive fever, Mrs. Mary R. JONES,

wife of John Rice JONES, aged 37 years; she was the mother of six children, five of whom are quite young and one an infant at the breast; an early inhabitant of this eventful country. Drowned in Galveston bay on 27th ult., Newton W. MABRY, about 17. The unfortunate young man accidentally fell from steamer "Branch T. Archer" near Redfish bar. The Nashville and Tuscaloosa papers will please copy.

Saturday, September 23, 1837

Duel fought on 24th between Lt. Joseph H. RHOADES and Lt. HOWL of the Texas Army, in which RHOADES suffered a wound to the head and from which injuries he died on August 31. The paper published a letter from Richard POLLARD, Charge d'Affairs for U.S. to Republic of Chile, in which POLLARD refers to the dead man as his son.
Runaways. $100 reward will be given for the apprehension and delivery to me on the Brazos timber, 3 miles above Col. HALL's plantation or to Col. Wm. T. AUSTIN, Brazoria, for negroes by name of ARTHUR and GEORGE. ARTHUR left my plantation on night of 12th; he is 5'10", about 36, wore a Mexican cassinett roundabout and blue cottonade pantaloons. It is believed he stole a tall bay horse with a star in her forehead and 3 shotguns. GEORGE left here on night of 18th inst; he is 5'6" or 7", about 36-37 years old, stout made, grim coutenance, red eyes, large whiskers, and very communicative when addressed. He has similar clothes plus an old fur hat and carrying an old brass mounted rifle. Evergreen, Sept. 19. P. BERTRAND.
Subscriber, having determined to move furthur west, proposes to sell plantation and present residence on the San Bernard with 3000 acres of land, 500 of which are under cultivation, located just below the proposed town of San Bernard; with stock and 10-100 Negroes, as suits the purchaser. M. EDWARDS. Inquiries can also be made of I. N. MORELAND, Houston.

On Saturday evening last, Mr. L. KELCEY of this city was killed by Mr. Z. HUBBARD, a dispute having developed 2 or 3 weeks ago between the two business partners. After exchange of angry words, KELCY pulled pistol and shot HUBBARD in the knee. HUBBARD rushed KELCY with a sword cane and stabbed him 10 times. Trial was held Wednesday, and jury brought in a verdict of justifiable homicide.

Died in this city on 16th inst., Col. Jonathon B. FROST, 32, of congestive fever.

Died in this city on 12th inst., suddenly, Capt. Wm. S. STILLWELL, of the Texas Army, aged about 28. New Orleans and New York papers will please notice.

Died in Harrisburg a few weeks since, Wm. H. PENDELTON, later of the Texas Army, and formerly a U.S. Navy midshipman. Baltimore and Washington city papers will please copy.

Oliver JONES named adm. of est. of Lawrence Martin DEES, Austin County, Sept. 16.

Henry A. ROBERTSON named adm. of John BUCKLEY est., Houston.

Ben Fort SMITH named adm. of Sarah D. TERRY est., Brazoria County, Sept. 16.

Saturday, September 30, 1837

Edmund ANDREWS named adm. of Henry BURT est. at Brazoria County, Sept. 21.

A Negro taken up on night of 5th inst. at house of John MILLICAN, on east side of Brazos, 10 miles above Washington. He says his name is LUKE and his master, Eli BORDLOW, lives in La. on east side of Red River, and 7 miles above Campty; he is about 40, 5'10", nose short and thick, brow high, hair mixed with gray, common complexion; has a scar about 3 inches long over his right eye, caused by a blow with a stick by a mulatto; has a slight impediment in his speech; he no longer has any of the clothes he wore when first starting out, which appears to have been last May. Washington Co., Sept. 12.

Wednesday, October 3, 1837

Died on Chocolate bayou, Sept. 18, Mrs. Parmelia ANGIER, wife of Dr. Samuel T. Mobile Register & Patriot will please notice.
Suit. Delilah SHAW vs. Wm. SHAW. It appears to the satisfaction of Dist. Ct. of Harrisburg Co. that defendant Wm. SHAW is now a resident of Rep. of Tx. but outside the juris. of this court, he is thereby ordered to appear before next term of said court to plead, answer or demure or else judgement will be given against him "pro confesso." Signed by James S. HOLMAN, District Clerk, Harrisburg Co., Sept. Term.
Notice. By virtue of an order of Probate Court, Harrisburg Co., I shall expose to public sale at 2nd store in new row of bldgs. in town of Houston on Oct. 10th, all goods, wares, merchandise, provisions, belongings, groceries &c. belonging to est. of C. KELLY, determined by said court to be "an insane person." Signed by L. H. BANCROFT, Curator.

Saturday, October 7, 1837

Died in this city on Wed. last, of the prevailing fever, Lucius L. BUCKNELL, who resided here only a few months but had a "high reputation of his legal attainment."
Died Sept. 21st, James M. BISHOP of Troy, formerly of Philadelphia.
Died in this city on 3rd inst., Wm. GRAVES, formerly of Jackson, Mississippi.
Almira BOWEN named adm. of est. of Sylvester BOWEN, Sept. 28.

Wednesday, October 11, 1837

Died on Galveston Island on Sept. 3 of yellow fever contracted during a short residence in New Orleans, Alfred R. GUILD, a native of Boston, Massachusetts.
Died at San Antonio on Aug. 21, John S. WIGEN, formerly of Norfolk, Virginia.

Notice. I will conduct a public sale at the storeroom of Boswell & Adams in Houston on 20th Oct., of certain goods, furniture, liquors, &c. belonging to estate of late Alfred R. GUILD. Houston, Oct. 10. John A. NEWLAND, Adm'r.
Samuel G. POWELL named adm. of est. of Jos. J. POWELL, Houston, Oct. 11.

Saturday, October 14, 1837

Ira INGRAM, only recently elected mayor of Matagorda and a former member of House of Rep., died recently at Matagorda and left $70,000 or so to charitable interests in that place.
Henry A. ROBERTSON named adm. of estates of Jacob OKERMAN and Thos. K. GUBTILL, Houston.
Ashbel SMITH named adm. of est. of Dr. Chancey GOODRICH, Houston, Oct. 11.
James McADAMS assassinated from ambush while traveling 10 miles from Milam in Sabine Co; the reports were that 20 people were involved in a plot to kill McADAMS and 4 or 5 others on the same road. Officers have arrested one person. McADAMS was struck with 6 or 7 rifle balls.

Wednesday, October 18, 1837

Died on evening of 14th inst., Lemuel H. BANCROFT, native of Salisbury, Conn. and several years a resident of New Orleans. N.O. and N.Y. papers will please notice.
Died at his residence on Galveston Bay, on 9th inst., Wm. SCOTT, one of oldest settlers in this country. He leaves a large family. Richmond and Cincinnati papers will please copy.
C. B. BANISTER named adm. of Daniel BUCKLY and Wm. A. MOORE estates, Brazoria.
Henry ROBERTSON named adm. of estates of Gasten WENDENBURG and M. J. CRITTENDEN, Houston, October 12.
Letter from Thos. M. THOMPSON, dated City of Houston, Oct. 15: I observe in your paper of the 4th inst., an article signed Henry L. THOMPSON, in which he states he isn't "Mexican" THOMPSON. I regret this publication for many

reasons, but especially because it forces me to go before the public in my self-defense. Many years ago, long before the war with Texas, being poor and having a family to support, and Mexico offering more profitable employment to me than the United States, I embarked in her service. Some years before me, this Henry L. THOMPSON entered also the Mexican service. A little before the war between Mexico and Texas broke out, I was ordered to the Texas coast in command of the schooner Correo to protect the revenue laws. In the discharge of my duty, undertaking to capture an American vessel which was violating those laws, I was made prisoner by Capt. HURD of the San Felipe, aided by the steamboat Laura. I was taken to N.O. in irons, imprisoned for nearly half a year, tried for piracy, and acquitted. Many Texans attended the trial. Notwithstanding the persecution I suffered, I offered my services to Dr. B. T. ARCHER, who was one of the commissioners at the time. My services were not accepted. I wished to enter the Texas cause from the beginning, and came away from the Mexican service as soon as I could. I could not get away when I pleased, for I had a family in Matamoros. My conduct towards the Texian prisoners at Matamoros can be known by referring to the Hon. Wm. H. WHARTON, Capt. WHEELRIGHT, Dr. LEVY, John SHARP of Brazoria, or any of those who were so unfortunte as to be consigned to captivity there.

A Card. We the undersigned passengers on board the packet brig Halcyon (D. V. SOULLARD, Master) from New York to Galveston Bay, deem it but justice to publicly express our thanks for his kind attention and seaman-like manner in the management of his vessel in the tremendous hurricane of the 16th ult. A. ANDREWS and Lady, New Haven, Conn.; Jos. S. MARTIN, Washington, TX; John S. PRESTON, Orange Grove, TX; Wm. H. BURGESS, Baltimore, MD; Harvey SANDERSON, N.Y.; Wm. TWISE, Springfield; John WOODWARD, Ithaca, N.Y.; and also in behalf of the steerage passengers. Houston, Oct. 17.

Saturday, October 21, 1837

Died at San Antonio on evening of 1st inst., Peter McKENNEY, a native of Scotland; death was from accidental discharge of gun while removing it from rack. Deceased lingered for 24 hours. New York papers will please publish.

Saturday, October 28, 1837

Died at Marion on 9th inst., Susannah E. HALL, 28, wife of Edward R. Hall, after illness of 9 days. Native of Georgia.

Saturday, November 4, 1837

Died in this city, Nov. 1, after a long illness, H. L. THOMPSON, late commodore of the Tx. Navy. The funeral took place on Thursday. His remains were accompanied to the grave by the largest group of citizens ever assembled here. An oration was delivered at graveside by Gen. Thomas J. RUSK.

Died in this city on 24th inst., John W. GAYLE, late purser of the Texas privateer "Tom Toby," after a long and painfull illness of 5 weeks. Louisville, Ky. papers please copy.

Died on 25th inst., Evan R. EVANS. Philadelphia papers will please publish.

J. H. POLLEY and D. M. MILBURN named admr's of est. of J. B. BAILEY, Oct. 28.

C. MILLON seeking letters of adm. to est. of L. L. BECKNELL.

Wm. G. COOK seeking letters of adm. to est. of Lemuel H. BANCROFT.

A. WYNNS and W. LAWRENCE seeking letters of adm. for est. of Stephen WINSHIP, Harrisburg Co., Oct. 29. Anyone who wishes to challenge has 10 days to make objections to Probate Ct.

Basil G. IJAMS named adm. of Stephen M. HALL est., Columbia, Sept. 29.

Notice. By virtue of certain writing in my favor by Samuel WILLIAMS, executed on Oct. 29, I will on Sat., Nov. 18 expose to public auction to highest bidder all right, title and interest which Samuel WILLIAMS had on the 29th of Oct., to a certain Negro woman named JANE and her infant child, to satisfy a debt of $450, along with expenses of keeping the Negroes from Oct. 29 to the time of the sale, which will be held at 12 o'clock at the warehouse of DOSWELL and Adams. Andrew BRISCOE.

Saturday, November 11, 1837

Murder. On the 30th day of Sept., Robert L. LOVELAND and Abraham SMITH were traveling from U.S. to Tx. on Trammel's Trace; five miles with in the Sabine River, they found a body in the road; tracks indicated two men had left the scene; they followed their trail and apprehended men named QUARLES and CARSON. QUARLES later confessed they had murdered two different men. They returned to the scene again, and QUARLES pointed out the other body. The two dead men are identified as Camb McFARLAND and a Mr. TURNER, both said to be from Missouri.

Md. at Orange Grove, the residence of Col. MORGAN, on 1st inst., by Rev. Richard SALMON, John W. CLOUD of Brazoria Co. to Miss Rebecca JOHNSTON.

Died at San Patricio on 12th ult. Capt. John McCLURE of the Buckeye Rangers.

Died at Peach Point near Brazoria, at residence of James F. PERRY, on Oct. 6th, John H.P. BRENT of same company, of Virginia; Fredericksburg, Va. and Cincinnati papers please notice.

E. BAILEY named adm. of est. of M. W. SMITH and authorizes Josiah J. CROSBY to settle the est., Washington, Tx., Oct. 25.

John STAFFORD named adm. of Harvey STAFFORD est, Nov. 9.

Samuel M. FROST named adm. of Jonathon B. FROST est., Houston, Nov. 10.

H. KESLER named adm. of est. of Ernst. V. BERNUTH, Houston, November 1.

Wm. BURCH named adm. of John MERRY est.

Saturday, November 18, 1837

Murder. William WOOD stabbed to death with Bowie knife by man named JONES, after JONES asked WOOD to try out his horse for speed. It appears WOOD did not stop riding the horse when JONES asked, angry words exchanged, and stabbing resulted.

On the 12th ult., a gang of Indians, well mounted, entered Mina and drove off 10 horses. They were immediately pursued by the inhabitants, who captured 12 horses, several mules and other property. On the 14th, 30 Indians charged upon three men just below HORNSBEG's on the Colorado and followed them 3 miles. Two of the men, FLOYD and CRAFT, escaped; the third, Joseph ROGERS, was speared to death by Indians.

Departed this life in town of Brazoria on 11th inst., Walter C. WHITE, one of the oldest and most respected citizens of Austin's Colony. Deceased immigrated to Tx. with Gen. LONG in 1821 and landed on Galveston island. He and a companion later penetrated the wilderness forests of Trinity river and made first crop of corn ever cultivated there.

Adam STAFFORD named adm. of Harvey STAFFORD est., Nov. 9.

Saturday, November 25, 1837

Res. of respect adopted at meeting of the bar held Oct. 14th in Dist. Ct., San Augustine Co., for late Major Samuel DEXTER of Nacogdoches; res. notes that DEXTER was buried on 5th of Oct. Deceased had served as aide-de-camp to Gen. Thos. J. RUSK during Tx. Rev.; provides for publishing res. in Nacogdoches Chronicle, Telegraph & Texas Reg., & Mobile, Ala. papers.

James WRIGHT, adm., serves notices that all persons indebted to firm of WRIGHT & McCRORY should call at law offices of WYNN & LAWRENCE, either of which is authorized to settle for the said firm or myself, Houston, Nov. 23.

Saturday, December 2, 1837

Deaf SMITH, one of the great heroes of the late revolution, died at Fort Bend on the 30th.

John GRIGG named adm. of estates of Samuel ELLIS and Samuel FARNEY, Nov. 23.

C. B. STEWART, adm. of James BUCKANON decd., announces public auction of 500 acre tract, part of a league granted to decd. Sale to be at town of Washington on 1st Monday in January. STEWART all announces he will be selling items and property from the estates of F. D. HARRISON and J. S. R. HARRISON, both soldiers of Tx. who fell in service of their country in Feb. and Mar. 1836. Adv. dated Nov. 23.

Mary McCRORY challenges adv. in last week's edition by James WRIGHT, in which he claimed to be adm. of late James McCRORY. Subscriber says she is the widow of McCRORY and the adm. of his estate. Houston, Nov. 28.

John BELDIN named adm. of estates of John FREDERICK & Wm. S. STILWELL, Houston, Nov. 24.

Land for Sale. John Rice JONES offers for sale 1 league of land lying on Cummin's creek, 10 or 12 miles from the Colorado river. Tract granted to him by the Mex. govt. as a colonist in 1830; also ¼ league lying near Groce's Retreat, granted by Mex. govt. to James DARWIN, decd., on which there is a first rate gin and other bldgs., about 50 acres under fence and a peach orchard; also the farm on which he lives in Bailey's prairie, on which there is a frame dwelling, gin, &c., and about 200 acres under fence; also several bldg. lots in the town of Marion, plus a 10 acre out lot; and also an African negro boy, about 16 years; all or any part of the above property may be purchased for cash. Nov. 23, 1837. John Rice JONES.

Saturday, December 6, 1837

Anyone with claims against est. of M. W. SMITH, decd., late of Harrisburg, may bring them to Messrs. GAZLEY and BIRDSALL of Houston for examination. Houston, Nov. 28. CROSBY & HUDSON, Agents for Admr.

Notice. This is to certify that I had stolen from me, or in some way lost, at San Felipe on the 26th inst., the following described discharges and furloughs, viz: Discharge in favor of Wm. L.MOSS, for services in summer of 1836, signed by T. J. GREEN, Brig. Gen, T.A.; discharge in favor of Jas. L. MOSS for 3 mos. service in spring & summer of 1836, signed by Capt. REID & T. J. GREEN; discharge in favor of Andrew L. MILLICAN for 3 mos. service in summer of 1837, signed by Capt. Lee SMITH & Major Wm. SMITH; discharge in favor of David W. COLLINS, for 6 mos. service in 1837, signed by 1st Lt. Jos. MATHER & Major Wm. H. SMITH; one furlough in favor of ----- MILLBROOKS, belonging to Capt. PEOPLE's company, furloughed in June last. Any person returning to the subscriber either of the above mentioned discharges or furloughs or discharges will be liberally rewarded. Nov. 29. William T. MILLICAN.

Saturday, December 9, 1837

Edwin WALLER named adm. of Chas. E. HAWKINS, ded., Brazoria Co., Dec. 6.

Geo. W. PATRICK and James MORGAN named admrs of James RUTT est., New Washington, Harrisburg County, Dec. 7.

R. BARR and John McCLANAHAN named admrs. of Henry FOLEY est., Houston, Dec. 7.

Edwin WALLER and Elizabeth SMITH named adm's of est. of Cornelius SMITH, Brazoria Co.

Horrid Outrage. An Indian of the Coshattie tribe was wantomly shot with a pistol in this city last evening. The ball perforated the breastbone near its right edge, causing a most dangerous wound. Should it prove fatal the scalp of some helpless infant or mother on our frontier may pay the forfeit of this villainy. The person charged with the crime has been arrested and his trial is now pending.

Died on the 28th ult., at the residence of Dr. PARROT on the Brazos, Capt. John J. MATHIAS (formerly of Loudon Co., Va.); Louisville, Ky. papers will please publish.

Capt. LeRAY was killed by Major TINSLEY in a duel at Bexar in October. Decd. was an officer and early volunteer in Texas Army.

Saturday, December 16, 1837

A severe battle was fought on Nov. 10 near the head waters of the Trinity between a party of 18 Rangers under the command of Lts. A. B. VAN BENTHUYSEN and A. H. MILES. The battle took some 2 hours, at the end of which time the Rangers were compelled to retreat. About 50 Indians were killed. Names of Rangers killed were: Lt. A. H. MILES, Jos. COOPER, J. JOSDIN, Alex. BOSTWICK, Dr. Wm. SANDERS, Jesse BLAIR, Lewis P. SCHEUSTER, James CHRISTIAN, Wm. NICK-ELSON, and Westly NICHOLSON. Rept. filed by Lt. VAN BENTHUYSEN states battle was fought at 33½ degrees North latitude. Indians were "Toweash, Wahco, and a few Keechies and Caddoes."

Obit. of MILES, as mentioned above, states he was formerly of Richmond, Va.; a veteran of battle of San Jacinto; and the actual capturer of Gen. SANTA ANNA. He had in his possession certains documents from the Secy. of War and Adj. Gen. of the Texas Army verifying the fact. He leaves behind a sister and his mother.

Harry CANFIELD is hereby notified that some interesting information from his widowed mother has been received at this office. Houston, Dec. 12.

A public sale set for 23d. inst. in town of Washington for a superior printing press, with all the necessary appendages, ink, paper, &c., belonging to est. of Dr. John H. COOK, decd. J. R. CUMMINS, Admr., Dec. 2.

Clement B. PENROSE, one of the earliest settlers of Texas, died in Oct. at the residence of Capt. Wm. B. G. TAYLOR at Balize, La.

Niles F. SMITH and Mary Ann FOLEY named as admr's of Geo. FOLEY est., Houston, Dec. 12.
The Indian wounded last week in this city has since died on 13th inst. James WRIGHT, the man accused of the crime, was apprehended, admitted to bail by the Justice of the Peace for $2000, and has since made his escape. This is an example to others who approve bail.

Saturday, December 30, 1837

Died at his residence in Brazoria Co., on 16th inst., Benn HEAD, aged 39 years. Mississippi papers will please publish.
Died on night of 12th inst., Maria, 4 year old dtr. of Barnard E. BEE, Secy. of War. The child had just landed on our shore in company with her mother when it pleased the Almighty to close her career. She came to Galveston on board the steamer "Columbia," on a trip from Charleston, S.C. to Galveston.
Died at Columbia on Nov. 2nd, Mrs. Sarah TYLER, aged 54, an exemplary member of the Baptist church for 30 years.
W. Y. McFARLAND, admr. of est. of Evan R. EVANS, calls on all persons indebted to said estate to present payment to him. Washington, December 27.
Public sale announced for Feb. 1 on half-league of land on Bray's Bayou, situated 1 mile from Houston and extending to within 2 miles of Harrisburg. Land belongs the succ. of late Luke MOORE & was granted to decd. as his headright. Houston, Dec. 23. Thos. EARLE, Admr.

Saturday, January 6, 1838

W. P. LIGHTFOOT named adm. of J. W. LIGHTFOOT est., Richmond, Nov. 27.
Benj. F. HANNA md. to Miss Isabel HARRIS, at Harrisburg, on Thursday evening by Isaac BATTERSON, Esq. All parties of this county.
A. FERGUSON named adm. of est. of Edward NELSON, decd., Jan. 6.

A gentleman by the name of Henry ULRY left a trunk at some house in Houston and has since died. If any person can provide info. to the Hon. Andrew BRISCOE, judge of probate, where said trunk can be found, they will confer a favor. Jan. 6. Peter J. DUNCAN, Admr. for Henry ULRY Estate.

John WOODRUFF and Mary McCRORY named adm'rs of Hugh McCRORY est., Houston, Dec. 14.

Saturday, January 13, 1838

Died at Zavala's Point, near Lynchburg, in Dec. last, Henry ULRY of Pennsylvania. Pittsburg papers will please notice.

Sale of lots in town of Randolph set for Jan. 20th, by order of John P. COLES, Washington Co. Town is situated on west side of the Trinity River at the San Antonio Road. John ROBBINS and Lucy ROBBINS, Admr's of Est. of N. ROBBINS, Proprietors. Randolph, Dec. 23.

Anderson SCOTT named adm. of est. of Samuel FREDERICK, Jackson Co., Jan. 10.

Man named W. M. BRIGHAM was mortally wounded with a dirk by John C. C. QUICK on evening of Wed. last in a brawl which occurred at a gambling table at the Houston House in this city. BRIGHAM died later from his wounds.

John L. BRYAN named adm. of est. of Haylett COURTLAND, Brazoria Co., Jan. 14.

Peter J. DUNCAN has been named adm. of the estates of Henry ULRY, Wm. Henry HASLEY, and David BARKLEY, Houston, Dec. 12.

W. B. ALDRIDGE named adm. of Walter C. WHITE (decd.), Columbia, Jan. 1.

Dr. EVANS (from New York) respectfully informs the citizens of Houston that he has located next to Mr. SANDERSON's store, where he intends to practice physic and surgery in general, Jan. 6 advertisement.

Saturday, January 20, 1838

Notice. Mrs. PLUMMER from Robertson's Colony, Texas, was lately purchased from the Comanche Indians. She is now at Independence, Mo., and states her 3 children and a sister are still with the same tribe. She has red hair. For full information, apply to Wm. T. SMITH, Columbia, Boone co., Mo. We learn that Mrs. HARRIS has been likewise purchased from the Indians and can be found at the same place.

Almon COTTLE named adm. of est. of Jonathon COTTLE, Houston.

Notice is hereby given to the owner of two Negroes named JOE and HENRY that they have been captured at Columbus, Colorado Co., and are now in the charge of the undersigned. Both Negroes were stolen from La. in July last. They say they belong to a Mr. BARR, who resides about 60 miles above N.O. Stephen TOWNSEND, Sheriff of Colorado County. Columbus, Jan. 13.

$100 reward will be given by B. CANFIELD of Piney Point to anyone who returns to him a "mulatto boy named SHELBY (familiarly styled) DOCTOR." He is abotu 20 years old, 5'8", stout build, with a long scar on right eye slanting down toward his nose. Escaped from me on the night of the 4th inst.

Saturday, January 27, 1838

Married at Magnolia Hall, the residence of A. J. YATES, on Galveston bay, on Thursday the 18th inst., by Rev. E. A. HUNTINGTON, Major Samuel WHITING and Mrs. Elizabeth MUNSON, both of Trinity.

Died on Tuesday the 23rd ult., after 4 to 5 months illness, Miss Louisa FROST, of bilious fever.

Died in Brazoria on 10th of Dec., 1837, George B. McKINSTRY, 32, judge of probate court of Brazoria. Decd. was a native of Ireland and had resided in Tx. for 7 or 8 years. Pittsburg and Cincinnati papers will please publish.

Geo. W. GRANT named adm. of succession of Edw. WINGATE and Edw. FITZSIMMONS, Houston.

Wm. DUTY named adm. of estates of Matthew and Geo. DUTY, Bastrop Co., Jan. 22.

James KERR named curator of vacant succ. of John McKAY, decd.

A. FERGUSON named adm. of EDWARD NELSON est.

Notice. On the 23rd June last, James C. THOMPSON sold his bounty land coming to him for services rendered as a pvt. in Capt. K. D. M'CASKY's company, 1st regt. infantry, from 2nd Feb. 1836 to 22d June 1837 (1280 acres) to Geo. W. HENSLEY. The auditor marked in the face of the copy which had been issued to claimant that he had sold the land to HENSLEY; he gave Geo. W. HENSLEY another copy with the endorsement of the transfer. The original, which should have remained on file, was surreptitiously obtained from this office. It appears that the whole papers have travelled to the U.S., and there it seems to have been reassigned to Jas. C. THOMPSON, and by him conveyed to H. R. A. WIGGINTON. The auditor requests that THOMPSON and HENSLEY inform him how these transfers were made; signed by J. W. MOODY, 1st Auditor, Dec. 29, 1837.

Saturday, February 3, 1838

$20 reward for apprehension and delivery to me or to Major I. N. MORELAND in Houston of a Negro girl named JULIA, about 20 years, griffe complexion, small scars on her neck and shoulders, speaks French and English; was purchased of Mrs. CLARK who recently left here for N.O., Harrisburg, Jan. 26. Wm. P. HARRIS.

Jas. PERRY named adm. of Alex. McCOY, decd.

John TURNER named adm. of Robert TOLLER est.

Henry A. READ named adm. of Robert GRIFFIN estate.

Maria DEMPSEY named adm. of Francis W. DEMPSEY est., Houston, Jan. 20.

James KERR named adm. of John CONREY est., Jackson County, January 13.

Saturday, February 10, 1838

From Louisville Advertiser we learn that the most shameful recontre took place recently in the Arkansas House of Assembly. The Speaker, Mr. WILSON, believing he had been insulted by a member, came down from the chair armed with a Bowie knife, and was met by his antagonist with another. His opponent, Mr. ANTHONY, soon lay dead upon the floor. Mr. WILSON, the Speaker, had one hand nearly separated from his arm and the other badly wounded.

Sale of land. To be auctioned to highest bidder on March 6th, 321 acres belonging to the succ. of the late Hugh KILGORE and situated on the Brazos River adjoining the property of Capt. Daniel PERRY; to be sold at sheriff's office in Houston by order of probate ct. Houston, Feb. 3. Edward WRAY, Admr.

Major Wm. GODDEN, formerly of N.Y., died on 12th ult. at Capt. Wm. WALKER's plantation on the Brazos River.

Died in this city on 6th inst. of congestive fever, Clifton PREWITT of Kentucky.

Saturday, February 17, 1838

Info. sought about John A. HITSELBERGER, who left Baltimore in summer of 1836 as one of the Baltimore Texian Guards, commanded by Capt. G. FRAILEY. If this meets his eye or that of anyone who knows him, please address a line on this subject to T. J. HITSELBERGER of N.O., Jan. 15. All Texas papers will please copy.

About a fortnight ago a fellow named Alexander ABRAMS undertook to cowhide a servant named A. FELTMAN at FORD's Hotel; ABRAMS was holding the cowhide in one hand and a Bowie knife in the other. In dodging the blows, FELTMAN fell against the knife and died several days later of his wounds. ABRAMS immediately mounted his horse and fled. Should the law succeed in taking him, a halter should be his reward.

Lorenzo DE ZAVALA Jr. named adm. of est. of Lorenzo DE ZAVALA decd., Harrisburg, Feb. 3.

$20 reward. Ranaway from the subscriber on Jan 20th, a Negro man named BEN; he is 6 feet tall, stout, light complexion for a Negro, forward in his manners, and when in liquor (which he is very fond of) impudent; he is a rough carpenter. BEN was brought to Houston in early Dec. by Dr. BERRY, remained there 10-12 days, and is most likely there now; above reward will be given for his apprehension and delivery to me at Marion. Columbus, Feb. 13. Robert M. FORBES for D. A. BARRY.

Married on 25th inst. at Centre Hill, Rev. Robt. ALEXANDER to Miss Eliza P. AYERS.

Married on 5th inst. by Judge BRISCOE, Jackson SMITH to Miss Sarah Maria CROSBY, dtr. of Platt H. CROSBY.

Robt. STEPHENSON named adm. of Lewis A. REYNOLDS est., Washington, Feb. 1.

By virtue of a decree from the Probate Court of Harrisburg Co., I will expose to public sale on March 10th, the lot adjoining the store now occupied by John CARLOS in this city and part of the est. of late Alfred R. GUILD. Houston, Feb. 17. John Alex. NEWLANDS, Admr.

Lost. An order on the Treasury for $34, and a certificate for 320 acres, for my service in the Army from the 25th of April to 23d of July, 1836. Robert KLEBERG. San Felipe, Jan.20.

Off Sabine River, Jan. 25, 1838. We the undersigned passengers on board the steamer Constitution, express our heartfelt thanks to Capt. AULD and his crew for their handling of that vessel when it was discovered she was in a sinking condition during our recent voyage from N.O.: A. Miles LEWIS, Selma, Ala.; Geo. S. WEAVER, do; L. B. JOHNSTON, do; Jas. WAPLES, Snow Hill, Md.; A. LESTER, Ohio; M. CUDY, New Orleans; John FAWCETT, Cincinnati; Thos. H. HASLICK, England; P. H. McMAHON, N.O.; F. A. SHERMAN, do; A. M. COWAN, Pontiac, Miss.; James BURNHAM, Maine; Wm. P. O'NEILL, N. O.; D. S. CLARK, New York; Geo. W. YOUNG, Ga.; Chas. L. LEWIS: John STEEL; Horace CURTIS, Wisconsin Territory; Francis B. WRIGHT, Texas Navy.

Saturday, February 24, 1838

Property belonging to est. of late John H. SCOTT to be exposed to public sale on 3rd Sat. of March next; lands are situated on Navidad river; also to be sold at same time are lands belonging to est. of late Caroline BROWN; all property located in Jackson Co. Terms cash. Andrew SCOTT, Admr.

Joint Resolution of Texas House & Senate to authorize audit of the claim of the Widow Kitty McCOY for beef and corn valued at $378 in scrip was approved on Dec. 18.

Jt. Res. approved by both Houses on Dec. 1, for relief of Manual CARBAJAL as compensation for compiling the laws of Texas and Coahuila, sum not to exceed $1200.

Jt. Res. of both Houses for the relief of F. W. THORNTON for sum of $1722 for purchase of provisions for the army in 1836, approved on Dec. 28.

Jt. Res. approved Dec. 18 by both Houses to approve an annual payment of $500 to the widow and family of late Erastus "Deaf" SMITH, until such time that she marries again or the courts of the country have confirmed their title to lands and town lots heretofore granted for compensation to Deaf SMITH for his services.

Jt. Res. approved by both Houses on Dec. 28, for the relief of Stilman S. CURTIS for horses and other property lost in the service of Texas during the winter and spring of 1836; the sum should not exceed $338.

Asahel TUTTLE named admr. of est. of Thos. AYERS.

Saturday, March 3, 1838

Mrs. PLUMMER, who was captured by the Comanches in the spring of 1836, has returned to her relatives and written an account of her travels with these Indians.

Oliver JONES and Joseph BARTLETT named admrs of est. of Jesse BARTLETT, decd., Washington, February 26.

R. B. JARMON named adm. of est. of Wm. HOUSE in Houston.

Wm. B. GOODMAN named adm. of Giles A. GIDDENS estate, Houston.

Murder! Murder! We will give a reward of $2,000 for the apprehension and delivery of LaFayette, Chamberlayne, Caesar A. and Achilles JONES to the sheriff of Shelby Co., Tenn.; four assassins are all brothers who maliciously and premediatedly murdered their own uncle, Col. Edward WARD on the 22nd inst. at the residence of A. G. WARD near Memphis. Adv. signed by John W. JONES, Robt. B. JONES, J. W. FOWLER, A. G. WARD and M. T. B. UPSHAW. Postscript adds that murderers left the residence of Mr. ROSS, 5 miles above Randolph, Ark. on morning of the 2nd inst.

Drowned on evening of 28th ult., in a bayou near this city, Fleming HALSEY, about 28, of Lynchburg, Va. and clerk on the steamer Branch T. Archer.

Thos. S. ALLCORN named adm. of est. of Elijah CAPLE, Houston. Thos. J. GAZLEY of Houston authorized to receive claims against the est.

Mary HOFFMAN named adm. of est. of Daniel A. HOFFMAN, Texana, Jackson Co., Feb. 12.

John L. BRYAN named adm. of est. of Fayette COPLAN, Brazoria Co., Feb. 23. Geo. W. PLEASANTS authorized to serve as agent for the adm. during his absence from the Republic.

Reward. John GOODMAN of Richmond authorizes $200 reward for arrest and return there of one Wm. H. HOWARD, who lately taught school in this vicinity, and one PEWETT, formerly of the Texas Army. Both men stole several horses from the plantation of the subscriber on the morning of February 20.

Saturday, March 10, 1838

Wm. M. LOGAN, adm. of est. of Henry B. PRENTISS, gives notice forbidding anyone from settling on a certain 11 League Grant on west side of the Trinity River, opposite the LONG KING's village, as well as another 11 League Grant be-

tween the Upper and Lower Coshatte villages, as said lands belong to the PRENTISS est. Adv. dated at Liberty on March 1.
A. WYNNS named adm. of Garret TOW, Houston.
A. WYNNS and Wm. LAWRENCE named admr's of estates of J. B. MURPHY, Isaac ALRIDGE, and James B. RODGERS, Houston.
Jt. Res. of Texas Congress approved on Nov. 18th authorizes Ellen O'DONNOVAN to take poss. of a stock of goods belonging to est. of her late husband, upon her giving bond in amount of $250 for the duties thereon.
Joint act of Texas Congress dated Dec. 18th provides that Thos. Wm. WARD, James C. NEILL, Jas. BELDEN, John THOM, and Washington SOMERS & all others who have been permanently disabled by the loss of an eye, arm or limb or such other bodily injury in the service of Texas, are hereby entitled to one league of land, as by certificate of board of land commissioners.
Administrator's Sale. I shall expose to public sale on 18th inst. at res. of Eli WILLIAMS in town of Harrisburg, all the personal property belonging to est. of late Denis EDSON, consisting of 14 gals of whiskey, 16 gals rum, 22 glas brandy, 15 gals Madeira wine, 1 box of almonds, 36 lbs of tobacco, 5 decanters, 1 pot, 1 tent, 1 mattress & blanket, $163 military scrip, &c. March 10. W. E. MILLER, Admr.
Sylvanus HATCH named adm. of est. of James ROSE, Jackson Co., Feb. 28.
$30 reward. Ranaway from subscriber in the city of Houston, Negro man named PLANNER, about 5'8", dark complexion, sharp features. Said Negro will prob. make for the plantation of Dr. Walter BRASHEAR in the Dutch settlement, St. Mary's Parish, La. $30 given if taken outside of Harrisburg Co. $20 if taken within. Deliver to D. WALDEN or R. B. BRASHEAR. Signed by P. W. HUMPREYS.

Saturday, March 17, 1838

Died on Feb. 4th on Galveston Island, after a long illness, Capt. Horrance P. CHAMBERLIN, late of the Texian Army and native of Buffalo, New York.

Geo. S. STRATTON named adm. of estates of Robt. WILKINS and John R. JENNINGS, Houston.

J. L. SLEIGHT named adm. of Enoch LATHAM est., Houston.

Notice. All persons are hereby forewarned against purchasing from any individual a certain site of land known as the Turtle Bayou League, situated on Turtle Bayou and Galveston Bay, adjoining the town of Anahuac, as the same is claimed by the subscriber, by virtue of a purchase from Green BLOUNT, to whom said league was granted by the Mexican government as his head right. Liberty, March 1. Wm. M. LOGAN.

Saturday, March 24, 1838

A letter has been received at this office with important info. for Kinear S. BENNET.

Notice. Daniel E. BROCK intends to run a keel boat regularly in the Trinity River from Cincinnati to Anahuac & will be at latter by the 25th. Dated March 15.

Robert D. JOHNSON has located permanently at Galveston and will attend to the sale of Lots on the Island. Galveston, March 1.

Married in this city on Thursday the 22nd inst., by John SHEA, Henry KESLER to Miss Mary BONZANO.

Thos. WARD named adm. to estates of James M. GEE, Wm. BLAZELY, and John JONES. March 23.

Nathaniel PECK named adm. of Seymour BOTTSFORD est., Washington Co.

A Runaway. There is now in my possession at my plantation near Washington, a Negro man aged about 40 years, about 5'5", calling himself Palmer JACKSON, and says he belongs to a Mr. BUSHARE of Attakapas, La., that he was brought to Texas last Sept. in a small boat by Robert BUSHARE, that he has been living in Houston ever since he arrived here, and that he is a free man. The owner can have him by applying to me and paying expenses. Robert STEVENSON, Sheriff of Washington County.

Look out for a Scoundrel! The public is advised to be on guard against a certain Col. Arthur WHITFIELD, who left Nash Co., N.C. some two days after having forged a note to the Tarboro branch of the State bank for $1400 or $1600. WHITFIELD is a fine figure of a man, about 5'10", dark hair, well mannered and well spoken, a man of business in every respect, and prone to ingratiate himself to strangers. It is supposed that he will make his way to Texas, and I feel it is my duty to forewarn the people against this fellow. Raleigh, N.C., Feb. 24, signed by Peter R. LILLY.

Proclamation by Alexander G. McNUTT, Governor of Mississippi: Whereas it has come to my attention that on or about Dec. 25, 1837, one Hiram HARDEN murdered his wife and has since become a fugitie from justice, I do hereby authorize a reward of $300 for any person or persons who may apprehend HARDEN and secure him in the jail of Marion County. HARDEN is about 5'9", stout built and very active, weighs about 170 pounds, fair complexion, light hair, light blue or grey eyes, about 21 years old; given to drinking and quarrelsome when drunk; he is a fiddler and carries a rifle. It is thought he has gone to Alabama or Florida. Proclamation dated Feb. 29, 1838.

Saturday, March 31, 1838

Some 2000 persons on Wednesday last witnessed the hangings of J. C. QUICK and David JONES for the murders of M. W. BRIGHAM and Mafred WOODS. Sentences had been handed down 4 days earlier by District Court, Harrisburg Co. Both QUICK and JONES were veterans of the late revolution. The latter was in the battle of San Jacinto after escaping the massacre at Goliad.

Geo. W. SCOTT and W. H. SCOTT named admr's of William SCOTT, decd., Harrisburg.

Samuel G. POWELL named adm. of est. of Leeman KELCEY, Houston, March 26.

Information Wanted. About 18 mos. ago, Mr. A. T. GAYLE, of Va., came to this country on the schooner Wm. Bryant. He was in this city last on Dec. 15th. Any one who may know anything concerning him will confer a particular favour on me and his friends by dropping a line to the undersigned at this office. Should this meet his eye, he may find me at this place until the 25th. Wm. B. GAYLE, March 27.

Houston, March 18. The undersigned passengers of the Correo express their high sense of gratitude to Capt. KING and his officers for the gentlemanly and urbane treatment they received on the passage from N.O. to Galveston, as well for their peculiar navigation from Gal. to this city: Mitchell BULLOCK, G. W. SCOTT, C. C. BROWN, E. M. JARVIS, Wm. F. WILSON, John GEACH, J. H. HOLLAND, D. SHERMAN, H. A. SMITH, John C. HUTCHINGSON, Francis MOORE, J. R. TILESTON, Miles H. WOODS, Jacob COFFMAN, E. J. ARNOLD, Green TAYLOR.

Appointments by the President.---Henry H. WILLIAMS, Consul of the Republic of Texas for the port of Baltimore; John F. CORTES, Consul for port of Natchitoches; John L. HODGE, Consul for the port of Philadelphia; and James D. HAMILTON, Consul for port of Charleston.

Saturday, April 7, 1838

Married Tuesday evening by Benj. F. HANNA, Mr. Henry TIERWESTER and Miss Ana WHITE of this county.

Manasseh SEVEY named adm. of James D. EGBERT and Thos, HOGAN estates, Houston.

Elizabeth ORRICK warns against trading for a league and a labor of land issued by the land commissioners of Washington Co. on Jan. 6, to the heirs of James ORRICK, late of this county. This certificate was obtained from me under "false representations" by one Jos. S. SMITH, Washington, March 23.

Notice. By order of the Probate Court of Harris County, will be sold to highest bidder, at the res. of Jonathon B. FROST, decd., on April 16th, 16 lots of ground containing nearly one acre each; 4 of them front on Buffaloe Bayou, others front a street adjacent to the city of Houston; 1 of them has a comfortable house, smokehouse, kitchen & a well on it; one of them has a dwelling house on it; many of the lots are under cultivation. Also selling 4 Negroes, viz: a man & a boy, a woman & a child. Terms cash, if they will bring their appraised value, if not they will be sold on 6-12 mos. credit, the purchaser to give bond & provide security. Will likely sell 5 other Negroes, 1 woman, two grown men, 1 boy, and 1 man who is a good carpenter, blacksmith, &c.; also will be selling a wagon, a car, five yoke oxen, some horses, some household and kitchen furniture, and blacksmith tools. Sale will be extended to Monday if necessary. S. M. FROST, Adm'r., March 29.

For sale, a likely Negro man, aged about 28 years, plane carpenter, for further particulars please apply at this office.

If Amos P. RANDALL and John S. WESTBROOK are residing anywhere in the Rep. of Tx., they are hereby requested to inform the undersigned. All persons hereby cautioned against purchasing the headrights of either of these men as they sold the same to me more than 12 mos. ago and a regular record of same was made in the office of the Clerk of the County of Brazoria. Signed R. M. FORBES, Columbia, April 5.

Saturday, April 14, 1838

Valuable Land for Sale. By virtue of an order of the Probate Court, Harrisburg County, there will be offered at public sale, at the store of Thos. SHELDON, on the 2d Thursday of April next, a tract of land containing ½ league of land (except for 1 labor) situated on Bray's Bayou about 1 mile from Houston and 2 miles from Harrisburg. This land belongs to Succ. of Luke MOORE, decd., and was the headright granted to the decd. Terms: one-fourth in cash, remainder to be made in six payments over either 12 to 24 months, with a mortgage on property. Signed by Thos. EARLE, Admr. of Luke MOORE Est.

Wednesday, April 18, 1838

Joseph D. CLEMENTS named adm. of Thomas R. MILLER estate, Gonzales, April 2.
John Rice JONES named adm. of est. of Stephen D. HURST, Marion, Brazoria Co., April 26.
J. MORGAN named adm. of est. of Styles G. FOWLER and Rich. BUSHEL est's, New Washington.
John S. BLACK named adm. of Marcus L. BLACK est., Washington County, April 7.
$100 reward and all reasonable charges for apprehension & delivery of a Negro man, DUDLEY, who was brought to Tx. by Wm. KEENER and by him sold to subscriber. He ranaway from New Year's Creek last Nov. DUDLEY is 23, spare built, well made, & weighs 150 lbs, remarkably active, and has beautiful set of teeth. David AYERS, Center Hill, March 30.
Notice. Came to the plantation of the subscriber about March 16th, a Negro boy (said to be an African, as his language cannot be understood), about 5'10", 25 years, spare made, skin very black, does not know his master's name, calls himself SACKEY & cannot talk with other Africans. Owner requested to come forward to pay charges & take him away. Henry JAMES, Fort Bend County, April 2.
Notice. I shall leave Texas on the 8th of next month for South Carolina & expect to be absent 2 mos.; during that time Geo. W. HORTON, Esq. will attend to my business both personal & professional & may always be found at my office in Washington town. Josiah J. CROSBY, Mar. 26.
Married at Galveston island on 8th inst., by Rev. HUNTINGDON, Mr. John N. REED to Emily M. LEWIS, both of Galveston.
Notice. D. M. STAPP is my agent during my absence from this Republic & has full power to transact all my business & to sell 2/3 a league situated on the Navidad, which was granted to me by the Mexican gov. John ALLEY, April 18.

Saturday, April 21, 1838

Died in this city on morning of 17th inst., of congestive fever, Nathaniel James DOBIE, of the commercial house of DOBIE & McCASKILL, aged 26 years. Decd. had been a resident of this county four years and was native of Sussex Co., Va., where his relatives still reside. Papers in N.O., Richmond & Petersburg, VA please copy.

Wednesday, April 25, 1838

The inhabitants of the frontier about 60 miles above Washington are forsaking farms and gathering at the forts on account of several incursions by small parties of Indians, who have lately killed 1 or 2 surveyors and a young man by the name of MOSS.

Escaped from the custody of sheriff of Montgomery Co., on the evening of 17th inst., Geo. NEWTON (alias Geo. JOHNSON, John RIGLEY, and John DICKSON) and Wm. BAKER, committed on chge. of counterfeiting Rep. of Tx. Treasury Notes. NEWTON is 5'8" or 10", sallow complexion, has a blemish in one eye, a blacksmith by trade, and 35-40 years old. BAKER is a good looking and impudent young man, about 20 or 21 years old, and bids fair to make a tip top rascal. Reward of $100 offered for capture of both, or $50 for either. Joshua ROBBINS, Sheriff of Montgomery County, Tx., April 21.

Wm. A. MATTHEWS named adm. of Almeron DICKERSON est., Gonzales Co. Prob. Ct, March Term.

Agee SHARPE named adm. of Benidic JOHNSON est., April 25.

Saturday, April 28, 1838

Married on the 25th inst., Charles MASON to Miss Evaline DEWITT, both of this city.

Saturday, May 2, 1838

Colonel Richards SPARKS has fallen victim to the Indians. Two weeks since he left Nacogdoches to locate land on the Trinity. He was

preceded from Fort Parker by a surveying party, with which he managed to join up near Three Forks, when the Indians attacked the entire group. SPARKS was shot through the head; two other man Hunter F. HOLLAND & a surveyor named BARRY were also killed. Believed to be work of Kickapoos---Nacogdoches Chronicle (The editor of the Telegraph contends the Indians were probably "Keachies or Wacos.")
Whitney BRITTAN named adm. of est. of Geo A. PITTUCK, Harrisburg County, May 2.

Saturday, May 5, 1838

A man by the name of CAMPBELL, convicted of the murder of a Mr. LINSEY, was hanged at Victoria on Saturday last.

Sale of Negroes. By virtue of a decree of Probate Ct., Harrisburg Co., dated May 3, and in accordance with the power vested in us by the Last Will & Testament of James ROUTH, decd., we will sell at public auction on June 6th at New Washington the following slaves, to wit: Negro man BILL; man BILL & his wife JINNEY; man LEWIS or LEW, his wife MARIA & their 6 children; and a girl HARRIET; or so many as will bring about the amount of $3000 to be sold for the purpose of paying the debts of the est. of James ROUTH, decd. J. MORGAN & Geo. M. PATRICK, Exct'rs.

Administrators Sale. By order of Probate Ct. of Harrisburg Co., I shall sell at public outcry on 14th inst., all personal prop. belonging to est. of Elisha BURRIT, late of sd. county, consisting of diverse articles of clothing, Mathematical instruments & books, a lot of mapping paper & other articles. Terms, cash. DOSWELL & ADAMS, Auctioneers. W. Pinkney HILL, Administrator.

Sheriff's sale. By order of Co. Ct., Harrisburg Co., I will expose to public sale at the Courthouse on the 23rd all right, title & interest of J. G. WELCHMYER & Michael DeCHAUMS in the following property: 1 Negro girl named JANE & several town lots, sold to satisfy a judgement in favor of D.W.C. HARRIS. Signed by J. W. MOORE, Sheriff, Harrisburg County.

By joint action of the House & Senate on the 25th April, the following vacancies on various Boards of Land Commissioners were made for the following counties: Chichester CHAPLIN, President, & W. R. WARD, assoc. comm., San Augustine Co.; H. HALL, assoc. comm., Bexar Co.; James H. STARR, Pres. & John R. HUBBARD, assoc. comm., Nacogdoches Co.; O. A. DELANO, assoc. comm., Jefferson Co.; W. W. ARRINGTON, assoc. comm., Washington Co.; C. H. HOWARD, Pres., Matagorda Co.; Hortz HOFFLER, Pres., Houston Co.; Adam ZUMWART, assoc. comm., Gonzales Co.; Darwin M. STAPP, assoc. comm., Jackson Co.; Jesse WEBB and P. H. CARRAWAY, assoc. commr's, Milam Co.; Wm. CLARKE, Jr., assoc. comm., Sabine Co.; James ARMSTRONG, Pres., & H. W. TUDLOTH, assoc. comm., Jasper Co.; Rowlett Samuel McFARLAND, assoc. comm., Fannin Co.; Daniel PERRY, Pres., & J. F. PAYNE and a Mr. BONDS, assoc. commr's, Fort Bend Co.

Wednesday, May 9, 1838

James B. ALLEN and Elizabeth ALLEN named as admr's of est. of Martin ALLEN, Austin Co., April 2.
Randal JONES named adm. of est. of John L. MONK, Richmond, Fort Bend Co., April 30.
Admr. Sale. A public auction will be held on June 2nd at the res. of the subscriber for all property belonging to the est. of John JAMES, late of this county. Henry JONES, Adm., Fort Bend Co., May 1.
Notice. If this adv. should meet the eye of Robt. F. RANDALL his immediate attention is desired. "He is the residuary legatee under the will of a gentleman who has lately died, & his interest is supposed be worth $20,000." A suit is now pending which he will he be divested of his rights unless he comes forward. S. HEYDENFELT, Atty. at Law, Montgomery Co., Ala. The Matagorda **Bulletin** & Nacogdoches **Chronicle** will please run this notice once and forward the acct. to the **Telegraph** office for collection.
Notice. J. B. CHANCE of Washington announces that he has been apptd. Deputy Surveyor for

Robertson Co. for 2nd Dist. & will spend the ensuing months in making locations in that part of the country. Notes that he has been a resident of Tx. for 9 years, 3 of which engaged in surveying. "I will leave this place between 1st and 10th of May on a surveying expedition to the above named district."

Ashbel SMITH announces his intention to seek letters of adm. for est. of late Ebenezer R. HALE, late soldier and "armorour in the service of the Republic of Texas;" and he will contest the application of Frederick NEIBLING of Brazoria Co. for same.

Saturday, May 12, 1838

Samuel DEXTER named adm. of est. of George GRANT, decd., Harrisburg Co.

Frederick NEIBLING agrees to have his name removed as admr. of est. of late Ebenezer R. HALE in favor of the application of Ashbel SMITH. All of said acts of NEIBLING as adm. up to this date are acknowledged. SMITH serves notice that he has been appointed as "attorney of the heir at law of the decedent" and that he has been placed in full possession of the effects of said HALE. Notice also includes a statement that HALE died at Dimmit's Landing on October 5, 1836.

Died at Richmond on the Brazos on evening of 10th inst., Mrs. Elizabeth BORDEN, consort of John P. BORDEN, General Land Commissioner.

List of Medical Censors, as elected by Joint Vote of both Houses of Congress: Ashbel SMITH, for dist. of Harrisburg & Liberty; A. C. HOXIE, MD, for Washington dist.; Geo. W. HILL, MD, for Milam dist.; J. M. Neil STEWART, MD, for Brazoria dist.; J. P. JANUARY, MD, for dist. of San Patricio, Refugio & Goliad; R. A. IRION, MD, for dist. of Nacogdoches and Houston; Joel JOHNSON, MD, for dist. of Austin and Colorado; Isaac JONES, MD, for Red River dist.; H. BISSEL, MD, for Bexar dist.; and A. M. LEVY, MD, for dist. of Matagorda, Victoria & Jackson.

Wednesday, May 16, 1838

On Wednesday last a man named BOYD in Washington Co., Miss., killed W. F. JEFFRIES and Simon MILLER with a Bowie knife. The terrible outrage was committed at a "doggery" or drinking house.

John BELDEN, adm. of est. of John FREDERICK, announces plans to sale 1280 acres of bounty land belonging to said est. The sale will be on June 20th in front of the Houston House, Harrisburg County.

Law notice. John D. MORRIS, atty. & counselor at law, has located himself at San Antonio and will attend to the courts of Bexar, Goliad, Victoria and San Patricio.

Notice. As there has been much said about the contract between Gen. Sam HOUSTON and myself, I think it proper to publish the same. Agreement dated Aug. 24, 1836 between HOUSTON and Peter E. BEAN, both of the Nacogdoches municipality. Document states that BEAN sells to HOUSTON a tract of land (about 1 league), located about 2 leagues east of Nacogdoches, and known by the name of Bean's Plantation; HOUSTON agrees to pay BEAN $5,000; upon payment of that sum, BEAN promises to give title to HOUSTON; if BEAN does not make the title to HOUSTON, BEAN agrees to pay $3000 to HOUSTON. Signed by Sam HOUSTON and P. E. BEAN.

Notice. I hereby revoke all powers of atty. given by me during my recent absence from this city. J. CORNICK, Jr.

Executors sale. Will be sold, by order of the Probate Ct., Brazoria County, to the highest bidder, the following valuable property, belonging to the succ. of Stephen F. AUSTIN, decd. Terms---one-fourth cash, balance on a credit of 12 mos., with approved security and a lien on the prop. until final payment, viz: At Houston on June 15th at FLOYD & COLLINS' Hotel, two tracts of land, one totaling 2,200 acres of land and situated on Bray's Bayou, and another totalling 3,300 acres and situated on Buffalo Bayou, about 8 miles from Houston and known as the Pine Point League, being the nearest good pine timber to the Brazos valley; at San Felipe de Austin, on June 22, two tracts of land containing 9 Labors, situated on the west margin of the man Bernardo, adjoining lands of J. B. PHELPS, D. HAMILTON and others; and at Bastrop, in front of the Courthouse on June 20, several out lots, containing from 10 to 20 acres of land, below and adjoining the aforesaid town. Signed by James F. PERRY, Executor.

Saturday, May 19, 1838

Died in this city on 12th inst., Mrs. Elizabeth STANLEY, aged 22 years. She leaves a husband and two sons to deplore her loss.

H. C. DAVIS named adm. of est. of Geo. ROSS.

Trunk found. Found concealed in the woods near this city, a small red trunk containing a pocket map of the state of Mississippi marked David MUNROE, also a pistol and powder flask. The owner of these articles will find them with O. J. COCHRAN.

Adm. Notice. County of Bexar, Republic of Texas. All persons are hereby notified that lands advertised to be sold in May by John W. SMITH, clerk of said county, as adm. of est. of the late Baron de BASTROP do not belong to said estate. This land is situated on SW side of the "Gaudaloupe" river, at the spring called Ojo de Agua del Comal. Said lands belong to the est. of the late Juan Martin de VERAMENDI. Luciana NAVARRO, adm. and guardian of Marco A. VERAMENDI, heir of the estate. Dated April 23.

Wm. P. SMITH named adm. of estates of Wm. M. CAREY, Abner C. DAVIS, J. GWYNN, Ross McLELAND, J. D. WEBB, Geo. A. SHELLAN, and Benedict JOHNSON, Washington, May 2.

Wm. H. POOL named adm. of estates of Jas. M. ROBINSON and P. Henry ANDERSON, Fort Bend Co.

Dr. James Anson DUNN will attend to the practice of Medicine & Surgery in this place & vicinity, with an office in H. SANDERSON's new building on Main Street and across from FLOYD's Hotel.

Wednesday, May 23, 1838

Thos. W. BUNDICK named adm. of est. of M. H. BUNDICK, Harrisburg County.
Notice. We will sell at a public auction on July 4th, ¼ league of land belonging to est. of M. HENRY. Sale will be conducted at Velasco; & land fronts on the Brazos River near the town of Velasco, above and below Brown's labor. Asa MITCHELL and Wm. H. WHARTON, Administrators.
Wm. PIERPOINT named adm. of Wm. FRANCIS est.

Saturday, May 26, 1838

Martin RUTER, D.D., supt. of the Methodist-Episcopal mission from the U.S., after a severe illness of 3 weeks, died at Washington on May 16 at 2 p.m. and was laid to rest at 5 p.m. of same day. Funeral to be held later.
Adam ZUMWALT named adm. of Samuel McCOY est. at Gonzales County.

Saturday, June 2, 1838

A skirmish took place a few days since near Tenoxtitlan between a party of settlers from the vicinity of Fort Oldham and a number of Indians concealed in a thicket. A charge was made by the Indians, who killed two men, Dr. BIGHAM and Joseph REED, and wounded a Mr. LAWSON. Neither of the men were scalped.
A party of "Comanchies" visited this city on Saturday last and met with President HOUSTON at his house. The principal Chief wore a Mexican officer's hat, of which he was quite proud; Mr. LeGRAND who has resided with the Comanches for seveal years refers to them as the "Comanches of the Woods," who inhabit a hilly tract northeast of Bexar.
Died at Victoria on the 26th ult., Daniel SCANNELI, late of New York City, aged 20, of bilious fever.
Notice. Will be sold on July 5th at door of the Courthouse, Harrisburg Co., 1280 acres of bounty land belonging to the succ. of J. W. KINGSLEY. David HARRY, Administrator.

Texas Congress authorizes 1st Auditor of Public Accounts to audit the claim of John R. FOSTER for personal services in the Army of the Republic of Texas from Oct. 8, 1835 to Feb. 14, 1836. Approved May 24.

Joint Act of Tx. Congress acknowledges that a mistake was made at land office in which the property described below was given to John HODGE on Jan. 14, 1831 and should have gone to Robt. HODGE; therefore be it enacted that the Comm. of the General Land Office should strike the name of John HODGE and replace it with Robt HODGE on the original grant and on the copy in the poss. of Robt. HODGE; this tract of land is located east of San Bernard and lying in back of Leagues 1, 2 and 3. Approved May 16.

Joint Res. of Tx. Congress approves audit of claim of Wm. KUYKENDALL for $205 for horse and corn furnish the army of the Rep. of Tx.; adopted May 24.

Joint Res. of Congress for relief of A. C. HORTON to be paid $350 per month for his service as a Navy Agent from Dec. 3, 1837 to the time of his return; approved May 24.

Joint Res. for the benefit of P. S. WYATT for the sum of $1200 as compensation for arms & monies expended by him in bringing a company of men to Texas in 1835; the resolution provides that $600 of the appropriation should be held in reserve by the Treasurer of the Republic until a similar demand has been made by State of Alabama by P. S. WYATT; Approved May 24.

$50 reward. My negro man BOB ranaway from me on the 23rd inst.; he is about 5'9", high, yellow complexion; took with him a rifle gun, shot pouch, and powder horn, and a strong Bowie knife. He left in company with a tall black man belonging to Mrs. R. HARDEMAN, three miles above me on Caney in Austin's colony; C. EAGEN.

To the Public. I take this opportunity of informing the public in general that I have made arrangements with Mr. CORRI, who has lately arrived in this city with "a corps Dramatic hailing from different Theatres of the United States." Another adv. by Mr. CORRI states that he is "late of the St. Charles, New Orleans, Mobile Theatres" and has established a Houston Theatre. Other performers are: Mr. BARKER, late of St. Charles, N.O. and Mobile; Mr. JACKSON, late of N.Y. and Boston; Mr. SARGENT, late of Mobile; Mr. NEWTON, late of Tremont Theatre, Boston; Mr. ORMOND, late of Philadelphia; Mr. CHAMBERS, late the Principal Dancer at Mobile Theatre; Mr. HORN, late of Mobile and N.O.; Mrs. BARKER, late of St. Chas., N.O. & Mobile; Mrs. HUBBARD, late of Camp Street and Mobile; Miss VOST, late of N.Y. and Mobile; Madame THIELMAN from St. Chas. Theatre, N.O.; a full and efficient orchestra is also engaged. Leader & 1st violin is Mr. BOLTON of N.O.; dresses made especially for the occasion by Madame DIROENS of New Orleans. Adv. signed by John CARLOS, Houston.

Jt. Act of Congress orders the Quartermaster Gen. to settle with F. NEBLIN for his service as asst. commissary general during the spring & summer of 1836. Approved May 7.

Saturday, June 9, 1838

Married on evening of May 24th, at Lake Providence, U.S., Augustus M. TOMPKINS of this city and Miss E. E. GRAHAM of Louisiana.

Married in Washington on 31st ult., by Hon. J. P. COLE, Mr. Thos. P. SHEPARD of the firm of HOOD, SHEPARD & Co., to Miss Anne HOPE, all of this city.

Died in this city on 28th ult., at 10 p.m., of the bilious fever, Dr. Hezekiah BISSEL, formerly of Wooster, Ohio. The Cincinnati Gazette will please notice.

H. PRATT is seeking letters of adm. for est. of D. GILMARTIN, a decd. soldier. Unless good objections are raised within 60 days, the pet.

will be granted by the Probate Court of Harrisburg County, June 8.
Michael CRONICAN named adm. of estates of Chas. SARGENT & Daniel BUCKLEY, Harrisburg Co.
Elisha FLOYD named adm. of est. of R. MONTGOMERY, Harrisburg County.
David HARRY, adm. of L. W. KINGSLEY est., announces 1280 acres belonging to said succ. will be sold on July 5th at Courthouse door.
We the undersigned passengers of the steamboat "Sam Houston," from Galveston to Houston, cannot leave the boat without expressing thanks to the Capt. S. B. EVES and his officers for their gentlemanly and polite conduct to us during our journey. Signed: B.L. HANKS, Thos. M. LEAGUE, N. JOHNSON, Peter F. BIGG, P. L. LEMAN, Josiah BISHOP, Thos. J. JOHNSTON, M. A. DIBBLE, J. BENNET, Niles S. BENNET (of Cincinnati, OH), A. TURNER, Thos. J. STANSBURRY, A. M. TOMKINS, Geo. W. GRANT, G. EVERITTE, T. M. L. STANSSBERRY, N. WINTERSMITH, E. E. TOMKINS, and John WOODRUFF.
Notice. Was taken up & confined in the Caleboose of Bexar County on 18th inst., Negro Man who says his name is WASHINGTON, or is generally called WASH, and says he belongs to Col. S. BOSHEA of Natchitoches, La. He is about 20 years old, about 5'3", light brown complexion, and has lost two upper front teeth. The owner is required to come forward and comply with the law. James F. JOHNSON, Deputy Sheriff (for J.F. HOOD, City of Bexar), San Antonio, May 21.

Saturday, June 16, 1838

John W. SMITH named adm. of estates of Baron DE BASTROP and Filipe Enrique NERI, both decd., Bexar County, 26th April 1838.
James W. PARKER named adm. of estates of Benjamin PARKER and Stephen BOYINGTON, Huntsville, Montgomery Co., June 14.
Jonathon & Sarah McGARY named admr's of est. of George A. LAMB.
William G. COOKE named adm. of ests. of Wm. MOTLEY and Henry L. THOMPSON, Harrisburg Co.

C. Herman JAEGER named adm. of estates of Edward HARCOURT & Ernst RICHTER, Columbia, Brazoria County, May 28.
Amelia BATTERSON named adm. of Isaac BATTERSON est., June 14.
Henry S. MAYS named adm. of Saml. A.I. MAYS.
Joseph BARNARD named adm. of the estates of Otis G. EELES, Z. M. SHORT, Seth CLARK, and Alfred DORSEY, all of whom were under the command of Col. FANNIN at Goliad and were either killed in battle of 19th March 1836 or the massacre on 27th of same month. Richmond, Texas.
Thirteen Americans, accompanied by 2 Comanches left San Antonio on May 12th and traveled 125 miles to the NW to village of ISOWACONY, the principal chief of the Comanche nation; the village was located on N bank of Rio Blanco and consisted of 400-500 tents and 900-1000 of the Indians.
Sacrilege!!! $1000 Reward! On the night of 25th inst., the Catholic Church at this place was feloniously entered and the following articles were stolen: the plate used in Divine services, a large crucifix about 8 feet tall, 4 large candlesticks about 30 inches tall, and 1 very tall candlestick about 6 feet tall. Signed by: R. R. ROYALL, Chmn.; Thos. THATCHAER, L. SMITHERS, M. B. SKERITT, L. B. FRANKS, Comm. San Antonio, May 26th.

Saturday, June 23, 1838

"Be it resolved by the Senate and House of Rep. of the Rep. of Tx. in Congress assembled, that John VINCE son of Allen VINCE and Matilda WILBOURNE is hereby declared legitimate and capable of inheriting his parents property in the same manner as if he had been born in lawful wedlock." Approved May 24.
John SHARPE named adm. of est. of M. C. BOWIE, Velasco.
Joseph JOHNSON named adm. of est. of Joseph EMERY, decd. soldier, June 16.
William W. HAWKINS named adm. of est. for Ashley R. STEVENS, decd., June 16.

Joint Res. of Tx. Congress provides that Wm. BRASHEAR and I. C. DUVAL, upon the testimony of 2 or more respected witnesses testifying that they are the brothers of R. C. BRASHEAR and B. H. DUVAL (who were of the unfortunate command of Col. FANNIN), should be permitted to receive their pay, bounty lands & headrights in the same manner as if they had complied with the law requiring them to administrate and to publish acts of adm. Approved May 24.

Joint Res. of Congress provides for 1280 ac. of bounty land to John TALBOT for his service as armorer at Galveston island. Aprvd. May 21.

Joint Act of House and Senate approves pension of $200 per annum shall be paid to Mary MILLSAPS & her children. Approved May 21.

Saturday, June 30, 1838

"We learn from the Courier that James HUMPHREYS, who killed Capt. Jo. POWELL at Columbia, Texas, some time ago, was arrested on Wed. last by Capt. JONES of the Third Municipality. He is in the Calaboose, has confessed to the murder, & will be sent back to Texas."-- [New Orleans] Picayune.

Extraordinary Decision. In the Arkansas Advocate of the 15th, it is stated that, in the case of the State vs. WILSON, for the murder of J. J. ANTHONY, a member of the lower branch of the legislatures, the jury returned a verdict of "not guilty of murder, but excusable homicide."

Married at Harrisburg, on Tuesday evening last, Capt. Thos. W. MARSHALL to Miss Virginia MILLSAPS, both of this city.

Died in this city on 24th inst., D. W. C. CURTIS, aged about 19, of fever; NY papers will please publish.

Died in this city on 24th, Samuel H. WILKINS of fever, aged about 26. Mobile papers will please notice.

Died on 26th, Jos. L. LOCKHART of dropsy.

Jane LOCKHART named adm. of est. of John LOCKHART, Harrisburg County.

C. B. STEWART named adm. of est. of James BUCHANAN, a decd. soldier of Washington Co., by Probate Court of Montgomery Co.

Dugald McPHERSON and DENIS NEIL named admr's of est. of Chas. M. BYRNE, Harrisburg Co.

Musgrove EVANS seeks letters of adm. to est. of Saml. B. EVANS, decd. soldier, Harrisburg Co.

Saturday, July 7, 1838

Thos. R. DAVIS named adm. of est. of Travis DAVIS, decd. soldier, Columbia.

Md. on Wed. evening, July 4th, John W. ELDRIDGE to Sarah, dtr. of Christopher MILLER.

Elizabeth ROWE petitions Probate Court of Gonzales Co. on June 25th, for letters of adm. in 2 cases, viz: est. of her late former husband James GEORGE, who died at the Alamo, and also in case of her bro. Wm. DEARDUFF, who also died in same battle; Ct. will grant petition after adv. has run 60 days and if no objection are made.

John M. and Mary SHIPMAN named admr's of the Moses SHIPMAN estate.

J. W. PORTER and Rachel CULLENS named admr's of Anson CULLENS est.; Rachel is the wife of the decd., Milam County Probate Ct.

Augustus H. GILLAND seeks letters of adm. in est. of his bro. Geo. M. GILLAND, a decd. soldier in army of Tx., Harrisburg Co., July 6.

Sterling N. DOBIE seeks letters of adm. in est. of Isaac RYAN, decd. soldier in Tx. Army, Harrisburg Co.; pet. filed July 4th.

Col. Jesse BENTON seeking letters of adm. in est. of Geo. W. CHILDRESS, decd. soldier in Tx. Army, Harrisburg Co., pet. filed July 6.

Monday, July 9, 1838

Dr. T. HUMPHREYS, charged with murder of Capt. POWELL and who was lately arrested in New Orleans, is now lodged in jail in this city.

John MORRIS named adm. of late Thos. HARMAN est., Columbia, Brazoria Co., May 28; decd. was a soldier in the army and MORRIS will seek land due for his service.

Info. is wanted of Alexander COOK, who formerly lived in Texas---first at Anahuac & then near the La Bacca. Mr. COOK will hear of something much to his interest, if he will make his residence known to the editor of this paper.

John CHASSAIGNE begs to inform the inhabitants of Houston that he has recently arrived in the city from N.O. and brought a large supply of groceries & liquors, which he will sell cheap. He is located in the store formerly occupied by Wm. H. COLE on Main Street.

Land Agency. All persons who have heretofore authorized me to locate their headrights will please forward their certificates to me at the post office of Fort Oldham or at my residence in San Antonio Prairie. Frederick NEIBLING, July 7.

W. H. H. BALDRIDGE named adm. of Andrew KENT est., Gonzales Co., July 5.

A. M. CLARE named adm. of Henry P. MILLS estate, June 20.

Francis FITZHUGH seeks letters of adm. for est. of Wesley FITZHUGH, decd. soldier of Tx. Army; filed June 20 at Gonzales Co. Prob. Ct.

N. W. SHEPHERD named adm. of est. of John BRICKER, decd. soldier, of Washington Co., filed in Montgomery County, June 27.

I am compelled on acct. of bad health to travel and offer for sale any of my lands on the Brazos, Bernard & Colorado rivers. Those on the Brazos are scattered on both sides of the river to the old Bexar Road; & I will also include my plantation where I now reside. Bargains can be had, but delay & all chance in lost. Jared E. GROCE, Pleasant Hill, June 28.

W. W. GANT named adm. of estates of James S. EDGAR and Asa WALKER, Washington Co., June 24.

Hugh GRANT of N.O. announces that Daniel I. TOLER has no auth. to dispose of any property belonging to my late bro., Dr. James GRANT, who died while in the army of Tx. in March 1836. I recd. a letter from TOLER at Nacogdoches dated Aug. 20, of same year, in which he said he had recd. my brother's will, dated at Bexar on 30th of Dec., 1835, setting forth that he and I were named as executors. In the same letter, TOLER mentioned that he had the will registered. I have strong proof that he never had it probated and I have been unable to get a copy over the past 2 years. Dated June 27, New Orleans.

Saturday, July 14, 1838

Died on the 7th at her res. near Richmond of child birth, together with her infant, Martha Ann, wife of Major Cornelius C. SEBRING, aged 25 years, late of New York.
Died in this city on the 11th inst., Mrs. Mary WILLIAMS, consort of Eli WILLIAMS.
Departed this life on June 17th in city of Bexar, C. M. STEVENSON from Greene Co., Ala.
J. D. CLEMENTS named adm. of est. of Isaac BAKER, a decd. soldier, Gonzales County.
John GRAY named adm. of est. of Wm. GUYMAN, Harrisburg Co., June 25th.
Andrew PONTON is adm. of Silas FUQUEA est.
Joseph JOHNSTON named adm. of est. of Wm. LANGHUDGE, a decd. soldier, Washington County Probate Court, on April 30th last. Adv. is dated July 4th from Robertson County.

Saturday, July 21, 1838

A funeral discourse honoring the late Gail LOCKHART will be delivered at the Capitol on Sabbath next by Dr. J. MERRILL at the usual hour of public workship.
Wm. H. KING named adm. of est. of Jacob CASPARI, decd. soldier, San Antonio Prairie, adv. dated July 16th.
Frederick NEIBLIN and Wm. H. KING named adm. of est. of Chas. MUIRHARD, decd. soldier, San Antonio Prairie, July 16th.
Other estates: John A. IRVINE, adm. of est. of Capt. Benj. C. WALLACE; Andrew PONTON, adm. of Wm. LEACH est.; and F. MOREHOUSE to be adm. of George S. DENNISON at Jackson Co. Other two adv's. do not list name of county.

Saturday, July 28, 1838

The funeral of the late Chief Justice COLLINSWORTH took place on Tuesday last, with an oration delivered by A. M. TOMPKINS. The remains were followed to the grave by a large concourse of our citizens. His body was discovered on Galveston beach several days ago.
Died at Galveston on 21st inst., Chas. Jos. BUTLER, aged about 30 years, son of Joseph BUTLER of New Harford, Oneida Co., NY. Editors at Natchez, Miss. will please notice this.
Andrew SCOTT named adm. of John G. COE est.; COE was a decd. soldier, Jackson Co., July 22.
Lucy PARKER named adm. of est. of Silas M. PARKER, decd. soldier in Army of Texas.
Harvey PARKER named adm. of est. of William PARKER, a decd. soldier in Army of Texas.
Wm. WALKER named adm. of Wm. GODDEN est.
Notice. Whereas I hold the bond of Elizabeth JONES, John JONES, Mary RANKEN, Deborah JONES & Nancy JONES, the condition of which bond makes it incumbent on me to clear out of the land office and discharge all dues upon the head right of John JONES, decd., ancestor of the obligers; also a power of atty. to act for them in all cases touching these presents...I hereby notify the aforesaid persons, and all others whom it may concern, to come forward and discharge their obligations, or the penalties of the bond will be rigorously enacted. Pierre BLANCHET, July 28.
Curtis M. JACKSON seeks letters of adm. in the estates of John M. MORGAN & Wm. S. PARKER, both decd. soldiers, Milam, Sabine County.
Alancon FERGUSON named adm. of estates of H. H. HUNTER and Oliver H. SMITH.
Jacob MITCHUSSON named adm. of E. MITCHUSON, Nacogdoches County.
Alexander SUMMERAL seeks letters of adm. in est. of Jos. HICKS, Richmond, Fort Bend Co., July 20. Hearing set for Sept. term of Probate Court.

Mr. BARKER, one of the Theatre currently engaged by Mr. CORRI, committed suicide in this city on the evening of Tues. last---dying from effects of drinking half a bottle of Laudanum, dying in front of his wife.

Monday, July 30, 1838

A Negro Man. Taken up near Sabine Bay by Solomon COLE on or about July 1st, a Negro man who calls himself GABRIEL & says he was sold by a man named VERGESS in Wilmington, NC to a man from Ky.; 2 nights after he was sold he ran off with a man named DAVIS, who then tried to sell him. He escaped while on a steamboat on the Mississippi. He is about 5'7", about 32 years old, no marks visible except small scars on left ear and left hand, weighs about 170 lbs., affable in manner. Owner is requested to come forward, prove his property, pay charges, and take him away. Wm. STEPHENSON, Sheriff of Jefferson County. Beaumont, July 20th.

A. NEILL named adm. of est. of John McCLURE, a decd. soldier, Gonzales Co. Probate Court.

Notice. This is to notify Mr. Isaac JONES to leave the tracts of land [one league and one fourth a league] situated on the North by lands belonging to Johnathon LINDLEY, on South by lands belonging to Mr. STEPHENS; on East by Trinity river; and on west by lands of Rudolp McGEE; and in the County of Liberty. The foresaid fourth league is situated between said league and the Batist Village on the east by Trinity river and on west by lands belonging to James LEE. The league was granted to Padro MADEIRA on 23d July 1835---the fourth a league was granted to Johnathon LINDLEY on 17th July 1835. The above statements can be proven by the General Land Office. I therefore warn JONES against cutting or destroying anything on said tracts of land. I further forewarn all others from using this land in any way. Should any person lay himself liable to a prosecution it certainly will be tended to by Piere BLANCHET, Houston, July 19th.

Saturday, August 11, 1838

Col. Peter W. GRAYSON, candidate for President of Rep. of Tx., has died by his own hand; he shot himself through the head with a pistol at Bean's Station, Ky. on night of 18th ult.; he was 47 years old and had been lately offered the position of Minister to the United States.

Died at Galveston, July 28th, Mrs. Margaret SHACKERLY, 27, wife of Wm. H. SHACKERLY.

Information wanted. Any info. that can be given relative to James MITCHELL, who emigrated to this country from Kennebunk, State of Maine, will be thankfully received by the undersigned at Galveston. James BURKHAM.

Henry FISHER seeks letters of adm. to estate of Lewis DILLEN, decd., Harrisburg Co., Aug. 9.

Any information on Geo. CALLIOTT will be thankfully recd. at this office. He joined the Texian army before the fall of Bexar and hasn't been heard from since then.

Married at Nacogdoches on 1st inst., Wm. G. LEWIS to Miss Louisa SIMS, late of Winston-Salem, North Carolina.

Henry PARKER named adm. of est. of Wm. PARK, a deceased soldier of army of Texas.

Notice. James H. KENNICOTT, atty. & counselor at law, has established himself at Houston and will attend to a legal practice here. Mr. KENNICOTT has several years experience in N.O. and is acquainted with the Spanish language.

Saturday, August 18, 1838

Died at res. of C. DYKEMAN, Montgomery Co., on 3rd inst., after short illness, Mr. Ishael SACKET, aged about 30, formerly of Cincinnati.

Departed this life on July 18th, at res. of A. C. ALLEN, his brother, Major John K. ALLEN, 29, a native of N.Y. who came to Tx. with his bro. in 1833. Decd. had been much exposed to the sun during his recent visit to the East and was attacked on his return by bilious fever, with which he was confined for 11 days.

Died on 31st ult., in New Washington, at the res. of her uncle Col. James MORGAN, Mrs. Sarah P. PATRICK, consort of Dr. Geo. M. PATRICK, at the age of 23 years. Decd. was born in Hertford Co., N.C. and lived there until removing to this country in 1834. Soon after her arrival, she was married to Dr. PATRICK.

Notice. A list of administrators who have filed on the estates of decd. soldiers in the Dept. of War for the first quarter ending the 18th inst. Names of the decd. are listed in parentheses: Ashbel SMITH (for Ebenezer R. HALE, decd.); Henry MAYES (Samuel G. MAYS); Wm. SCURLOCK (Mial SCURLOCK); J. W. CUMMINGS (C. P. CUMMINGS); Ashbel SMITH (Chauncey GOODRICH); M. EVANS (Samuel R. EVANS); Jeremiah TIMMINS (Caleb M. TIMMINS); Thos. H. McINTIRE (Hugh M. FRAZIER); Augustus BARKER (Ira WESTOVER); Adolphus STERNE (Conrad EIGINAMER); Mary ROBBINS (E. ROBBINS); Thos. H. McINTYRE (L. W. GATES); Jas. HAGGARD (Nevill HAGGARD); Asa MITCHELL (Nathan MITCHELL); Wm. A. FARIS (Travis DAVIS); Wm. MANN (Walter L. MANN); Adam STAFFORD (Harvey STAFFORD); W. M. COOK (Robt. C. MORRIS); Wm. S. RICHERSON (Wm. T. MALONE); James D. CLEMMONS (Isaac BAKER); Andrew PONTON (Galba FUQUA); Andrew NEILL (John McCLURE); A. NEILL (Wm. TAYLOR): James W. BROOKS (S. PENDLETON); George VAUGHN (Wm. E. VAUGHN); G. W. GRANT (Edward WYNGATE); John HART (James M. MILLER); David HARRY (L. W. KINGSBURY); A. WYNNS & W. LAWRENCE (James B. MURPHY, James RODGERS, Thos. G. ALDRIDGE & Garret LAW); and Isaac HOSKINS (Francis JOHNSON). Published in accordance with an Act of Congress passed May 18th, 1837. Signed Geo. W. HOCKLEY, Secretary of War, Aug. 18th.

Saturday, August 25, 1838

Henry R. ALLEN seeks letters of adm. on est. of John K. ALLEN, Harrisburg Co., Probate Ct., August 20.

Joel LEE, pltff. vs. Catherine LEE, defendant, action for divorce, Harrisburg Co., Dist. Ct., March Term. Adv. dated Aug. 24.

Solomon PAGE, pltff. vs. Harriet PAGE, def., action for divorce, Harrisburg Co., Dist. Ct., March term, adv. dated August 24.

Richard Henry LEACH, pltff. vs. Mary McQUART def., action for divorce, Harrisburg Co. Dist. Ct., March Term. Adv. dated Aug. 24.

Sophia AUGHIBAUGH, pltff. vs. Jesse A. AUGHINBAUGH, def., action for divorce, petition filed with Harrisburg Co. Dist. Ct. on July 25.

All of the above cases have been scheduled to be heard for November Term.

The notorious James WRIGHT has been arrested at Columbia and will soon be removed to the co. jail here to await trial.

For Sale a new 2 story frame dwelling house situated near the Custom house in city of Galveston. Apply to J. W. CRUGER, Houston, or to L. H. HITCHCOCK, Galveston. Aug. 24 adv.

John BURGESS named adm. of est. of John HAINEY, Brazoria County, July 21.

John R. KING seeks letters of adm. in Gonzales Co. for est. of Wm. P. KING, a decd. soldier who fell at the Alamo.

W. W. SHEPHERD named adm. of est. of M. P. CLARK, Aug. 24 adv. date.

Public Sale. Will be sold at public auction on Monday the 31st in city of Richmond, the following property: two Negro slaves---REUBEN, aged about 24, a smart & active man who can make himself useful in a variety of ways; and ELIZA, about 19, a good cook and washer. David AUSTIN, Auctioneer.

A camp meeting will commence on 1st Thursday of October next on Pina Creek, Austin Co., two miles south of Centre Hill. All members of the gospel in good standing in their different denominations are invited. R. ALEXANDER, missionary Methodist Episcopal Church.

Arrived at Galveston 9 a.m., brig Emprasario 40 hours from SW Pass of the Mississippi. Passengers on board---James R. BROWN, D. VANCALT, W. JONES, E. V. RUSSEL, D. COLL, D. E. SMITH, S. A. ROBERTS, H. ATKINSON, P. CHASTINE, T. S. LEWIS, H. R. CARTWELL, Thos. P. CARMELL, Miss MORGAN, Miss FITCHETT, Miss E.

JONES, D. F. FITCHETT, J. G. WILLIAMS, George LONGCOPE, and 33 Negroes.

Jos. ATORFF begs leave to inform his friends and the public that he has purchased the Baking Est. formerly owned by C. C. WOODWARD & lately occupied by J. P. LUM; will be providing fresh bread, family stores & best liquors, Aug. 14.

Preaching at Courthouse tomorrow by the Rev. Mr. MERRILL. We are requested to notice that a bell has been procured by members of the Baptist Church which will be rang to notify citizens of the time of assembly for worship.

The following intelligence has arrived by messenger from Nacogdoches: On the approach of Generals RUSK and DOUGLASS with a large division of militia from this section, the Mexicans and their allies the Biloxies, fled from their encampment on the Angelina and took refuge in the Cherokee village; they were pursued by Gen. RUSK who, in order to avoid bloodshed and war, halted his troops a few miles from the village and sent a message to the principle Cherokee chief BOWLES, requesting him to give them up; BOWLES desires permission to hold a council of his nation and will provide an answer by the following Saturday. No further intelligence has been received.

Important Information. The Nacogdoches Chronicle reports that a dozen leaders of the Mexican population in Nacogdoches have renounced the Constitution and expressed their desire to have revenge. Other reports state 200 men are now in arms. Horse thieves are active here and Mr. F. HAMILTON, a worthy citizen of this county, was killed returning with his stolen horses. The day before yesterday the two Messrs. ROBERTS were shot down on the road, and a third man in their company escaped to Nacogdoches, although his clothes had been pierced by a bullet. He claims the assassins were Indians, although we think he was mistaken.

Saturday, September 1, 1838

Died in this city on 28th ult., Mr. RAFFIN, aged 65 years, a native of Nantz.

On the 10th ult., a party of 200 Comanche warriors made an attack near "Aronjo Seco" upon a company of 21 men commanded by Col. KARNES & were completely defeated. It is believed that one of their chiefs, ISAMANI, was killed & another chief CASEMIRO was dangerously wounded.

Died in this city Sunday evening, Aug. 26th, Wm. D. DURHAM, 24, native of Norfolk, England. His remains were escorted to the grave by the Milam Guards, of which Corps he was a 2nd Lt. He came to Tx. in Oct. 1835 with the N.O. Grays and served valiantly in the siege of San Antonio in December 1835.

Alex. McDONALD named adm. of est. of Geo. DICKSON, a deceased soldier. August 31.

W. B. SCATES named adm. of est. of Geo. EVANS, decd.

Prudence KIMBELL named admx. of est. of Geo. C. KIMBELL, decd. soldier of Gonzales Co.

$30 reward will be given to anyone apprehending a deserter from the army named PATRIDGE (alias John W. WILSON); PATRIDGE was born in Washington, D.C., aged 29 years, fair complex., blue eyes, light brown hair, and a printer employed at National <u>Banner</u> at time he enrolled. Signed by 2nd. Lt. Samuel ELLISON, Regt. Officer.

John KOEPF seeks letters of adm. in the est. of Geo. M. BIERMAN, Harrisburg Co. Probate Ct., August 23.

W. W. SHEPHERD named adm. of est. of M. P. CLARK, decd.

James A. SYLVESTER named adm. of est. of Saml. FREDERICK, decd. soldier, August 24 adv.

Notice. All persons indebted to the estates of Solomon SIBLEY & Chas. J. BUCKLEY, lately decd. at Galveston city, are requested to present payments & those having claims to present them to Stewart NEWELL, U.S. Counsel, Galveston, August 15.

Notice. All persons indebted to the est. of D. C. BRENT, lately decd. at Houston, are requested to present payments & those with claims to present same to Stewart NEWELL, U.S. Counsel at Galveston, Aug. 15.

Curtis M. JACKSON and John M. MORGAN seeking letters of adm. in est. of Wm. S. PARKER, decd. soldier, Probate Court, Milam, Sabine County, July 28.

Thos. G. WEST, admr. of Caleb BENNETT est., Harrisburg Co., will hold a public sale at the Courthouse door at 12 o'clock Sept. 5th; will sell all of BENNETT's rights and claims to a league of land in Refugio Co., August 3.

Saturday, September 8, 1838

Health Officers' Report, number of deaths in City of Houston for week ending Aug. 31st: Mrs. Wm. DEVENPORT, of congestion; W. D. DURHAM, 24, disease of the heart; one man drowned, name unknown. Signed: "E. H. WINFIELD, Sec., B. Health."

$25 reward will be given for the apprehension of a Negro man named MARK, who ran away from the subscriber about Aug. 5th, said Negro is black complected, about 6 feet high, stout made, and has an extremely large foot---he has been seen with a gun in the neighborhood of Dr. Wm. PUNCHARD's. The above reward will be paid upon his delivery to Dr. Wm. PUNCHARD, Austin Co., or if found in this county delivered to me at Houston. Samuel W. PUNCHARD., Sept. 8.

$100 reward for the apprehension of my Negro man DUDLEY, who ran away from Mr. KESCE on New Year's Creek, Austin Co. last December. DUDLEY was brought from Atlanta last fall by Mr. KESCE and was raised in Pickens Co., Ga. He is 5'6" or 5'8", well built, jet black, has beautiful teeth and small hands and feet. He is about 23 years old. Whoever delivers him to me at Centre Hill will receive the above reward and all reasonable charges. David AYRES, Sept. 8.

J. RENAULT, Architect & Civil Engineer, respectfully offers his services to the people of Texas, having lately held various high offices in this capacity in both France and the U.S. He can be found at Mrs. MILON's boarding house, opposite the public square in Houston, Sept. 1.

E. M. PEASE named adm. of est. of late L. T. PEASE, Jr., Brazoria, Brazoria Co.

Article on life of Texas Commodore Charles HAWKINS. During the Mexican Revolution, he resigned his commission in U.S. Navy and entered the Mexican service. He participated in the siege of Bexar in 1835. He became ill in early 1837 while visiting New Orleans and died there at the age of about 36 years.

J. H. DAVIS granted letters of adm. to following estates: John CHRISKO, Chas. DOYLE, Wm. MINOR, Cortes BUTTERFIELD, W. W. EMERY, Newton HERNDON, Chancey PERDEES, and S. S. McKINNEY, all decd. soldiers, by action of Probate Ct. of Jackson County.

Francis J. HASKINS granted letters of adm. by Probate Ct., Brazoria Co., in these estates: Robt. W. CARTER, Chas. FILLSHER, Geo. WRIGHT, John E. BOLD, James T. SPROWL, Henry WELLS, James PENNINGTON and S. W. YEAGER, all of which are decd. soldiers.

Alexander RUSSELL named adm. of est. of Jas. BRADLY, Velasco, Brazoria Co.

J. B. CHANCE named adm. by Probate Ct. of Washington Co. for the vacant successions of John LOYERS of Pulaski Co., Ky.; Wm. B. BRENT, late of Davidson Co., Tenn.; & Wm. M. WILLIAMS.

Notice. Stuart PERRY warns all persons from trespassing upon lands in Refugio Co. belonging to the est. of late Robt. P. HEARN. The lands amount on a league and a third of league, all situated between Copano and Melon creeks and touching on the bay. The Hon. John DUNN, who resides in that vicinity, can instruct anyone as to the lands, and also to the patriotism and service of him who some years ago located here. The heirs to that estate are three little orphans now under my care in this city---I being executor of the est. Stuart PERRY, New Orleans, June 15.

Sheriffs Sale. By virtue of a "Fi Fa" to me directed by the Hon. John P. COLE, chief justice of Washington Co., I will expose at public auction, for cash, in the town of Washington on 1st Monday of Oct. next, one Negro girl slave named HET, levied on as the property of Wm. B. McCAMPBELL to satisfy a mortgage made by said

McCAMPBELL in Dec. 30, 1837. Robt. STEVENSON, Sheriff, August 24.

Saturday, September 15, 1838

Died in this city on 8th inst., John R. SLEEPER, 65, a native of Philadelphia. N. O. papers will please notice.
I caution the public against trading for notes of hand, drawn and signed by me in favor of James M. WILLIAMS. The notes were given in part payment of a share in the town of Washington. Said WILLIAMS has failed to comply with his contract. L. B. PARRIS, Sept. 6.
Alfred MORROW and Nancy MORROW named admr's. of est. of Andrew WINTER, a decd. soldier.
R. R. ROYAL seeks letters of adm. in est's. of Memory B. TATEM, Montgomery D. KING, and Wm. SINGLETON, all decd. soldiers, Probate Court, Goliad County, Sept. 4.
Andrew J. F. PHELAN and John W. DANCY named admr's. of est. of Hezekiah BISSELL, deceased soldier, Probate Ct., Bexar Co., Aug. 11.
Daniel McCOY seeks letters of adm. on est. of Jesse McCOY, decd. soldier of the Texian Army, Probate Ct., Gonzales Co.
HALL and IJAMS named admr's. of est. of Wm. W. SIMPSON, decd. soldier of Texas Army, East Columbia.
Thos. SIMON named adm. of est. of Warren ABORN, decd., Texana.
John W. SMITH named adm. of Eugeneo NAVARRO, Bexar County.

Saturday, September 22, 1838

Health Officer's Report, deaths in City of Houston for week ending Sept. 2d. Henry DOUGLASS, of fever; N. H. ANDRUS, of fever; Mr. RAY of fever; Negress, name unknown, of fever; child, name unknown, of fever.
For sale on advantageous terms, a number of shares in the Houston Steam Mill Company, the property of the succession of Elijah M. BURRETT and Jabez CORNWALL, decd. Enquire of BURNET & MORELAND, Agents for the the Adm., Sept. 22.

James BERRY named adm. of estates of Orlando FORREST, Dr. Thos. NESBETT, C. C. EMERY, John DODIMEAD, Michael LAURY, James CULBERT & Thos. DUFFY, all decd. soldiers, Jackson Co.

A soldier by the name of DUTCHER was recently arrested in this city and held in jail, and charged with the murder of the lamented Col. TEAL. He is being committed for trial, which should begin soon.

Thos. W. BUNDICK named adm. of est. of Marcellus BUNDICK, Probate Ct., Harrisburg Co., September 17.

John McKELVERE seeks letters of adm. in est. of James CHRISTIAN, a decd. soldier, Galveston County Probate Court.

J. N. REED seeks letters of adm. in est. of Wm. EGBERT, decd. soldier of the Tx. Army, Galveston County Probate Court, Sept. 14.

Gail BORDEN, Jr. seeks letters of adm. in est. of John JAMES, decd. soldier, Galveston County Probate Court, Sept. 14.

Notice. I have been informed that Mecum MAIN of Houston Co. has been attempting to sell a part or the whole of a certain league of land granted to said MAIN as a citizen and colonist of Burnet's Colony. Whereas I hold in my possession the bond of the said Mecom MAIN for titles to one equal half of said league, this is to notify all persons against trading for said lands or any part thereof, until I receive my title. Stephen CRIST, Fort Houston, Sept. 8.

Saturday, September 29, 1838

Married on Sunday the 23rd by John HAYES, John DUNN to Miss Elizabeth HAYES.

Married on the 27th inst., Thomas J. JORDAN to Miss Stacy CHOAT, dtr. of Thos. CHOAT, all of Harrisburg.

Alonson FERGUSON named adm. of estates of Micajah FRAZIER and Obed MARSHALL, both decd. soldiers.

Andrew NORTHINGTON named adm. of est. of Palham J. YARBOROUGH, a decd. soldier, Austin County, Sept. 28.

Geo. W. DAVIS named adm. of est. of James DAVIS, a decd. soldier, Bastrop Co., Nov. term of Probate Court, 1837.

Jane LOCKHART names Geo. FISHER as her sole legally authorized agent for the estates of her decd. husbands Samuel SAWYER and Joel LOCKHART, September 8.

N. T. BYARS named adm. of est. of William B. CALDWELL, decd., July Term, Bastrop Co. Probate Court.

We have lately received the first number of the "Red Lander," a paper recently established at San Augustine, under the auspices of W. W. PARKER, who purchased the establishment of the "Texas Chronicle" and continues the latter under this new cognomen.

Saturday, October 6, 1838

The country between the Colorado and Gonzales is very much infested with Indians. It is not safe to go from Columbus to Gonzales in companies smaller than 5 or 10 persons. A citizen of the neighborhood by the name of DAVIS, who had been on the Colorado on business, was killed on the 11th inst. by Comanches while on his way home.

John C. P. KENNYMORE seeks letters of adm. on est. of John S. THOM, a decd. soldier, Galveston Co. Probate Ct., Sept. 27.

John ANDREWS named adm. of estates of John ANDREWS Sr. and Joseph F. McLAUREN, decd., Texana, Jackson County, Sept. 25.

Samuel A. ROBERT seeks letters of adm. on estates of Memory B. TOTEM and Wm. HASTIE, both decd. soldiers, Harrisburg Co. Probate Ct.

John M. BOYER named adm. of est. of Louis F. SHRUSTER, decd. soldier, Harrisburg Co.

Clark L. OWEN named adm. of est. of Wm. H. RODGERS, decd. soldier, Harrisburg Co. Probate Court, Oct. 4.

Abraham GOSNEY named adm. of est. of David GRAVES, Harrisburg Co. Probate Ct., Oct. 2.

Walter H. GILBERT named adm. of est. of Wm. GILBERT, Washington Co. Probate Ct., Sept. 5.

James McGLOIN named adm. of est. of Patrick NAVAN, decd. soldier, Bexar County.

Died in this city on 4th inst., of a lingering illness, Marshall MANN, 45 years of age.

Died on 5th inst., Mrs. DAGET, consort of M. DAGET, both of this city.

Died Wednesday on 29th ult., in this city of a short illness, Capt. H. C. McCLUNG, late captain of steamboat Sam Houston, formerly of Wetumska, Alabama.

$500 reward. The subscriber will give the above reward for the apprehension and delivery to my home seven miles from Shreveport two Negroes who have fled to Texas. One is named JEFFERSON, about 23 years old, black complexion, 5'8" or 10", has a serious and determined look, somewhat shy, and has the marks of the whip on his back, and the mark of having worn an iron on the heel-string of his right leg; the other is named WINTER, he is dark but not black, about 35 years old, has small piece cut out of his left ear and 4 or 5 buckshot holes in one of his legs; he is very polite, speaks broken, and wings his body when walking. James MARKS, Shreveport, La., Sept. 18th.

Negroes for Sale. A gentleman who is much in want of money has placed in my charge two likely Negro fellows for sale. They are aged about 23 and 24 years, are first rate field hands and is very acquainted with use of carpenter tools. Price of the two is $2000 in La. funds. They can be seen at my residence in Brazoria Co., 6 miles below the home of Major BINGHAM. Wm. T. AUSTIN, October 1st.

Wm. TWOMY named adm. of est. of Wm. LONG, a deceased soldier of the Texas Army.

Saturday, October 13, 1838

Jas. W. JONES named adm. of est. of Gehazel VAN NORMAN, decd., Richmond, Fort Bend County, Septermber 25.

James E. SILVEY named adm. of Peter G. SILVEY estate, Sept. 13.

Geo. SIMPTON has piloted the U.S. schooner, Grampus, under my command on the 7th inst. into and out of this port. I am persuaded he has a perfect knowledge of the bar and recommend as one on whom all commanders of vessels may depend. Off Galveston, 7th Oct 1838. Signed: John S. PAYNE, Lieut. Comm.; G. G. WILLIAMSON, 1st Lt.; D. McDOUGAL, acting Lt.; W. Ross GORDON, acting Master.

Mr. Thos. TOBY has been appointed consul of Texas for the port of New Orleans.

Notice. Henry FANTHROP of Montgomery Co. and Jacksom SMITH of Harrisburg Co., are my authorized agents until my return from the U.S. Benj. F. SMITH, October 10.

Plantation for sale or rent. The well known place (Farmington) at present occupied by James HALL, the third of the main road to, and within ten miles of, Washington. The tract contains 732 acres, two-thirds of which is well timbered and located on banks of New Year's Creek. The improvements consist of 70 acres under new cedar fence, a good dwelling house, spring-house, outhouses with large commodious barn and stables. HANDY & LUSK, Richmond, Oct. 9.

Saturday, October 20, 1838

Married on the evening of 17th inst., by Judge BRISCOE, Henry LEVENHAGEN to Miss Frances GERLACK, dtr. of Ferdinand, all of this city.

$1000 reward offered for apprehension of two men who escaped from Yazoo Co., Miss. Jail on Sept. 24; Magnus T. RODGERS, who was committed to jail on charge of murdering James T. RAINY, is 5'6", fair complexion, blue eyes, light auburn hair, about 28 years, remarkable for sound sense, square, well built; and Thos. J. BYRD, who disappeared same time while serving as a jailer and assisted in RODGER's escape. BYRD is about 30 years old with blue eyes and wears a wig, quite corpulent. Signed: Sheriff Parham BURFORD, Yazoo County, Miss.

Harvey N. GASTON seeks letters of adm. in est. of Wm. GASTON, decd. soldier, Harrisburg

County Probate Court, October 15.
Died on 28th ult., at Texana, Francis Flornoy WELLS, only son of F. F. WELLS, aged 3 yrs, 8 mos, after an illness of 15 days.
Died in New Orleans on 28th ult., Capt. HURD (former commander of Texian schooner Brutus.
C. J. HEDENBERG named adm. of estates of Nathaniel H. ANDRESS and H. H. DOUGLASS, both decd. soldiers.
James W. HENDERSON seeks letters of adm. in est. of Edward L. GRAHAM, decd., Harrisburg Co. Probate Court.
John DAVIS named adm. of est. of Samuel DAVIS, a decd. soldier.
James TUMLINSON named adm. of est. of Geo. TUMLINSON, decd. soldier, Washington County, Sept. 26.
James CAMPBELL seeks letters of adm. in est. of James McKAY and David HARDING, Gonzales Co. Probate Court, Oct. 11.
Lysander WELLS seeks letters adm. in est. of Major James M. TINSLEY, decd. soldier, San Antonio de Bexar.
James TUMLINSON seeks letters of admd. in est. of John E. GARVIN, Gonzales Co. Probate Court, Sept. 26.
A man named QUIN has been recently convicted at Brazoria of manslaughter and sentenced to be whipped and branded.
We have been informed by Capt. HENDERSHOT that SAVARIAGO and his party recently visited the "ranches" of Mr. ALEXANDER situated about 20 miles SW of Bexar and carried away every portable article of value they found. They even took the rings off the fingers of the young ladies in the house. Mr. ALEXANDER and a Mr. BULL were both taken prisoner. It is supposed they returned to Matamoros.
Three of our citizens havely escaped from the prisons of Matamoros. CARNES, who was captured on the Nueces about a year ago, is one of the three. Mr. BRENAN, the former representative from Goliad, is still in prison there.
For sale a likely Negro girl, an excellent nurse, good cook, washer and ironer, brought up

in the house, and sold for no fault, aged 20, less than $1000 in N.O. money. Inquire at this office for particulars.

The Traveller's Inn & Social Hall, situated in the town of Huntsville, Montgomery Co., has always a full table and stables well supplied with corn and fodder. It is situated on the road leading from Houston through Montgomery to Cincinnati and Nacogdoches, and on the road crossing the Trinity at DUNCAN's Ferry. The house is kept by one of the first settlers of the country, Pleasant GRAY, Huntsville.

Plantation near Galveston Bay For Rent. The plantation whereon James ROUTH formerly lived, situated on the San Jacinto River near Galveston Bay, 5 miles above New Washington. On said planation are a dwelling house, kitchen, meat houses and other out houses; besides a large and commodious cotton gin, which has a grist mill attached to it. There are about 100 acres under fence, most of which are under cultivation. For terms apply to: J. MORGAN and G. M. PATRICK, Exec'rs., New Washington, Oct. 17.

Probate Sale. I will offer for sale at the court house door in Brazoria on Nov. 19th, the following property belonging to the succession of Benj. READ, decd., viz: an individual interest of a half in tract of land on which C. G. READ now resides, containing 740 acres; also one unlocated headright of a league and labor, and following Negro slaves, to wit: ANDREW, WILLIAM, EMILA, ROBERT, ANDREW 2D, HENRY, CAROLINE, CHARLOTTE, WINNY, and AGGA; also one wagon, 10 yoke of oxen, 10 cows and calves, more or less. The sale will take place between the hours of 10 a.m. and 4 p.m. Wm. P. SCOTT, Judge of Probate, Brazoria, Oct. 20.

Caution. Alexander LESSIAN, who was a member of Capt. W. W. HILL's company in the spring service of 1836; on the 30th of May of same year, transferred to Moses F. ROBERTS his right to 320 acres of land for said 3 months service; which transfer is in my possession; all persons are hereby warned from purchasing or trading for the certificate issued for said service. W. W. GANT atty. for M. F. ROBERTS, Washington.

Saturday, October 27, 1838

We are informed by a gentleman lately arrived from the North that Col. R. POTTER was killed a few weeks ago near the Arkansas boundary.

$50 reward for apprehension of our negro man THORNTON who ranaway on the night of 25th inst. He is a bright mulatto, 5'6", with a downcast look, last seen wearing white hat with hole burned in the rim, an overcoat, heavy boots and other clothing we cannot recollect. We will pay the above plus all reasonable charges for delivering him to us in Houston. BOSWELL, ADAMS & COMPANY, October 12.

The statement relative to QUIN in our last issue was derived from a respectable physician, who had just arrived from Brazoria, but the story was in error. QUIN was only sentenced to two years in the penitentiary, and not branded or whipped.

Geo. VAIL seeks letters of adm. in est. of Edward SMITH, Galveston Co. Probate Ct. Oct. 9.

Notice. The subscriber purchased of Samuel BARBER of Old River, Liberty Co., in July 1836 his head right to a league of land, and took his bond in penalty of $5000 to ensure compliance. Said BARBER has been paid for said head right, and now not only refuses to comply with his contract, but is offering to sell said head right again. A bill of injunction has been obtained, and notice served on the commissioner general to prevent said BARBER from obtaining a patent for said head right. This notice is given to prevent litigation and trouble, presuming no one will purchase of said BARBER knowing the circumstances above stated. Signed J. MORGAN, New Washington, Oct. 20.

Auction sale. Milam Hotel will he sold at public auction on Nov. 12th at 10 a.m.; said property belongs to est. of Charles MILLER, decd., and is situated on Main street near the steamboat landing at the top of the hill in block no. 2. Above will be sold subject to a lease of 5 years. Sale to take place on premises. HEDENBERG & VEDDER, Auct., Oct. 27th.

Saturday, November 3, 1838

Col. WELLS has just arrived from Bexar and brings the melancholy news that 10 Americans have been killed 3 miles from that place, and 3 Mexican citizens were captured in the precincts of that city by a party of Comanches. The Indians first made their appearance at Bexar on the afternoon of the 20th ult., when they made an attack on a party of 5 surveyors about 4 miles out of town. One of the men came back in town to report the Indians but had no idea of their number. A party of 13 citizens rode out, and had proceeded 3 miles when they discovered several Comanches hovering about them. Gen. DUNLAP, noting they were in open prairie, proposed retiring to the timber and fight under the protection of the trees. But Capt. CAGE, who was wounded a few weeks since by these Indians on the San Leon, would have nothing of this and proposed engaging the Comanches there. The small party was soon surrounded by over a hundred Indians. Eight of the 13 were killed, and 4 of the remaining 5 were wounded and with the utmost difficulty escaped into Bexar. The dead are: Capt. CAGE, Dr. McLUNG, R. M. LEE, COONROD, O. BOYLE, PICKERING, KING and GREEN. Gen. DUNLAP received a wound from a spear but is rapidly recovering. Citizens of Bexar went out the next morning and found the bodies of those slain in the engagement, as well as bodies of two of the surveyors, Messrs. LAPHAM and JONES. The remains of the 10 victims were brought into the city and decently interred on the 22d. A funeral oration was delivered on the occasion by Judge ROBERTSON. The remaining 2 surveyors had escaped into the city. Col. WELLS believes the Comanches are still in the vicinity of Bexar.

Killed in encounter with the Comanches near San Antonio de Bexar on the 20th ult., Robert Montgomery LEE, of the firm of W. D. & R. M. LEE of this city. R. M. LEE was late of Norwich, Connecticut and 24 years of age.

Died in this city on Thursday morning, 25th ult., Mrs. Deborah F. GAZLEY, consort of Mr. A. GAZLEY, in the 25th year of her life.

It should be noted that R. M. LEE, who was killed in the battle with Comanches on the 20th ult., was on a visit to San Antonio de Bexar in hopes of establishing a mercantile business at that place and was planning to return here in one or two days. He had been gone only an hour or two when his horse came rushing back into town with an arrow sticking upright in the saddle, which was covered with blood. He possessed an amiable disposition and was generally beloved for his mild virtues and fascinating manners. He was a personal friend and we feel authorized in paying this tribute to him.

Dr. G. I. COWLES, late of Florence, Ala., is now permanently located in city of Houston and hopes to establish a liberal patronage here; he can presently be found at the residence of Dr. GAZLEY, Nov. 3 advertisement date.

Thos. H. BREESE named adm. of est. of late John R. SLEEPER, decd. Nov. 2 adv. date.

W. W. HILL named adm. of est. of S. S. CURTIS, decd., Washington Co. Probate Ct.

C. C. DYER and Sarah W. BRANCH have been appointed admr's. of est. of Edward M. BRANCH, decd., by Probate Ct. of Fort Bend Co.

Administrator's Sale will take place on 24th inst. at the plantation of Wm. STAFFORD on the Brazos, 15 miles below Richmond, about 1500 bushels of corn, 2 good horses, 1 yoke of oxen, together with household and kitchen furniture too tedious to mention. All of which belongs to est. of late E. T. BRANCH; terms made known day of sale. C. C. DYER and Sarah W. BRANCH, Admr's., Fort Bend Co.

Benj. F. McMILLEN named adm. of Alexander McMILLEN est., Colorado County, Oct. 7.

For the United States.---A Negro man of mine absconded from this place on night of 1st inst. no doubt in company with a trifling white man, who promised to take him to the states by way of the Red Lands, but will probably sell him whenever he has an opportunity; this Negro will endeavor to make his way to Dallas Co., Alabama. His name is ABRAM, he is about 45 years of age, he is quite dark with a thick beard and a sly look, of middle size, and is ruptured. He appears to be dull, but is quite shrewd and an accomplished scoundrel. Please direct any information leading to his detection and return to me at Lagrange, Fayette Co. Signed A. P. MANLEY, Washington, Oct. 10.

Saturday, November 10, 1838

Auction. Valuable lands belonging to est. of late Stephen F. AUSTIN will be sold in an Executor's Sale on Dec. 11 of this year at the City Hotel in Houston. James F. PERRY, Admr.

We have been informed by the Hon. Mr. WRIGHT from Red River Co., that Mr. NEAL, an Indian trader, has recently visited the villages of the hostile Indians on the head waters of the Trinity. He states that the chief village of these Indians is situated near the Three Forks of the Trinity and contains about 700 warriors, who have congregated from the remnants of the tribes of Caddoes, Wacos, Keachies, Towacanies, Ironies, Cherokees and a few Seminoles. To the westward of this village is another composed of some 300 warriors.

Married on the evening of the 31st ult., by the Hon. A. BRISCOE, Charles BOWMAN to Miss Catherine, eldest dtr. of Ferdinand GERLACH, all of this city.

Asa WHEELER named adm. of the vacant succession of Rodney WHEELER, decd., by Washington Co. Probate Court, Oct. 28.

Plantation for sale. I offer for sale my plantation on the Brazos River, in the county of Brazoria; the amount of land contained in the tract is 1111 acres, 10 of which is cleared and under good fence; there is also a good dwelling house, kitchen, meathouse, corn crib, and all of which are new. The above land is contigious to the plantation of R. MILLS, near Bailey's prairie, and was formerly the property of Joseph FESSENDEN. For further particulars, contact the Hon. John A. WHARTON, now in Houston, or myself at Velasco. Edwin WALLER, Velasco, Nov. 1.

Wednesday, November 14, 1838

Capt. Benjamin F. CAGE who fell on 20th ult. in the affair with the Comanches near San Antonio, had been lured to that city in the spring of the year and was engaged in almost every battle with the Indians in that neighborhood since last June. He was with young CAMPBELL when he was killed by the Indians, on which occasion CAGE was seriously wounded. He was also second in command under Col. KARNES in the recent engagement with the Comanches on the Arroyo Seco. He was also a veteran of the battle of San Jacinto.

The undersigned have entered into a co-partnership for the purpose of running a general store and commission business in this city under the name of Harris & Lee. Thos. H. HARRIS, W. Douglass LEE, Nov. 3.

Died in this city on 12th inst. at 2 p.m., Stephen James, eldest son of Thomas & Martha MULRINE.

Thos. KEATING seeks letters of adm. in est. of Thomas QUIRK, decd. soldier of TX Army, Victoria Co. Probate Court, October Term.

Bridget QUINN seeks letters of adm. in est. of Timothy Hart, Victoria Co. Probate Court, October Term.

Probate Court, Montgomery Co.--Public notice is hereby given to Jesse B. M'NEALY and whomsoever it may concern, to appear at Dec. Term of this court and show cause, if any, as to why commissioners shall not then and there be appointed to divide the league of land granted to M'NEALY in April 1831, lying in Austin's Colony, near the town of Washington, in conformity with a bond contract by him executed in favor of Thomas TAYLOR, decd., in his life time. Geo. MORRISON, Clerk of Probate Court.

Wiley PARKER named adm. of est. of Francis

FULCHER, decd., by action of Montgomery Co. Probate Court, October 3.

$25 Reward will be given to any person who will apprehend 2 deserters from the Army of Texas, Burris SIMS and Richard MURRAY. Sims was born in VA, aged 24 years, 5'11½", fair complexion, blue eyes, sandy hair, and by profession a farmer. MURRAY was born in Baltimore, aged 24 years, 5'8½", fair complexion, blue eyes, sandy hair, and by occupation a laborer. Signed: J. W. JORDAN, Capt. com'd, Rect'g Station, Houston, Nov. 14th.

$25 Reward---Whereas, a certain David ANDERSON, formerly a teamster in the Texian Army, employed to hall a load of goods for me from Matagorda to Colorado City, in Sept. last, broke open boxes, trunks, &c., and disposed of my goods without license, I will give the above reward to anyone who will apprehend him and lodge him in any jail so he may be brought to justice. ANDERSON is about 6 feet tall, light, sun burnt hair, dark eyes and bad countenance. Said ANDERSON is also guilty of passing counterfeit money in LaGrange. Samuel ALLEN, Colorado City, Nov. 10.

P. CALDWELL given letters of adm. in following estates: Robert HENDERSON, Geo. WEBB, John SHIREY, and Wm. S. ROBERTS. Texana, Nov. 10.

Saturday, November 17, 1838

$100 Reward. Ranaway from my plantation near Brazoria on night of Nov. 11th, a Negro man named BUCK, 25 years, large size, about six feet tall, dark complexion, and has a large scar on back part of elbow, one or more scars over one eye lid, and both ears pierced for ear-rings, and had a small ring in one ear when he left. He run off from me about a month ago and was harbored by some free negroes in Houston. He will aim for the United States, as he has lived in New Orleans for past 8 years and will seek passage on some ship to that country. Alexander M. M'NEEL, Brazoria, Nov. 12.

J. R. CUMMINS named adm. of est. of Nathaniel R. BRISTER, decd., Washington, Nov. 7.
A man by the name of Vaulton CHILDRESS was found dead in the prairie 8 miles east of San Felipe near the house of Mr. MIXON on the 12th inst.; there was found with him a pocket book containing $43 in cash, notes and receipts in the amount of $480, and sundry articles of clothing; it appears from letters found in his possesion that he has two sons, John & Josiah, living at or near Nacogdoches. Articles found with him are in the charge of Mr. MIXON.
List of administrators and estates of decd. soldiers as filed in the Dept. of War during the second quarter ending Nov. 18, 1838: Hanson FERGUSON (estates of Oliver SMITH, Wm. H. HUNTER, Micajah FRAZIER, Obed MARSHALL); Jesse BENTON (G. W. CHILDRESS); Alex. SOMERVELL (Jas. W. HICKS); Peter McGREAL (Samuel A. PETUS); Edward QUIRK (Thomas QUIRK); Sarah HENDRICK (W.S. HENDRICK); and M. H. ROBINSON (Isaac ROBINSON). Signed by Geo. W. HOCKLEY, Secretary of War, 16 November 1838.

Wednesday, November 21, 1838

A Mexican trader from the Rio Grande lately arrived at Bexar and reports that Messrs. ALEXANDER and BULL, who were captured a few weeks since on their plantation below Bexar by a party of Mexicans from Laredo, have been basely murdered by their captors near the Nueces.
Stop the Villain.---Public warned against trading for two notes executed by me to Beanard JANSEN, said to be a resident of Matagorda, one for $2000 & the other for $$10,212, hearing the date of 10th Nov. 1838, the first note payable on 1st June 1840 in town of Washington and payable in produce, and the other payable at the same place on 1st June 1841. Both notes were fraudently obtained and I do not intend to pay them. I have moreover executed a power of attorney authorizing said JANSEN, in my name, to have perfected a deed to a league of land in Milam Co. Samuel SEWARD.

Sale at Auction. On Nov. 22nd at 10 o'clock at the City Hotel, will be sold a number of valuable bldg. lots in this city; also about 550 acres of fine timbered and prairie land, about ½ mile from the centre of Houston, being a grant made to Wm. J. MORTON. Terms, ¼ cash, the balance in 6, 12 or 18 months. Offered by HEDENBURG & VEDDER.

President Sam HOUSTON recognizes John A. MONROE, recently appointed as Consul of the USA for the port of Matagorda. 6th Nov. 1838.

HOUSTON recognizes Young J. PORTER as Consul of the USA for port of Brazoria. 6th Nov 1838.

Wednesday, November 28, 1838

Wm. Henry DAINGERFIELD seeks letters of adm. in est. of Capt. Le RAY, late of Texian Army, Bexar, Nov. 25.

$50 Reward. Ranaway from subscriber a Negro girl MARANDA of dark complexion, rather low and heavy built, about 19 years old, formerly the property of Lewis KNIGHT of this co.; said girl carried off when she left, 2 domestic dresses, 1 plaid blue & 1 red domestic dress, 1 black silk dress, and 1 black muslim dress. The above reward will be paid to anyone who detains her until I may obtain her. Robert F. MILLARD, Nacogdoches, Nov. 3.

Wright N. KIRK seeks letters of adm. in est. of John H. BARCLAY, decd. soldier; petition to be heard at Jan. 1839 Term of Probate Court, Richmond, Fort Bend Co., Nov. 22.

President Sam HOUSTON recognizes Elisha A. RHODES as Consul of USA to port of Galveston, Nov. 6th, 1838.

Saturday, December 1, 1838

Notice. All persons are hereby forewarned not to trespass on lands formerly belonging to the est. of Joshua DAVIS, decd., and which are situated on the Guadaloupe and San Antonio rivers; and further forewarn against cutting any timber on said property, as I have become the purchaser thereof. James GRANT, Goliad.

W.Y. McFARLAND named adm. of Evan R. EVANS est., Washington Co. Probate Ct., Nov. Term.

G. H. BEAM named adm. of estates of George BIRD and Wm. TAYLOR, both decd. soldiers, Brazoria County.

Several of the crew of the "Motto" have arrived at Galveston and bring the sad intelligence that the boilers of that vessel burst and killed 4 of the crew and wounded Capt. BOYLUM, who was acting as pilot, so severly that his life was considered in danger when they left the wreck. The accident took place near the East pass of Galveston Bay, and the survivors escaped in the long boat to the beach.

Saturday, December 8, 1838

A. F. MOSS named adm. of est. of Leander HART, Robertson County.

J. T. CALLIHAN, adm. of est. of Ezekiah THOMAS, decd., to sale his 10-12 acres of cleared land to highest bidder on Dec. 31st, 1838; the land is located 2 miles below Harrisburg.

Thos. SIMONS, adm. for est. of John FLICK, cautions against trading for Cert. No. 815 for 640 acres of land granted to FLICK on or about Dec. 1st, 1836; said FLICK removed from state of Mississippi during winter of 1834-35 & died in Jackson Co., Rep. of TX in summer of 1837; he is belived to hand kinfolks in Miss. and left family in Indiana.

Information wanted on Marinus FITCH who left Cincinnati, Ohio 2 years ago on Sept. 24th 1836 bound for TX; since that time his friends have not heard from him; FITCH would be 23-24 years of age, 5'8" or 5'9", black hair, black eyes; he was naturally studious and found of books. Any information can be communicated to his mother Eunance FITCH, Pittsford, Monroe Co., NY or his brother Willis O. FITCH, Rochester, NY.

John Jacob MATHERN of Frankfort, Germany seeks succ. of est. of Peter MATTERN, who was killed at the Alamo in March 1836. Harrisburg Co., Probate Court, Nov. 22.

Wednesday, December 12, 1838

For Sale. A valuable plantation of 2160 acres, situated about 2 miles above Columbia on east bank of Brazos River, and near the head of the tide water, with all improvements thereon, consisting of a house, cotton gin, corn crib, stables, negro cabins &c., 300 acres under good fence in high state of cultivation. Those who wish to see, may examine the place. Charles D. SAYER.

Jesse BILLINGSLEY named adm. of est. of David THOMAS, decd. late attorney general of the Rep. of TX, Bastrop Co. Probate Court.

Saturday, December 15, 1838

Married in this city on the evening of the 12th inst., Rufus MUNCAS of this city and Miss Amelia POWELL of NY.

Died in this city on Sunday morning 9th inst., Samuel BROOKS, aged about 27 years, late and active & enterprising merchant of Roma, Illinois, who recently established himself as a merchant here. His wife and children survive.

N. J. DEVENNEY seeks letters of adm. in est. of Chas. McKINNEY, decd. soldier of TX Army, Bexar County Probate Court.

Miranda H. ROBINSON named adm. of est. of Isaac ROBINSON, Houston, Harrisburg Co.

John FORBES named adm. of M. B. CLARK est.

Henry DAINGERFIELD named adm. of est. of Alexander LeRAY de CHAUMONT, decd., San Antonio de Bexar, Nov. 10.

G. COLE seeks letters of adm. in est. of Geo. ALEXANDER, a decd. soldier, Austin County.

Notice. All persons are forewarned not to purchase or trade for a certain tract of land containing one and a half leagues, lying west of the Guadalupe River and adjoining the town of Victoria, purporting to have been sold by me to Richard N. and Alex. DUNLAP, as the considerations for which sale was made have entirely failed, and I intend to not give up the land unless compelled by law. Margaret T. WRIGHT.

Charles D. SAYER offers for sale a very valuable 2,100 acre plantation situated about two miles above Columbia on east bank of Brazos River, and near the head of the tide water, with comfortable dwelling, cotton gin, corn crib, negro cabins, 300 acres under cultivation, and 17 acclimated Negroes. Those interested are requested to call at the premises.

The proprietor of the National Banner, has discontinued that paper and now issues in lieu of it a new paper called the National Intelligencer. The editor of the new paper is Jas. S. JONES, formerly editor of the Matagorda Bulletin. We wish him success.

A man of the name of John W. CARTER, alias COLLINS, has been apprehended in Lauderdale Co. (Miss.), who it is believed assisted in the murder last Sept. of Silas D. RIVES near Hillsborough in Scott Co. Another villain by name of Johnson COOK is also implicated and has fled to Texas. COOK is 26-30 years old, 140 lbs, with keen blue eyes, very narrow between the eyes, and his face and hands are badly scarred from dirks and knives. COOK has 2 friends in Texas named Augustus & Willis AUSTIN.

Wednesday, December 19, 1838

Died at his home in Brazoria Co. on the 17th inst., the Hon. John A. WHARTON, a member of the present Congress, after a lengthy illness. Funeral services planned for 18th before the assembled Houses of Congress. Decd. served as adj. general at battle of San Jacinto and was a brother to Hon. William H. WHARTON.

Following individuals have taken out letters testamentary on estate of decd. soldiers, as noted: James L. BRYANT (est. of Henry A. JOHNSON); Geo. POLLET (Chas. HASKELL & Daniel WILSON); John DORSETT (Jacob ROTH); John S. McDONALD (Marques SWORD); Wm. L. ALLISON (W. HACKODAY); Chas. McARTHUR (John BLAIR); and Henry RAQUET (Wm. IRVIN). Nacogdoches.

W. G. Henry THOMPSON is seeking info. on John McVICOR, who set out from New Orleans at end of July last, bound for Houston.

Saturday, December 22, 1838

House of Rep. on Dec. 13th debates claims of Miss Frances TRASK, Washington Co., who says she is entitled by law to land due her brother, who was killed in the battle of San Jacinto and was believed to be her only relation in Texas; debate further indicates that Miss TRASK taught school from 1824 to 1826. Ayes and nayes tied on vote, Speaker of House casts deciding vote in her favor.

Information on residence in TX of gentleman named BONELY or BONELEE sought, contact J. C. WATROUS at his office near the Capital.

Probate sale at Courthouse Door in Brazoria, Jan 14th 1839, for property of J. C. BARRETT, decd., to wit: 4 town lots with improvements in Quintana, adj. to tavern of SETTLE & WILLIAMS, plus following slaves: HENRY, JUDGE, EDWARD, MARY and JUDA. Signed by Wm. SCOTT, Probate Judge, Brazoria County.

W. M. WILLIAMS named adm. of estates of John FIZER, Samuel WORTHINGTON, Aaron VANVINEL, Jos. STRICKLAND, John DICK, John PROFFET, and Granville MORRIS, Red River Co. Probate Court.

James C. ALLEN named adm. of est. of Archibald DUNLAP, decd. soldier, Victoria County.

H. A. ALSBURY named adm. of est. of Peter CONRAD, decd. soldier, Victoria Co.

James BURUS named adm. of est. of John CHIVERS, Victoria County.

Sheriff's sale ordered on prop. of Andrew G. HOLLAND at Courthouse door in Houston on Dec. 31st; property includes following slaves: BEN, age 50; ABRAM, 26; MARLA, 28; NIECE, 20; PRISCILLA, 3; BETSY, 6 mos. The HOLLAND property was seized to satisfy debts and sundry executions in favor of Robt. CLOSSON, Jos. COALDRY, McCASKILL & DOBIE, and others. Signed by Sheriff John W. MOORE, Harrisburg Co.

Medical Notice. Dr. HARTRIDGE (from Ga.) is tendering his professional services to citizens of this city and its vicinity. He may be found day or night in his offices over the store of HEDENBERG & VEDDER, Main Street.

W. M. WILLIAMS, atty. at law, has located at Clarksville and will practice law in the courts of Shelby, Red River and Fannin counties.

Wednesday, December 26, 1838

In response to article in this paper on the 15th inst., Wm. T. AUSTIN of Brazoria Co., says he has a brother named Willis AUSTIN living in Philadelphia, who is not the same person mentioned in the story as an accomplice of the murderer CARTER. My brother has never been in Texas.

A party of 100 Comanches recently attacked the home of Mr. Andrew LOCKHART, between Gonzales and Victoria, and captured his eldest dtr. and 4 children of a Mr. PUTNAM. A company of citizens is now in pursuit.

Saturday, December 29, 1838

WHITE PATH, a celebrated chief of the Cherokees, died near Hopkinsville, KY a short time since. He was "enterred" near the Nashville Rd and a monument of wood painted to resemble marble was erected over his grave, giving his name and station in life.

Wm. BRYAN has been appointed consul for his Republic to the port of New Orleans.

Notice to all concerned: I, as adm. of my brother's est., and which includes all the certificates that were in his hand for location, I have made arrangements with Wm. JACKSON for the location of these same lands and with Wm. HENDERSON, dep. surveyor of Robertson Co., so these may be done as soon as possible. Signed Thos. WHEELER, adm. of the est. of Rodney WHEELER, December 26.

Hamilton HALL has removed his real estate agency from 14 Exchange Place in NO, to San Antonio de Bexar, and can be found at the city hotel No. 6; December 22.

Surgeon dentist. H. MARKS announces to citizens of Houston that he intends to make this city his permanent residence; his office is on Main Street, three doors below the city hotel.

Guadulupe SMITH, widow of Erastus SMITH, has applied for guardianship of the minor heirs of the decd.; letters of guardianship previously granted to Joseph W. GARRATY are revoked by the Probate Court, Bexar Co., November Term.

Almina COTTLE named adm. of est. of Thomas JACKSON, a decd. soldier.

The murderer COOK from Mississippi, who was advertised in a late edition of this paper, has been apprehended in Galveston. He also states that his accomplice, as named in that paper, was Willis ALSTON not Willis AUSTIN.

Wednesday, January 2, 1839

Married on 30th Dec., by Rev. Wm. Y. ALLEN, John Alexander NEWLAND to Mrs. Caroline MELONE, all of this city.

Dr. ROBERTS, recently from Mobile, Ala., has been appointed Collector for the port of Galveston, replacing Gail BORDEN, Jr., who has stepped down.

N. G. NORTH, one of the editors of the New Orleans Picayune, is now engaged in the editing dept. of the Natchez Courier.

Saturday, January 5, 1839

Probate Court of Gonzales names George W. DAVIS as adm. of the estates of John GASTON and Benj. KELLOGG, both decd. soldiers, Jan. 2.

Wm. PIERPONT, adm. of est. of Larkine WEST, serves notice for any person with claims on the est. to present them to him.

Married in this city on evening of 31st ult. by Rev. W. Y. ALLEN, R. R. ROYALL to Miss Elizabeth A. LOVE

Wednesday, January 9, 1839

Jt. Res. of TX House & Senate requires Board of Land Comm. of Red River Co. to grant certificate for 320 acres to Saml. B. MARSHALL to be located on any vacant land of the Republic; approved Dec. 21, 1838.

House & Senate adopt Jt. Res. for relief of Antonio MANCHACA in compensation of losses sustained by him in consequence of his adherence to cause of Texian independence; and in view of fact that one the houses and lots belonging to him in San Antonio de Bexar may be confiscated for the public use; the Chief Justice of the county is hereby required to give him a certificate of occupancy and possession to the house and lot; said property is also exempted from direct tax under provisions of recent Act of Congress preventing direct taxation of those citizens who have been compelled to abandon their property because of incursions by Mexicans and Indians; approved Dec. 21.

A gentleman lately arrived from the Falls of the Brazos has brought the unpleasant intelligence that a party of about 15 Indians a few days since attacked the home of a Mr. [George] MORGAN, killed him and captured 3 women, one of whom was his dtr-in-law; his son, Wm. MORGAN, is also missing, whether killed or carried away it is not known. This event occurred immediately after the ranger corps from this city [The Milam Guards] left that section to return to Houston.

Saturday, January 12, 1839

Married in this city on Thursday evening in the home of Hon. Wm. H. WHARTON, by Rev. W. Y. ALLEN, James Henry DAVIS, Esq., late of Albemarle, VA, and Miss Mary Jane HAWKINS, late of Winchester, KY.

Anson LEWELLEN seeks letters of adm. to est. of Thos. LEWELLEN; hearing on this petition set for last Monday in April in San Augustine; this est. is same one in which Wm. JONES had been previously named adm., and same was revoked last Monday of Oct. 1838 by Probate Court of San Augustine County.

John LEVERING named adm. of Col. Robert Eden HANDY's est., Fort Bend Co.; decd. was a partner in the firm of HANDY & LUSK.

Wednesday, January 16, 1839

House & Senate approve an Act establishing a mail route from the city of Houston to town of San Augustine by way of Capt. HIRAM's on Trinity River, BELT's ferry on Neches, B.W. HARVEY's on the Angelina, and Nathaniel HUNT's on Ayish Bayou; approved December 24.

Jt. Res. by House & Senator requires audit of claims of Capt. John GARRETT in the amount of $1,963.50 for 10 mos. service as Captain of Infantry; approved December 24.

John H. ALLCORN named adm. of Antonio MANCHO est., Washington County.

Mr. J. HEDRICK and Mr. DAVIS, two of our men imprisoned at Matamoros last year, made their escape on the 20th; Mr. HEDRICK arrived in our city on Sunday last.

Daniel I. TOLER and Hugh GRANT named admr's. of est. of Dr. James GRANT, with James OGELRY named as the legal authorized agent for Hugh GRANT; info. is requested by the executors of the above est. of the following, viz: of the existence or the deaths of Col. Edward EDWARDS, a native of England, and of one John Jose DELGADO, a resident of Perras in Coahuila, who were in the company of the decd. in Feb. 1838 and were supposed to be possessed of many valuable document belonging to their employer.

Geo. W. LONG named adm. of Richard H. PARK, a decd. soldier of TX Army, Richmond, Texas.

A. T. MILES named adm. of est. of Philip MARK, decd. soldier, Bastrop County.

Andrew PONTON named adm. of Jacob STIFLER, decd., Colorado County.

J. R. JONES named adm. of Col. Stephen D. HURST, decd. officer in Col. FANNIN's command; Brazoria County, Jan. 5.

James H. ASHBY seeks letters of adm. in est. of John R. DAVIS, Jackson County Probate Court, December 1838 Term.

Saturday, January 19, 1839

House & Senate adopt Jt. Res. authorizing John Finley CALLIER to change his name to John Finley ROBERTS; also authorizes John S. ROBERTS to adopt the said John Finley ROBERTS as his son; approved January 10.

House & Senate adopt Jt. Res. authorizing an audit of the claims of H. A. ALLSBURY, allowing him all of the pay & rations of a Major of Infantry for term of 63 days, deducting $20, for his service as interpreter for the post of Bexar in 1836; approved December 29.

Joint Act for the relief of certain orphan children, requires Board of Land Commissioners, Shelby Co., to issue a certificate for 1200 acres of land to Mary, Ann, Richard P., Elizabeth & Francis MANNING, the legitimate heirs of Dr. Joseph M. & Elizabeth MANNING, both decd.; neither the guardian or any other person be allowed to sell or dispose of said land until such time as the youngest child comes of age, at which time it will be equally distributed among all the heirs; approved January 10.

Jt. Res. requires audit of claims of Col. Wm. WARD, decd., for claims of $5600 for expenses paid by Col. WARD in raising, equipping and bringing troops to Texas in 1836; approved by House & Senate on Jan. 12.

Died at Camp Arnold on the Navasota River on 14th inst., Sgt. Robert Hamet BREEDIN, formerly of Mobile, Ala., by accidental discharge of a rifle in the hands of one of his comrades. He was a member of the Milam Guards who left Houston a few days since to join Gen. RUSK in an expedition against the Indians. "He sleeps in a quiet and lonely grave on the banks of the Navasota."

Died at Warm Springs, Ark., Hon. Samuel P. CARSON, a native son of North Carolina who served in the legislature of that state in early life and later in the U.S. Congress; more recently as Secy. of State to Rep. of Texas, and which important post he was forced to resign to flee to protection of his wife and children.

Married, by Hon. Wm. P. Scott, on evening of 7th inst., Mr. Ammon UNDERWOOD to Miss Rachael Jane CARSON, all of Columbia.
Almera POWELL named as adm. of the estate of Philip McELROY, Austin County.
Peter MacGREAL named as adm. of estate of Samuel O. PETTERS, decd. soldier, Brazoria Co.
Notice. By virtue of a deed of trust to me executed in July 1838 by Wm. H. STEELE, in favor of Nathaniel TOWNSEND, I will expose for sale at the Courthouse in city of Houston on 15th Feb. next the following property, to wit: 1 league of land on San Antonio river, ½ league on Brazos river, and ½ league on San Antonio Road; all within the limits of what was termed the Nashville Colony. The above were located in 1834 & 1835 and are choice selections. Thomas P. SMITH, Trustee.

Wednesday, January 23, 1839

The house of Mr. MARLIN, at the Falls of the Brazos, on east side of the river, was attacked on 3rd inst. by a party of about 70 Indians. There were 5 men in the house who defended it with remarkable courage, not one of the defendants was injured. Immediately after Indians retreated, a message was dispatched to nearest settlement, and a party of 48 men set out after the Indians. The men had traveled only 6 miles when they were fired upon by Indians hiding in ambush in the thicket; 13 men were killed.
Robert M. FORBES named adm. of Wm. H. CARSON est., Brazoria County.
Mary A. SACKET and John I. NICHELSON seeking letters of adm. on est. of Israel SACKET, decd, Harrisburg County.
J. FREESON, atty. & counselor at law, & late partner of D. C. BARRETT, decd., will continue his office at Brazoria.
A. B. SHELBY, atty. & counselor at law, late of Miss. and formerly of Tenn., has located at Houston & will attend to this business and particularly to land claims; he has practiced law for the past 28 years and will be officed on

the east side of public square, the same occupied by P. C. JACK and Jackson SMITH, Esqrs.

John W. HALL offers for sale 1000 acres of land in immediate vicinity of Washington, including the ferry and embracing lands on both sides of the "Brassos River," & also his interest in the city of Washington.

Law notice. The undersigned have formed a co-partnership in practice of law and offer our services to the public; we will attend the Courts of the 3rd Judicial Dist., also those of Colorado & Austin, offices at Washington; signed John T. MILLS and George W. HORTON.

Richmond Hotel. The subscriber respectfully informs his friends & the public that he has taken possession of this extensive & commodious house, which being now finished, he is prepared to accommodate travelers in the best style the country affords. His stables are well supplied with provender & his bar with the choicest liquors. C. C. DYER, Richmond, Jan. 23.

Saturday, January 26, 1839

Jt. Res. of House & Senate requires audit of claims for relief of Capt. James SMITH for his personal service as Capt. of Cavalry from 11th April 1836 to 6th May ensuing, from which period until 5th Sept. of same year he served as Inspector General, and from the latter period to 1st Nov. as Col. of Cavalry under appointment of Commander in Chief; approved Jan. 15.

Jt. Res. of House & Senate for relief and audit of claims of Thos. Wm. WARD as Major of Infantry from 18th May 1836 to 18th Dec. 1837; approved January 15th.

Jt. Res. of House & Senate allows Manasseh SEVEY to change his name to Wm. SEVEY; approved January 15th.

Jt. Res. of House & Senate requires audit of claims of Lee C. SMITH for 6 mos. service as Capt. of Cavalry, & requiring the Secy. of War to issue land certificates for corresponding term of service; approved January 15th.

Jt. Res. of House & Senate requires audit of

the account and emoluments of Louis P. COOKE in accordance with the commission he has held and discharged as an officer of the Republic of TX up to Dec. 1837; approved Jan. 15.
    Jt. Res. of Congress requires audit of claim of Dr. S. BOOKER for 6 mos., 23 days as asst. surgeon of Army of TX; approved Jan. 15.
    "The Comm. on Claims & Accts., to whom was referred the petition of F. A. SNIDER, have had the subject under consideration & find from the testimony of respectable persons, that the petitioner was appointed a 2nd Lt. of the corps of engineers in April 1836." SNIDER proceeded to New York, obtained a vessel for use in the defense of the coast. The Comm. recommends toTX House that petition be granted and that SNIDER should be reimbursed for $400 in personal loss on the sale of the vessel. Report from Committee, TX House, dated Jan. 7.
    Look Out for Rogues!! A small package of papers, containing among them $300-$400 in TX Treasury notes, was stolen from my pantaloons pocket on Tuesday morning last, in my own room, from the boarding house of Mary HAMILTON, whose husband bears the same name; the papers are valuable to me, & if the rogues will deposit them in the post office at this place or forward them to me at San Augustine, I will be extremely thankful. E. W. CULLEN.
    C. VAN NESS named adm. of the estates of Juran Manual ZAMBRANO and Vicente ALDRETE, both decd., Bexar County.
    Rebecca B. BROWN named adm. of est. of late Jeremiah BROWN, Brazoria County.
    J. D. ANDREWS named adm. of est. of Saml. O. PETTUS, late soldier of the Army of TX, Harrisburg County.

Wednesday, January 30, 1839

    Henry J. HILL named adm. of est. of Benjamin HILL, a decd. soldier of Texas Army; Robertson County, Jan. 30.

Lodged in my hands a runaway slave, a mulatto man who says his name is WASH, aged about 20 years, 5'8", lost some upper fore teeth, said boy says he is free and formerly resided with a Mr. BOSHER in Natchitoches. Ask owner of said Negro to come forward, prove property, and pay charges, or else he will be dealt with according to law. John DAVIS, Jackson Co., Jan. 2.

Wednesday, February 6, 1839

Jt. Res. of TX Congress grants divorce to Louisa BEASLY & Seymore S. BEASLY. Approved on January 23.

Jt. Res. of TX Congress requires Secy. of War to grant hon. discharges to Wm. K. RIVIER and James STONUM for terms of 3 mos. service in TX Army under command of Capt. John HART's volunteer cavalry of Red River co. in year 1835. Approved January 23.

Jt. Res. of TX Congress requires audit of claim of Moses MARTINDALE for 3 mos. in Army of TX and that Secy. of War should grant him a certificate for corresponding amount of land. Approved January 24.

We have learned that a Female Seminary will open at Quintana on March 1st. under charge of Mrs. GIBBS & daughters, who recently emigrated from Tuscumbia, Ala., where they operated the Tuscumbia Female Academy for past 2 years.

Died, John DE BROT, a merchant of this city, on Jan. 26th.; decd. was a native of "Loriain," France, and arrived in Philadephia at age 14; he later moved to St. Mary's, GA and then returned to Philadelphia, where his bereaved family is still residing. Decd. came to TX in 1837 and in the winter of the following year established himself as a merchant at Houston.

Wednesday, February 13, 1839

Jt. Res. of TX Congress requires audit of claims of John A. ZAMBRANO as a capt. of cavalry for TX Army from Dec. 4, 1835 to Sept. 31, 1836. Approved January 24.

Jt. Res. of TX Congress requires audit of claim of James C. BOYD for 6 mos. service as a spy to the cavalry at $25 per month, deducting $48 already paid and allowing him $120 for a horse lost in service; and requiring the Secy. of War to allow him a certificate for a corresponding quantity of land; approved Jan. 24.

Col. Bernard E. BEE has resigned as Secy. of State in consequence of his appt. as Minister to the U.S.; Judge James WEBB, formerly of Key West, Florida, has been appointed as successor.

The following passengers on board the steamer "New York, Capt. J. T. WRIGHT, from N.O. to Galveston arrived 3rd inst., in 35 hours "from the Balize:" Mrs. GADSON; B. TOWNSEND & Lady & svts.; Stephen JORDON & Lady; M. W. CROMWELL & Lady; J. W. HARRISON; John WILSON; Hugh KERR; A. MYERS; W. D. SCATES; A. S. TERRY; Mr. LUCAS; I. S. UNDERWOOD & Lady; H. C. SEBRING; Samuel JORDAN; A. F. PENNALL; S. MESHER; I. P. MAGEE; G. W. LEWELLEN; H. M. SMITH; A. GARDINER; Judge SMITH; Thos. G. MASTERSON; I. B. HANCHETT; Jas. IMIN; N. A. WARE; T. R. EDSON; H. WOLSEY; L. H. COE; S. JACKSON; W. A. HARNETT; J. D. NIXON; T. BRUARBY; T. D. MURRAY; J. W. PATIS; J. D. HORD; P. R. WAGONER; M. HOPKINS & Svt.; J. TAYLOR; A. HELM; H. W. GODFREY; Francis BROOKFIELD; L. J. PILLIR; M. WILSON; Wm. TEMPLIN; 21 steerage and 16 deck passengers.

Medical Notice. H. H. CONE, M.D. has located here after practicing for last 16 years in GA and serving as surgeon in TX Army; has set up practice here with Dr. HARTRIDGE in city of Houston; he will found at night at the boarding house of Mrs. MORGAN & by day at their office over the store of Hedenberg & Vedder, Main St.

Notice. All persons are warned not to trade for claims of Chas. WRIGHT, as he has sold his certificate of land, it being the headright granted to him by the Bd. of Land Commissioners of Harrisburg Co; said claim was sold to the undersigned at Texana, Jackson Co., & is now in my possession. Charles BIGELOW.

Mary A. SACKETT & John L. NICKELSON named as admr's. of est. of Jos. SACKETT, Harrisburg Co.

Edward HALL, adm. of est. of Wm. S. BROWN, decd., of Brazoria Co., serves notices that all persons with claims or debts against said est., should present them to either Edmund ANDREWS at Brazoria or the Edward HALL at Houston.

L. J. PELIE, engineer, architect & former surveyor general of LA, informs the public that he is ready to undertake surveying, planning of private & public bldgs, superintending bldgs, &c. He can be found at Dr. MERRILL's, corner of Franklin & Travis sts., Houston.

Wednesday, February 20, 1839

Jt. Res. of TX Congress instructs Board of Land Commissioners, Harrisburg Co., to issue a certificate for a league of land to Jas. GOURLY "on same terms as emigrants of 1835." Approved January 26.

Jt. Res. of Congress requires audit of claim of Nathaniel TOWNSEND in amount of $177.33 for articles furnish the 1st Congress while at Columbia, as per voucher. Approved Jan. 28.

Jt. Res. of Congress provides bounty land for James Anson DUNN for his service from 8th Feb. to 28th Dec. 1837; approved Jan. 28.

Jt. Res. of Congress requires audit to settle with the heirs of Capt. Wm. A. HURD, decd., in accordance with the existing law at time of said claim; approed Jan. 26.

Murder!! A Frenchman named PEPIN was murdered near this city on yesterday afternoon by a Italian man named Francis MERIGONCE; some called it a duel, but it was clearly an assassination. Two men have been arrested.

Died on 13th inst. Mrs. Sarah F. HARRY, late wife of John H. HARRY and former resident of Lincolntown, NC. Raleigh papers please copy.

Notice. Wm. PIERPONT of Houston & John WHITE of New York City, have associated themselves in business in a firm bearing the name of Wm. PIERPONT & Co., Houston.

Notice. Friends & family in U.S. anxious to hear of Wm. E. COUNCILL, formerly of Tenn. and late of San Augustine; it is probable that he

is now either in Brazoria or back in San Augustine. Signed: Green Q. TAYLOR.
    Died on 8th inst. in San Augustine, the Hon. Shelby CORZINE, Judge of the Dist. Court embracing the Eastern dist. of TX; leaving a family and numerous friends.
    Married, in Washington Co., on 19th ult., Hon. Holland COFFEE, late member of Congress of Red River Co., to Mrs. Sophia AUGHINBAUGH, late of Houston.
    Married on Tuesday evening, by John Alex. NEWLANDS, Mr. Archibald CUMMINGS to Grace SCOTT, all of this city.
    Mrs. VAN HORN respectfully informs the public that has moved in with Mrs. TWIGS on Commerce st., where she intends to take in sewing.
    J. A. NEWLANDS, adm. of est. of Alfred R. GUILD, will apply to be discharged from those duties at next term of Probate Court, Harrisburg County.
    C. MILLON, adm. for est. of late L. BICKNELL will apply to be discharged from those duties at next term of Probate Court, Harrisburg Co.

Wednesday, February 27, 1839

    Information wanted on Mr. John DAVIS, son of John DAVIS of Baltimore, who emigrated to this country about 2 years since. It appears by a recent paragraph in this paper there were two men named HENDRICK and DAVIS who escaped a few weeks since from jail at Matamoros, the latter of which is supposed to be the same. Any intelligence respecting him will be gratefully received by his distressed parents. Signed: Thos. M. LEAGUE, Postmaster, Houston.
    Married, on 17th inst., by J. SHEA, Esq., Got. D. F. WEYMOUTH to Mrs. Fanny ROBERTSON of this city.
    Married on Thursday, 21st inst., by the Rev. Wm. Y. ALLEN, Major John W. MOORE to Mrs. Eliza BELKNAP, all of this city.
    Married on the same evening (21st) by Rev. Mr. ALLEN, Capt. George C. BRISCOE to Mrs. Dorcasina WALKER, all of this city.

Wm. E. HOUTH seeks letters of adm. for Benj. CAGE and Cornelius SKINNER estates.

Wednesday, March 6, 1839

Sheriff's Sale. By virtue of an execution from the County Court of Liberty Co., I shall offer for sale at court house door in Liberty, on 1st Tuesday of April next, 2 leagues of land or as much thereof as will be sufficient to satisfy a judgement in favor of E.H.R. WALLIS, against the succ. of Geo. ORR, decd.; 1 league, situated on west side of Trinity River, 16 or 18 miles above Liberty, granted by Commissioner MADERO to S. M. FELAN, and by said FELAN transferred to said ORR. The other league laying adjoining the town of Liberty, above, granted unto said ORR as his head-right. Terms: cash. Signed: B. W. HARDIN, Sheriff, Feb. 28.

Sheriffs Sale. To be offered at same time, all of the right, title & interest of Robert WISEMAN, in & to a league of land more or less. Said land is represented as being of excellent quality, well watered & timbered, & is situated on Old River about 15 miles from town of Liberty; served and taken in execution as property of said Robt. WISEMAN, to satisfy said executions, one in favor of Charles WILLCOX & other in favor of Wm. MOORE. Terms: cash. Signed: A. G. VAN PRADELLES, Dep'ty Sheriff, Liberty County, Feb. 28.

E. H. BARSTOW will apply to Probate Court of Brazoria Co. for letters of adm. in est. of his brother Joshua BARSTOW, late of said co., decd.

J. FREON, attorney at law, late partner of D. C. BARRETT, decd., will continue his office at Brazoria.

Gabriel COLE named adm. of est. of George ALEXANDER, decd. soldier of TX Army, Austin Co.

To Planters. For sale, 380 acres of Caney & Bernard land, situated about 40 miles from Matagorda & about 8 miles from the Colorado River. Said land was settled in 1824 & not exceeded by any in the country. It will be sold low for Gold, Silver or Specie. S. INGRAM, Matagorda.

Wednesday, March 13, 1839

General Henry S. FOOTE & his Lady, of Miss., arrived in this city on Saturday last.

Died at his residence on the Brazos, T. E. GROCE, on the 28th after a lingering illness of several months.

Died in this city on 10th inst. of lingering illness, Mary MORTIMER, the consort of Thos. V.

Edward WAY seeks letters of adm. in est. of James WILCOX, decd.; hearing set for March term of Probate Court, Harrisburg County.

J. A. SWETT seeks letters of adm. in est. of Alexander LE GRAND, decd., Harrisburg County.

We have just received 2 issues of the Brazos "Courier," a new paper established in Brazoria by Mr. R. L. WIER. It resembles in the style the paper called "The People," formerly published there. This is the third attempt to establish a paper in that county.

To the Public. Whereas a certain malicious person has reported things derogatory to the character of Asa MITCHELL of Washington Co., & given me as the author, I feel it is my duty, having known Mr. MITCHELL in Penn., to give it an unqualified contradiction & hereby certify the statement as false in every particular. Alonzo B. SWEITZER.

Information is wanted of John ROAME of NY, who came to TX soon after the battle of San Jacinto & served as a soldier in the company of Capt. SPROAL. Should this notice meet the eye of any person who can give information respecting his present situation, he will confer a favor by addressing the subscriber at Brazoria. Charles ROAME.

Notice. I offer for sale a large frame house handsomely calculated for a public tavern plus 1 or 2 storeooms attached, & 2 lots of ground all fronting the river. The above property can be had cheap. P. S. And a stock of cattle and hogs. Also a house & its appendages to rent & well situated for merchandising or a family dwelling. Phil DIMITT, Port of La Baca.

By virtue of an order of Hon. Wylie MARTIN, Judge of Probate for county of Fort Bend, we will sell at public auction at the court house, in the city of Richmond, on Tuesday, April 2nd, all the personal property of the late firm of HANDY & LUSK, consisting in part of the following effects: Two Negro women RACHEL & ESTHER; 3 yoke of oxen; 6 valuable horses; 1 bay mare & colt; a good plantation wagon; 1 dray and harness; 1 very good horse cart; plough & harrow; pitt & cross-cut saw; carpenter tools & grindstone; a quantity of corn; & a variety of other articles. Likewise: 2 millstones; 2 cast-steel mill saws; all of the machinery for grist and saw mill, new and complete; &c. Also to be sold at same time some of the personal effects of Col R. E. HANDY, decd. J. W. LEVERING, Adm. of the succ. R. E. HANDY & Wm. LUSK, surviving assigner. Richmond, March 3.

Notice. A $20 reward will be given for the recovery of a cypress-built Boat or Skiff, 10 feet long, painted green inside & out, with a white molding for stem to her stern; & built by John TAYLOR of Lynchburg. She was taken from my place by John HARVEY; circumstances have come to my knowledge since his departure that induce me to believe he has sold my boat & made his way to the U.S. The boat has been gone since Jan. 28th, 1839. Benj. F. HANNA, near Harrisburg, March 4th.

Notice is hereby given that I have in my possession, as sheriff of Victoria Co., 3 African Negro men, supposed to be runaways of the following description: The first, calling himself BARKER, about 38 to 40 years old, 5'3"; the second calling himself DOC, about 23 years old, 5'6", high round full face and sprightly countenance; the last calling himself LUFFER is about 28 year, 5'8", thick projecting lips with gaps between his front teeth, both above and below. They do not understand English. The owners are requested to come forward, prove their property, pay charges & take them away; Malcome A. JOHNSON, Victoria, 9 Feb.

Wednesday, March 20, 1839

The Hon. Wm. BRENNAN, who was captured near San Patricio several months ago & subsequently imprisoned at Matamoros, is now in this city. He escaped from there six weeks ago.

The Hon. W. H. WHARTON died on 14th inst. at Groce's Retreat of accidental pistol discharge. He was on a visit to that place and was preparing to return to his residence at Eagle Island. While adjusting his holsters and attempting to draw out one pistol to examine it, the weapon went off, shot off two fingers, and the ball lodged in his abdomen. Symptoms of tetanus appeared on the 3rd day after the accident and he died. The death is most shocking, particularly in view of the recent demise of his brother, the Hon. John A. WHARTON a fews weeks ago.

Notice. Dr. James GLASS, after many years of practice in Miss., has located in Houston & will office on Congress st. near the residence of John Alex. NEWLANDS.

Notice. Any information on Thomas H. O. S. ADDICKS will be thanfully received by his brother T. E. ADDICKS who is now in Philadelphia. Any letters to him should be addressed to care of L. HARWOOD, 108 Market St., Philadelphia.

Probate Sale. Probate Court Judge Andrew BRISCOE, Harrisburg Co., orders probate sale on April 26th at the premises on all the right, title & interest of the succ. of Chas. MILLER, on a certain half lot in city of Houston on which the Milam Hotel is situated. Terms are $850 cash & Balance on 6 mos. credit.

$1000 reward will be given for any information concerning the following Negroes, viz: VIOLET, about 25 years, cross-eyed, quite-spoken; PETER, the husband of VIOLET, about 38 years, one tooth out before; SYRUS, about 25, an African; JACOB, about 21, with bad teeth. The Negroes were taken from Mobile to N.O. by A. L. SHACKELFORD, Presley C. RICHARD, & Alfred GIBSON, & a part of them were sold there, & others on the Coast. Said Negroes have been in TX since that time, & from the information I have PETER & VIOLET have been in the neighborborhood of the city of Houston; any information on one of them would doubtless enable me to secure all of them. H. VAUGHAN, Feb. 16.

Married on 20th Feb., by Judge A. BRISCOE, Ira A. HARRIS to Miss Delia W., daughter of Dr. P. W. ROSE, all of this county.

Married (no date given) by Rev. Mr. CHAPMAN, Mr. Algeron THOMPSON to Mrs. Louisa L. STANLEY.

Notice. Israel S. DODGE has petitioned this Court praying that Wm. F. GRAY be named adm. of est. of Samuel BROOKS, decd.; hearing set for March Term, Harrisburg Co., Probate Ct.

Sheriffs Sale. By virtue of order of County Court of Liberty Co., I will expose to public sale on April 2, 1839 at Court House door in Liberty, all the right, title, interest & claim of Saml. WHITING to a certain Negro woman JUDY, aged 35 to 40 years, to satisfy judgment in favor of Wm. M. LOGAN, adm. of est. of H. B. PRENTICE decd. B. W. HARDIN, Sheriff, Mar. 11.

Notice. Samuel L. & Henry H. ALLEN seeking letters of adm. in est. of Samuel PIPER, decd. soldier; Harrisburg Co. Probate Ct., Mar. 12.

Thos. W. MARSHALL seeks letters of adm. in est. of Wm. VICKERS, decd., Harrisburg Co. Probate Court, March 18.

Wednesday, March 27, 1839

Eight Mexicans went on trial Monday, the 7th inst. at San Augustine for "levying war against the Republic of Texas." The eight are: Andres TORRES, Juan Babtiste MONSOLA, Jose PROCELLA, Juan PENADA, Antonio MANCHACA, Vicente MENDES, Esteban MOROU, and Jose Antonio PERES, who have pled not guilty.

Col. Pierce BUTLER, late governor of South Carolina; Gen. HAMILTON, of same state; and Joseph M. WHITE of Florida, during their recent visit to Houston filed declarations recording their intentions to become citizens of Texas.

John P. WYATT named adm. of est. of Stephen R. WILSON, decd. soldier, Washington County.

Notice. Public is forewarned from cutting timber or trespassing on the upper half league of land situated on Cedar Bayou & being part of a league granted by Mexican govt. in 1824 unto Wm. BLOODGOOD as his heard-right. Said land now belongs to the heirs of Page BALLEW, deceased. Enoch BRINSON, Administrator.

Benj. P. AYERS named adm. of est. of Henderson COWART, who was killed under the command of Col. FANNIN, Shelbyville, Shelby Co., Feb. 22.

Notice. Any person who give information regarding Wm. G. POINDEXTER, who emigrated to this country about 2 years since, will please call at my office (2nd floor over HEDDENBERG & VEDDER's auction house). Mr. P. B. GEORGE of TX informed the father of Mr. POINDEXTER of his death some months ago. Should this notice meet his eyes, he will oblige me by calling or writing to me at Houston. Richard MORRIS.

Notice. The public are cautioned not to buy any of the property or lands belonging to est. of the "Barron de BASTROP" of any person's except said BASTROP's heirs who are now in this Republic. Yzidoro CLAUZEL, Mar. 22.

Wednesday, April 6, 1839

Beware of Imposters!! We the members of the Quarterly Meeting Conference of the Methodist Episcopal Church, Washington circuit expose to public journals that James BROWN and W. W. WALLINGFORD are imposters. BROWN, an Englishman, about 30, of light complexion and middle size staure, & is remarkably boisterous in reading hymns & preaching; said BROWN came to the Red Lands in spring of 1838 and preached in the vicinity of Nacogdoches until Oct., when he departed under suspicion. BROWN has a certificate renewing his license to preach, signed by Wm. WINAMS OF Miss. and dated March 1838, which was obtained by fraud. He also has an amiable wife in the U.S., but claimed to have no family when he came to TX. BROWN was last heard of in Houston. WALLINGFORD obtained a license to preach in Austin Co. last fall, since then his guilt has been exposed. He has several wives in the U.S. and deserves to be shunned by the religious community. Littleton FOWLER, Centre Hill, Austin Co.

A daily paper entitled "Evening Star" will be published from this office by E. HUMPHREYS & Co. on Monday next, devoted to the Commercial, Agricultural & Mercantile interest of the county. John W. ELDRIDGE will serve as editor.

Married on Sat. evening last, by J. W. BRONAUGH, Esq., Henry OBERMEYER to Miss Wendeline POCK, all of this city.

Dancing & Waltzing Academy. Mr. J. R. CODET of NY City, announces to ladies & gentlemen of Houston that he will commence instruction on Monday, April 8. Those desiring to become patrons may leave a note for the subscriber at Mr. John CARLOS's, at city exchange, Houston. J. R. CODET, April 3.

C. McANELLY, M.D., late of Nashville, Tenn., graduate of Transylvania University & Worthington Medical College, member of the society of surgeons & physicians in Lexington, KY, announces he will be permanently locating himself here. His office is on Franlin st., four doors east of Main st., & next door to the store of Messrs. HAFFORD & MILLS.

Runaway Negroes. Ranaway from plantatiion of P. D. McNEEL & R. MILLS, in Brazoria County, early in January, 3 African Negro men: SANCO, about 30, 5'8" or 9 ", small eyes, fine marks running down the cheeks and a high bold forehead; DOO, black, about 30, stout built & not much inclined to talk; and LUTHER or LUFFA, black, about 28, large & stout built, very thick lips. These Negroes can speak little English. They were taken near Victoria & delivered to the sheriff & made their escape from him on March 14. A liberal reward will be offered. R. MILLS, Brazoria, April 3.

For Sale. The executors of the late John DE BROT are now selling off nearly at cost his extensive stock of goods, consisting of a large assortment of groceries, provisions, hardware, glass and earthenware, dry goods, &c. Store on Main st., next door and above W. D. LEE's.

Elizabeth ROWE serves notice that she has administered the est. of her bro., Wm. DEARDUFF, decd., & will apply to the court in Gonzales

County for the entire estate in 6 months from this date unless some other heir of her brother should come forward in that period. Dennis NEAL named adm. of est. of Charles M. BRYNE, decd., Harrisburg County.

Wednesday, April 10, 1839

Medical Notice. Dr. J. H. GARDINER, late of LA., intends to make Houston his permanent residence and will office on Main st.
Caution. Whereas I have purchased ½ league of land from Thos. CRISIP in Montgomery Co., I forewarn all parties from trading for the same. I have had it surveyed & the field notes are in the courthouse in Montgomery. James POWELL.
Law Notice. S. P. ANDERSON, late of N.O., has removed to TX and will practice his profession in the courts of the Republic. He can be found at present at Mr. NEWLANDS', opposite the Court House in Houston.
Married by Rev. W. Y. ALLEN on evening of 4th inst., Dr. J. Wilson COPES, late of the TX Army, to Miss Elizabeth L. BELL of Brazoria Co.
REV. Jesse HOND, minister of the Methodist Episcopal church, will preach in the senate chamber on Sabbath, 14th April, at which time a church will be organized by said minister.

Wednesday, April 17, 1839

Newspaper publishes a report from Col. [Edward] BURLESON to the Secy. of War. Albert S. JOHNSTON, dated Bastrop Co., April 3. The report states BURLESON recd. intelligence on 27th March about a large body of Indians encamped at the foot of the mountains on the Colorado. "I proceeded immediately & collected a body of 80 mounted men & proceeded to the encampment;" the soldiers then located their trail & followed it for 2 days before being overtaken by 2 citizens in company with a man named ROBISON who said he had been captured by the Indians in August and had recently escaped. ROBISON said the party we were following consisted of Mexicans with the celebrated [Vicente] CORDOVA, the leader of the Mexicans who rebelled against the citizens of Nacogdoches, at their head. I proceeded on their trail to the Guadalupe River & "overtook them about an hour by sun in the evening." We killed about 20 of them in the engagement, and among the slain was one by name of CANZE, who was identified by ROBISON. There were about 5 slaves with this party, and we took one by the name of RAPHAEL, who confirmed what ROBISON had said. After a court martial, RAPHAEL was condemned & executed at the town of Leygun on the Guadalupe. Capt. BILLINGSLY and Capt. Wm. M. ANDREWS conducted their divisions with great courage. I have the honor to be, sir, your obedient servant. Edward BURLESON.

The following is a list of the men composing Gen. BURLESON's command: John B. ROBINSON, Martin WALKER, John CALDWELL, A. J. ADKISSON, Nelson FLESHER, Preston CONLEY, Wm. M. HORNSBY, M. M. HORNSBY, Richard J. LLOY, M. Hicks WILSON, S. C. BENNETT, Jos. BARNHART, Wm. P. HARDEMAN, James FENTRESS, Thos. SANDERS, C. M. HEMPHILL, W.A. HEMPHILL, Napoleon CONN, D. C. SHELP, Jas. MILLER, G. W. SCOTT, Winslow TURNER, James P. GORMAN, Enoch S. JOHNSON, John L. LYNCH, D. C. GILMORE, J. W. PENDLETON, J. L. SMITH, Samuel HIGHSMITH, R. W. MILLER, J. D. ANDERSON, G. J. GLASSCOCK, John GT. DURST, John L. FOSTER, Geo. ALLEN, J. O. RICE, Henry ALDERSON, James L. MABRY, A. C. BROWN, Henry G. WOODS, W. NEWCOMB, Lewis ENGLEHART, G. W. SHARP, Jonathon BURLESON, P. D. ALEXANDER, Wm. CARTER, John DANCER, Saml. COLVER, J. NORRES, Thos. McKARNAN, John BURLESON, John W. BROWN, John J. EAKEN, R. M. MILLS, Ross BYERS, M. ANDREWS, Isaac McGARY, S. S. GILLET, F. P. WHITING, J. R. CUNNINGHAM, Wm. HOLMES, Wm. A. CLOPTON, Hugh M. CHILDRESS, B. A. CAMPBELL, Henry CROCHERON, H. S. MORGAN, Wm. CAROTHERS, Logan VANDEVER, Warjn. BARTON, Jepu BILLINGBERY, Thos. A. MOORE, J. S. LESTER, W. M. ROBINSON, John MOORE, J. N. ROBISON, and Dr. S. G. HARGNIE.

Moreau FORREST named adm. of est. of John C. BOYD, decd., unless objections are filed with

Probate Ct., Harrisburg Co., on or before the 5th Monday of present month. D. W. Clinton HARRIS, Clerk of Court.

G. W. MORGAN named adm. of est. of Geo. MORGAN, decd.

John T. PORTER named adm. of est. of John H. CARTER, decd. & late soldier in TX Army, Milam County.

Administrator's Sale. By virtue of an order of the county court, Fort Bend Co., I will expose to public sale on June 4th, a certificate for 1/3 league of land granted to Richard H. PARKER, decd., by the board of land commissioners of this co. G. W. LONG, Adm., Richmond.

Fayetteville Hotel. The subscriber informs the public that he has completely fitted up the large & commodious house recently erected by Jesse H. CARTWRIGHT, which he intends to keep as a public house. The house is situated 25 miles from Houston and 22 from San Felipe, on the east side of the Brazos timber. Michael CRONICAN, Fayetteville.

Administrator's sale. Will be sold at the late residence of Wm. FIKE, decd., near Hodge's bend, east side of the Brazos, all of the personal property belonging to the est. of the decd., consisting of about 40 head of cattle, a yoke of oxen and cart, a small stock of hogs, some farming tools, and other things. The sale will take place on 1st Tuesday in May next on a credit of 6 mos., the purchaser giving notes with approved security. Jesse H. CARTWRIGHT.

P. W. ROSE seeks letters of adm. in est. of Abraham GALLATIN, decd., Harrisburg Co. Probate Court, April 15.

Wednesday, April 24, 1839

Married on Friday the 19th by the Rev. W. Y. ALLEN, at the residence of Samuel WHITING, Mr. Edmund PREWITT to Miss Martha Caroline MUNSON, all of Liberty County.

James W. SMITH, adm. for est. of Young J. PORTER, decd., will offer 250 acres of land for sale at town of Washington on 1st Tuesday of July next. The land is situated in the lower part of Washington Co., & adjoining Jesse BARTLETT's league. Terms made known on day of the sale. James W. SMITH.

J. Wilson COPES, M.D., late surgeon of Texas Army, has located himself at E. Columbia. His practice of several years in Miss. & TX. has made him familiar with diseases of our climate.

Alexander RAMSEY seeks letters of adm. in the est. of N. Winter SMITH, late of Harrisburg Co. Hearing set for May Term of Probate Court.

We learn from Col. BONELL, who has recently arrived from Bastrop, that Col. KARNES and Capt. MANCHACA have captured 16 Mexicans of CORDOVA's band. It is believed that CORDOVA was killed or seriously wounded, as when last seen he was reeling in his saddle from loss of blood.

Catherine ROONEY seeks letters of adm. in est. of her brother Cornelius ROONEY, a decd. soldier of TX Army. April Term of Galveston Co. Probate Ct. sets hearing for 60 days.

Wednesday, May 1, 1839

TX Congress jointly approves resolution of thanks to O. de A. SANTANGELO for the firm and zealous support he has provided to he cause of TX Independence in his periodical entitled "El Correo Atlantico." Be it further resolved that the Board of Land Commissioners for Harrisburg Co. are hereby required to issue to him a certificate for one league and one labor of land as donation by the Rep. of TX; approved May 1.

Administrators Sale. I will sell to the highest bidder on the public square in the town of Montgomery on Sat., May 27, one claim of wooded land being the head-right of James SHARP (decd.) for 640 acres, to satisfy the debt of the said est. Terms of sale: 6 mos. credit plus security. James L. BENNETT, Admr.

Wednesday, May 8, 1839

Notice. Info. is wanted of Wm. H. VAN HORNE by Edgar R. VAN HORNE at Van Buren, NY.

Caution. All persons are forewarned from locating or surveying on a certain tract of land by the name of "Nacamche Ranche," which lies 20 miles north of Nacogdoches & consisting of four square leagues as per the title of Ranando NOVES, now on record at general land office. Anyone who trespasses on said property can rely on being sued at the next district court from said county, as the said property by transfer belongs to the subscriber. James GAINES.

We have received the first number of the "Richmond Telescope & Literary Register," published at Richmond on the Brazos. Mr. David L. WOODS is the editor.

Died on the evening of April 23, at his residence on Cumming's Creek, Fayette co., after an illness of 20 days, Mr. John T. SHIELDS, 23, late of Marengo co., Ala. Decd. leaves a wife and 2 children. The editors of the Marengo Gazette, Southern Advocate of Huntsville, Ala. & Decatur Observer will please copy the above.

Adm. Sale set for June 4 at court house door in Houston on following property: 3 old cows & 3 calves; 2 cows & calf; 1 steer, 3 years old; 2 steers, 1 year old; 1 labor of land adjoining GROCE's on the Brazos; all property belonging to the Succ. of Violet HAMLET, decd. Terms are cash. John W. MOORE, Admr.

Wednesday, May 15, 1839

A card. Mrs. A. SACKMAN, mantle & dress maker, late of NY, would inform the ladies of Houston that any favor in her line would be kindly received. Residence on Franklin st., nearly opposite the telegraph office.

H. E. SACKMAN, book binder, late of NY, has opened a shop near the printing office of the "Telegraph" & is prepared to do all types of binding in the neatest manner.

Notice. W. W. HILL, admr. of est. of Stillman S. CURTIS, decd., has placed 50 land certificates in my hand to locate, which was the number in the hands of S. S. CURTIS at the time of his death. Any of his employees can contact

T. C. LeCOMTE, Hair Cutter from Paris, expresses his appreciation to the people of Houston for encouragement "I have received during my stay in Houston. Being the first barber of Houston and of this republic, I am sure the good people will not pass by one of their fellow citizens and a soldier. My price is 25¢ for shaving, 75¢ for hair cutting, & no charge if not pleased." His residence is by the city hotel on Main st., no. 2, Anderson building.

Thos. COCHRAN, admr. of Amasa IVES est. will hold a public sale of property on 1st Tuesday of June at court house door in Austin. Horses, cattle & other personal property to be sold.

Wednesday, May 22, 1839

Administrator's sale set for July 2 at court house door in Montgomery on a quarter league & labor of land lying on the east side of the San Jacinto River, about 12 miles southeast of the county, belonging to est. of Martin P. CLARK, decd. Terms 3-6 mos. credit with appropriate security. W. W. SHEPHERD, Admr., Montomgery.

James M. BRANHAM, atty. & counsellor at law, has established himself at Galveston and will attend the courts in Brazoria, Harrisburg, Galveston & Liberty counties. Gives references in Vicksburg, Miss. and New Orleans.

Look Out for a Thief. Stolen from the house of Mr. TEAL's in Houston a pair of saddle bags containing about $60 in clothing, supposed to be stolen by one John SELLERS, about 45, sallow complexion, black eyes, very much addicted to intoxication & very talkative while under its influence, about 5'8" or 9". Geo. NELSON.

Wednesday, May 29, 1839

Dr. James H. STAR, former President of Board of Land Commissioners, Nacogdoches, has been appointed Secretary of the Treasury.

Republic of TX, Victoria Co., in April Term, Probate Ct.: Whereas David HARRINGTON, late of the firm of R. STONE & Co., of Newport, Ark.,

was unfortunately wounded in an affray in the town of Victoria during the month of Oct. 1838, of which injuries he later died; notice hereby given to all persons legitimately interested to come forward and claim the property of the deceased."
Quarterly Report of the Hospital Surgeons, Feb. 20th through May 20, 1839: James FRANKLIN admitted Feb 20th, age 22, native of N.C., pleuritis, discharged cured, March 9. John CLARK, Feb. 28th, native of Penn., age 31, ulceration of the leg, discharged cured May 4th. Antonio RENDRANDO, March 2d, age 25, native of Rio Grande, stabbed with a dirk, discharged cured March 10. Daniel KENNEDY admitted March 4th, nat. of Ireland, age 25, burns, of which he died March 10. Robert MORRIS admitted March 16th, nat. of Ireland, age 30, lacerated scalp and cephilitis, discharged March 21. Joseph J. BELL, nat. of NY, age 26, disenteria, discharged March 27. Edward SMITH admitted March 21st, native of NY, age 26, phythyics pulmunalis, died March 25th. John SHERROD admitted March 27th, native of Ireland, age 24, sore lip, discharged cured April 2. Thos. MARTIN admitted March 31st, native of Ohio, age 20, ulcerated legs, discharged cured April 29. James MANLEY admitted April 21st, native of Ireland, age 27, deleriums tremens, discharged cured April 28. Report is signed by Dr. W. W. CARTER, who further states KENNEDY suffered a fit, fell into the fire and was horriby burnt. The other decd. person, SMITH, was too far gone with consumption by the time he was admitted in the hospital on March 21st.

Wednesday, June 5, 1839

Spring Term, Grand Jury issues final report and recommendations, Harrisburg Co. Members are: Ashbel SMITH (foreman), John CHENOWETH, John WOODRUFF, Jos. A. PARKER, Jas. RUTHERFORD, Wm. M. BURCH, James McGABEY, Harmon DACKMANN, Henry F. FISHER, Edwin BELDEN, John S. BLACK, O. T. TYLER and Watkin CLAY.

Henry HUMPHREYS, Esq. has been appointed as Chief Justice of Harrisburg Co., in the place of Andrew BRISCOE, resigned.

Married in this city on 6th inst., by Rev. Mr. ALLEN, John HOFFMAN and Mrs. Sarah BARKER, all of this city.

Notice. Warner L. UNDERWOOD and Charles S. TAYLOR, attorneys and counsellors at law, Nacogdoches, TX.

Runaway from me on April 6th, a brown colored Negro man by name of ISAAC, age 24, near upon 6 feet tall, chunky made, has large eyes and a bushy head somewhat, no brands, his clothing is velvet round-about, cassinet pantaloons, and cotton and red pantaloons, a fur hat (short brim with a buckle and riband), check shirt and cotton shirt. He belongs on the White Oak Bayou, East Fork, half a mile of the Montgomery road, 9 miles from Houston city. I will give $15 if brought to me---and if stolen, and with the thief, $400. I purchased him in Feb. last at Vicksburg, Miss. JAMES DOWELL, living on White Oak Bayou.

Notice. Mr. Ephraim BOLLENGER, when he was murdered and robbed on the 14th ult. near the Cibolo by a party of Mexicans and Indians, was carrying numerous papers belonging to the undersigned. (Numerous documents listed.) He intends to file duplicate papers as soon as possible. A. NEILL, Bexar, May 23d.

C. W. BUCKLEY seeks letters of adm. in est. of Warren J. MITCHELL, decd., late a soldier in army of TX. Harrisburg Co., June Term of Probate Court. 60 day notice.

C. W. BUCKLEY at same time files for letters of adm. in est. of John O. MOORE, decd., late a soldier in TX Army. Same county, same period.

Thomas BLAIR seeks letters of adm. in est. of Hilliard Terry HORTON, decd. soldier in TX Army, Bastrop County Probate Ct., May Term.

Notice to all those interested in the Succ. of Joseph L. DUGAT, decd.: I, MARY C., widow & admrx. of the Succ. of Joseph L. DUGAT, decd., will petition the Probate Ct. of Liberty Co. at its next term, to set aside dower in accordance with law in such cases. Mary C. DUGAT, Liberty. Notice to all persons interested. I have been appointed by Probate Ct., Brazoria Co., as admr. of est. of Philip STROM, a decd. soldier. Signed by J. A. HUESER.

Republic of TX, Victoria Co.: In Dist. Ct., March Term. A suit is pending in the case of Thos. G. WESTERN, admr. of est. of Caleb BENNETT, vs. Felix DE LEON. This suit has been set for 3rd Monday in November. John McCRABB, District Clerk.

Members of the Bar, District Ct. in Bastrop Co. adopt a resolution of respect for the late Wm. T. BRENT, late a member of this Bar. The res. refers to BRENT as "a Virginian by birth & education," but provides no other details. The resolution adopted on May 3rd by following members of the Bar of the 3rd Judicial District: Thos. R. JACKSON, C. B. SHEPPARD, F. A. MORRIS, W. Pinkney HILL, J. W. BUNTON, Thos. J. GAZLEY, L. B. JOHNSON and Henderson C. HUDSON.

Law Notice. The undersigned have formed a law firm styled JASPER & COOPER to practice in the various courts of the Republic and to also attend to Locating of Lands. Offices in Montgomery. S. L. B. JASPER and Richard COOPER.

James McGLOUN named admr. of estates of Edwin ALEXANDER and E. BULL, late decd., San Antonio, 19th January 1839.

George WEEDON announces administrator's sale on Tuesday, July 2nd at court house door in Montgomery on 640 acres of land belonging to the succ. of Richard BRADY, decd. Terms cash.

Probate Sale set for 1st Tuesday of July by order of Probate Court, Brazoria Co., for all of the real and personal property belonging to the est. of William J. EATON, decd., viz: the undivided half of a tract of land belonging to Washington M. SECREST and the succ. of the said EATON, lying on the east side of the Colorado river, 3 miles above Columbus, plus the dwelling house and all outhouses and having 60 acres under fence. Also a likely Negro woman named EVELINA, 23 or 24 year old. Terms cash, constitutional currency. Willard WADHAM, Judge.

George DEWEY named admr. of est. of Paul PIER, decd., Probate Court, Liberty County.

Stolen. On Tuesday night last from house of Wm. SHEPHERD, south-west of the Capitol, among other articles one large and valuable Writing Desk, with the name of the owner J. W. SIMMONS engraved on a brass plate upon the top. The desk contains manuscripts and documents of no value to the thief. A suitable reward will be given for return of the desk. James W. SIMMONS

Wednesday, June 12, 1839

The Eptimomist. A weekly newspaper to be printed in the city of Austin, the new seat of government for the Republic of TX, to be conducted by an association of literary gentlemen, and edited and published by James BURKE, former reporter for the house of representatives.

A. A. ANDERSON, attorney & counselor at law, late from the Alabama Bar, has located himself in Bastrop and will intend to any business entrusted in his care.

Wednesday, June 19, 1839

Married on Tuesday evening, by Rev. W. Y. ALLEN, Geo. W. MILLER and Mrs. Caroline A. STEVENS, all of this city.

Died after a short illness, in city of Houston, on 18th inst., Virginia, aged 2 years and 6 months, the daughter of Mrs. Mary A. SACKETT, late of Cincinnati, Ohio.

Died in the city of Galveston on 12th inst., of hyrdocephalns, Nicholas Dashiell, infant son of Lt. Thruston M. TAYLOR, TX Navy, aged 11 months and 22 days. Baltimore papers are requesed to please copy.

Caution. All persons are cautioned against purchasing from any persons other than myself a certain tract of land I now hold, described as lying in the county of Jasper and part of the head-right of John BEVILL. I hereby inform the public that Elijah M. COLLINS, representing himself as a "claimer," and Wm. MEANS, claiming to be sheriff of Sabine Co., fraudently obtained my signature on a document transferring to said COLLINS my right to said land. A. M. COLEMAN, Jasper, May 29.

Fifty dollars reward offered for the apprehension & delivery to me of my Negro Man, TOM, who ran away from me at Harrisburg, on night of 13th inst. Said Negro is about 26 or 28 years old, black complexion, good face, rather long nose for a negro, and remarkable for the beauty and symmetry of his athletic proportions, and a sweet, soft voice. I lately purchased him of Thos. C. WOODLIEF of Washington Co. He may be slightly wounded with a small shot, but this is uncertain, as I have not seen him since I fired at him. A. BRISCOE, Harrisburg.

David LAUGHLIN named admr. of est. of James J. WILLIAMS, decd. soldier in TX Army.

Wednesday, June 26, 1839

Notice. David Y. and John W. PORTIS, attorneys at law, will practice in the several courts of Harrisburg Co., and will office in No. 6 Exchange Buildings over HEDENBERG & VEDDER's auction room.

Probate Court, Harrisburg Co., grants petition of H. R. and S. L. ALLEN seeking to be discharged from the administration of est. of Simon PEPIN, decd., representing that there is no property belonging to said estate, June 24th.

Richard MORRIS seeks letters of adm. in est. of William G. POINDEXTER; court gives 10 days notice to individuals interested in the est., Harrisburg Co., Probate Court, June 24.

State of Mississippi, Yazoo County, Probate Court, April Term 1839---Magnus T. RODGERS, the executor of last will & testament of Robert DICK, decd., has removed out of this state, and has become a resident of TX. A hearing is now scheduled for July Term of said court to show cause why these letters testamentary should not be revoked. Robert C. CAMPBELL, Judge.

Notice. The land certificates lately advertised as having been taken from Ephraim BALLINGER, when he was killed, have been retaken and are now at Bexar, where they will be attended to for those concerned, and duplicates are not required. A. NEILL, Gonzales, May 29.

BENBROOK & MILLER, General Land Agents, office on Main Street, Houston, and Main Street, Natchez, Miss, at which places they are purchasing and selling every description of land claims. The highest prices given for 1st class Headrights and Soldier's Bounty Claims. Daniel G. BENBROOK and Geo. W. MILLER.

$300 Reward. Ran away from the subscribers on or about April 1st, two Negro fellows, named JACOB and EPHRAIM. Jacob is about 28-30 years, black complexion, about 5'1", rather slow in speech, belongs to John H. THOMPSON near Fort Jessup, LA. Ephraim belongs to Wm. J. SNUD who lives near San Augustine, and is about 30 years old, 5'7½", very black, has a speech impediment and stammers when alarmed. The above reward & all reasonable expenses will be paid for the apprehension & delivery of Negroes to Wm. J. SNUD, near San Augustine. It is supposed that said Negroes are making their way to San Antonio, as they were once taken and made their escape from F. FRANKLIN, Robinson Co.

Wednesday, July 3, 1839

Private House. The subscriber has taken over the old and well known stand of Capt. Joseph TAYLOR in Galveston and made arrangements for rendering it a desirable home to travellers and resident boarders. The situation is elevated, airy, quiet and convenient to business. The table will be supplied with vegetables from NO, Houston and the country. R. R. MUNCUS, Galv.

N. AMORY named admr. of est. of J. S. STEPHENSON, Harrisburg County.

Ranaway from the subscriber near Fort Bend on the Brazos, on 14th inst., a Negro man named CATO, 5'8" or 10", slim built, very black, is a carpenter by trade, and heavy whisskers. A liberal reward will given and all reasonable expenses for his apprehension and delivery to me. Johnson HUNTER, June 29.

Sheriff's sale. By virtue of three executions to me directed, two from the dist. ct. of Galveston Co. & in favor of D. W. Clinton HARRIS, and the other in favor of Amelia BATTERSON; and one from dist. ct. of Liberty Co. in favor of J. C. DAVIS and all against John M. SMITH, Mrs. SMITH, Mrs. CARROLL, & Sally SMITH, alias Sally BLACKMAN---I have levied on and will expose to public sale on 1st Tuesday in August at the Court House door in Liberty, to the highest bidder for cash, all the right, title, interest and claim of the above named defendants in & to a certain Negro woman, named ANN, about 30, and her child RICHARD, about 4 years old, one bay mule and one old cart, to satisfy said executions. B. W. HARDIN, Sheriff, Liberty Co.

Wednesday, July 10, 1839

On the Sabbath, 12th ult., Rev. HOES of the American Bible Society preached in the Stone House to a large and respectable crowd. Afterward, the Nacogdoches County Bible Society, an auxilliary to the American Bible Society, was organized. Col. Frost THORN was elected president; Col. Haden EDWARDS, Gen. K. H. DOUGLASS and Wm. SPARKS, vice presidents; Wm. HART, secretary; Chas. M. GOULD, recording secy.; Gen. Thos. J. RUSK, treasurer; and Major D. S. KAUFMAN, John R. HUBERT and A. S. HAMILTON distributing committee.

Married on 3rd inst., by Wm. FERGUSON, Esq., Barnard CERCHER to Miss Maria O'ROURKE, only daughter of Patrick O'ROURKE, all of this city.

$100 reward. Runaway from me on 17th inst., an American Negro Man named DICK, about 5'10" or 11", he belongs to Munroe EDWARDS, and has been sequested in the case of C. DART vs. Munroe EDWARDS. The above reward will be paid on his apprehension & delivery to me in Brazoria, or $150 if out of the county. R. J. CALDER, Sheriff, Brazoria, June 18.

$100 reward. Runaway from me on the 14th of this month, a negro man named TOM. He is upwards of 30 years old, dark complexion, about 5'9" or 10", spare built, with small face, down look, holds his head down, and stammers considerably. The end of one of his thumbs has been mashed and is disfigured. I will give the reward above for his apprehension and delivery to me on my plantation, 9 miles below Brazoria, or $50 more if he is taken east of the Colorado river. Leander H. McNEEL, Brazoria, June 24.

C. W. BUCKLEY seeks letters of adm. in est. of Randolph SLATTER, late a soldier in the army of TX, who fell with FANNIN at Goliad in 1836. Hearing set for 60 days; Harrisburg Co. Probate Court, July 2, 1839.

Law Notice. The subscriber tenders his professional services to the community, having served as judge of the U.S. Superior Court for the Southern district of Florida for 10 years. He has particular experience with Spanish land titles and may be found at the office of the Attorney General in Houston. James WEBB.

H. R. A. WIGGINTON seeks letters of adm. in est. of Wm. SPEAKE, decd., late a soldier in the army of TX. Fort Bend Co., July 1.

N. B. BREEDING named adm. in est. of Jas. N. SMALL, decd., late a soldier in the army and of this county. La Grange, June 28.

Samuel SWISHER seeks letters of adm. in est. of Harvey COCKS, late a soldier in FANNIN's command. Harrisburg Co. Probate Court, July 8.

A Proclamation by Alexander G. McNUTT, Governor of Mississippi, offers reward of $300 each for apprehension of James G. SCOTT, Wm. T. SCOTT and John W. SCOTT, who it is believed murdered Samuel CARPENTER in Copiah Co., Miss., on May 10th, 1839. James SCOTT is slender built, dark complexion, black eyes, thin visage and leans forward. He is about 25 years old. Wm. T. SCOTT is a small, chunky man, about 5'8" or 9" high, fair complexion, light hair, red cheeks, aged about 28-29 years, uses his left hand generally. John W. SCOTT is rather heavy built, about 5'10", light complexion, blue eyes and light hair; Proclamation issued at Jackson, Miss. on June 21, 1839.

Notice. John HEMPHILL and Charles H. RAYMOND will practice law in co-partnership in counties of Milam & Robinson. Office of the former at Bastrop, and the latter at Franklin. A Proclamation by Gov. Alexander G. McNUTT, Mississippi, offers reward of $300 for the apprehension & delivery to a U.S. Jail of Nathaniel H. PEGRAM, who while residing in Hindes Co. of said state, is believed to have murdered one Green SPEIGHTS on Dec. 7th, 1839, and is now a fugitive from justice. PEGRAM is described as of slender person, about 6 feet high, and about 30 years old; red face, swarthy complexion, remarkably short front teeth, has a speech impediment, is quick spoken and stammers. Proclamation issued at Jackson, Miss., June 21, 1839.

Sheriff's Sale, Montgomery Co.: By virtue of an execution to me directed by the honorable county court, I have levied on and will expose to public sale at the Court House door in Montgomery on the last Tuesday in August next, one Negro girl named NANCY, levied on as the property of Andrew ROBINSON, to satisfy an execution in favor of Joseph L. BARNETT, for use Alexander WHITAKER. A. McNEILL, Sheriff.

Wednesday, July 17, 1839

We learn that Joseph BRATTON, Esq., to whom TX is much indebted for the valuable Academy at Independence, was killed by Dr. CANNON, one of his fellow citizens at that place. Dr. CANNON, it seems, was away from home and on his return, was informed by Mrs. CANNON that Mr. BRATTON had used some "hasty language" towards her. He took his double-barreled shotgun and proceeded to BRATTON's house to settle the difficulty. BRATTON told him he was unarmed. CANNON retorted by discharging the contents of his gun into BRATTON's side. He expired immediately; CANNON was taken to the jail at La Grange to await his trial---From the Richmond *Telescope*.

$200 reward offered for return of a runaway Negro Man named CALEB, either to myself or Mr. S. N. DOBIE, Houston. Said Negro is about 33 years of age, 5'4" or 5", black but not jet black, well built, very quick and active in his movements. The above Negro was persuaded away by an unknown white man and taken to TX. For the apprehension of both, I will give $500 in promissory notes of the govt. of TX. Daniel McCASKILL, Parish of La Fayette, Louisiana.

Lost. A certain bounty land warrant, granted by War Dept. at Houston to Wm. BAILEY as original claimant, and myself as the assignee of said BAILEY, for 320 acres of land. I therefore caution all persons from trading for said land warrant, as I am the bone fide owner of said claim. Thos. JEWETT, Warren, Fannin Co.

Abigail H. THOMPSON has filed a petition with the Probate Court, Harrisburg Co., claiming one half of the property belonging to the succ. of Henry L. THOMPSON, as widow and heir of said THOMPSON; with half claimed on behalf of their daughter, Rebecca Amanda THOMPSON, a minor and heir of the decd. Hearing on petition set for July Term. Petition originally filed on June 13, 1839.

A company under the command of Capt. Reuben ROSS left this city a few days since for the West. They are to be mounted and will assist the civil authorities of San Patricio, Refugio and Victoria counties against a banditti composed of Americans, Mexicans and Indians who have for some time committed the most desperate outrages against the Rio Grande Traders.

Wednesday, July 24, 1839

Glorious News From the East!! After negotiations between our Commissioners and the Cherokee leader BOWLES collapsed, our troops attacked on July 15th and routed the Cherokees from a strong position, leaving 18 of their warriors dead on the field, while we had only two killed, 1 mortally and 6 slightly wounded. On the next day, the 16th, another battle took place, which was desperately contested & lasted one and a half hours, terminating with a fierce charge in which the Indians sustained a considerable loss. BOWLES, their chief, was found among the dead. Our loss in this battle was 2 killed and about 20 wounded, among whom were

David RUSK, Major AUGUSTINE, Major KAUFMAN, Col. McLEOD, Dr. ROGERS and Col. CRANE. The officers and men are said to have acted with extraordinary bravery and coolness.

The paper also publishes a letter from Secy. of War A. Sidney JOHNSTON, who was dispatched there as one of the Commissioners, dated July 16th, from "West Fork of the Neches," in which he states that Mr. CRANE from Trinity and Dr. ROGERS of Nacogdoches (formerly of Bowling Green, KY) were killed during the engagement on the 16th.

The funeral of the Hon. John BIRDSALL yesterday was attended by a large concourse of people. The body was taken to the Capitol where the funeral was performed. After the services, the hearse and the procession, escorted by the Milam Guards, proceeded on the way to the family burying grounds at Harrisburg.

A probate sale has been scheduled for Aug. 6th at the Court House door in Victoria on so much of the personal est. of the late David A. HOFFMAN, sufficient to pay $800 owed by the estate. Said property is located on the La Bacca river in Jackson Co. By order of Wm. P. MILLER, Judge of Probate, Victoria Co., July 1.

James B. ALLEN named adm. of est. of John REESE, decd., San Felipe, July 19.

Information wanted on John P. RIDGWAY, who left Wheeling on July 3rd, 1837, as an engineer on a steamboat for New Orleans. He was last seen in NO on Dec. 6, 1837, where he had arrived from the Red River and has not been heard from since. The undersigned, his brother, would be thankful for information on his whereabouts. Joseph W. RIDGWAY, Wheeling, June 15.

Information wanted on the residence of Mr. Arthur SWIFT. Anyone with any such information is asked to contact the undersigned at Houston. Louis P. COOKE, July 4.

Property belonging to the est. of the late Mary THAYER, will be sold at the Court House door in Texana on the first Tuesday of August, next. Thomas SIMONS, Admr.

Died at the residence of Mrs. BELL, near Columbia, on 2nd inst., Rev. J. L. J. STRICKLAND, after a short illness.

At the same place and about the same time, very unexpectedly, Mr. Bird LOCKHART, one of the most valuable private citzens in TX, died.

Wednesday, July 31, 1839

Deadly Encounter. We learn from a passenger on the steamer Rodney, arrived this morning from Alexandria (LA) that J. W. MOORE, Editor & proprietor of the Red River <u>Whig</u>, was shot dead in the streets of that city on the 1st inst. A gentleman named King HOLSTEIN, connected with the office of the <u>Republican</u> in that place, was the author of that terrible deed.

It is with much regret that we announce the death of Mrs. Rebecca LAMAR, the venerable mother of Gen. M. B. LAMAR, which took place at the country seat of the President on July 26th, after a severe attack of congestive fever.

The Texian schooner of war "San Jacinto" set sail from Galveston on Friday last, bound for New Orleans. The following is a list of her officers: Capt. LOTHROP, Lt. HENDERSON, 2nd Lt. ESTES; Surgeon, Dr. GARDINER; Purser, STEPHENS; Sailing Master, BAKER; Midshipmen, SNOW, WAITE, CRISP, CUMMINGS and BENNETT.

Notice. The subscriber will in the future accommodate those who may favor him with a call with something to eat and horse feed, at his residence. Wm. BEARD, Big Creek, July 12.

Perry DAVIS named admr. of estates of Fields DAVIS and Jackson DAVIS, both decd. soldiers, Matagorda County Probate Court, July 26.

Wednesday, August 7, 1839

The Rev. Dr. BRACKENRIDGE, who was for some time a resident of this country, is delivering lectures on the state of society, the history & agricultural resources of TX, at Clinton Hall, New York.

The "Asp," another Schooner of War built for our government is on her way from Baltimore to Galveston. She is now commanded by Capt. KANE.

Died in this city yesterday evening, after a lingering illness, D. Juan Antonio PADILLA, the former Secretary of State of Coahuila and Texas and friend of the late ZAVALLA. He was a native of Mexico and lately a resident of Nacogdoches, where his family is now living.

Sheriff's Sale on property belonging to est. of Thomas R. MILLER, decd., will be held at the Court House door in Gonzales on 1st Tuesday in Sept. next. Admr. listed as Joseph D. CLEMENTS and property includes a half league above & adjoining the town of Seguin; one fourth a league on west side of San Marcos river about 15 miles above Gonzales, formerly granted to Benj. FUQUY by Mexican govt. All old deeded land, title indisputable. Wm. A. HALL, Sheriff, Gonzales County, July 20.

Notice. Eli WILLIAMS of this city is my legally authorized agent to attend to all business of mine, during my absence. Reuben ROSS.

John McCREARY seeks letters of adm. in est. of Wm. L. ALSTON, decd. soldier of TX Army, Washington Co. Probate Court, July 29.

All persons having claims against the est. of Chas. MILLER, decd., will present them to me in one form. C. C. WOODWARD, Admr.

Notice. Judge John SCOTT is my legally authorized Attorney for the city of Houston. H. E. HARTRIDGE, M.D., Montgomery Co., July 30.

The following described Negroes have runaway from the subscriber, they left while at a camp meeting in Montgomery co. on Sunday, July 31; a liberal reward will be paid. FRANK, a stout well made man, quick speech, 22 years old, had on narrow brim black hat, black cloth coat and copper colored pants. RALPH, 22, tall & spare built, very black, rather talkative, quick spoken. A woman, CATY, 50, rather yellow, outmouthed, hollow eyes, common height. A woman, SARAH, well made, rather spare, tolerably handsome, very backward in speech, rather down look and pregnant, wearing a calico dress. They took with them wearing apparel and bed clothes and are believed headed to United States. If they went west, they must have been kidnapped. H. G. JOHNSON, Spring Creek, July 24.

Cherokee War. Additional correspondence on military engagments on July 15-16 against the Cherokees, states that both Col. BOWLES and THE EGG, two of their principal chiefs were killed. An elegant sword and side-dirk were taken from the body of BOWLES, being the same presented to him by Ex-President HOUSTON.

Article from the "Constitutionalist," newspaper published at Bath, NY, describes Dr. Francis MOORE, editor of the <u>Telegraph & Texas Register</u>, who came to this country in spring of 1836. Dr. MOORE was for several years an esteemed citizen of the village of Bath. An enthusiastic supporter of liberty, he left us in 1836, in company with a young friend Mr. Jacob CRUGER, to join the Texian Army. For a time, Dr. M. served as a surgeon but settled permanently in the new Republic. Messrs. MOORE and CRUGER purchased the "Texas Telegraph," the only paper at that time in the Republic, and have since been very successful in the accumulation of property. He is presently the Mayor of Houston and a candidate for the TX Senate.

Notice. In the spring of 1837, Henry ULERY, of Washington Co., Penn., went to TX with a cargo of flour & whiskey; he landed at Galveston in late May and proceeded to Houston. This is according to a statement of Benj. CRAWFORD, who went down the river with him. CRAWFORD says ULERY left Houston for San Antonio and has never been heard from since. If he is still living, he is requested to answer this advertisement. If any person can give any information on his whereabouts, a liberal compensation will be given by his brother. Address letters to Beallsville, Washington co., Penn. Jacob ULERY, August 6.

Property belonging to est. of E. M. BRANCH, decd., will be sold at public auction at my house on first Tuesday in Sept. The residue of the property belong to the decd. includes one yoke of oxen, running in the bottom, the right of the est. to 1 bounty land certificate calling for 640 acres, and a part of a frame bldg. standing on the premises where the decd. lived. My residence, where the sale will be held, is located 15 miles below Richmond. Sarah JARVIS, Adm'x., E. M. JARVIS, Surety for Adm'x. Fort Bend County.

Wedesday, August 14, 1839

Information wanted on Michael Angelo WELCH, who left NY 2-3 years ago and came to TX; he is a lithographer by profession. Any person having information on him, will confer a favor by informing me at Galveston. Thos. P. RUSSELL.
Died on July 26th, near Fort Lamar, Neches Saline, Lt. Timothy O'NEILL of the 1st Infantry Regiment, TX Army. While scouting the country west of Neches with a detachment of his men, O'NEILL was killed and his body horribly mangled by a party of Indians hiding in the Neches swamp. The decd. came to TX in the fall of 1835, one of the volunteer corps raised in the city of New York by Col. E. H. STANLEY. He was buried with the honors of war, by his company at Fort Lamar.
Died on July 16th at Franklin, Robinson Co., Rev. Robert BROTHERTON, a minister of Gospel in connection with the Presbyterian church. He was a native of Greencastle, Penn., spent several years in the South, principally Miss., and came to TX earlier this year.
Wm. B. JAQUES named admr. of est. of Wm. P. DELMOUR, decd., Bexar County.

Wednesday, August 21, 1839

Died in this city after a short illness, Major J. W. MOODY, of congestive fever, aged about 48 years. The decd. has been 1st Auditor of the TX government for many years.
The New York papers assert positively that Lt. [Edwin Ward] MOORE, formerly of the sloop of war Boston, has resigned his commission in the U. S. Navy and accepted the appointment of commander of the Texian Navy.

C. W. BUCKLEY appointed Curator of vacant successions of Warren J. MITCHELL and John O. MOORE, decd., by Harrisburg Co. Probate Court. John S. EWELL seeks letters of adm. in est. of Samuel W. SCHOOLFIELD, late decd. of this county, Harrisburg Co. Probate Ct, Aug. 21; the petition to be granted in 60 days barring any objections.

Died in this city on 19th inst., William L. RHOTON, age 18, formerly of Lexington, KY.

Benjamin C. FRANKLIN, having resigned the office of Judge of 2nd Judicial District, will practice law in the several Courts of Republic of TX, in connection with Wm. W. FRANKLIN, Esq. Communications may be addressed to B. C. and W. W. FRANKLIN at Galveston or left at office of Henry HUMPHREYS, Chief Justice of County of Harrisburg.

Wednesday, August 28, 1839

Van Buren, Ark., July 31, Messrs. Editors: We have just received information of the execution of RICHAMOND, TURNER & BARNES, 3 of the murderers of the Wright family in Washington County in this sate. They were hung at Cane Hill, which is about 35 miles from this place & 8 miles from the Cherokee nation. The men were found guilty of murdering the Wright family, burning their house and their mutilated bodies. There were many others involved. Two of the principals are BAILY, who is gone to TX, and NICHOLSON, who is in the nation; several others have been told to quit this place within 10 days.--New Orleans <u>Bulletin</u>.

Proceeding of a general court martial held at camp near Fort Houston, August 14. The court martial consisting of Capt. CLENDENIN, President; Capt. HOWARD, Lts. CARRON, OGDEN & DUNNINGTON. Lt. ACKERMAN will act as special judge advocate. Pvt. Wm. TYNDELL, of Company C, 1st Infantry Regt., found guilty of desertion on July 20th, 1839 from Camp Harris, Cherokee Nation, sentenced to be shot to death. Pvt. John HARRIS, of same company, found guilty of desertion on June 24 from Bastrop and sentenced to be shot to death; signed by 1st Lt. D. Verplank ACKERMAN, Judge Advocate, and Capt. Adam CLENDENEN, President.

Died at the residence of W. Douglass LEE, in this city, Arthur CONROY, native of Ireland and late of Tennessee.

Died on July 15th, at the residence of Wm. PENN on the Trinity river, opposite Carolina, of congestive fever, Joseph WALDEN, formerly of NY. He came to this country last spring & had commenced a cotton planation on the Trinity.

$100 reward. Stolen or runaway on the 10th inst., from my plantation on the Colorado river 10 miles above Columbus, a Negro girl, MINTA, about 16 years, rather dark, down look when spoken to, small mouth, her under lip sticks out rather more than common; she carried away with her 1 red calico dress, 1 white muslin dress and 1 blue domestic. I will give the above reward for her and the thief, or $25 for her alone, delivered to me at my plantation, or to Field SECREST in Houston. W. H. SECREST.

Notice to Shippers of Goods in TX. The undersigned has established himself at Linnville, Port of Labacca, being the most convenient landing for the new seat of government, Bastrop, LaGrange, Gonzales, Upper Labacca, and San Antonio. He will attend to the receiving & forwarding of Goods to all points. he will also attend to the Custom House business. Charges will be moderate. John HAYES, August 1.

Wednesday, September 4, 1839

Remember Tampico!! The surviving members of the Expedition of the late Gen. Jose Antonion MEXIA, decd., against Tampico in the fall of 1835, are requested to report their names and present places of residence, by letter or otherwise, to the undersigned in this city as soon as possible, and hopefully before the commencement of Congress in November. Reports should include name, rank & commanding officer. Geo. FISHER, late Secy. to said Expedition, Houston, August 31st.

Sheriffs Sale. By virtue of an execution to me directed by Liberty Co. Dist. Court, I have levied upon and will expose to public sale at the Court House door in Liberty on 1st Tuesday in October next, a negro boy, JIM, about 25, levied upon as the property of Jos. DUGAT decd. to satisfy said execution in favor of Wm. M. LOGAN against Pierre and Mary BLANCHET, admr's. of Jos. DUGAT. Terms cash. B. W. HARDIN, Sheriff, Liberty, August 27.

Probate Ct., Harrisburg Co., Aug. 21st: Mr. Samuel B. EVES seeks letters of adm. in est. of John CUNNINGHAM; final hearing in 60 days.

Wednesday, September 11, 1839

We understand that the Hon. H. W. FONTAINE has resigned the office of District Judge.

Col. A. NEILL arrived from Bexar this morning in company with General Juan Pablo ANAYA & his party. This gentleman has paid a visit, as we understand, to negotiate with this govt. for aid in establishing a new republic out of a portion of eastern Mexico. ANAYA was a particular friend of Gen. JACKSON in LA in 1814 and fought at his side in the battles of Dec. 1814 and Jan. 1815. He has since served as General of Division in the armies of Mexico.

Probate Ct., Harrisburg Co., Sept. 4th: Otto C. SACKMAN has filed letters of adm. in est. of James GOBBEN, decd. Hearing set in 10 days.

Probate Ct., Harrisburg Co., Sept. 8th: Mr. John Alex. NEWLANDS seeks letters of adm. in vacant succ. of Joseph REUX, decd. Final hearing set for 10 days.

Wm. LAWRENCE prays to be associated with Mrs. Francis LYNCH as adm. in succ. of Nathaniel LYNCH, decd. The petition will be granted in 10 days unless objections are raised.

A letter has been received by the Secy. of War from Lt. WILLIAMS, of Fannin co., on Red River, containing the information that the Cherokees have crossed Red River and gone into Arkansas. Lt. WILLIAMS had a fight with them and killed three on the banks of that river.

Wednesday, September 18, 1839

John SCOTT, an attorney of high standing, has been named Judge of 2nd Judicial District, replacing H. W. FONTAINE; John R. REID has been named District Attorney for same district, replacing A. M. TOMPKINS, removed.

Fabraius REYNOLD vs. H. A. E. REYNOLDS, suit for divorce, Harrisburg District Court, if the defendant wishes to make a defence, she must appear at December Term of this court.

Probate Sale, Colorado County, will be held at town of Columbus on 1st Tuesday of Nov., all the lands belonging to the vacant succ. of Henry HARRISON, decd., viz: 2 tracts of 585 acres each, a part of the James ARMMINGS headright, granted in 1824; three several quarters in the county of Matagorda from the league of Thomas BOYCE, granted to said BOYCE in 1830; one quarter league on west side of San Bernard, being the lower quarter of a league granted in 1824 to Thos. GRAY and John M. MOORE. By order of Probate Judge Willard WADHAM, Sept. 15.

M. B. SHACKLEFORD, having learned that letters disreputable to his good name were found among the Cherokees is desirous that they be laid before the public.

Dispatch from Newton County, Mo., dated June 29. On the 22nd inst., about 40 half and full blooded Cherokees came to the house of John RIDGE, a distinguished Cherokee, was drug from his home and was viciously butchered. The party, after killing Mr. John RIDGE, took up the line of march in pursuit of Major RIDGE, his father, who was visiting friends in Van Buren, Ark. Reports reach us that the party overtook Major Ridge on the night of the 22nd and killed him on his horse by shooting him. It is also reported that Elias BOUDINOT, a member of the Ridge Party, was also killed. Major RIDGE was a gentleman of highly cultivated mind and had attended college in Connecticut, where he met and married a Miss NORTHROP of that state. He was formerly a principal chief of his nation & fought under Gen. JACKSON against the Creeks. John RIDGE was about 37 years of age and leaves a wife and six children. It is generally believed that the faction led by Chief John ROSS was behind the murders. The deaths of the two RIDGES will long be regretted by their friends and acquaintances.

Died in this city on Sept. 8th, Mr. John E. LUCAS, late of Clarke Co., Alabama but a resident of TX for past 10 months.

Robert WATSON has filed petition to be named admr. of est. of Hugh GRAY, decd., Harrisburg County, Sept. 13th; hearing will be in 10 days.

Ann HINDS seeks letters of adm. in est. of her husband, Thos. F. HINDS, decd., Harrisburg County Probate Court, Sept. 13th.

Watkins CLAY seeks letters of adm. in est. of John ISAM, decd., Harrisburg County Probate Court, September 8th.

Wednesday, September 25, 1839

The Tremont House at Galveston has been opened by Mr. NORWOOD. It is the largest house in TX and we have received very favorable accounts of the manner in which it is kept from those who have visited the Island city.

Died in this city yesterday morning at the residence of Geo. W. LIVELY, after a long and protracted illness, William T. LIVELY, 35, late of GA. The Columbus paper will please notice.

A Runaway Negro. Taken up on the 20th Sept. at my house on Bray's bayou, 5 miles from Houston, on the Brazoria road, a negro woman, tall, slim built, who says she belongs to A. KLESON, in San Felipe, her owner will please call, prove her, pay all charges, and take her away. P. W. ROSE.

The subscriber, having made arrangements to move west, will on Oct. 21st offer for sale at public auction in the town of Liberty, all his property in said town, consisting of 12 inner lots, 2 of which have comfortable dwellings on them. Also to be sold the late residence of S. KIRKHAM in West Liberty, consisting of three 12 acre lots under fence & cultivation and cultivation, a good dwelling, kitchen & outbuildings together with a fine stock of hogs, harming utensils, &c. The subscriber will also offer for sale all his household & kitchen furniture, bedding, &c. E. LIGHTLE, Liberty, Sept. 5.

Andrew BRISCOE and D. W. Clinton HARRIS are named admr's. of the est. of John BIRDSALL, decd., Houston, Sept. 14. Persons who left their legal business in Mr. BIRDSALL's hands may obtain their documents by calling upon us.

Wednesday, October 2, 1839

Probate Court, Harrisburg Co., Sept. 13th: For various causes move before the hon. Probate Court of this county, by counsel for the absent heirs of the succ. of Charles MILLER, decd., it is ordered and decreed that Coroden C. WOODWARD, heretofore appointed as the admr. to the succ. of said MILLER, be dismissed from adm. of the same.

James H. SPILLMAN named admr. of the est. of George B. WILSON, decd.

Wednesday, October 9, 1839

The Columbia arrived at Galveston on Friday last. Among the passengers who came on board her were Commodore MOORE, formerly of the U.S. Navy, & now commander of our naval force; Col. DEXTER, who was appointed by our govt. as one of the commissioners to act with the agent of the U.S. to run our north-eastern boundary; and Commodore RIBEAU of the Federal Party of Mexico, who was recently in this country, compelled to put into Matagorda, on board the Pontchartrain, on account of bursting of her boilers.

Married on Tuesday, 8th inst., D. W. BABCOCK and Miss Margaret GRANDISON, both of this city.

Died at the residence of Major BINGHAM, in Brazoria co. on 2nd inst., Moumor R. WIGGINTON, late of N.O. Louisville, KY papers will please notice the above.

Lewis COX named admr. of est. of Isaac B. BROWN, decd., Montgomery County.

Administrators Sale set for 1st Tuesday in November next at court-house door in city of

Houston, to be sold to highest bidder, 2 certificates of head-right for one-third of a league of land, and two bounty claims for 320 acres each, being the property of the succ. of Wm. W. WATROUS, decd., sold for benefit of creditors of said succession. P. REILY, Administrator.

Probate Ct., Harrisburg Co., Oct. 3---Henry KESLER seeks letters of adm. in est. of Wm. G. LONG, decd. Appointment will be made ten days from this date unless objections raised.

Peter DICKMANN seeks letters of adm. in est. of Harmann DICKMANN, decd., Harrisburg Co. Probate Court. Appointment to be made in 10 days unless objections are raised.

$3.00 (Texas Money) Reward. Runaway from the subscriber at Richmond on 19th inst., a mulatto boy named GABRIEL, about 13 years old, 5 feet, 7 inches tall, has a receding forehead, and dark hair inclined to be straight; he had on when he left home a pair of linen pantaloons but no coat or hat. He has a scar under one of his eyes. Geo. W. TONY, Sept. 27.

$150 Reward in Texian Money. Ranaway from my plantation on the night of the 7th ult., the following Negroes: WILLARD, a dark mulatto, about 25 years, about 5'8", stout built, has two forefingers on his right hand broke. Also, CHARLOTTE, a black, about 30 years, very thick projecting lips, clips her words when speaking, her right leg shorter than other one; and CAIN, her sopn, about 13 years, black, thick lips, has small scar on his forehead over his left eye and was wearing a light mixed Kentucky jeans hunting shirt. The above reward will be paid upon delivery of the slaves to me or to Col. Wm. T. AUSTIN at Velasco. P. BERTRAND, Brazoria co., Oct. 1.

The public are hereby cautioned against trading for certain notes of hand, executed by the subscriber to Samuel B. MIXON, as they were given in consideration of property the title of which is doubtful. Joanah DUNLAP.

If J. Porter BROWN will call on J. L. NICKELSON at the Telegraph printing office, he may be put in possession of useful information.

Wednesday, October 16, 1839

His excellency, James CLARK, Governor of Kentucky, died at his residence on the morning of the 27th ult. after a lingering and painful illness. He was 55 or 56 years old & was elected as governor in August 1836.

We are under the painful necessity to record the decease of three of our most worthy citizens during the last week --- the Hon. Henry HUMPHREYS, Chief Justice of this county; the Hon. Robert BARR, Postmaster General; and Dr. A. A. ANDERSON, late of Vicksburg, Miss. The community has sustained an almost irreparable loss in these deaths.

By a gentleman from Austin, who arrived this morning, we have letters from that place containing the following particulars of depradations by a party of Indians: "About 10 days since a party consisting of 13 men, 1 woman and 2 children started from the settlement of Mr. HORNSBY 10 miles below Austin, with a view of making a permanent location on the San Gabriel River about 60 miles above Austin. After having travelled about 30 miles, they were attacked by a body of Indians, and the whole 13 men killed on the spot, and their bodies left lying within a few feet of each other. The woman and her 2 children were not found and of course the supposition is that they were taken prisoners. The attack was made in an open prairie. . .The names of the individuals killed are as follows: Two REESEs of Brazoria, John WEBSTER, John STILLWELL, Willson FLESHER of Va., Martin WATSON of Scotland, BAZLEY, Nicholas BOYLER, Milton HICKS of Ky., Wm. RICE of Va., Albert SILLSBEY of Ky., James MORTON of TX, LEUSHER, a musician, and a negro man the property of WILSON." The above melancholy intelligence comes from Dr. D. C. GILMORE, who was one of a surveying party of 20 persons, who left this city on last Saturday, the 5th inst., with a view to locating lands between this river and the Brazos.

C. W. BUCKLEY named curator of est. of Randolph SLATTER, decd.

R. MORRIS named Curator of the vacant succ. of W. G. POINDEXTER, decd.

Lost. Sometime about the 1st of Aug. 1839, a pocket book containing a bond for titles to a labor of land, executed sometime in Oct. 1838, by James WALLACE in favor of myself---the headright of Charles TASE to 1 league & 1 labor of land. Any person finding any of the above papers shall receive a reasonable reward by delivering them to me, on the road to Washington near Groce's Retreat. R. A. PORTER.

Probate Court, Gonzales County, Sept. 26th: Notice is hereby given that Alonzo B. SWITZER has filed a petition with this court for the appointment as Curator of the vacant succession of J. L. SCHOONHOVER and J. SMITH, decd. soldiers. If any person opposes this appointment they have 60 days to advise this court; otherwise the petition will be granted.

Wednesday, October 23, 1839

Died in this city on Oct. 2nd, of the prevailing epidemic, S. J. COOK, late of Cooperstown, NY. It will be gratifying to his relations to learn that many attended him to his last home and that the impressive rites of the Episcopal church were performed over his narrow grave. He was indeed "By Strangers honored and by Strangers mourned."

Died at the residence of Mr. MARTIN, Spring Creek, Thos. C. DABBS, a respectable citizen of this city. The Nashville, Tenn. papers will please copy the above.

Died on Sunday morning, Otto FINKE, about 30 years, a native of Germany, but late of Butler County, Penn. Pittsburg papers please copy.

Died in this city this morning at 1 o'clock, Mrs. Aurelia MILLER, consort of Christopher MILLER, Esq., formerly of Hartford, Conn.

Died at the residence of David RANDON on the Brazos, on the 14th ult., W. Augustus PASSMORE, a native of Mercer Co., KY. Although the decd. had been here but a short time, he has acquired a large circle of friends.

Died at my residence on the Navidad, Frederick POOL, a native of Germany. Those who are interested are hereby informed that I have now in my possession the following property of said decd.: 1 horse bridle & saddle, 1 gun, and a pocket book containing a $10 bill, Texas money, with other sundry papers. George SUTHERLAND, Jackson County, Oct. 23.

Died on Wednesday, 16th inst., at the residence of his father, Mr. E. F. STANSBURY, late of the city of Cincinnati, Ohio.

Wednesday, October 30, 1839

Dissolution. The Co-partnership heretofore existing between MARTIN & EDMONDSON was on Oct. 20th, by mutual consent, dissolved. Any person having claims against said firm will present their accounts to John Edmondson for payment, and all persons owing said firm will make payment to same. Geo. W. MARTIN, John EDMONDSON.

The Turning & Bedstead Making business will be continued by me at the old stand. John EDMONDSON, October 23.

In County Court, Oct. 30th. Present Benjamin P. BUCKNER, Chief Justice; E. H. WINFIELD, Assoc. Justice; John W. MOORE, Sheriff; & J. A. SOUTHMAYD, Deputy Clerk. Col. W. F. GRAY, in a brief address, communicated the death of Robert PAGE, Esq., a young and promising member of this Bar. As a token of our respect, we the Members of the Bar & the officers of this Court will attend the funeral of the decd. and send a copy of this resolution to his grieving family in Virginia.

Notice. All persons to whom the late firm of HASSETT & GRAVES is indebted are requested to present their accounts; and those owing said firm, will come forward and liquidate the same. Or their accounts will be turned over to a collection officer. Charles H. GRAVES, Admr. and surviving partner of the said firm.

Henry KESLER has filed his petition & prays for appointment of curator to the vacant succesiosn of Robert BARR & John SCHLOCHTENBERGER, both decd., and if any opposition is intended, it must be made within 10 days of this date (Oct. 21st). E. H. WINFIELD, Acting Judge, Probate Court, Harrisburg County.

Charles KESLER seeks position of curator of vacant succ. of Wm. HENNINGS, decd., Harrisburg County, Probate Court, Oct. 25th.

John S. EWELL seeks appointment as curator of vacant succ. of Abram HILTON, decd., Harrisburg Co., Probate Court, Oct. 25th.

Thos. W. HOUSE seeks appointment as curator to vacant succ. of Thos. MITCHELL, decd., Harrisburg County, Probate Court, Oct. 28th.

Chas. BOWMAN & Ferdinand GERLACH have applied for the adm. of the succ. of Charles B. FANGER, decd. Harrisburg Co. Probate Ct., Oct. 30.

John CONROY prays for appointment as curator of vacant succ. of Arthur CONROY, decd. Harrisburg County, Probate Court, Oct. 28th.

Administrators Sale. Will be sold at the court-house door in town of Liberty on the 1st Tuesday of December next, three likely Negro men, belonging to the succ. of Joseph DUGAT, decd.; sold by order of probate ct. of Liberty County, to satisfy a mortgage against the property of the decedent. Mary C. DUGAT, Admrx. of Joseph DUGAT, decd.

Wednesday, November 6, 1839

Probate Sale. Will be sold at court-house door in town of Liberty on 1st Tuesday in December next, one quarter of a league of land belonging to the succession of Patrick CARNOLD, decd., lying upon the waters of Menard's Creek in county of Liberty. Sold to pay the debts of said succ. Terms cash. Hugh B. JOHNSTON, Judge of Probate, Liberty, Nov. 4th.

Sheriff's Sale set for 1st Tuesday of December next, at court-house door in Liberty, all the right, title, claim & interest that the succ. of M. B. MUNSON, decd., has in and to a certain Negro woman named MILLY, about 10 years old, and her child MOSES, about 15 months old. Levied upon as property of said succ. to satisfy executions in favor of Alex. S. ROBERTS and Daniel P. COIT against said succ. Terms will be cash. B. W. HARDIN, Sheriff, Liberty Co., November 2.

Public sale of valuable lands. Bu virtue of a decree from Hon. Wyley MARTIN, Judge of Probate of Fort Bend county, we will offer at public sale on Dec. 3rd, at the court-house in the town of Richmond, the following valuable landed property, belonging to the late firm of HANDY & LUSK, and the succ. of R. E. HANDY: 1 league, known as the DELGADO league, lying west of the Brazos river, about 9 miles below San Felipe, adjoining the land of the late Martin ALLEN. A league on the waters of the Tegua, in Washington co., being the land granted to Bazil M. HATFIELD. A league in Gonzales co., granted to Jos. D. CLEMENTS in 1835. 200 acres of land on Cedar Lake and Caney, being part of the league granted to Daniel DECROW & Thos. McCOY in 1836. A quarter of a league on Peach Creek, Bastrop co., land granted to Samuel HAYSLETT in 1835. A league on Pin Oak creek east of the Colorado, granted to Geo. W. WHITESIDE in 1832. A half league on the Rio Blanco in Milam's colony, being land granted to Benj. WILLIAMS. A quarter of a league on Big Creek, Fort Bend co., land granted to Asa WICKSON by the Mexican government. A fine plantation & improvements on north side of New Year's Creek, in Washington co., containing about 760 acres, formerly occupied by James HALL, 3rd. About 1/3 a league on the Colorado, near La Grange, part of a league granted to Geo. DUTY by the Mexican government in 1824. A ½ league on east side of Brazos, between GROCE's Plantation and Retreat, being the land granted to Samuel H. HARDING by the government of Coahuila and Texas. One tract of land on west side of Brazos in Fort Bend co., containing about 860 acres, with a small improvement, being part of the land granted to John JONES by the Mexican government. Terms of sale--12 and 18 months credit, with bond & approved security. John LEVERING, Admr. of the succ. of R. E. HANDY, & William LUSK, surviving partner of HANDY & LUSK. Richmond, Oct. 23.

Sheriff's sale set for 1st Tuesday of Dec. next at court-house door in Liberty, for all right, title, interest & claim of Samuel WHITING in & to a Negro woman named LAVINIA, about 25 years of age, and her child, JOE, about nine months old, to satisfy an execution in favor of Wm. M. LOGAN, admr. of H. B. PRENTISS, decd., against said WHITING. Terms cash. B. W. HARDIN, Sheriff of Liberty County, Nov. 5th.

Charles BOWMAN seeks appointment as Curator to vacant succ. of Peter KRAIG, decd., Probate Court, Harrisburg Co.

E. HUMPHREYS seeks appointment as Curator of the succ. of Jas. H. WARFIELD, decd., Harrisburg County, Probate Court.

Isaiah CALL and Jane D. BODHAM seek appointment as Curators of the vacant succ. of Austin R. BODMAN, decd., Harrisburg Co. Probate Court.

Robert BROWN seeks appointment as Curator of the vacant succ. of John B. SIMPSON, decd., Harrisburg Co. Probate Court.

W. Douglass LEE seeks appointment as Curator to vacant succ. of Isaac READ, decd., Harrisburg County Probate Court.

Erastus S. PERKINS seeks appointment as Curator of vacant succ. of James PICKUP, decd., Harrisburg County Probate Court.

Wednesday, November 13, 1839

[Compiler's note: This particular issue is missing from the files of this newspaper.]

Wednesday, November 20, 1839

The recognition of the independence of Texas by France is already well known; and we learn from the "Globe" that M. DE SALIGNY, one of the secretaries of the French mission in the U.S., will be appointed Charge d'affairs in this country.

J. CASTANIE, General Broker, 42 Canal st., New Orleans, undertakes the sale & purchase of real estate, merchandise, produce, etc. Having resided 3 years in Texas, he is well acquainted with the validity of titles & claims in that republic, and will also translate in French or English, all Spanish grants and claims.

Notice. The Co-partnership existing between S. and T. F. BREWER is not dissolved by the death of the senior partner, but will be continued by the surviving partner, as usual under the same firm. T. Francis BREWER.

Died in this city on the 12th inst., Ezekiel HUMPHREYS, a native of Conn. & late of Warren, Ohio, about 28 years of age. Mr. H. came to this country early in 1836, as a volunteer in the corps commanded by Capt. QUITMAN of Natchez, Miss. After becoming a resident of this city, he resumed his profession, a printer, and upon the establishment of the **Morning Star**, became its publisher, in which capacity he continued until his decease.

Notice. The undersigned, intending to reside at the city of Austin for some months, notifies the citizens of Houston and the public at large that he will attend to any business at the city of Austin. Thomas Wm. WARD.

Wednesday, November 27, 1839

Notice. The undersigned have formed a Co-partnership for the practice of Law in the Probate, District & Supreme Cts. of the Republic. The office of John HEMPHILL at Austin; of C. B. HEFORD at Bastrop; the latter will also keep open his former office at San Felipe. John HEMPHILL, C. B. HEFORD , Nov. 25th.

Wednesday, December 4, 1839

The Senate have refused to confirm the nomination of Hon. Richard DUNLAP as Minister Plenipotentiary to the U.S.; and he will therefore be immediately recalled.

Samuel ROBERTS, Esq., Secretary of Legation to the U.S. resigned some weeks since.

Dr. Willis ROBERTS, late Collector of the port of Galveston, has been removed.

The following gentlemen compose the Grand Jury for Harrisburg Co. empaneled yesterday:

James MORGAN, W. D. LEE, A. J. DAVIS, James M. McGEE, Michael McCORMICK, John W. NILES, Ransom HOUSE, Wm. MATTHEWS, Henry LEVENHAGEN, Geo. H. ROBERTS, Buckner COMPFIELD, Andrew LAWSON, Wm. BLOODGOOD, Singleton HOUSE, Robt. DUNMAN, Henry EVANS, and H. R. ALLEN.

Died yesterday afternoon at the residence of Alden A. M. JACKSON, in this city, Col. A. S. LEWIS, formerly of NY, and late of Montgomery. Col. LEWIS came to the aid of TX in her darkest hour and took part in most of the engagements during the war.

Died in this city yesterday, Dec. 2nd, Mrs. Hannah VEDDER, wife of Philip V. VEDDER, late of Schenectady, New York.

John HALL seeks appointment as Curator of the vacant succ. of Charles L. CARRERE, decd., Harrisburg County, Probate Court, Nov. 29th.

I. F. THIELL seeks appointment as Curator of the vacant succ. of D. H. STOVAL, decd., Nov. 30th, Harrisburg County Probate Court.

Rutersville. Rev. Mr. RICHARDSON and Lady have arrived & will take charge of the Rutersville Academies on the 2d Monday of Jan. 1840. Tuition & board will be as at other similar institutions of the Republic. Wm. P. SMITH, Sec. Board of Trustees, Nov. 25th.

Wednesday, December 11, 1839

MORRIS, a corporal in the army, was executed at Austin on the 28th ult., in pursuance of the sentence of a court martial. His offence was the stabbing of Capt. KENNYMORE. An attempt to murder the officer of the day was clearly and conclusively proved against him, and he had met the punishment he deserved.

The Galveston volunteers under Capt. WILSON, lately had a skirmish with the Indians on the Pedernalles, killing 11 of them, & taking about 40 horses. Some of the Indians displayed garments supposed to have been taken from Mr. WEBSTER and his party, who were murdered near the San Gabriel.

From a New Orleans Paper. Mr. Editor, at the request of a large number of Texians & particularly officers of the navy in this city, I beg leave to explain the reasons behind an advertisement which appeared some time since in your paper. I was arrested at the suit of John CORMICK, Jr., as endorser on a draft, without recourse on me, for $800. After my arrest, and while in custody of the officer, the yellow fever broke out to an alarming extent and I, not being acclimated, felt alarmed. I went to the deputy sheriff and offered him such security as I had to double the amount, but he said TX property was useless to him. I then applied to other individuals in the city, whom the sheriff refused; & then went to the late H. BETTS, who remarked to me that as my business was confined up the river, and yellow fever very rampant in town, I might leave, and write him what to do---which I did---& on my return all would be satisfactory. Shortly after I left, BETTS died of the prevailing epidemic, and I did not hear from New Orleans until my return; and on my return was met by a friend who told of the advertisement stating that I had absconded. I then proceeded forthwith to the office of the sheriff. I hope the following statement will exculpate me from anything like dishonor in the transaction. Your obt. servant, John O'BRIAN.

At the request of Mr. John O'BRIAN, who was advertised sometime since by me, as having absconded from the sheriff's officer who arrested him, I certify that on Nov. 21st inst., he came to the sheriff's office, & surrendered himself again into the hands of the sheriff honorably. Sheriff's office, New Orleans, Nov. 23rd, 1839. W. E. MURPHY, Deputy Sheriff, Orleans Parish.

Look at this! For sale by the subscriber 20,000 acres of Land all of which is located, a part on the Colorado, & in various places west; on the Nueces, Corpus christi bay, or near there. I would take in exchange negro property, a few fine horses, goods or produce. Purchasers would do well to give me a call, I can generally be found 8 miles above Lagrange on the Colorado. Z. F. MORRELL, Nov. 20.

Wednesday, December 18, 1839

A. A. M. JACKSON of this city has been appointed as Collector of the Port of Galveston.

Judge WALLER has been nominated by the President for office of Post Master General; when the vote was taken in the Senate, it was equally divided on the nomination, and the Vice President cast the deciding vote in his favor.

We have been informed by Mr. BARTON, who accompanied Col. BOWIE in an expedition to the head waters of the San Saba 8 or 9 years ago, that a large well-built fort is situated on the northern bank of that stream, about 70 miles from its juncture with the Colorado. It is believed that this fort was constructed by the Spanish many years ago.

Runaway or stolen from the subscriber in May last, from New Orleans, a yellow boy, named LEVI, about 5'10", slender built, about 23 years, has little to say unless spoken to. He was raised in Nashville, TN. I will give $200 reward for his capture and returned to me, or if taken up in TX and delivered to a jail so as I can get him. Address me at Mobile, Ala. until May 1st next, and then to Louisville, KY. M. COTTER, Dec. 16th.

All persons indebted to the late Wm. LANGTHORP, decd., are to call upon the undersigned and make payment; and all persons with claims against the same are requested to present them properly authenticated for payment to the same. S. N. DOBIE, Harrisburg Co., Dec. 16th.

Mansion House, Market Square, city of Houston---Robert WALKER informs his friends & the public that he has taken the extensive establishment formerly occupied by Mrs. BROWN, on Market Square, and is now prepared to receive company.

Midway for Sale. I offer for sale the tract of land, containing 6,356 acres, which is situated upon Clear Creek, on a direct line and half way between Houston and Galveston. This tract adjoins headright of Col. W. D. C. HALL. Also for sale 1476 acres of land upon the coast side of San Jacinto river, about 12 miles above its mouth, being an old survey, the head right of Andres DE ROJAS, adjoining the lands of ROARK and others. For further particulars, refernce to Major COCKE at Houston, or to myself at Velasco. Thos. J. GREEN, Dec. 13.

Wednesday, December 25, 1839

Colonels ROSS and SWITZER of the Federal Army of Mexico arrived at Austin on the 15th. They state that Matamoros had not been captured when they left the Rio Grande; but that the Army of the Federalists had advanced to within 9 or 10 miles of the city and had entirely cut off all communication with the interior.

Another account has reached this place of the fall of Matamoros. The news was brought by a respectable citizen of Goliad. Great slaughter was made on both sides and many Centralists were taken prisoners, but CANALIZE, their leader, escaped. No other particulars are known.

Caution. We the undersigned hereby notify the public that a quantity of counterfeit Land Claims, well executed, are now offered for sale in this market, they purport to be issued by Chichester CHAPLIN & Nathaniel HUNT, Commissioners, and John C. BROOKE, Clerk of the Board of Land Commissioners for the county of San Augustine. N. K. KELLUM, John H. McRAE, Isaac CAMPBELL, Houston, 21st Dec. 1839.

Public Notice. The undersigned will continue to locate lands for his friends, & promises to give entire satisfaction to those who may engage his services. Address---T. P. HAWKINS, Peach Creek, Montgomery Co., TX, Dec. 23.

Wednesday, January 1, 1840

The newspaper publishes a poem "written by a friend, on the death of Wm. H. LEVINS, a Lieutenant of Texian schooner of war Invincible, who, after the capture of that vessel by the Mexicans, was shot to death at the Brazos Santiago (Mexico) by the order of General SANTA ANNA on the 6th of April 1837.

N. AMORY, Esq., has been appointed Secretary of Legation to the United States.

Juan Pablo de ANAYA, the Mexican Federal General, who has been in this city for the last six months, left here last week. It is understood that he set out for Matamoros, having received authentic information of the capture of that place by his party.

Died on the 27th Dec., at his residence on Bray's Bayou, Dr. P. W. ROSE, formerly of St. Louis, Mo., in his 59th year.

Information Wanted!! In July 1837, Wm. H. DAVIS, formerly of Baltimore, was in the service of the TX govt., and sailed from Galveston in a national vessel of war, called the Invincible. He was afterwards put on board a prize, called the Telegraph, in the character of prize master, which vessel was reported to have been recaptured by the Mexicans and carried into the prot of Tampico. The American Consul at Vera Cruz, under date of June 1839, states that a person by the name of DAVIS was brought there as a prisoner, and released after the attack upon Vera Cruz by the French Squadron. It is said that some persons, amongst whom was one by the name of DAVIS, were confined in Havana, and addressed a letter in the summer of 1839 to the commander of the U.S. vessel of war, the Boston. The parents of Mr. DAVIS are anxious to learn something further respecting his fate, and would be thankful to any person who can give them information respecting him. Address: John DAVIS, No. 77 Pratt street, Baltimore.

C. C. NORTON seeks appointment as curator to the vacant succ. of Virgil COLLINS, decd., Harrisburg County, Probate Ct., Dec. 28th.

Take Notice that I executed a power of atty. in Mexico City in Feb. 1834 to James WHITESIDES and Walter C. WHITE, to make and execute a title to Anthony BUTLER, for a quarter league of land situated on Kronkeway Bayou in Austin's Colony. I hereby declare the power of attorney as null & void, as the consideration for which it was given has entirely failed. F. STACK.

For sale in city of Sabine a valuable house & lot on Lot 8, Block 53. S. JONES.

Wednesday, January 8, 1840

We have received a bundle of papers from Judge ROBINSON, given to him by CASTRO, the Lipan chief taken in Gonzales county about the 25th of Oct. last from the Comanches, in fight with them, in which one of the latter was killed, and one Mexican boy about 15 years old escaped, and came into Victoria---he has been a prisoner of the Comanches for about four years. The papers are receipts for land taxes, a land certificate granted by the Board of Land Commissioners for Bastrop co., and other papers, all of which can be had on application to this office. From the names, they would appear to be the property of the 13 persons killed by the Indians, 15 miles from this place, on this side of Brushy Creek.---Austin *Gazette*.

Two companies of troops lately raised in New Orleans left this place on Tuesday for the frontier under the command of Capt. REDD. Several companies have preceded them within the last six weeks, destined for service on the same field.

We have conversed with Mr. HODGE, a gentleman who arrived yesterday from Austin, who gave an account of an engagement which took place some 10 days since between troops under Colonel BURLESON and a party of Cherokees. The Indians were routed with the loss of 6 killed and 24 women & children captured; it is said that EGG, one of their chiefs was among the slain, and the wife of young BOWLES and other relatives of his were among the captured.

M. DE SALIGNY, the French minister to this country, & his suite arrived in NY by the Liverpool, on his way to Texas.

The city election, yesterday, resulted in the choice of these officers for 1840: Charles BIGELOW, Mayor; D. W. BABCOCK, Recorder; Aldermen, John CARLOS, Geo. STEVENS, Henry R. ALLEN, E. OSBORNE, John W. NILES, Ferdinand GERLACH, Wm. M. CARPER, John W. MOORE; and Lewis WAY, Constable.

James D. COCKE seeks letters of adm. in the est. of A. S. LEWIS, decd., Montgomery County, Probate Court, Dec. Term, 1839.

For Sale. 10 valuable acclimated negroes, 30,000 acres primarily bounty land claims, 900 acres, (in tracts to suit purchasers) rich and heavily timbered land, part of which lies in one half mile of Houston & part in two miles of Harrisburg on Bray's Bayou to which steamboats can run to Houston; it is also contiguous to C. P. CLEMMON's sawmill; 160 acres on Green's Bayou; 10,000 acres of land in small, desirable tracts in Robertson & Milam counties; much other property. S. M. FROST.

The Austin City Gazette, after a suspension of 3 weeks, has made its appearance again under date of Dec. 25th. We were somewhat surprised to observe an article in that paper announcing the election on the 4th ult., of its publisher, Major Samuel WHITING, as public printer for 1840, without mentioning the reconsideration of the vote, which took place the same day. On the reconsideration CRUGER & BONNELL, publishers of the Texas Centinel, were elected by a majority of six votes over Major WHITING, and were at the time of the publication of that article and are now public printers for 1840. Such pitiful attempts to gain importance in the eyes of the community, are altogether unworthy a conductor of the public press.

Notice. The subscriber has made arrangements with the proprietor of the City Hotel, to take charge of the stables attached to the same and assures the public that no one who shall leave with him his horse, shall ever it said that his nag has not been well attended to by Alex. H. MOORE, Houston.

Wednesday, February 5, 1840

Mexican mode of Warfare Against the Comanche and Apache Indians. We find in a late file of Mexican papers, notice of the junto, or society formed in the Department of Chihuahua, on the river del Norte, for repulsing the Apache and other Indian tribes from Texas. This junto is an association of some 200 men, 150 of which are from North America, and the other 50 from Mexico. The command & entire direction of this force is confided to James KICKER, a German who settled at the fort Paseo de Norte, on the river of that name, in lat. 32 deg. 30 min. north. He has contracted to furnish men, ammunition, & provisions for this guerilla war.---<u>Globe</u>.

Among the trophies won from the Cherokees in the recent skirmish near Pecan bayou was the military hat of the late Cherokee chief BOWLES. Col. BURLESON, on learning that it had been captured, forwarded it to the Adjutant general Col. H. McLEOD at Austin, with a polite request to present it to Gen. HOUSTON. Col. McLEOD did so, but HOUSTON, based on his longtime friendship with the Cherokees, regarded it as a direct insult.

W. D. WALLACH has purchased the Colorado <u>Gazette & Advertiser</u>, now published at Matagorda.

Runaway from the subscriber on Jan. 13th, a negro man named LEM or LEMUEL, his height about 5'8", aged about 40 years, his apparel consisted of an old brown frock coat, blue linsey pants and a somewhat worn and mended black hat. A reward of $25 will be paid for delivery of said negro to my house or the nearest jail. Margaret McCORMICK, Jan. 30.

Wm. PIERPONT named admr. of the est. of G.B. SEYMOUR, decd., Harrisburg County, Jan. 21.

Information wanted of a gentleman by the name of John A. DAVENPORT, aged about 23 years, and who probably emigrated to this country some time last year. Should this be seen by him or any of his acquaintances, they will favor the subscribers by giving such information respecting him as they are possessed of. S. & T. F. BREWER, Feb. 2.

Notice to Surveyors & Others. During the winter of 1838, while at the city of Houston, the undersigned enclosed by letter to John F. GRAHAM, of Nacogdoches co., a certificate for 1 league & 1 labor of land, said certificate was issued by the board of land commissioners for the county of San Augustine, to E. W. CULLEN, assignee of -----------; one half of which was assigned to John F. GRAHAM; the letter containing said certificate was handed by the undersigned to Mr. Presley GEORGE now of Tenn., with a request to deliver it to John F. GRAHAM; but Mr. GEORGE did not go to Nacogdoches as he expected, and is now residing in the U.S. From the high and unimpeachable character of Mr. GEORGE, the undersigned has no doubt he either put the letter containing said certificate in some post office, or placed it in some person's hands to deliver it to GRAHAM. Should the said certificate fall into any surveyor's hands, he is respectfully requested to inform the said John F. GRAHAM of the same as he is entitled to all the benefits assigned to him by John M. WHITE. Signed K. H. MUSE.

Law Notice. The undersigned announces his intention to decline the practice of law --- he has now concluded to give his full attention to his profession, he has associated with him in the practice James S. JONES, Esq.; business will frequently take him from home, but Mr. JONES may always be consulted at his office. Josiah J. CROSBY, Washington, Jan. 1840.

[Several issues are missing here --- compiler's note.]

Wednesday, April 8, 1840

The following is a list of Acts & Joint Resolutions passed by the Fourth Congress, commencing the 11th November 1839:

Joint Res. for relief of Richard J. WOODWARD.
Joint Res. for relief of Saml. W. WYBRANTS.
An act for the relief of Joseph TATE.
Joint Res. authorizing & requiring the Auditor to audit the claim of Gabriel JACKSON.
Joint Res. authorizing James HAMILTON to take the oath of allegiance & to become a citizen of the Republic of Texas.
Joint Res. for the relief of Messrs. James GRAHAM, Israel L. LUDLOW, and David T. DISNEY.
Joint Res. for relief of H. W. AUGUSTINE.
An act for the relief of H. M. BREWER.

An act for the relief of J. W. SMITH and the heirs of Thomas SAUL.
Joint Resolutions for the relief of Isaac D. HAMILTON, Jonathon A. McGARY, Crawford GRIGSBY, John EDEN, Wm. SMALL, Jesse AMMONS, Dr. Jas. G. WRIGHT, Wm. P. RUTLEDGE, Neserin MANCHE, Peter KERR, Macum MAIN, John DAVIS, Herman D. KOOPMAN, Allen C. BULLOCK, the heirs of Jas. BRACKEN, John MARLIN, Harriet A. HURD, David SAMPLE, Benj. ROBERTS, Edward LINN, Capt. Isham SIMS & others, Theodore DORSETT, Dr. Anson JONES, and Jacob HARRELL.
An act for the relief of James FOSTER and McLin BRACY.
An act to authorize CAREY, a free man of color to remain within the Republic of Texas.
An act for the benefit of Albert MITCHELL, a free boy of color.
Joint Res. for the relief of Thomas J. RUSK, and the company under command of G. E. BLACK.
An act for the relief of Jonathon IKIN.
An act to authorize Wiley MARTIN to emancipate his slave PETER.
Joint Resolutions for the relief of Dread DAWSON, John P. T. FITZHUGH, Joseph CECIL, H.W. KARNES, David F. WEBB, Erasmo SEGUIN, George S. STRATTON, Jos. L. BENNETT, Rebecca WESTOVER, Wm. H. HILL, Wm. F. SPARKS, David SILCRIGGS, the heirs of Samuel T. Brown decd., Wm. H. STARK, George JOHNSON, and John MUTCHINSON.
Joint Res. for the relief of Wm. H. SMITH, admr. of Wm. H. SMITH, decd.
An act authorizing Varlan RICHENSON to construct a bridge across the Guadalupe River, at or near Victoria.
Joint Res. for the relief of Jesse BENTON & the heirs of Wm. LAUGHBRIDGE, decd.
Joint Res. for relief of John P. T. FITZHUGH as legal representative of Westley FITZHUGH, decd.
An act granting divorce to S. G. HAYNIE.
Joint Res. for relief of heirs of Samuel T. BROWN, decd.
Joint Resolution for the relief of Salina ARNOLD, relict and administratrix of Hayden ARNOLD, decd.

Ellen BROWN vs. William BROWN, Victoria Co., It is ordered by the Court that an injunction issue, enforcing Wm. BROWN, & all others claiming under said BROWN, from proceeding against the est. of the plaintiff in this action, until the final determination of this suit. And it is further ordered that six weeks' publication be made in the Houston Telegraph, previous to the next term of the district court of Victoria Co., summoning said BROWN to appear and answer. John McCRABB, District Clerk, V.C.

The undersigned, having taken the stand adjoining Mr. CAREY's bar room, offers his professional services to the citizens of Galveston as a Barber. T. D. FARRIS.

Bloody End to the Comanche Treaty. We have before us the official Report of Adjutant Gen. McLEOD, to the President, on the subject of the late slaughter at San Antonio. About a month since a few Comanche Indians, who came into San Antonio to treat of peace with this country, were informed by our commissioners that if they bring in the 13 white prisoners which they held in bondage, terms of peace should be granted to them. They promised to do this; and appointed for the time of the next full moon, which was about the 15th of last month. Our commissioners, Col. Wm. G. COOKE and Adjutant General H. McLEOD, together with several men from this place, and Austin, repaired to San Antonio at the time agreed upon. On the 19th inst., the Comanches arrived to the number of 65, but they brought only 1 prisoner, the daughter of Mr. LOCKHART. Twelve chief were received by our commissioners in the govt. house, & claimed the other prisoners were with other tribes; a pause ensued in the council at this falsehood, but an order was relayed to one of the companies of soldiers outside to advance into the room. In the meantime, the terms that would have been offered were explained to the chiefs. And as the troops under Capt. HOWARD had become stationed, the 12 chiefs were informed that they were prisoners, and would be detained until the rest of their company could secure the other prisoners. As the commissioners were retiring from the room, one of the chiefs sprang forward to pass the sentinel, at the back door, who, in attempting to prevent him, was stabbed with the Indian's knife. Capt. HOWARD received a severe wound in the same way. The rest of the chiefs, meanwhile, drew their knives or bows and arrows and made a general attack. The soldiers fired and killed all 12, while the warriors in the yard fought with desperation. The company under Capt. REDD soon repulsed them, and forced them to take shelter in the stone buildings nearby. A party after awhile escaped across the river, but were pursued by some mounted men under Colonel WELLS, and all killed except one renegade Mexican, who was suffered to escape. The Indian dead included 32 men, 3 women and 2 children, who fell in the midst of the melee; 27 women and children, plus 2 old men were taken prisoner. Our loss was as follows:

Killed---Lieut. W. M. DUNNINGHAM, 1st infantry; Private Kaminski of A Company; Private WHITNEY of E Company; Judge THOMPSON, of Houston; Judge HOOD, of Bexar; Mr. CASEY, of Matagorda Co.; and a Mexican, name unknown. Total killed seven.

Wounded--Capt. Geo. T. HOWARD, 1st Infantry; Capt. Matthew CALDWELL, 1st Infantry; Lieut. Edward A. THOMPSON; Private KELLY, Company I; Judge ROBINSON, Mr. HIGGINBOTHAM; Mr. MORGAN; & Mr. CARSON. Total wounded, eight.

Administrator's Sale. I will expose to public auction on 1st Tuesday of April next, at the door of the court-house in the city of Houston, all the real & personal property belonging to the succ. of Samuel & George LEFFEL, consisting generally of extensive assortment of millwright's & carpenter's tools, head-rights, &c., &c. Gabriel JAYNE, Admr.

Jesse P. HITCHCOCK, Attorney at Law, from Columbus, GA., has located in Bastrop, TX, and will attend the district courts of surrounding counties, March 17.

Curator's Sale, Harris County: By virtue of an order for sale issued to me by the Probate Court, bearing the date of 28th Feb. 1840, I will offer for sale at the Court House door in Houston on the 1st Thursday of April next, all the personal property belonging to the succ. of Thos. STANFORD, decd., consisting cf 1 wagon, 1 yoke of oxen, wearing apparel, rifle, &c. For cash, good money. John SIMMONS.

$50 Reward. Absconded from my premises in Rutersville, on the 9th inst., a negro man named BOB, aged 30 to 35 years, about 5 feet high, thin visage; his right thumb has been injured, and the nail nearly entirely wanting; wears a small bunch of hair on the top of his head as a cue tied with a bit of ribbon or string. Also, a girl accompanied this fellow, who is about 14 years old, tolerably well grown, & rather slim built; she will call her name PEN or PENNY. Clasky P. MORROW, Rutersville, Jan. 12.

Notice.---All persons having claims against the succ. of Wm. M. LOGAN, decd., are hereby notified to present the same properly authenticated, within the time prescribed by law, or they will be barred; those indebted to the est. are required to make immediate payment to the undersigned at Liberty. B. TOWNSEND, Jan. 21.

Wednesday, April 15, 1840

Notice. All persons having claims against the est. of Wm. FRANCIS, decd., or indebted to the same are requested to come forward. Wm. PIERPONT, Admr., Houston, March 30th.

Curator's sale for property belonging to the succ. of Warren J. MITCHELL, decd., set for 1st Thursday in May next at Court House door in Houston. C. W. BUCKLEY, Curator.

Isaac SUTTON will attend to the commission business at Carolina on the Trinity River, and solicits consignments. Carolina, Jan. 1.

Wednesday, April 22, 1840

Notice. The public is cautioned not to trade for a note I gave to Thos. FITZGERALD in November last for $50. Wm. WALKER, April 16.

Lost. On or about Oct. 10th, 1836, on east side of the Brassos, somewhere between Bolivar & Col. HEAD's plantation, three Land Certificates, one to Thos J. JORDAN for 640 acres; one to John MINTON for 640 acres; and one to Wm. H. MOORE for 300 acres. All persons are hereby cautioned against trading for same. Any person finding them will be amply rewarded by Thos. J. JORDAN at this office, April 16.

$100 Reward. Runaway or else stolen from the subscriber a few weeks since at Austin, a Negro man named PLANNER; he is about 35 or 40 years old, and stands about 5'6". No particular or marks or traits recollected. The above reward will be made for his delivery to Messrs. DOBIE & DAVIS, Houston, or for any information leading to his return. W. P. BRASHEAR, Jan. 22.

Extract of a letter from Hon. C. VAN NESS to Adjutant & Inspector General H. McLEOD, dated San Antonio, 7th April 1840: "Dear Sir: About a week since we received the intelligence of the defeat & almost complete destruction of the Federalist, their flight in this direction, and of the proposed visit of ARISTA, with about 2300 men. . .but the visit of ARISTA is doubted. CANALES, with about 130 followers, is some 15 miles of us, and the balance of his forces (200 men) are on this side of the Nueces. . ."

Extract of letter from Wm. S. FISHER, Lieut. Colonel, commanding detachment of 1st Infantry, dated Mission San Jose in San Antonio, April 8: "On the 6th inst., a party of Comanche Indians, about 30 in number, made their appearance in San Antonio, and expressed through me their desire to effect an exchange of prisoners. Being at the time confined to my bed, unable to move, in consequence of a severe fall, I despatched Capt. HOWARD, in command of 'C' and 'F' companies, 1st infantry, to San Antonio with instructions to effect an exchange. . .General CANALES has arrived on the Medina, with 150 men; and another party of the federalists have crossed lower down on the route to Goliad. Of all those with whom I have conversed the majority are of the opinion that they will be followed by ARISTA or APULIA, as far as San Antonio; and their object would be to rob San Antonio, Live Oak Point, Lamar, Goliad, and other small towns in the extreme west. I have this day despatched to Gen. CANALES a communication informing him of the terms upon which he would be allowed to remain in Texas."

Lost or mislaid by the undersigned, a certificate for 640 acres of land, the same being a donation claim, granted to Lancelot ABBOTTS under an act passed in 1837, granting lands to those who were in the "Battle of San Jacinto & other battles." Any person finding the same will confer a favor by delivering it to this office. Joseph BAKER.

Wednesday, April 29, 1840

Lengthy article on the Council House Fight, between the Comanches and the Texians, provides more information, but nothing of a genealogical interest.

A. BRIGHAM, Treasurer of the Republic of TX, has been suspended from his office.

Sad accident. It becomes our sad duty to announce the death of Mr. A. H. WETHERBY. On the morning of yesterday, at 3 o'clock, after having finished his duties for the night as a reporter, he sat himself down on the window sill on the third story of the Bulletin office, whence he fell accidentally on the pavement below. The skull was fractured in the fall, and the lamented died three hours later. Although a printer by trade, WETHERBY had for several years collected news for the Bulletin and other papers in this city. The corpse is exposed in the Committee Room of Banks' Arcade. The funeral takes place at 10 o'clock this morning, and the attendance of his typographical brethren is expected.

From the Richmond <u>Telescope</u> of the 18th inst., we gather much information concerning the recent overthrow of the Federalists at Morales. The facts were derived from Capt. ALLEN of the Federal Army. It seems that on the 15th of March, the Federal forces left their encampment at the Presidio del Rio Grande, & took up their line of march toward Monclova. When some 35 miles from the Presidio del Rio Grande, CANALES, the Federalist commander, received information that a party of Comanches were about to attack Morales, a town about 9 miles from San Fernando. CANALES then despatched Col. Antonio SABATA with 30 men to assist the citizens in defending the place. SABATA was to remain 1 day, but he stayed for 5, contrary to orders. ARISTA, aware of the division of the Federalist forces, brought in 100 cavalry, attacked SABATA and forced him to surrender. CANALES pushed on and it was late in the day by the time he attacked ARISTA; daylight found CANALES surrounded by ARISTA's whole army, consisting of 1300 men. CANALES, with only 400, fought on bravely and only 15 or 16 of the Federalists escaped. The Centralists paid dearly for their victory, with 500 killed and almost that number wounded.

Wednesday, May 6, 1840

The Republic of Texas, County of Robertson, District Court, Fall Term 1840. Republic of TX vs. Franc'o RUIS & Others. Whereas at a Term of the District Court. . .in the town of Franklin. . .before the Hon. John T. MILLS, Judge of the 3d Judicial District. Information having been filed by Henderson C. HUDSON, Dist. Atty. . . .giving the Court to understand that divers large tracts of land, lying within the county aforesaid & the jurisdiction of this court, and claimed by certain individuals, under color of pretended grants from Governments of Mexico and of Coahuila & Texas. And whereas this Court is the proper tribunal to pass upon the validity of the aforesaid grants, & to determine whether or not the conditions attached to the said grants have been complied with, and whether the lands are the property of the grantees or their assigns, or of the Republic of Texas.

It is therefore ordered by the Court that the following individuals, to wit: Francisco RUIS, who claims a 6 league grant on the right bank of the Brazos river, Robertson Co.; Antonio MANCHACA, who by his atty. Allen REYNOLDS, claims 6 leagues on east bank of the Brazos; George A. NIXON, who claims 11 leagues on the east bank of the Brazos; Gregorio BASQUES, who by his atty. Jonathon C. PEYTON, claims 11 leagues on the east bank of the Brazos; Mariano de la CORDA, who by his atty. M. R. WILLIAMS, claims 11 leagues on the east bank of the Brazos; J. A. MANCHACA, who by his atty. Robert BARR, claims 7 leagues on the east bank of the Brazos; Jose de la SANCHEZ, who by his atty. Frost THORN, claims 4 leagues on the east bank of the Brazos; Ignacio GALENA, who by his atty. Wm. H. WHARTON, claims 3 leagues on the east bank of the Brazos; Tomaso VEGA, who by his atty. Samuel M. WILLIAMS, claims 11 leagues on the east bank of the Brazos; Piero Pieriera Jose Jesus y Mariann GRANDE, who claims 11 leagues on the Navasota river; Maria Concepcion MUSQUES, who claims 11 leagues on the Navasota; ManuelC. RIGON, who claims 11 leagues on the Navasota; J. S. CHAVART, who claims 11 leagues on the Navasota; Maria Riva PALACEAS, claiming 5 leagues on the Navasota; Juan N. ACOSTA, who claims 5 leagues on Navasota; Andrew BARCLA, who claims 11 leagues on the Navasota; Pedro VARELA, who claims 11 leagues on the Navasota; Jose Maria VIESCA, who claims 11 leagues on the Navasota; Rafael PENA, who claims 11 leagues on the Trinity river; Thomas J. CHAMBERS, claiming 11 leagues on the Brazos; Gordeano BANDILLO, by his atty. A. DEXTER, who claims 4 leagues on the Trinity. And all, and singular, their heirs, executors, administrators, or assigns, of the above named individuals, be notified of this information, and are hereby commanded and required to personally appear before the honorable, the District Court to be held in the town of Franklin, on the fourth Monday in September, 1840, and show cause, if any they can, why the said information shall not be acted upon. Given under my hand, this 22nd day of April, 1840, Joseph LOVE, District Clerk, pro tem.

The following is a list of Grand Jurors empaneled for the District Court of Harris County for the present term which commenced its session on Monday last: Geo. W. ADAMS, Foreman; Joseph DUNMAN, Henry LEVENHAGEN, A. M. CLOPPER, Thos. CHOAT, John BELDEN, Sterling N. DOBIE, John S. EWELL, L. C. STANLEY, Henry KING, Thos. EARLE, Sr., Lorenzo de ZAVALLA, Samuel M. HARRIS, Lewis B. HARRIS, Chas. J. HEDENBERG, Wm. A. ELLIOT, Sam MILLET, Field SECREST, and Jesse WHITE.

It will be recollected that a small company of 3 or 4 Indians recently fell upon the house of a Mr. WRIGHT near Nacogdoches & killed two men. We have learned further particulars about this affair. A third man was shot through the lungs, but he contrived to evade the savages by running some 80 rods and hiding in the bushes, where he was discovered the next morning by Mrs. WRIGHT and her children. The Indians also scalped both victims and burnt the house. Some citizens followed the trail and camp upon the wretches at their camp on the Neches. Although the Indians fled before the camp was reached, the guns, blankets and scalps taken from the family were discovered in the camp.

$200 reward offered for my boy JOE, who absconded from my farm on Cumming's Creek in Fayette co. on April 5th. Said boy is 27 years of age, 5'10" and has a yellow complexion. The small finger of his right hand is cut off, and he is left handed in any work he does, & weighs 160 lbs. I believe the boy has been deceived by some villain and they are making their way to the Red River or LA. R. B. JARMON, May 4.

Montgomery County Sheriff's Sale. By virtue of an execution directed to me by Mills WHITLEY, a Justice of the Peace, I will expose to a public sale before the Court House doors in the town of Montgomery, on the 1st Tuesday in June next, one Negro girl named ELLEN, levied on as the property of James P. McCORMICK, to satisfy said execution, issued in favor of John HAMILTON vs. Jas. P. McCORMICK et al. For cash, sale in hours prescribed by law. A. McNEILL, Sheriff, Montgomery, April 29.

Wednesday, June 10, 1840

640 Acres Valuable Colorado Land For Sale.--by order of Probate Court of Austin County, will be sold at public auction, on six months credit, with mortgage, in town of Columbus, on the 1st Tuesday in July next, a valuable situation on east side of the Colorado river; two miles from Columbus, former residence of late Wm. ROBINSON, decd., upon which there is a comfortable frame house and outbuildings, & about 50 acres under cultivation; this was one of the first places settled in Austin's colony, & has always been admitted to be one of the most desirable locations on the river. Robert STEVENSON, Adm'r. of Wm ROBINSON, Decd.

Administrator's Sale set for 1st Tuesday in July at Court House door in the town of Montgomery, Montgomery Co., for 500 acres of land belonging to the estate of John CRANE, decd., & situated in the same county on the road leading from the town of Washington in Washington Co. to the town of Caroline in Montgomery Co., being a part of the head-right of said John CRANE, decd. Sale on a six months credit, with the purchaser giving bond & security. Polly CRANE, Admr. of John CRANE, May 8.

Executors Sale set for 1st Tuesday in July next, at Court House of Austin County, on 231 acres of land belonging to the succ. of Amason IRIS, decd., situated on Caney Creek in this county. Also a Certificate for 1 labor of land (unlocated) issued to the decd. Thos. COCHRANE Executor, Austin Co., May 25.

Runaway Taken Up. Committed to the Jail of Fayette Co. TX, by McKree WHITE on May 5th, 1840, a Negro Man who says his name is HENRY, & says he belongs to Beaties GIDDREST (or Batiste GIDRE), living in the parish of Opelousas, LA, on Bayou Boeuf about 40 miles below Chinaville. Said slave is about 25 years old, 5'4", & would weigh about 135 lbs. He has a scar on his left arm, chin & forehead, all occasioned from a burn. He says he is carpenter, speaks French language, & on the whole is a very smart, pert boy. Owner should come forward & claim his property, pay all charges and take him away in 6 months, or he will be sold according to law, to satisfy expenses. William NABERS, Sheriff of Fayette Co., La Grange, May 6th.

Robert KLEBERG named adm. of est. of Rudolph VON ROEDER, Austin County, May 1st.

Notice to All Baptist Churches & Ministers: Resolution of the Union Baptist Church at Independence, Washington Co.. We consider it important & necessary that there be an organization of Baptist churches in western Texas, and that the Thursday before the first Sunday in June next (and days following) be the time appointed for the meeting of a Convention with the Union Baptist Church at Independence, for the purpose of forming an Association. All Baptist churches friendly to such an organization should send 3 or more delegates to said meeting. The Baptist Ministers throughout the country are respectfully requested to attend. T. Washington COX, Moderator; T. TREMMIER, Clerk. Independence, April 2d, 1840.

Centre Hill Hotel. Mrs. MATTHEWS informs the public that the above house of entertainment is now open for the accommodation of visitors. Appended to the establishment is a bath house, well fitted up & supplied with fine soft water. No individual in Texas will regret a ride of 12-15 miles, in addition to a four bit fee for this luxury. Those who patronize the house may have the bath at no charge.

Reward of $300 offered by Alex. G. McNUTT, Governor of Mississippi, for the apprehension of Benj. F. REYNOLDS, a resident of Tishemingo Co., Miss., who is believed to have murdered Stephen W. SMITH on April 4th, 1840, and is now a fugitive from justice. Description: The said REYNOLDS is about 21 years old, light hair, fair complexion, blue eyes, 5'6", full face and rather corpulent for a man of his age. He received a severe wound to his right foot with an axe a few days before the murder, which causes him to limp. He cannot wear a shoe on the foot.

Administrator's sale. Will be sold at Court House door in Montgomery, on the 1st Tuesday in

July next, a Certificate for 640 acres of land, belonging to the est. of Sanders GROOMS, decd., it being the headright of said decd. Hugh McGUFFIN, Admr., May 29.

$50 reward. Ranaway from the subscriber on 12th inst., a Negro fellow named SAM, light complexioned, bald headed, and squint eyed; dress, short jacket, dark pants, cloth cap. Whoever will arrest the said Negro & lodge him in jail shall receive the above reward by applying to Col. A. TURNER or to subscriber, Wm. TURNER, May 9th.

Probate Notice. Lucretia PONCHARD makes an application to Probate Court of Austin Co. to be declared the heir of the est. of Geo. MADISON, decd. Hearing on this petition set for last Monday in June next at Court House in San Felipe, Austin Co., May 27. J. Benton JOHNSON, Probate Clerk.

Notice. To John W. DANCY, Enoch JONES and Lewis MATTHEWS: I have this day filed my petition in the District Court of Fayette County, praying for a petition of the land known as the Colorado City tract. You are hereby notified to be in attendance at the fall term of said court, 1840, and show cause why said petition shall not be granted. Henry MANTON, Colorado City, May 9th.

The subscriber hereby notifies all whom it may concern that he holds an undivided share with Wm. TAYLOR in the following half-leagues of land in Montgomery Co.---and that such share amounts to nine-tenths of each half-league; viz: John SHANNON's, Owen SHANNON's, J. B. McKEELY's, Benj. RIGBY's, and W. C. CLARK's league. The subscriber has taken measures to obtain an order for the division of aforesaid land from next District court, and in the mean time hereby warns all parties who may have claims against W. TAYLOR from trespassing on the premises. J. B. LYNCH, May 9.

Will be sold at Court House door in Montgomery on the 1st Tuesday in July next, all the personal property pertaining to the est. of Jesse HYATT, decd., consisting of carpenter's tools, household and kitchen furniture, &c. on

a credit of 3 months, to satisfy debts against the estate. Timothy CADE, Admr., May 8th.
   Caution. The undersign cautions the public against the purchase of a certain tract of land of Col. Wm. B. P. GAINES, situated on the San Bernard river, and known as the place formerly occupied by Monroe EDWARDS as a plantation, which said land purports to have been sold on 1st Jan. 1838 by said EDWARDS to said GAINES, for the consideration of $40,000 cash. Also a part of the town of San Bernard, sold in like manner, for sum of $5,000. C. DART, Brazoria, TX, April 20th.
   Daniel BARNETT named adm. of est. of Daniel SYMONDS, decd., Austin County, on last Monday in April, 1840.

Wednesday, June 24, 1840

   Lt. Wm. Ross POSTELL referred to as commander of the Texas Navy schooner San Jacinto.
   Died at Cottage Hill Plantation, near Lynchburg, Mrs. Sopronia PIERPONT, consort of Hon. Wm. PIERPONT, on 28th ult., aged 42 years. This lady was the daughter of Dr. Saml. FRISBY, of Vernon, Oneida Co., NY, and had been a resident of Texas for the past four years.

Wednesday, July 1, 1840

   The Austin mail came in early yesterday afternoon. We glean from the Gazette of Wednesday last some news of interest.
   Gen. Felix HUSTON has arrived in Austin.
   Capt. PIERCE of the Pitkin Guards is said to have accidentally shot himself at San Antonio.
   Judge CAMPBELL of Seguin has been murdered by a party of Indians---particulars not known.
   Indian Prisoners. The Cherokee women and children, 18 in number, were brought near town yesterday. These, it will be recollected, were made prisoners last winter, at the engagement between a company under Col. BURLESON & a party of Cherokees above Austin. Among them are the wife & sister of BOWLES; Maj. RANSOM has charge of these prisoners, & is on his way to deliver

them into the hands of the Indian agent at Fort Jessup for the United States government.

Wednesday, July 8, 1840

In our last number, we casually mentioned we believed that Gen. Memucan HUNT arrived in TX at the close of 1836, about 8 months after the battle of San Jacinto. We were mistaken. He arrived in the country in May 1836, about one month after the said battle, but returned almost immediately to the United States.

The Hon. M. DE SALIGNY, Charge de Affairs, from France left this city last evening for Austin where he intends to reside permanently.

Probate Notice. I will attend the probate court of this county, to be holden on the last Monday in July inst. Then & there to render my account, & make a final settlement on the est. of Martin ALLEN, decd. James B. ALLEN, Admr., Austin County, 1st July 1840.

Probate Notice. I shall, as admr. of Sylvanus CASTLEMAN, decd., present my account for final settlement & allowance at the next term of the probate court of Austin co., & pray to be discharged from any further administration. Elizabeth CASTLEMAN, Admrx., San Felipe, Austin County, July 1, 1840.

Administratrix's Notice. The undersigned, having been duly appointed admrx. upon the est. of John R. V. HIGGINBOTHAM, decd., hereby notifies all persons indebted to the est. to make immediate payments to John O. SEIBELS, who is my authorized atty.; and all persons having any claims against said est. must present them to my attorney within the time prescribed by law. Her appointment made by Hon. Jesse GRIMES, Probate Judge for Montgomery County. Signed Mary Ellen HIGGINBOTHAM, Groce's Retreat, July 1.

John O. SEIBELS is my authorized atty. during my temporary absence from the Republic. Mary Ellen HIGGINBOTHAM, Groce's Retreat.

Surveying, Civil Engineering & General Land Agency. The undersigned have opened an office in Main street, near the Post Office, and solicit a share of public patronage. Frederick A.

STUART, Wm. F. WEEKS, Houston, July 1st.
Succession of Sam Rogers. By virtue of a decree made by the Hon. John W. MILES, Judge of Probates, Liberty Co., I shall offer for sale, at public auction, at the courthouse in Liberty on the 1st Tuesday in August next, all the lands belonging to the succ. of Samuel ROGERS, decd., consisting of from 15 to 20,000 acres, lying & being situated on Village Creek and its tributaries, in the counties of Liberty & Jefferson. Terms, 12 months credit, with security required, & a lien upon property until final payment. H. B. LITTLEFIELD, Admr., Liberty, June 13.

Will be sold on 21st day of present month, under the direction of the Probate Court of Harris Co., at the house formerly occupied by Field SECREST; all the personal property belonging to the succ. of Field SECREST, decd., [except negroes] consisting of household and kitchen furniture, clothing, &c., and one cow & calf, for cash to highest bidder. W. H. SECREST, Admr., Houston, July 1.

$100 Reward will be paid for the apprehension of the Negro man, FREDERICK alias FRED, a Griffe, aged about 30 years, 5'11", good looking, has a little beard & whiskers, has lost one of his front upper teeth; has a sour look, and is very impudent when spoken to by strangers. He took away with him his wife, a black woman named PATSY, belonging to Mr. Charles GENOIS, of this city; and likewise his female child, about 6 years, a cripple, and very small for her age. Mr. GENOIS will give the same reward for his woman. FRERET & Bros., Near the St. Charles Hotel, New Orleans, May 30.

Notices. The Trustees of the Presbyterian Society of the city of Houston, respectfully inform all those who subscribed for the purpose of erecting a church, that they have contracted with Capt. J. DANIELS, for the erection of a house; and they earnestly solicit all those who have not yet paid, to call upon Mr. J. M. ROBINSON, Long row. Trustees: A. C. ALLEN, Jos. BAILY, John R. REID.

Wednesday, July 15, 1840

General Land Agency. The subscribers have associated themselves together for the purpose of doing a General Land Agency in the city of Austin. Their offices are opposite the capitol on Congress avenue, City of Austin. Jos. MORELAND, Thomas G. GORDON, June 18.

P. J. ALSTON, Attorney & Counsellor at Law, Houston, Texas, June 16.

N. C. RAYMOND, Attorney & Counsellor at Law, Nashville, TX. Refer to John B. JONES, Galveston & John C. WATROUS, Austin.

J. H. WINCHELL, Notary Public and General Agent, San Antonio de Bexar, will attend to any business that may be entrusted to his charge. He will also execute instruments of writing of every description. To emigrants, he has the agency of upwards of 20,000 acres of first quality land, situated on the rivers Medina, San Antonio, &c.

We learn from the <u>Sentinel</u>, that Gen. Felix HUSTON has been ordered to Nashville, to take command of the militia embodied there. It is expected that an expedition will be made up the Brazos, against the Indians in that quarter.

Resignation. Judge BRANCH has resigned the office of judge for the Fifth judicial district and it is rumored that Gen. TERRY will be named to fill the vacancy.

A neat little sheet called the <u>Musquito</u> made its appearance in this city last Sunday, edited by G. H. FRENCH. It buzzed around quite harmlessly on its first appearance, but we think it will show a sting before many weeks.

Administrator's Sale, by order of Probate Court of Harris Co., will be held on 1st Tuesday in August next, at the court house door in city of Houston, at public auction to highest bidder all right, title & interest to the following property, belonging to the est. of Robert BARR, decd., viz: Lot No. 1, Block 20, known as the Star Coffee house & Wild Bull. Henry KESLER, Administrator.

Probate Sale, by an order from Probate Court of Fort Bend Co., will be held at court house door in Houston, on August 4th, to be sold for cash to highest bidder, 50 bales of cotton more or less belonging to the succ. of Wm. WALKER, late of Fort Bend Co., decd., during the hours prescribed by law. Mary WALKER, Admrx.; J. M. BRISCOE, Admr., July 8.

Administrator's Sale, by order of Probate Court of Harris Co., will be held on 1st Tuesday of August next at court house door in Houston, at public auction, to highest bidder, all the property belonging to the estates of Otto FINCKE and Joseph SCHLACHTENBERGER, viz: 640 acres of land situated & fronting on the west side of the Nueces river, in San Patricio Co.; a certificate for 1240 acres of land; and 2 lots near city of Houston, being lots Nos. 1 & 2 in Block No. 164. H. KESLER, July 11.

Administrators sale, by order of Probate Ct. of Austin Co., will be held at the court house door in San Felipe de Austin, on Aug. 1st, at public auction, to highest bidder, all the personal property belonging to est. of Daniel M. SANOGDS: a lot of Negroes, cattle, hogs, farming utensils, household & kitchen furniture, feather beds, clothing, wagons, teams, &c. Terms of sale, 6 months credit with approved security. David BURNETT, Admr., San Felipe de Austin, June 29th.

Curator's Sale, Harris County: Will be sold on 1st Tuesday in August at the Court House door in Houston, by virtue of an order of the probate court of said county, all the property of the succ. of Abraham GAZLEY, decd., consisting of 1 town lot in city of Houston, being lot No. 7 in block 88, & a certificate for 1280 acres of land, now in the hands of Thos. J. GAZLEY, being the head right of decd. Terms, cash. Geo. GAZLEY, Curator, July 4.

T. K. BROWN named admr. of estates of John RICHARDSON and Joseph A. PARKER, both decd., Houston, Harris County, TX, July 1.

John W. PITKIN seeks letters of adm. in the est. of C. B. DUNBAR, decd., Harris County Probate Court, June 24.

Justice Court. Geo. FISHER has opened his Magistrate's Docket at his office next to Post

Office, April 13th.
 For Sale, Lease or Rent. The Yellow House, formerly occupied by the Ordnance, Quarter Master-General, & General Post Office Department, fronting on Milam Street, with a convenient kitchen, stable, &c., well calculated, either for offices or private dwelling. Apply to Geo. FISHER, General Agent, June 30.

Wednesday, July 22, 1840

 $1,500 Reward. Stop the Murderer. The above reward will be given for the apprehension & delivery to the Sheriff of Wilkinson Co., Miss., of Arad WOODARD, who on 28th June 1840, murdered George E. FRAZIER on the public highway near Woodville. The said WOODARD is about 6'2", slim, raw-boned, brown hair, face square & bony with large nose, upper front teeth somewhat decayed, eyes light hazel to grey, with a downcast and depressive look, speaks slowly and is about 25 years of age. Wm. FRAZIER, Woodville, June 29th, 1840. N.B.: $500 of this reward is to be paid by Wm. FRAZIER, and the remainder by the citizens of Woodville.
 Taken Up. On the Coleto, near Victoria, on July 2nd, and now in the possession of the subscriber, a yellow boy, calls himself JESSE, said boy is about 5'8" or 9", about 24 years of age, has a scar on his breast & large moles on his face; says he belongs to George PARKER, two miles below Houston. Owner requested to come forward, claim property, pay charges & take him away. John POLLAN, Deputy Sheriff, Victoria, July 3rd, 1840.
 Charlotte SCARBOROUGH seeks letters of adm. in the succ. of Charles SCARBOROUGH, decd., and that any opposition to such an appointment must be made within ten days, at the end of which time the application will be acted upon; by order of Probate Judge I. N. MORELAND, Harris Co.
 Lost in the City of Houston during month of Jan. 1839, a Bounty Certificate, for 640 acres of land, issued to me by the Secy. of War, for military service and numbered 407. Notice is hereby given that unless intelligence of said

certificate is received at the Dept. of War in three months time, I will apply for a duplicate copy of same. James HOCKETT, Houston, July 22.
San Augustine Female Academy. The Trustees of this institution have the honor to inform the public that they have engaged Miss A. E. MADDEN to take charge of this school. Miss MADDEN comes well recommended, having been employed as a teacher in the United States for the past 5 years. The terms of tuition will be in her possession. Trustees: Samuel STIVERS, J. D. THOMAS, A. HORTON, J. T. PATTERSON, A. HUSTON, J. G. LITTLEFIELD, G. A. NIXON, T. G. BROOCKS, W. G. ANDERSON, W. W. PARKER, Wyatt HANKS, and A. E. BAKER.

Wednesday, July 29, 1840

On Sunday evening last, an express reached town from San Antonio, bringing information of a skirmish with the Indians. Capt. CLENDENIN, who had gone in pursuit of a body of Comanches, with 19 regulars and 3 Tonkaways, came up with the party, 20 in number, encamped on a creek west of Rio Frio. The Captain placed his men in a position around the camp, with instructions to remain quiet and attack only after a pre-concerted signal was given. One of the men fired his gun, alerting the Indians, who fled the camp. Captain C. was unable to pursue, his men being unmounted and tired. It is believed that 17 out of the 20 Indians were either killed or wounded.---Austin City Gazette
Died, in Rutersville, TX, June 30th, Robert CRAWFORD, 45, late of New Iberia, LA, and formerly of Westchester, NY.
Died at Washington, of congestive fever, Miss Elizabeth WHEELER, dtr. of Green J. WHEELER, aged 10 years. The Charleston Courier will please notice this.
Died in this city on Sunday, July 26th, Mary GODFREY (late JAMES), wife of Joseph P. WILSON, aged 35 years, a native of Hampton, NH, late a resident of New Orleans.
Married at Galveston, at the house of Madame NEWLANDS, on the 20th inst., by Judge JOHNSON,

Mr. Geo. FISHER, Esq. to Mrs. M. C. PAGE, late of New Orleans.

Mr. John L. DORAN, a principal clerk in the Auditor of State's office under Mr. BRYAN's administration, was arrested at the theatre Thursday night, by Mr. SAFFIN, city marshal, and by J. O'NEIL, constable, charged with having passed counterfeit money on several merchants here. Mr. DORAN was an eminent attorney in Ohio.

$200 Reward (Texas Money). Ranaway or stolen from my premises at Harrisburg my negro man, ABRAM, 5'11" or 6' tall, light and trim built, black complexion, about 30 years old, has lost some of his back teeth, with small whiskers high on his cheek, with a very humble & conciliating manner. He left with a trunk of fine clothing. Since his leaving was without provocation or complaint, I am afraid he was taken by some white speculators and may be offered for sale in Louisiana. A. BRISCOE, June 27.

Rutersville College, Fayette Co. The Fall session of the Preparatory & Female depts. of this institution will commence on the 1st Monday in August, and close on Dec. 18th. Rev. C. RICHARDSON, A.M., Principal; Mrs. Martha G. RICHARDSON, Vice Principal. Terms per session: Elementary branch, $15; Higher English, $20; Higher English with Language, $35. Board can be had in good private families for $10 to $13 per month. Thos. D. FISHER, Secy., July 15.

Wednesday, August 5, 1840

M. DE SALIGNY, the French Minister, arrived in Austin on the 25th

The Secretary of War has commenced running the military road, from the Colorado to the Red River. Two companies have been detailed for this service, and the work will probably be completed as far as the Brazos by this month. It is expected the road will intersect the Brazos at the mouth of the Bosque, near the Waco village, and terminate near the mouth of Bois d'Arc creek. Blockhouses will probably be erected 40 miles from the frontier settlements.

The Austin Gazette says that a ship was to have left London for Texas on June 28th with 70 families. This vessel will be followed by a steamship freighted with "British spirits" for the western world!

Property for Sale---City of Chambersia. Although this city was projected for some time, the proprietor, Gen. CHAMBERS, was unwilling to offer it at public sale until the demand for lots should force it onto the market. The town is situated on an elevated bluff, 30 feet high, at the head of Galveston or Trinity Bay and the mouth of the Trinity River. This place was formerly known as Anahuac. One certificate for $100 entitles the purchaser to select two lots of his choice. The land has been owned by Gen. T. Jefferson CHAMBERS since 1830; G. S. THOMAS, Agent for the Proprietor, Chambersia, July 15.

City of Brazos.---This city is situated on the east side of the Brazos River, 53 miles northwest from Houston. The Houston & Brazos Railroad will terminate here. We ask people to examine this place and judge for themselves. Col. Thos. B. WHITE, located at the city of Brazos, is the general agent of the company; by order of the company. A. C. ALLEN, President, July 20, 1840.

Wednesday, August 12, 1840

The portion of the Lipan tribe that has during the past several years raided beyond the Rio Grande, has recently joined the main body under CASTRO. This accession of 70 warriors is sure to make them formidable foes of the Comanches. They are still residing in the vicinity of Bexar.

There is probably no settler on our frontier whose history is more interesting than Mr. [Josiah] WILBARGER, who resides about 6 miles above Bastrop. This enterprising man, in company with 3 others, removed to the spot where he now resides in the winter of 1830, when the whole section was completely in the possession of the savages. The nearest town was LaGrange, 60 miles distant. One of his companions was

Mr. BARKER, whose hospitality has rendered himself noted by travellers to Austin. The men immediately constructed a blockhouse where they could defend themselves against the hostil tribes. In the summer of 1833, WILBARGER & four companions were exploring the country upon the present site of Austin when their camp was attacked by about 100 Indians. Only WILBARGER survived, though stunned by a rifle ball that struck him in the neck. The Indians, presuming him dead, scalped him. He was discovered the next day by neighbors. He was taken to his home some 30 miles distant, where his wounds were dressed, and strangely enough survives to this day as one of the most enterprising farmers on the Colorado.

Wednesday, August 19, 1840

A Joint Act of Congress adopted on Feb. 4th, creating a new County of Milam, from that part of Washington Co. west of the Brazos river and north of the Yegua. The following men are named as commissioners to select a county seat: James SHAW, John W. PORTER, Geo. GREEN, Westley MOORE of Milam County---and Willet HOLMES, John ECHOLES, Wm. W. HILL & James HARVY of Washington County.

A party of 500 Comanches, and it is supposed some Cherokees & Mexicans, after traversing the section of country between Saint Marks and the coast undiscovered, attacked Linnville on the 8th inst., about 8 o'clock, murdered or captured several of the inhabitants, and reduced the place (consisting of 5 houses) to ashes. Some inhabitants fled to vessels in the bay. They also burned 2 or 3 houses at Dimmit's Landing & also attacked Victoria, while about 50 of the inhabitants were out in pursuit of the enemy. The inhabitants were driven into one corner of the Public square where they made a valiant defense. About 30 citizens of the place, including Capt. P. CALDWELL, were killed. News of the attack was communicated in a few hours to the settlements on the Colorado. Col. MOORE & over 100 men from La Grange set out in pursuit;

COL. BURLESON set out from Bastrop with 60 men; and 250 others left Austin on Monday. An express from the Border Guards arrived on Wednesday stating they were fighting the retreating foe about 15 miles below the Old San Antonio Road. Those dead at Linnville included Capt. WATTS and Major O'NEIL. It is also reported that Mrs. WATTS is a prisoner.

A. McNEILL appointed admr. at February term, Probate Court, Gonzales Co., in the est. of Colonel Reuben ROSS, decd.

A runaway Negro man was committed to the jail of Liberty Co., on July 25th; he says his name is DAVID and belongs to Wm. WOODWARD, formerly of Noxuba Co., Miss. He says he ranaway from Wm. BRANDON, Shelby Co., TX, in whose care he was left. He is about 30 years old, 5'4" or 5" tall, yellow complexion, has three scars on his breast & many on his back. He says he is a baker by trade. The owner is requested to come forward, claim his property, & pay all charges. B. W. HARDIN, Sheriff, Liberty, Aug. 11th.

We have received the Galveston *Courier* with additional intelligence from Matagorda. The Indians appeared in the vicinity of Victoria on Thursday, the 6th inst., & 40 men immediately went out to meet them, but nothing was heard of this company when the express left. Another express arrived at Matagorda on the 11th inst., at 12 o'clock noon, from Wm. MENIFEE, stating that the 40 men who had left Victoria, finding the Indians too strong for them, out-flanked them & joined Capt. OWEN, who also had 40 men, on the Rio Noso, 12 miles west of Texana, when they were attacked by the Indians on Sunday morning, the engagement continuing throughout the day. In the evening, the Indians withdrew, leaving 8 of their dead on the field. Among the Texians, Dr. BELL was killed & 4 others were missing; on that night the Texians received a reinforcement of 120 men, making in all 200 men. The engagement was renewed on Monday morning at 9 a.m. by the Indians & was still going at noon when the express left. The company from Matagorda left Mrs. KELLERS on Monday evening at 4 o'clock for the scene.

Another express arrived at Matagorda on the 12th inst., stating that on Monday evening the Indians retreated---that the plunder taken from Linnville was about 2 days in advance of the main body. B. H. MORDEICA, John MENIFEE, Col. CALDWELL & servant were killed near Victoria. STILL LATER. A gentleman from Lagrange has just arrived & states that on the morning of Thursday last, the troops from the Colorado and Gonzales, amounting to about 200, under Genl. Felix HUSTON, intercepted the Indians near the San Antonio road & after a fight of 4 hours, entirely defeated & dispersed them. They also killed 30 warriors & 1 Mexican, recaptured about 250 mules loaded with goods plundered at Linnville, and rescued Mrs. WATTS of Linnville, who was slightly wounded by the Indians. She states there was one other lady captured by the Indians, who was killed to prevent her from falling into the hands of their pursuers. Many homes across the prairies were destroyed.

Wednesday, August 26, 1840

Joint Act of Congress provides for the incorporation of the Milam Guards, adopted on 5th Feb 1840. Names Joseph DANIELS, J. D. COCKE, Jos. C. ELDREDGE, J. L. NICKELSON, A. J. DAVIS, C. J. HEDDENBERG, and Francis R. LUBBOCK among its members.

Joint Act of Congress on Feb. 4th approves the incorporation of Union Academy in Washington; trustees named are: Ephraim RODDY, Wm. LOCKRIDGE, Jesse B. ATKINSON, James G. SWISHER, Stephen R. ROBERTS, Samuel P. BROWN, Adolphus HOPE, Horatio CHRISMAN & Isom G. BELCHER.

Joint Act of Congress adopted on Feb. 5th provides for incorporation of Rutersville College. Trustees are named: Andrew RABB, Robert ALEXANDER, Chauncey RICHARDSON, A. P. MANLEY, J.S. LESTER, W. P. SMITH, Robt. CRAWFORD, John RABB, James W. COX, Joseph NAIL, and Gideon B. LOCKRIDGE.

The following, from the Austin City Gazette, is highly creditable to the militia of the Guadalupe, La Vacca & Colorado; it shows these to be brave men of great courage: "The immense amount of spoils taken by the enemy has been, in every instance, returned to the owner when it could be identified; but such was the destruction and waste which had taken place, by the Indians, that it was impossible to identify the whole, & in such instances they were distributed among those in the battle. Mrs. WATTS and her Negro woman & girl, who were recovered, have been furnished with every thing which could make them comfortable, and all the clothing which could be found has been sent back to Victoria that the owners may reclaim it."

Account of the "Plumb Creek" battle by Gen. Feliz HUSTON, as written to Secretary of War Branch T. ARCHER, is published. The letter is written from "Plumb Creek" and dated Aug. 12th. In the letter, HUSTON states that Mrs. WATTS was wounded by an arrow. The other woman, Mrs. CROSBY, had been killed by a spear.

Romantic Incident. Major H. O. WATTS, the husband of the lady lately captured by the Indians, was not killed in the skirmish at Linnville, as first reported. The dead man was his brother, Capt. WATTS. The Major was wounded severely & was unable to protect his lady & their servants.

Probate Sale. We will sell to the highest bidder on a credit of 3 months, at the Court House door in Liberty, on Oct. 27th, the following property belonging to the est. of John SWINNEY, decd., viz: 1 tract of land containing 150 acres, part of the head-right of Baker M. SPINKS; another tract on Old River, part of the head-right of C. C. P. WELCH, containing 1 quarter league, being an undivided interest in a half league, all land situated in Liberty Co. Sale for the benefit of creditors of said succ. Newton SWINNEY & Franklin HARDIN, Executors, Liberty, Aug. 22nd.

County of Harris, Orville T. TYLER vs. Jane BROOKS, alias Jane TYLER. Libel for divorce, District Court. It appearing that the above named defendant, being a non-resident of the Republic of TX, the court orders said defendant to appear at Fall Term of this court & answer why this petition should not be granted.

Lost in the spring of 1838, a copy of a discharge signed by A. Sidney JOHNSTON, Secy. of War, for 3 months service as a private in Lt. Elias EDEN's company, from 1st July to 1st Oct. 1836. Unless intelligence is received at the War Dept. in 3 months time, I will apply to the proper office for a duplicate copy. Houston County, Aug. 4. James NEVILLE.

Wednesday, September 2, 1840

It is with feelings of deepest regret that we announce the death of Col. H. W. KARNES, at Bexar on the 16th ult. of a protracted illness. This heroic man has been almost constantly in active service since the revolution and his name is associated with nearly every important battle with the Indians.
Military Road Expedition. Capt. KENNYMORE, in command of companies B, E & G, left on Monday last for Little River, where he will be joined by Capt. HOLLIDAY with his company; Col. COOK, immediately on his return from San Antonio, leaves for Little River to assume the command on Sept. 1st. The expedition plans to commence operation on the 5th; Col. C. anticipates reaching the Red River, blazing the road as he proceeds, by Oct. 15th.--Austin <u>Gazette</u>.
Maj. HOWARD, at the head of two companies, leaves San Antonio previous to 1st Sept., on an expedition against the Comanches.
We were agreeably surprised a few days since to notice among our exchange papers a new journal, styled the "San Luis Advocate," which in both dimensions & reading matter, exceeds any of our exchange papers within the republic. It is published by S. J. DURNET.
The following letter from the pen of Capt. Wm. H. WATTS, contradicts the report of his death, published in our last number & furnishes some interesting details of the attack on Linnville & the death of his lamented brother Major H. O. WATTS: "The Indians made their appearance on the Victoria road on the morning of Saturday the 8th inst., about 8 o'clock, and were discovered by some of the citizens while they were

about 2 miles from town; but not having heard or believing that a body of Indians would venture so low down the country. . .we were careless, and supposed they were Mexican traders with a large caravan, nor we were undeceived until they approached very near in the town, which they did riding nearly at full speed, and in the shape of a half moon for the purpose of surrounding the place. The citizens then had no other alternative but to flee to the bay, where the most of them were saved by getting into a lighter. Mr. and Mrs. WATTS, being in the lowest house, and not hearing the Indians as soon as the rest, could not make their escape. The number killed in Linnville were 3 whites and 2 negro men, viz: Maj. WATTS, collector of the Customs; Mr. O'NEIL, a waggoner by the name of STEVENS, & 2 negro men belonging to Maj. WATTS. . .The Indians appeared to be perfectly contented & remained in town till after dark, burning 1 house at a time. They destroyed nearly all the goods & all the houses; also, a large number of cattle & calves, which they drove into pens & burned, or cut to pieces with their knives & lances. . .Some of the citizens returned the next morning and buried the dead, the remainder continued on to the Pass, where they were kindly treated by Mr. DECKROW, boarding officer at that place. The number of the party which attacked Linnville. . .were at least 400 or 500. They were principally Comanches. Yours respectfully, Wm. H. WATTS."

Andrew BRISCOE & D. W. C. HARRIS, Executors of John BIRDSALL, decd., vs. Corordon C. WOODWARD. Foreclosed, District Court, Harris Co., Spring Term, June 12, 1840. "It appearing that the defendant in this action has died since the inception of this cause, & that there is no administration of said decd., nor guardian for the minor heir, on motion of C. W. BUCKLEY, counsel for plaintiff Charlotte L. JEFFREYS, formerly WOODWARD, the mother of said minor heir is hereby appointed guardian ad litem to defend this suit, & it is ordered by the court that the representatives of said decedent be ruled to pay into court on or before the first day of next court thereof, the principal, interest & costs, set forth in plaintiff's petition . . .It is further ordered that a copy of this rule be served upon Charlotte L. JEFFREYS, widow of decd., & guardian of said minor, 90 days before the 1st day of the next term of this court." James S. HOLMAN, Clerk.

Wednesday, September 9, 1840

Account of military activities during recent battle of Plum Creek, burning of Linnville and Victoria, offered by W. D. MILLER, who served in Capt. B. McCULLOCH's Company from Gonzales during the episode. MILLER's account bears the signatures of McCULLOCH and "David MURPHREE of Victoria," testifying to its truthfulness. The journal includes movements of men and battles. It states that Mr. MORDECAI of Victoria was killed on Aug. 9th in engagement with Indians 5 miles south of DE LEON's rancho near the Casa Blanca. Other deaths are noted below.

"The following may be relied on as a correct estimate of the losses of the several places named, derived from unquestionable authority. At Victoria & Vicinity---Killed Capt. Pinckney CALDWELL, Varlen RICHESON, Wm. McNUNER, Dr. GRAY, Mr. DANIELS, a German--name unknown; a Mexican, 4 Negroes of Col. POAGE---and 2 others owners not known, among whom may be included Mr. MORDECAI, killed in the battle of the 9th, and also Mrs. CROSBY & child, taken captive and killed by the Indians on Plum Creek. About 1,500 head or horses were driven off, many cattle killed, 1 house burned & several plundered. At Linnville, Killed, Maj. WATTS, Mr. O'NEIL, two Negroes of Maj. WATTS' and Mr. STEVENS, a waggoner between Linnville & Victoria. The town was plundered. . .many cattle killed. Dr. BELL was killed near KITCHEN's rancho,"

Administrator's Sale set for first Tuesday in October at court house door, Austin County, for personal property belonging to est. of John CUMMINGS, decd., consisting of horses, cattle, hogs, farming utensils, 5 Negroes, &c. Rebecca

CUMMINGS, Adm'x., San Felipe, Sept. 3. Lost---sometime in Aug. 1839, in Harris co., between Houston & Green's bayou, a certificate for bounty land issued to Thos. PRATT for 1280 acres, No. 1694, bearing date of 9th Jan. 1838, signed by Barnard E. BEE, secy. of war; said certificate was transferred to C. C. WOODWARD on 10th April 1838, & from WOODWARD to the undersigned on 21st Aug. 1838, the signed transfers of which are in my possession. This is to give notice that after 60 days from this date, I shall apply to the proper department for a duplicate copy of the same. John LAPRELLE, Sept. 9.

[Several issues are missing here.]

Wednesday, October 7, 1840

The following is a list of Postmasters in the Republic of Texas and Post Offices. Names of counties in parantheses: Austin (Travis), A. C. HYDE; Aransas (Refugio), J. McDANIEL; Bastrop (Bastrop), Andrew MAYS; Beaumont (Jefferson), J. P. PULSIFER; Big Creek (Fort Bend), A. C. DODD; Bolivar (Brazoria), H. AUSTIN; Brazoria (Brazoria), R. D. WEIR; Belgrade (Jasper) Samuel S. SCOTT; Ballards (Red River), B. M. BALLARD; Caney Crossings (Matagorda), R. H. WILLIAMS; Cedar Creek (Washington), James HALL; Centre Hill (Austin), D. AYRES; Crockett (Houston), J. H. KIRCHHOFFER; Columbia (Brazoria), A. UNDERWOOD; Carolina (Montgomery), Ed BAILEY; Coffee's Station (Fannin), J. A. CALDWELL; Comanche (Travis), J. HANIE; Clarkesville (Red River), D. SAMPLE; Cochran's Retreat (Jasper), N. H. COCHRAN; Columbus (Colorado), H. M. SALLEE; Colorado city (Fayette), H. MANTON; Dunn's (Robertson), J. DUNN; Douglas (Nacogdoches), P. H. PEARSON; DeCalb (Red River), A. W. KING; Egypt (Colorado), Eli MERCER; Epperson's ferry (Red River), M. EPPERSON; Fanthorp's (Montgomery), H. FANTHORP; Fair Hill (Travis), Henry JONES; Franklin (Robertson), H. OWENS; Franklin (Red River), S. M. FULTON; Fort Houston (Houston), W. McDONALD; Fort Oldham (Washington), C.

FITCH; Fort Bennett (Houston), G. E. DWIGHT;
Fort Inglish (Red River), B. INGLISH; Gaine's
Ferry (Sabine), James GAINES; Groce's Retreat
(Montgomery), D. S. DURHAM; Gonzales (Gonzales)
E. WILLIAMS; Gay Hill (Washington), J. B.
SWISCHER; Galveston (Galveston), Edwin B. SETTLE; Goliad (Goliad), W. THOMPSON; Huntsville
(Montgomery), E. M. GRAY; Hodge's Bend (Red River), A. HODGE; Hardman's (Nacogdoches), B.
HARDMAN; Hibbetville (Liberty), R. H. HIBBETT;
Holmes' (Jasper), T. HOLMES; Hamilton (Shelby),
E. KELLOGG; Houston (Harris), G. STUBBLEFIELD;
Hickory Grove (Bastrop), Eli DURHAM; Johnson's
(Red River), L. JOHNSON; Independence (Washington), F. J. C. SMILEY; Jonesboro (Red River),
R. H. GRAHAM; Jasper (Jasper), W. L. SMITH;
Jones (Fayette), M. F. JONES; La Baca (Jackson)
Eli STAPP; Lamar (Refugio), G. ARMSTRONG; La
Grange (Red River), M. W. MATTHEWS; Lynchburg
(Harris), W. GAFFIELD; LaGrange (Fayette), Jos.
SHAW; Liberty (Liberty), W. BROOKS; Lexington
(Fannin), D. RAWLETT; Lowell (Gonzales), L. L.
PECK; Mustang Prairie (Houston), C. ALDRICH;
Mt. Sterling (Nacogdoches), John DURST; Montgomery (Montgomery), W. SHEPPERD; Mt. Pleasant
(Bastrop), Moses GAGE; Matagorda (Matagorda),
G. W. WARD; Mt. Holland (Jefferson), R. BOOTH;
Myrtle Springs (Red River), R. PETERS; Montague
(Fannin), J. MURPHY; Menard's Mills (Liberty),
G. DREW; Myrtle Turf (Harris), H. A. NANCE; Mt.
Vernon (Montgomery), C. WEST; New Cincinnati
(Montgomery), G. WEEDEN; Nashville (Milam), W.
THOMPSON; Nacogdoches (Nacogdoches), G. STERNE;
Orazimba (Brazoria), J. A. E. PHELPS; Oak Grove
(Washington), E. W. EAST; Patillo's (Jefferson)
G. A. PATILLO; Palo Gache (San Augustine), B.J.
THOMPSON; Peach Creek (Colorado), A. B. PHILIPS;
Potter's Creek (Harrison), A. C. DAVIDSON; Pine
Island (Jefferson), T. D. YOCUM; Plum Grove
(Fayette), W. SCALLELD; Preston (Matagorda), T.
THOMPSON; Primm's (Bastrop), W. PRIMM; Quintana
(Brazoria), J. G. WILLIAMS; Quairo (Gonzales),
Geo. BLAIR; Richardson's (Jasper), B. RICHARDSON; Richmond (Fort Bend), J. LEVERING; Ruttersville (Fayette), Lee GRAY; Rusk (Montgomery),
M. MANNING; San Luis (Brazoria), E. ANDREWS;

Salem (Jasper), Seth SWIFT; Spilman's Island (Harris), J. H. SPILMAN; San Antonio (San Antonio), S. W. SMITH; Spring Hill (Shelby), W. WOOD:; Swartout (Liberty), T. STUBBLEFIELD; Smithfield (Liberty), S. C. HIROM; Spring Creek (Harris) J. W. ASBERRY; Sabine city (Jefferson) W. McGOFFEY; San Augustine (St. Augustine), J.G. BERRY; San Felipe (Austin), J. KINGSBERRY; Slate Bank (Red River), L. W. TINNIN; Smithfield (Red River), S. W. CHENY; Shelbyville (Shelby), A. LEWELLEN; Sabine Town (Sabine), H. H. LOVING; Shelton (Red River), J. SHELTON; Seguin (Gonzales), H. HENDERSON; Tenoxtitlan (Milam), A. DE ORR; Texana (Jackson), S. S. WELLS; Tuscumbia (Harrison), Levi JORDON; Tellet's Prairie (Red River), H. WILLIAMS; Velasco (Brazoria), H. A. WALCOTT; Victoria (Victoria), J. A. MOODY; Udolpho (Montgomery), J. MITCHELL; Wooten's (Nacogdoches), W. WOOTEN; Warsaw (Harris), D. McCALL; Washington (Washington), J. B. ROBERTSON; Ward's (Red River), J. WARD; Zavalla (Jasper), T. B. HULLING.

Mr. J. L. NICKELSON will leave Houston this week on a tour through the western counties for the purpose of collecting debts due our office; he is fully authorized to act as our agent in the settlement of all unliquidated accounts.

The armed schooner, San Jacinto, Lieut. James O. SHANNESSY commander, went to sea from Galveston on the 26th ult. to join the squadron on the coast of Mexico.

The Bermuda Slaves. "It will be recollected that the British Brig of War Pilot, visited our shores some time last winter,, having on board a commission to enquire into the reported sale & detention of 6 or 7 free negroes, said to have been brought to this country by John TAYLOR, a native of the Barbadoes. A late number of the Bermuda Royal Gazette, states that on the return of the commission with 6 of the negroes, & with documentary proof of TAYLOR's guilt, obtained in this country, the accused was brought to trial; & after a long but interesting investigation, was sentenced to 14 years of imprisonment. The Gazette justly observes 'The Texian government afforded the commissioner and those who accompanied him, every possible facility & convenience'."---Houston Morning Star.

We learn by letter from Austin that James SIMMONS, Esq. has been appointed Treasurer; and J. C. SHAW, comptroller.

From the Galveston Courier of Saturday last: We are under the painful necessity of recording the death of G. F. LAWRENCE, Esq. Recorder of the city of Galveston. His decease occured the night before last at his residence, the death resulting from the wound he received from a pistol a few days since while trying to end a riot there. There is no doubt the wound would have ended his life sooner had it not been for the efforts of Drs. WORK, SHEPHERD & PILATE; on Tuesday morning last, doctors had just dressed the wound and the patient had composed himself on his bed when a hemorrhage commenced from the large artery which had first been secured. The vessel burst open an inch or so from the first ligature. The doctors used a compress of lint & applied caustic medicines to the wound, but it was not successful. Death ensued about one o'clock yesterday morning. He was buried last evening with full Masonic honors; beloved as a husband, son, brother & associate.

Died at Centre Hill (Austin co.), Sept. 6th, 1840, Mr. James R. ISBELL.

From the San Augustine Journal: It has become our painful duty to announce the death of Mrs. Martha HART, consort of the Hon. Wm. HART, Chief Justice of Nacogdoches Co. She was the daughter of Mr. Robert HART of Rathfeiland, in Down co., Ireland, where she resided until her marriage in 1835. She emigrated with her husband to the United States and also located in Nacogdoches in 1836, where she lived until her death on July 25th. Mrs. HART is buried in the new Protestant cemetery, which is situated in a beautiful grove in the Eastern suburbs of Nacogdoches.

Administrator's sale set for Dec. 15th at the courthouse door, Bastrop Co., for one half league of land, fronting on the east side of the Colorado river in said co., being originally the headright of Josiah WILBARGER, a well known citizen of that region. Fifty acres out of this tract is in a fine state of cultivation now. Sarah McGEHEE, Adm'x in the Estate of John C. McGEHEE, Sept. 22.

John B. MURPHREE has obtained letters of adm. in the est. of his father, Stevhen MURPHREE, decd., Victoria County, Sept. 16th.

By virtue of an order from the Sept. term of the Liberty County Probate Court, I will sell for cash on the 1st Tuesday in November at the courthouse door in Liberty 1 league & 1 labor of land, being the headright of Nancy GOWENS, decd., or so much as shall be sufficient to pay the expenses of the administration. J. S. FIELDS, Admr., Liberty, Sept. 28th.

By virtue of an order of the August Term of the Probate Court, Liberty Co., I shall sell for cash on the 1st Tuesday in November at the courthouse door in Liberty, one-third a league of land, being the headright of Joseph SANGERMAIN. Said lands are situated on the Peninsula formed by the Gulf of Mexico & East Bay. Edward T. BRANCH, Admr.

Charles P. GERLACH named as admr. of estate of Ferdinand GERLACH, decd., Harris County.

Abram KUYKENDALL named admr. of the est. of Moses NORTON, decd., Austin co.

Jackson County, Probate Notice. The heirs & all persons interested in the est. of John H. SCOTT, decd., are hereby advertised that final settlement & division of said estate will take place before Probate Court of said county on Sept. 28th, 1840. Thos. SIMONS, Clerk of Probate, Sept. 15.

David R. COLE named admr. of the est. of Mr. Edmund B. ANDERSON, decd., Harrisburg Co.

Alabama---Texas. There will be a public sale of lots in the Town of Alabama, situated on the east bank of the Trinity river, on 2nd Monday of Feb. next. Terms will be one-fourth cash, & balance on 1, 2 & 3 years credit & lien on property until last payment. Geo. W. GRANT, Jacob ALLBRIGHT, G. H. HARRISON, Proprietors, Alabama, 30th August 1840.

John W. FOGG appointed on Jan. 20th last as admr. of the succ. of Dennis HOPKINS, decd.

Matagorda Academy. The Rev. C. S. IVES and Lady respectfully inform the public that they are now prepared to accept pupils of both sexes into their institution. Testimonial from Bishop T. C. BROWNELL of the Diocese of CT, states that Rev. IVES was a graduate of one the first colleges in the U.S.; Mrs. IVES taught a female seminary for several years in Hartford. Testimonial, Principal of the Mobile Institute, says that Rev. Caleb S. IVES served for past 2 years as an officer of his institution.

Wednesday, October 14, 1840

Exportation of Timber & Staves. --- We learn that J. H. FABER, Sr., a merchant of NYC, and connected with J. H. FABER, Jr., of this city, has sent out to this country Mr. HANSON of Hamburg, for the purpose of procuring & preparing cedar & live oak timber to be shipped to Bremen & other European ports. They calculate to do business to the amount of $100,000 the ensuing year. Thirty workmen are also expected daily from Europe, with machinery for making staves for exportation --- likewise a highly promising branch of trade.---Galveston Civilian.

Married in Newnan, Cowper Co., GA, on Tuesday, Sept. 8th, by the Hon. Hiram WARNER, C. W. BUCKLEY, Esq. of this city, to Miss Lurena Jane PHILIPS, of the former place. The bride and bridegroom arrived in town on Saturday last.

Married on Tuesday evening, the 6th inst. by Rev. REED, Mr. T. W. HOUSE of the firm of HOUSE & SHEARN to Miss Mary SHEARN, all of this city.

Died at New Washington on Oct. 1st, of Pulmonary Consumption, Mrs. Celia MORGAN, consort of Col. James MORGAN, & native of Hertford Co., SC., but a resident of Texas for most of the last nine years.

Melancholy Accident. Edgar Wm. THOMPSON, a brother of A. P. THOMPSON of this city, was recently drowned while bathing off the town of Calhoun. This promising young man had but a few days before reached this country from London, having been a passenger on the English Bark Elisabeth. It is supposed that he was seized with a cramp while in the water and was carried off with the current before any help could be rendered.

The above mentioned vessel, the English bark Elisabeth, which sailed from Liverpool, reached Matagorda. She is charted, we believe, by Mr. Jonathon IKIN of London, with a cargo of salt, coal, articles of husbandry & some choice lots of high bred English horses, cattle &c; upwards of 50 emigrants came on board this vessel & are proceeding to open farms at once in western TX.

Sheriff's Sale scheduled for Tuesday, Nov. 3 at courthouse door in Houston, on all right, title, & claim of Robert WILSON, in & to his undivided interest in Lots 1, 2 & 3, containing 286 acres each, and others lands totalling 1284.2 acres, making altogether 1372 acres; the above lands are adjoining & part of the land granted to Wm. P. HARRIS and Robert WILSON by the Mexican government, seized & take in execution as the property of Robert WILSON to satisfy judgements in favor of Chas. BIGELOW & Hiram WOODS. John W. MOORE, Sheriff, Harris County.

Property belonging to Edward OSBORN in city of Houston to be sold at courthouse door on 1st Tuesday in October to satisfy judgements ordered by District Court, Harris Co.

Property in city of Houston belonging to Clark WOOSTER to be sold at courthouse door on Nov. 3rd. to satisfy judgement in favor of Wm. BOYD, Harris County Sheriff's Sale.

Property on Buffalo Bayou (200 acres) belonging to Joseph CALLAHAN to be sold at Courthouse door in Houston on Nov. 3d to satisfy judgement in favor of A. B. SHELBY, Harris Co. Sheriff's Sale.

Property belonging to J. R. HORDE to be sold at Courthouse door in Houston on Nov. 3rd to satisfy judgement in favor of Thomas EARLE, Sr., curator of the heirs of Luke MOORE, decd. Said land consists of 132½ acres, being lot No. 10, in Luke MOORE Tract. Harris Co. Sheriff's Sale.

The north half of a league originally granted to John W. ASBERRY as his headright to be sold at Courthouse door in Houston on Nov. 3rd to satisfy judgment in favor of WYNNS, LAWRENCE & JEWETT. Said land surveyed in the name of John W. ASBERRY, by virtue of certificate No. 442, granted to him as his headright by board of land commissioners of Harrisburg Co. Said land located on east bank of San Jacinto river. John W. MOORE, Sheriff, Harris County.

Property belonging to James SEYMORE Est. to be sold at Courthouse door in Houston on Nov. 3 to satisfy judgement in favor of Allen VINCE, admr. of est. of Wm. VINCE. Said land totals 3,500 acres, fronting on Buffalo Bayou & above property of Thomas EARLE. John W. MOORE, Sheriff, Harris County.

Property in city of Houston belonging to Prudence HUSTON to be sold at Courthouse door on Nov. 3rd to satisfy judgement in favor of Andrew HODGE, Jr. Harris County Sheriff.

Property in city of Houston belonging to Nathan KEMPTON to be sold at Courthouse door on Nov. 3rd to satisfy judgment in favor of Andrew HODGE, Jr. Harris County Sheriff.

Property in the city of Houston belonging to Thos. RAFFERTY and W. B. Harrison to be sold at Courthouse door on Nov. 3rd to satisfy judgment in favor of Jacob MATOSSEY. Harris Co.

Wednesday, October 21, 1840

We were most agreeably entertained last evening while listening to a serenade of Mr. HEERBRUGGER and a few companions, who played several German & Swiss airs. We understand he intends to give a concert on the Thursday or Saturday evening next, & we cordially commend him to our fellow citizens as the ablest musician who ever visited our republic.

Heroic Conduct---During the late incursion of the Comanches, some 300 of the warriors surrounded the log cabin of Mr. KITCHEN, situated about 3 miles above Victoria. Mr. KITCHEN, his wife & their infant children were the only inmates, but the Comanches did not dare attack. Mr. KITCHEN took a station at one door with his rifle, while his wife stood at the other with a musket; although they never fired their pieces, they kept them pointed with unshaken firmess at their foe, who at length tired of their fruitless attempts to attack the home and retired.

J. L. RIDDELL, M.D., Professor of Chemistry at the Medical College of Louisiana, publishes a lengthy report on the mineral wealth of the Trinity River country made during an expedition to that district in April and May, 1839. Article mentions the lands on Salt Creek near Oceola belonging to Dr. Frederick B. PAGE on the Trinity, which contain large subterranean salt deposits.

Wm. R. RECTOR of Cincinnati, TX, serves notice that he has lost his headright certificate for 640 acres of land and will seek a duplicate within the time prescribed by law. The certificate was granted by the commissioners of Houston co. in Sept. or Oct. 1838.

Alexander HAWTHORN, late of the Republic of TX, has established himself at New Orleans as a commission merchant. Oct. 20 advertisement.

Notice to Travellers. As a good road is now open from Houston to Austin, by way of city of Brazos, on the Brazos river, & as there is the best graded banks and Ferry Boat there is on the river & free of all charges to all passengers, travellers would do well to follow this route. Thomas B. WHITE, Agent.

$60 reward for John J. O'MALEY & Edw. FITZGERALD, deserters from the Austin Arsenal. Description: FITZGERALD is 5'7", age 21, complexion fair, eyes dark, born in NY; O'MALEY, age 24, 5'8", complexion fair, eyes blue, hair red, occupation a clerk, a native of Ireland. The above reward will be given for both or $30 for each deserter. W. E. BERRY, Lieut., Com'g Arsenal, Austin Arsenal, Oct. 5th.

Lost---A land certificate of one-third of a league of land, No. 81, being the headright of Geo. STEPHENSON, issued by board of land commissioners of Jefferson co. After 60 days from this date, I will apply for a duplicate copy from the proper office. B. ALLEN, Oct. 16th.

Beththia W. ADAMS appointed admr. on est. of John W. ALEXANDER by the May term of the Probate Court, Montgomery Co.; Oct. 10 notice.

Waverly House, Houston. The subscribers beg leave to inform the public that they have taken the Hotel next door to the corner of Main and Congress streets, & it is now open to the reception of boarders. Their table will always be supplied with the best the market can afford and the choicest liquors & wines kept at the bar. M. HAYWOOD & Milo K. PINCKSTON, Proprietors. W. W. HAYWOOD, Mgr. Houston, Oct. 19.

Wednesday, October 28, 1840

Madame THIELMAN has commenced theatrical performances at Galveston.

A valise was washed ashore at Galveston some few days since, having the strap cut & a piece of iron in it, apparently for the purpose of sinking it. A letter of introduction for a young man recently from Maine, addressed to a Mr. James COCHRANE, was found inside.

Anonymous correspondent, "Texas," advances the name of Judge John HEMPHILL, of the 4th Judicial Dist., as a candidate for Chief Justice; states that he attended college in the U.S. and began practice of law in SC in 1827-28, came to TX in 1838, first locating in town of Washington; he had not been here barely 12 months before President LAMAR asked him to serve his cabinet as Secy. of Treasury, a position he declined. During the last session of Congress, friends prevailed upon Judge HEMPHILL to serve on the bench in the 4th Judicial District, since which time he has resided in San Antonio.

Information wanted of the widow of George A. PETTUCK, late of the town of San Patricio, who with family is supposed to be still in the Republic of TX. Any information in regard to the said lady or family will be thankfully received by the son of Geo. A. PETTUCK at Matamoros, Mexico or by R. GAMBLE, New Orleans, Oct. 27th.

The undersigned, wishing to embark into other business, offers for sale his Steam Mill at Bastrop, which he has successfully operated for the past 12 months; she produces 3,000 feet of lumber & will grind 200 bushels of corn in 12 hours. For further particulars & terms, apply to Thomas STANSBURY, of Houston, or at Bastrop to Willis TATUM, Oct. 19th, 1840.

The sale of the Steamboat "Sam Houston" is postponed until Nov. 27th. This steamboat was lately in the trade from Anahuac, to Houston & Galveston, & is offered for sale with her tackling, apparel &c., as she now lies partly sunk, in the west fork of Double bayou, about 8 miles from its mouth, & about 2 miles back from the city of Chambersia. The engine is well known to be an excellent & powerful one. Terms: one-half cash in hand, and the balance in 6 months. G. S. THOMAS, Agent for the Proprietor, City of Chambersia, Oct. 16th.

Wednesday, November 4, 1840

Capt. THOMPSON, better known in this community as Mexican THOMPSON, arrived in town Sunday on board the Gen. Houston. This man figured somewhat largely at the time of our revolution, & was captured off Velasco by a Texian vessel under Capt. HURD. He is now engaged in the cause of the Federalists in Mexico.

Drs. RICHARDSON & SMITH propose to publish a Medical & Surgical Journal in the office of the San Luis <u>Advocate</u>, at the city of San Luis. It will published quarterly, with the first number due out in January, & will contain about 64 pages octavo.

Col. SEGUIN, Senator from Bexar co., has resigned; Wm. H. DAINGERFIELD is a candidate to fill the vacancy.

Several French gentleman who visited this country with M. de SALIGNY, the French Charge d'Affaires, contemplate the establishment of mercantile houses & intend to open a communication with Santa Fe. M. DULONG, who was formerly connected with the Legation, having resigned his situation after coming to the Republic, has already opened a stock of goods there.

A work on Texas, styled "Texas and its Revolution," has lately been published in Paris. The author, Frederick LeCLERC, Chief Physician of the Hospital of Tours, was in TX during the latter part of 1838 & is quite knowledgeable.

The Dayton---This boat having undergone some thorough repairs & fitted up in great style, is resuming her situation on the Bayou. Her gentlemanly commander, Capt. STERRET, has an established character on our waters & treats all with great accommodation and courtesy.

Last night the schooner Augusta, Lord, arried in this harbor 23 days from Philadelphia; the brig Emprasario, LONGCOPE, arrived here yesterday from Baltimore. She performed the voyage in 14 days. Passengers by Empressario: W. D. LEE & lady; Wm. MANN, lady & 2 children; F. PENNY; C. HOFFMAN; B. DYER; L. B. WATKINS; Jas. HAVILAND; W. B. WAYSHAM; and J. OSTERMAN.

Canal Steam Boat---Mr. Mellen BATEL, an ingenious mechanic of this city, has succeeded after many years & much study, in perfecting machinery for propelling boats on the canal by steam, as tow boats or independent packet or freight boats. We have seen the machinery and have no hesitation in speaking of it as an important invention.

Houston House, corner of Main & Franklin streets, this well known establishment is now open for the accommodation of the public, having undergone a thorough repair; the subscriber seeks a liberal share of the public patronage. F. E. STURTEVANT, Nov. 3rd.

Notice. All persons indebted to the est. of Prettyman MERRY, decd., are requested to come forward & make payments; & those with claims will present them to the subscriber within the time prescribed by law. John W. MOORE, Admr.

Wednesday, November 11, 1840

A party of six Indians, supposed to be Keachies, recently ventured near Franklin in Robertson co., & stole several horses; they were immediately pursued by five citizens, four of them were killed & the horses recaptured. Two of the Indians were overtaken by a Mr. LOVE, who after shooting one, was fired upon by the other. The shot missed LOVE & he rushed the Indian, who fought with his clubbed musket. LOVE killed him finally with a Bowie knife.

Died, on the 26th ult., at Linnville, Frederick B. HERNDON (?), in his 19th year, who had just arrived from KY on a visit to his brother.

Notice. I will sell at public auction at the courthouse door in Montgomery, on the first Monday in December, one headright certificate for 640 acres of land. Also two land warrants for 320 acres each, said land claims are transferred to WEEDON & SAUL, & will be sold to close the concern; terms cash; Montgomery, Nov. 1st. Geo. WEEDON.

J. Harris CATLIN appointed admr. of the est. of Daniel M. SYMONDS, decd., at the Oct. term of the Probate Court, Austin county.

Runaway in Jail. Taken up by J. R. CLARK & committed to the Jail of this county, a boy calling himself SANDY, says he belongs to Washington EDWARDS, near Shreveport, LA. He is of copper color, 5'5", two scars on his forehead above his right eye, about 25 years old. The owner is requested to come forward, pay charges & take away said negro, or he will be dealt with according to law. John W. MOORE, Sheriff, Harris county, Nov. 11.

Notice. Taken up by James W. McCLELLAND and committed to the Jail of this county, a negro boy named SAM, age 18, 5 feet high, dark complexion, who says he belongs to a Mr. SHROCK, living on Caney, Matagorda co. The owner is requested to come forward, pay charges & claim said negro, or he will be dealt with according to the law. John W. MOORE, Sheriff, Harris Co.

To be sold at courthouse door in Houston on Dec. 1st., all right, title & claim of Thomas McDONALD to property known as Lynchburg steam saw mill, to satify judgment in favor of D. W. Clinton HARRIS and against said McDONALD and James W. McGAHEY. John W. MOORE, Sheriff of Harris Co.

Alexander S. WILKS can obtain the certificate for his headright, which he lost sometime since. Apply at the Telegraph office, Nov. 5.

Property belonging to A. C. ALLEN to be sold at courthouse door in Houston on 1st Tuesday in December by order of District Court of Harris co. Property includes: 534 acres granted to

Wm. SCOTT, located on Galveston bay, bounded on the east by Cedar bayou, north by Christian SMITH, west by Charles GRIMES, and south by Pinckney HENDERSON; also several lots in the city of Houston, including a Brick House on lot No. 11, Block 21. John W. MOORE, Sheriff of Harris County, Houston, Nov. 11th.

Information. Clement WATERS can obtain his certificate of headright, which he lost about a year ago, by applying to the Telegraph office, and paying the charges of this advertisement.

Wednesday, November 18, 1840

Fort on the San Saba---The old Spanish fortress on the San Saba, was discovered by Colonel MOORE, in the late expedition, & found to be in very good state of preservation. Most of the walls were still standing & a part of the timbers of the houses. The fort could be repaired at a trifling expense. It is about 100 miles from Austin and 70 miles above the mouth of the San Saba.

Colt's Patent Rifle --- In the late Indian fight, Capt. ANDREWS used one of COLT's patent rifles, which he discharged 10 times while a comrade could discharge his rifle only twice. He believes these rifles in proper hands would prove to be the most useful of all weapons in Indian warfare.

Official Report. The newspaper publishes a report from Col. MOORE's recent engagement with the Indians. The report of Col. John H. MOORE is dated Nov. 7th, 1840, from Austin & addressed to the Hon. Branch T. ARCHER, Secy. of War: "Upon receiving orders from your Honor, I marched on Monday [Oct. 5] from Walnut Creek, immediately up the Colorado river, through the mountains, until I passed the head waters of the San Gabriel. I then bore into the river & crossed over, bearing NW for the San Saba river, scouting the country upon my right & left generally. Upon reaching the San Saba, I was convinced that the enemy must be very near the head waters of said stream, or they had moved their encampment to another river known as the

Concho. During this time the weather was very unpleasant, owing to rain & north winds, which caused the troops to become very unhealthy; and unfortunately I was called upon to pay the last debt of gratitutde to a decd. volunteer Garrett HARRELL, of Fayette co., who died at Camp Rabb on the 16th ult., upon the waters of the Concho...Afterward I moved for the Concho. Upon arriving at this point, I proceeded on to the Colorado...At this point I discovered that a considerable trail bore immediately up said stream, & I determined to pursue the same until I should find their encampment. In moving forward directly up the Red fork of the river, I discovered that the enemy had been cutting pecan trees for the fruit. This was on Friday the 23rd day of October about 10 o'clock, A.M. I immediately ordered my troops to take shelter from the severe north wind." MOORE sends out 2 Lipan spies on horseback to search for the Comanches. They returned about 4:30 p.m., after traveling 18-20 miles, and reported the discovery of a large Comanche village. "I ordered my troops to prepare supper & make ready for marching. At half past 5 o'clock, the tropps marched directly north, for about 10 miles, where we reached the Colorado river, & went directly up said stream. After marching 4 miles I ordered my beef cattle to be herded in a musquite flat upon the bank of the river, where I left them to fortune's chance. I moved about four miles further, when I ordered my troops into a hollow, near the river, where they were ordered to dismount about 12 o'clock. Then I sent forward 2 of the spies to the Indian village, for the purpose of ascertaining the probable number of the enemy & the situation of their encampment. The wind continued a blow from the north and about 3 o'clock it commenced raining, which continued to fall until morning. About three o'clock the spies returned & reported that the village was situated on the south side of the Colorado...and they estimated their numbers to be about 125 warriors & 60 families... At the break of day on Saturday, 24th day of Oct.,

I ordered the troops to begin march. I soon ascended the hill Lieut. J. L. OWEN to take command of 15 men to act as cavalry to cut off any retreating enemy. I ordered Capt. Thos. J. RABB, with his command upon the right, Lieut. OWEN, to center, and Capt. Nicholas M. DAWSON, with his command, to the left. . .After crossing a small branch [of the river], I then ordered Lieut. OWEN & his command to the right of Capt. RABB's command. I then ordered a charge of the whole upon their village. . .The enemy fled for the river, which is in the shape of a half moon, encircling the village. Immediately upon charging the village a general & effective fire was opened upon the enemy, who soon commenced falling upon the right & left. After charging pretty near through their encampment, the men dismounted from their horses & continued to fire at the enemy, as they were retreating to the river. Many were slain before they were able to reach the water, where many others were killed or drowned. Some, however, succeeded in crossing the river & making off thru the prairie on the other side. At this time, Lieut. OWEN crossed over & commenced cutting off their retreat." The troops captured 34 prisoners, seven of which escaped during a stampede of our beeves on a very dark night; an examination of the scene came up with 48 bodies on the ground plus 80 killed or drowned in the river. We had two men wounded, Mr. DAUGHERTY of Colorado co., Mr. B. F. JONES of Fayette co. Great credit is due the Lipan chief CASTRO and his men, several of whom served ably as spies. I have the honor to remain your most obdt. servant, John H. MOORE, Col., Comm'dg Militia.

Jane CRAWFORD appointed executrix of estate of Robert CRAWFORD, decd. Oct. 10th notice.

Executors sale. By virtue of an order from Probate Court, Bexar County, I will sell on 1st Dec., next, at public auction to highest bidder, all of the personal property belonging to the est. of Henry W. KARNES, decd. A lot of horses, mules, farming utensils, firearms, &c. Terms of sale, cash. Thos. H. O. S. ADDICKS, Executor, San Antonio de Bexar, Nov. 5th.

Property belonging to Fabricius REYNOLDS in Harris co. to be sold at Courthouse door on 1st Dec., to satisfy judgment in favor of Daniel NUTTER. Said land consists of 40 acres, being the back tract half of a tract fronting on Buffalo bayou & joining the town tract on the upper line, & bound on the town line by the land of S. N. DOBIE, it being part of the head right of Samuel M. HARRIS. John W. MOORE, Sheriff.

Property belonging to Stephen RICHARDSON to be sold at Courthouse door in Houston on Dec. 1st., to satisfy judgement in favor of Wm. GOLDING and against James W. SCOTT, A. J. DAVIS, Stephen RICHARDSON, & Abram MOORE. John W. MOORE, Sheriff, Harris County.

Information wanted of John M. BAILEY who left the residence of his mother in Knoxville, Tenn., on 22d of Oct., 1839, for TX and has not been since heard from. He is supposed to have joined the army as a volunteer. If he is alive he would do well to return as his grandfather is dead & by his last will & testament has left him a large estate. Any information concerning him will be gratefully received by his aged mother Elizabeth BAILEY, Knoxville, TN, July 28.

C. C. DYER named admr. of the est. of Wm. STAFFORD, decd., by probate judge of Shelby Co. Said letters of administration have been transferred to county of Fort Bend for final settlement, Sept. 25th.

Wednesday, December 2, 1840

The *Courier* says that James FOULHOUSE, Esq. has been recognized by the President as Vice Consul of the King of France, for the port of Galveston.

Married in this city on the 25th inst., by the Rev. Mr. REED, John H. BROWN to Miss Sophia LOOMIS, at the home of Isaac CADE.

Married at Fayette co., on 1st inst., Alfred OBAR to Miss Sarah WALKER, both of La Grange.

Married on 18th inst., at the residence of Capt. James G. SWISHER, in Washington Co., by the Rev. Hugh WILSON, the Rev. Edward FONTAINE to Miss Nancy SWISHER.

Died on the evening of Nov. 11th at New Washington, Andrew VANCE, formerly a highly respected merchant of Clarksville, TN. Mr. VANCE had but lately come to TX & after travelling the country, had located himself & secured a residence for his family on Galveston Bay and was on his way to meet a steamboat to go on for them when he died.

Trinity River Packet. The new and light draught Steamboat "Vesta," having been purchased by Capt. GOULD expressly for the above trade will run regularly during the season between Galveston & Houston. W. C. GOULD, Capt.

Milam County, District Court, November Term. Alexander THOMPSON vs. Jos. J. DeWITT's Heirs, Action for Land Title. "Plaintiff's petition alleges that plaintiff & defts. intestate Jos. J. DeWITT entered into contract by which plaintiff was to furnish kettles & build a furnance and shelter, dig troughs, &c. and prepare for making salt on a certain half league of land of the said DeWITT; the same being a part of the headright lying on the Yegua, in Milam & Washington counties, & in consideration thereof, the said DeWITT agreed to make to plantiff a title to one-half of said league of land & that the said Joseph J. DeWITT died without having executed the title." Wm. L. MURRAY, Clerk. This notice requires heirs & legal representatives of the decd. to appear on first day of next term of the court & answer plaintiff's petition. Dec. 2.

Notice. Committed to jail on 23rd Oct., a negro man who calls himself CORNELIUS, who says he belongs to Theophilus & Robert SIMINGTON (late of Alabama) living in Robertson co., TX; said CORNELIUS is about 35 years of age, yellow complexions, 5'3", heavy built, with a scar on his left jaw & is quite intelligent; was taken up by Col. COOK's company of regulars, on their expedition from the Brazos to Red River; owners are requested to come forward, claim property, pay charges & take him away; or he will be disposed of according to the law. J. P. SIMPSON, Sheriff & Jailer, Warren, Fannin co.

Lost or Mislaid. A Land Certificate for one third league granted to Wm. T. EVANS, by board of Land Commissioners of Harrisburg co. on or about June 28, 1838, together with a power of attorney for Location, Survey & procuring a title, plus other related documents. Any person delivering the same to F. K. TAYLOR at Houston or to C. CHAMBERLAIN at Galveston will be liberally rewarded. C. CHAMBERLAIN, Wm. T. EVANS.

To All Whom it May Concern. Died at my home sometime early in Oct. last, a man calling himself Thos. PETTINGER, who says he came from and was raised in Shelby co., KY, and was last from Victoria on the Guadalupe. He has left some wearing apparel, between $20-30 in TX Treasury notes & change tickets, $2.50 in specie, & $300 in notes on the Chicago bank of Illinois, which he said was spurious & of no value. Any person coming legally authorized to receive & dispose of said articles can get them by paying charges for attendance in sickness, burial expenses &c. G. G. WILLIAMS, living near Egypt, Colorado co. November 26th, 1840.

Notice. Sometime in the spring of 1838, I deposited in the hands of Green Q. TAYLOR, a certificate of augmentation for 320 acres of land, which has been lost or mislaid; said certificate was issued by the board of Land Commissioners for Montgomery co., No. 130, signed June 20th 1838. I intend to file for a duplicate copy within 60 days, unless the original turns up. Thomas P. DAVY, Nov. 26th.

Sheriff's Sale scheduled for 1st Tuesday in Feb., next, for purpose of foreclosing a Mortgage executed by J. KINGSBERRY to E. B. NICHOLS and foreclosed for the use of Isaac CADE. I have levied upon a negro boy named NELSON, now in the possession of said KINGSBERRY. Sale to be held at courthouse door in San Felipe de Austin. Said negro boy NELSON is aged about 40 years. J. Harris CATLIN, Sheriff, Austin Co., Nov. 21, 1840.

Wednesday, December 9, 1840

   Colt's Patent Rifle. A young man named HOTCHKISS was dangerously wounded at Austin on the 17th ult., by the accidental discharge of one of Colt's patent rifles. Several accidents of this kind have occurred in that city since the introduction of these pieces.
   From the Houston <u>Morning Star</u>: A German society has been formed in this city whose objects are entirely philanthropic. We understand that a petition will be addressed to congress praying for an act to incorporate, with the view of enabling the association to hold real estate to the value of $10,000, which is contemplated to be a small farm in the vicinity of this city, to answer for the purposes of an Alms House, Hospital & Asylum for poor, sick & indigent German emigrants. Officers of the "German Union:" Geo. FISHER, President; Henry LEVENHAGEN, 1st Vice President; Theodore MILLER, 2nd Vice President; Henry F. FISHER, Secy.; and John KOOP, Treasurer. The regular meetings of the Association are on every Sunday evening at 7 o'clock.
   We have learned from a reliable source that there were 3 lads from Fayette county, in Col. MOORE's command, viz: Elisha IRONS, Leander HARRELL, and Henry EARTHMAN, Jr., all under 15 years of age; and that the severely underwent the fatigue & duties of the campaign with signal promtitude & participated in the battle with all the determination & bravery that characterized the more experienced & veteran members of the corps.---<u>Gazette</u>.
   The Second Annual Meeting of the Texas Bible Society convened at the Capitol on the evening of Sunday, Nov. 29th. Hon. David G. BURNET, as president, took the chair and called upon the Rev. John HAYNIE, Chaplain to the House of Representatives to open with a prayer. New officers were elected during the course of the session: BURNET, President; Rev. C. RICHARDSON, 1st Vice President; Hon. Wm. MENEFEE, 2nd VP; Hon. F. MOORE, 3rd VP; Hon. G. W. BARNETT, 4th VP; Rev. John HAYNIE, 5th VP; James BURKE, Cor-

responding Secy.; Wm. HOTCHKISS, Recording Secy.; Hon. M. EVANS, Treasurer. Executive Committee composed of Hon. D. S. KAUFMAN, Rich. BULLOCK, and Robert M. SPICER.

Shipwreck. We regret to learn that the schooner which was seen in the offing the night before last, was wrecked yesterday morning about 12 miles below the city. She proved to be the "Experiment," Capt. GRANT, from New Orleans; the vessel will be an entire loss. Galveston Courier of the 22nd.

Married on the 11th ult., by G. HUFF, Esq., John L. WHITAKER to Miss Sarah Ann ALLEN.

Married by the same on the 16th ult., Wm. J. ALBRIGHT to Mrs. Sarah BIRD.

Married by the same on the 22d ult., James LATHAM to Miss Hannah E. ALLBRIGHT.

W. W. WOOD named admr. of the est. of Bennet WOOD, decd., Montgomery Co., Nov. 15th.

Report of Col. Wm. G. COOKE to Hon. Branch T. ARCHER, Secy. of War, dated Nov. 18th, Bois d'Arc. MOORE states that he and his troops remained five days at Little River, arriving there on 9th Sept. Started for the Brazos where he had ordered Capt. HOLLIDAY to meet him and arrived at the Waco Village on the 17th and remained there until the Quarter Master came up with a line of supplies, at which time he and his men pushed on to the Trinity. "Owing to the dryness of the season, we were obliged to encamp in 2 or 3 instances without water. Upon one of these occasions at Chambers' Creek, some of our men went back upon the trail for water, contrary to orders, without their muskets; they were attacked by 10 or 15 Indians, and four of them were killed. Upon the same night a severe norther blew up, during which our cattle again broke away from the guard & escaped . . . From the Brazos to the Trinity we averaged about 6 to 8 miles per day, both on account of the difficulty of getting through the bottoms and the bad condition of our mules. . .As we approached the Trinity, game became scarce & before we had reached the main bottom, we were obliged to subsist for several days upon dogs, mules and horses. In this state of affairs I saw it was impossible to get to the settlements with the waggons, or even with the sick & being informed by the pilot that it was but 2 days ride to the settlements on Sulphur fork of Red River, I concluded to leave a part of my command & march on for supplies, calculating to reach the settlement in 4 days. Lieut. Col. CLENDENIN, at his own request was left on the west side of the Trinity, with the waggons, sick & 40 men as a guard. The 5th day after leaving the Trinity we struck a thicket, supposed by our guides to be upon the head waters of the Sabine, which we were 5 days in cutting through. On the 10th day after leaving Lieut. Col. CLENDENIN, we struck the trail of the Chihuahua traders which took us to the settlements on the Bois d'Arc fork, on Red River, where we were received very hospitably by Mr. Bailey ENGLISH, and furnished with supplies after having been without beef 22 days. Arrangements were immediately made to send assistance to the command on the Trinity, a company was sent back with beeves, oxen to draw the waggons &c. Four men who have returned, state that they arrived there on the 5th inst., but too late to meet Col. CLENDENIN's command. Capt's. SKERRIT and MAURAND wer there with 40 men who followed us from Austin . . . They stated that they had arrived on the 4th and found a note signed by Col. CLENDENIN dated the 3rd inst., stating he had been starved out, that he had eaten most of his mules and horses, that he was obliged to leave for the settlements & that he expected to return in 8-10 days time. I have heard nothing of Col. CLENDENIN, but expect that he has gone down the Trinity. He had when I left him some 20 horses & mules."

Wednesday, December 16, 1840

Letter from S. W. JORDAN to General CANALES, dated at Laredo, 2nd Nov. 1840. "Enclosed I send you a field report of my regiment after the battle of Saltillo." Report deals with an engagement against Gen. MONTOYA at Saltillo on

Oct. 23-28, 1840. Forces loyal to CANALES consisted of 231 men, and out of that number 111 were Americans led by the aforementioned JORDAN (although 4 of them were ill and unable to take part in the battle). JORDAN reports losses as: KILLED: Lieut. James GALLAGHER, O. S. STULTZ, Private WOODRUFF. WOUNDED: Capt. , severely; Capt. STILL; Pvt. BRATT, mortally; WIGGINS, severely & left behind; BECKHAM, slightly; Sergt. BLOOD; Pvt. HULL; BLANERHASET; Capt. DONNELLY, died at Laredo. MISSING: BYROM; ALSBROCKE; KELSENGER; MUSTARD; WALSH.

Arrival of the San Antonio. On Tuesday morning this Schooner of War came into the harbor of Galveston with her colors at half mast, and firing minute guns. She brought the body of Mr. TREAT, late the Texian agent at Mexico, who took passage on her at Vera Cruz, but died of consumption on the voyage; the services & money he provided the army during the summer of 1836, plus his recent exertions on our behalf, entitled him to the fullest honors. His wife, we understand, died only recently, and 3 children are now left destitute and without protectors.

Judge HEMPHILL was elected Chief Justice by 2 votes over Judge WEBB in the Senate.

Henry D. GALE of New York has been appointed by the President of the United States, Consul of that government to the port of Velasco.

Lost. A headright certificate for one-third league of land issued to John T. SMITH by Board of Land Commissioners of Harrisburg co., No. 432, which certificate was duly assigned to the subscriber, who will seek a duplicate 90 days after the date of this notice. Jos. P. WILSON, Houston, Dec. 1.

Lucy ROBBINS and John ROBBINS, Admrs. of the succ. of Nathaniel ROBBINS, decd., will present his accts. for allowance and final settlement to the probate court of Washington co. on Monday the 28th inst.

John ROBBINS, admr. for succ. of Thomas ROBBINS, decd., will present his accounts for allowance & final settlement to the probate court of Washington co., on Monday the 28th inst.

Runaway Taken Up. Committed to jail by Mr. WALLEY, a negro man named BOB, about 5'10", of yellow complexion, says he belongs to the est. of Wm. S. HALL, late of Brazoria co. The owner is notified to prove property, pay charges and take him away, or he will be dealt with according to to the law. John V. MORTON, Sheriff of Fort Bend co., Richmond, Dec. 9.

Cotton Farm for Rent. I wish to rent my farm, situated on the west side of the Brazos river, 6 miles below Richmond; there are 85 acres of Brazos bottom, well fenced & under cultivation; in the Prairie 45 acres, well-fenced; a pasture of 120 acres; a good dwelling house, smoke house, 2 Negro quarters, good corn cribs, stable, mill & gin. Alex F. JOHNSON.

Notice. A Runaway Negro taken up & committed to the jail of the northern division of Liberty co., who says his name is BILL, about 5'10" or 11", very large & stout, about 30 years of age, no particular marks visible. The owner is requesed to come forward, claim his property, and pay all charges, or he will be dealt with according to the law. David G. KINCAID, dep. sheriff for northern division of Liberty county, Swartout, Dec. 5.

Wm. DUGAN appointed admr. of the est. of George F. RICHARDSON on 23 Nov. 1840 by probate court for northern division of Liberty Co.

Sam. PATTERSON appointed admr. for the est. of Green R. KIRKHAM, decd., late of Washington co. Washington, Dec. 5th.

About the 1st inst., a body of men (supposed to be from Brazos Santiago) arrived in a large boat at 12 o'clock at night & boarded the sloop Phoenix, belonging to AUBREY & KINNEY, then lying at anchor in Corpus Christi bay, slipped her anchor & hoisted sail, but in attempting to tack she missed stays and went ashore; they then ordered the two men belonging to the sloop on deck & without allowing them to clothe themselves, took them on board their boat; before they left they destroyed the sails of the sloop. The mate, Mr. HURD, was secreted below and made his escape; and from him the particulars were obtained.

The names of the men taken from the sloop are John ALLEN of San Luis and James GIBSON of Galveston. Capt. LITTING of the sloop was fortunately on shore and escaped.

When Capt. THOMPSON, of the schooner "Wasp," left AUBREY & KINNEY's landing on the 3rd inst. they were hourly expecting an attack from a party of 300 men, under the command of one RODERIGUES who was dispatched for the purpose of destroying this Rancho. The party of the Rancho (comprising about 25 men) were in good spirits having a 12 pounder and plenty of small arms and ammunition.

Sheriff's sale set for 5th Jan. 1841 at the courthouse door in Houston, for all the right, title & interest of Andrew BRISCOE in and to a negro man named ISAAC, aged 19 years, seized by order of the District Court of Harris co., as the property of said BRISCOE, and will be sold to satisfy a judgment in favor of Seth CAREY. Terms of sale cash, in silver or gold, without appraisement. John W. MOORE, Sheriff, Dec. 15.

Property belonging to Wm. N. BRONAUGH to be sold in Sheriff's Sale at courthouse door in Houston on 5th Jan. 1841, to satisfy a judgment against him. Property consists of a house and lot in Houston. John W. MOORE, Sheriff of Harris co.

Wednesday, December 23, 1840

Card. George G. WOOD, Attorney & Counsellor at Law, will attend to the duties of his profession in the District Courts of the counties of Liberty & Montgomery. Swartout, Liberty county, Dec. 23rd.

Notice. Taken up by the Bidais Indians and brought to my house on 8th Dec. 1840, 2 Negroes (Africans), a man named FRANK and a woman named AMANDA, both appear to be well satisfied & between 20-25 years old. They speak little English & will not tell to whom they belong; Isaac DONOHO, Austin county.

Festus DOYLE named admr. for the estate of David HANSON, late of Fort Bend co., by probate court of said co. on 26th October 1840.

County of Washington, Probate Ct., Nov. Term. In the manner of proving the nuncupative will of Wm. W. GANT, decd. "Upon the petition of Harriet E. GANT for the probate of the nuncupative will of William W. GANT, decd., it is ordered & decreed by the court, that Monday, 25th Jan. 1841, be appointed as the day upon which the said nuncupative will of Wm. W. GANT will be heard & admitted to probate, & it is further ordered that notice be given to all persons and especially to those who would have been entitled by inheritance to the estate of the said Wm. W. GANT, if there had been no will. . ."

Died at the residence of Dr. HOXIE, near Independence, Washington co., on evening of 7th inst., the Rev. Francis RUTHERFORD of the Presbyterian church. His death was occasioned by a nail puncture to his foot, which resulted in tetanus. A few weeks prior to this, the decd. had followed the remains of his beloved wife to her grave. Two days before his death he became a member of the Presbytery of Brazos; & leaves no relatives in his adopted land.

Wednesday, December 30, 1840

$50 Reward New Orleans Money. Ranaway from the subscriber at Houston, sometime last June, my negro girl SARAH, who has probably been conveyed to another place by some white villain; I will give the above reward for the delivery of said girl to myself or to any Jailer in the Republic. Said negro is black in color, small of size, quick spoken, short, about 21 years old & has a visible scar on her one of her cheeks. Address to me at FANTHORP's Post Office, Montgomery co, Tx. Dec. 30. James SCOTT.

Lost. Sometime in the month of Aug. last, a mule of a bright roan color, with white tail & mane, branded on the left fore shoulder with the initials J. B. Said mule was left in the charge of the ferryman at San Luis & by him delivered to some unknown person. Any individual having the above will confer a favor by informing the undersigned & will be compensated for his trouble. John BROWN, Texana, Dec. 30th.

Notice. Sometime in the month of Aug. 1838, I employed Stillman CURTIS to locate a bounty land certificate No. 1,283, for 1,290 acres issued in my name for military service; said CURTIS has been killed by the Indians & since that time I have made diligent search for said certificate without success; this serves notice that I intend to seek a duplicate copy in sixty days from this date from the appropriate authorities. Francis J. DUFFAU, Oct. 15th.

Runaway Taken Up. Committed to the Jail of Harris co., by a Mr. PAYNE, on evening of 25th Dec., a negro boy by the name of JERRY, who was apprehended near the place of Matthew BURNETT on Cypress, mounted on a sorrel mare without saddle or bridle; he says he belongs to James COX of Montgomery co., who lives about 17 miles this side of the town of Washington; said negro is about 17 years old, of black complexion, has a gash on his nose, and stands about 5'4" or 5" tall. The owner requested to come forward and claim property, or he will be dealt with according to the law. John W. MOORE, Sheriff, Harris County, Dec. 28th.

The undersigned have formed a copartnership for the practice of law in Harris county. John TAYLOR, Algernon P. THOMPSON, Dec. 26th.

Wednesday, January 6, 1841

Col. Juan SEGUIN has returned in safety to Austin. The Centralist leader, Gen. ARISTA, endeavored by every means in his power to induce him to join his forces in Mexico, but in vain. He found both bribery and fear failed to move the heart of this noble hearted soldier. The same generous courage and patriotism which distinguished him in the campaign of 1835-36, distinguished him also in this trial.

"Description of ARISTA. Imagine a thick set, corpulent Mexican of ordinary stature, about 40 yearsw old, with red hair, large bushy whiskers and a beard about 10 inches long, also red; and you have in view ARISTA. This Mexican officer has passed through many vicisitudes of fortune, and has gained much knowledge in the school of experience. He is decidely the ablest and most enterprising of the generals now in the Mexican service."

Military Station. The company of rangers in the command of Maj. CLENDENIN, which have been stationed near the falls of the Brazos, have been ordered to remove to the Waco village, where they will probably be stationed until Col. COOK returns from Red River. In the mean time they will erect block houses at this post.

The first session of the Texas Conference of the Methodist Episcopal church was held at Rutersville, commencing on Dec. 25th & ending on the 29th, The Rev. Bishop WAUGH presiding; 19 Ministers, 9 members & 10 probationers were present---4 of the latter being admitted on probation at the Conference. The stations of the Preachers for the present year are as follows, to wit: San Augustine Dist., Littleton FOWLER, P'dg. Elder: San Augustine (Francis WILSON), Nacogdoches (to be supplied), Harrison (Nathan SHOOK), and Jasper (Henderson D. PALMER). Galveston Dist., Saml. A. WILLIAMS, P'dg. Elder: Galveston & Houston (Thos. O. SUMMERS), Brazoria (Abner P. MANLY), Montgomery (Richard OWEN, Jas. H. COLLARD), Liberty (to be supplied), Crockett (Daniel CARL), Nashville (Robert CRAWFORD). Rutersville Dist., Robert ALEXANDER, P'dg. Elder: Rutersville (to be supplied), Austin (John HAYNIE), Washington (Jesse HOOD), Centre Hill (Robt. H. HILL), Matagorda (Dan'l. N. V. SULLIVAN), Victoria (Joseph P. SNEAD). Chauncey RICHARDSON, President of Rutersville College. Abel STEVENS transferred to Providence Conference.

James H. SPILLMAN named as admr. of the est. of James SPILLMAN, decd., Jan. 1 advertisement.

Administrator's sale scheduled for 1st Tuesday in Feb. next, at Courthouse door in Houston on that valuable property known as Spillman's Island, situated in Harris co. and in the bay of San Jacinto, formerly the residence of James SPILLMAN, decd. Property to be sold at the order of the district ct., to pay off debts owed by said est. James H. SPILLMAN, Admr.

J. B. WOODS, Attorney & Counsellor at Law, Liberty, Dec. 16th advertisement date.
Notice. I hereby forewarn all persons from trading for a note drawn by B. W. HARDIN in favor of Charles COLVILLE & Andrew WYLIE, for the amount of $50, dated Oct. 7, 1837; for the said note was lost by men in December 1837. Thos. COLVILLE, Jan. 1st.
Benjamin ROBB named as admr. of the est. of John HUFFMAN, decd., Northern Division of Liberty County. Notice dated Oct. 29th, 1840.
G. A. PARKER appointed as admr. of the est. of Susan PARKER, decd., Fort Bend co., Jan. 3.
E. J. ARNOLD appointed admr. of the est. of Christopher VANDEYENDER, decd., by Probate Ct., Montgomery co., Sept. Term, 1840.
Lost. Sometime about 1st Aug. 1839, a pocket book containing a bond for titles to a labor of land, executed sometime in Oct. 1838 by Jas. WALLACE, in favor of myself---the headright of myself to one league & labor of land---a note of C. TASE's payable 1 day after date, in Nov. 1838, to Ira WITLERMANN, for $49. Anyone finding the above shall receive a reasonable reward by delivering them to me on the road to Washington near Groce's Retreat, or leaving them with D. Y. & J. W. PORTIS in Houston. R. A. PORTER.
Card. George T. WOOD, Attorney & Counsellor at Law, will attend to his profession in the District courts of Liberty & Montgomery co's.; Swartout, Liberty County, Dec. 23rd.

Wednesday, January 13, 1841

The death of Felix GRUNDY is announced in the New Orleans papers.
A letter from Federalist Gen. J. P. ANAYA, dated Sept. 30, 1840 from Tobasco, Mexico, to the Galveston <u>Civilian</u> reports that his forces under Lieut. Col. SAMMARAT attacked the town of Cuercacau, a Centralist stronghold, and executed the commander there, Everest SANCHEZ. Other forces under the command of Don Nickolas MALDONADO took the town of Tacoltapa and its garrison under Rosando Garcia SALAS, who was execut-

ed also by the Federalist forces.

Married in this city on the 12th inst., by Rev. W. Y. ALLEN, Leonard S. PERKINS to Miss Harriet B. PERKINS, both late of New York.

Monroe EDWARDS. This infamous forger is now in London. He pretends that certain negroes which he brought into this country in 1835, and which he sold here, were actually free blacks. Linking himself with the Abolitionists in the U.S. and England, he is striving to induce the British govt. to make a demand for their surrender. Monroe EDWARDS fled TX to escape punishment for forgery.

Quoting the New Orleans *Picayune*: Marcus Cicero STANLEY, said to be brother of the member of Congress from North Carolina, has been accused of committing several robberies in London, & was tried on a charge, made by Mr. CATLIN, of stealing from him, and was found guilty and sentenced to 6 months hard labor in the House of Corrections, 6 weeks of that time in solitary confinement. He was shortly to have been married to a rich heiress. At the solicitation of Mr. STEVENSON, the American minister, he was ably defended by the celebrated Charles PHILLIPS." Editor of the *Telegraph* notes that Marcus Cicero STANLEY was in TX for 18 months, during which time he was sought in 2 or 3 thefts. When finally arrested, he slipped bail and escaped to the States.

Wednesday, January 20, 1841

We understand that a Mr. MAILLARD, an Englishman who was for a short time last spring associated with a little sheet formerly published at Richmond, on the Brazos, called the "Richmond Telescope," is now making himself quite busy in the smaller papers of London, abusing Texas, her institutions and her people.

Additional information on Marcus Cicero STANLEY, states he formerly lived in Houston in 1837, sharing a room with GOODRICH and the lamented LAURENS, & some other men. On one occasion a $1000 belonging to GOODRICH turned up missing. GOODRICH, instigated by STANLEY, accused LAURENS of taking the money. LAURENS, being high minded and hoping to prove his innocence, met GOODRICH in a duel that resulted in his death. GOODRICH, completely stricken with what he had done, later blew out his own brains while STANLEY left TX for awhile. He returned in 1839, when he stole a $500 bill.

Wednesday, January 27, 1841

Texian Antiquities. We have been informed by Judge SCURRY that the remains of a large village or City have been found in Sabine co., on the estate of Mr. Wm. CLARK, at the junction of the "Tabo and Pancho" (?), about 17 miles east of San Augustine. It is not known if it was built by the Spanish or the French.

Administrator's sale ordered by Probate Ct. of Harris Co., on property belonging to est. of James D. EGBERT, decd., late of said co., and consisting of one-third a league situated on White Oak bayou, about 12 miles above the city of Houston. To be sold at public auction; no sale date listed. Wm. SEVEY, Admr., by C. W. BUCKLEY, attorney in fact.

The new steamer "Maryland," A. MARSH, master, has arrived at this port and will commence a regular trade between this city and Galveston. ENNIS & KIMBALL.

Wednesday, February 3, 1841

PLACIDIO, a "Tonquaway Chief," came in town on Saturday for the purpose of volunteering to join the expedition of Gen. MOREHOUSE against the northern Indians on the Upper Brazos. He reports that lately he came from their town, having been there with a few of his men as spies, and that the enemy consists of 400 to 600 men, in a strong enclosure in which they maintain their winter quarters. PLACIDIO will offer his services and those of 47 warriors, who are now lying on a tributary of the Brazos, between this city and Austin; and seeks the pay and rations of our soldiers.

Extract. From evidence taken before the Committee on Public Lands; General Land Office, Austin, Dec. 2nd, 1840. To Hon. Robert POTTER, Chairman, Com. on Public Lands. Yours of the 26th ult., requesting me to furnish the committee with a brief sketch of the history of land titles in what is termed the Nashville, or the Robertson's Colony, is before me. I have to state that the territory lying North of the San Antonio road, & known as Robertson's Colony, was originally contracted for by Robert LEFTWICH, as Empresario, in April 1825, who shortly after transferred all his right & authority to the Nashville company, who appointed 74 directors and they, through their agent, H. H. LEAGUE, petitioned the govt. to be recognized as the contractors, as well as to have an extension of time to complete the contract, to which the govt. assented. In Feb. 1831, Stephen F. AUSTIN and Samuel M. WILLIAMS made a contract to include the above colony, together with parts of Austin's old colony. Under this contract it appears the surveying and locating of the "eleven league grants" was sanctioned, and titles amounting to 194½ leagues within what is now known as Milam and Robertson counties, were issued by the Alcalde of San Felipe de Austin, during the year 1833. Instructions were given to Wm. H. STEELE, as commissioner, on 22nd May, 1834, in which it seems he was authorized to give possession to certain individuals as colonists, introduced by the Nashville company previous to the 15th Oct., 1833, & it will further appear that the commissioner had no right to grant titles to colonists for the same land which had previously been given to Mexicans by authority from AUSTIN & WILLIAMS, nor to issue titles for any land within the Nashville colony subsequent to 18th May, 1835. Reference to the titles issued by W. H. STEELE, now on file in this office, shows that the 292 being the whole number, 159 bear a date previous to 18th May, 1835, 133 subsequent to that period, & one on that date; 4 are dated after the closing of the Land offices. In addition, 23 leagues have been granted to T. Jefferson CHAMBERS, to wit:

5 leagues situated on the east side of the Brazos; 2 on the west side, including the Waco village; 1 at the mouth of Little River, it being a part of 11 leagues given to him for services rendered to the govt. as surveyor-general; 16 leagues were granted CHAMBERS for services rendered by him as Supreme Judge of TX, being part of 30 leagues claimed by him for said services---9 leagues of the above 30 are located in Robertson co.; 6 leagues have been located & titled under the agency of the said CHAMBERS, by virtue of a special grant to Jose Manuel BANKS, as a settler in 1830; 2 of the above 6 are situated on the east side of the Brazos, for which a pre-emption was given by Thos. BARNETT in Nov. 1830; 5 leagues have also been obtained by said CHAMBERS, as attorney for Alejandro DE LA GARZA, two of which are situated on the east side of the Brazos, near the San Antonio Road, located by consent of of Empresario ROBERTSON & title issued by Ira LEWIS, special commissioner, bearing date 20th Oct. 1834. The origin of this title is a grant to said GARZA by the governor of the state, dated 15th Feb. 1831. Within the territory of Robertson's colony are 2 other large grants---one of 11 leagues in favor of G. A. NIXON, situated on the Brazos opposite Nashville, including a part of a grant to Francisco HURD and A. MANCHACA, title for which issued by W. H. STEELE in Feb. 1835. The other 11 league grant is under the name of Manuel RABAGO on the west side of the Brazos, some 50 miles above the falls. For this title there was no corresponding original on file. John P. BORDEN, Commissioner, General Land Office.

Another report by BORDEN dated Dec. 12th, at Austin, states "it appears that eleven leagues of land were granted to Benjamin Robert MILAM, on 29th Dec. 1829, by the state of Coahuila and Texas. I also find that a survey for said MILAM, is referred to in a certified copy of title to Jose Antonio Valdez y GONZALES, as forming a part of the boundary of said GONZALEZ's land, which is the only evidence of MILAM's claim on file within my recollection."

Maj. HOWARD with a small party of soldiers recently overtook a party of 5 Comanches who have conducted depredations at the Ranches near Bexar, and during a small skirmish succeeded in killing 2 or 3 of them. Maj. HOWARD received a wound to his side from an arrow.

Wednesday, February 10, 1841

Property in the city of Houston belonging to W. W. HAYWOOD to be sold at courthouse door in Houston on 1st Tuesday in March, to satisfy a judgement by the Spring Term of the District Ct. of Harris Co. in favor of Andrew J. YATES.

Public Sale of Lands. By virtue of an order by Hon. Wyly MARTIN, Judge of Probate, Fort Bend co., bearing the date Jan. 27, 1841, we will sell at the courthouse door in Richmond at public auction, on the 1st Tuesday in March, next, the following described property belonging to the late firm of HANDY & LUSK, or so much thereof as will be sufficient to pay the debts of said firm. Terms: a credit of 12 months, with bond & approved security & a mortgage on the property until final payment: One quarter league adjoining J. V. MORTON; a quarter league on Peach Creek, near Bastrop; a league & 80 acres adjoining the late Mr. ALLEN, Austin co.,; 1 quarter league & 30 acres near La Grange; 200 acres on Cedar lake & Caney; 700 acres & improvements on New Year's creek; one quarter league on Big creek, Fort Bend co.; and a half league on Rio Blanco (originially granted to Benj. WILLIAMS).

Also to be sold at same time "Lands Belonging to HANDY & LUSK, not yet patented, viz:" One third league in Goliad co. (Abel SEGMAN's headright); 1280 acres in Goliad co. (Abel SEGMAN's bounty land); 3139 acres located land (James POWELL's headright) in Goliad co.; one third of a league (J. BRIDGEMAN's headright) in Goliad co.; 494 acres (John McDERMOTT's headright land) in Goliad co.; one third league (John P. PAYNE's headright) in Goliad co.; one half league & half labor (James T. KILGORE's bounty land) in Goliad co.; 320 acres (Michael

GREEN's bounty land) in Goliad co.; 320 acres (D. McGARY's bounty land) in Goliad co.; 320 acres (Robert STEVENSON's bounty land), Goliad co.; four certificates of 640 acres each, not located yet, to wit: 760 acres on Navasota, part of C. O. EDWARDS' headright; 320 acres on Pin Oak creek, bounty land; 2 lots in Galveston Island; Nos. 22,293 in Section 4; four lots in Matagorda; 1 lot in city of Bastrop; interest in the plan of Powhatan, town lots in Richmond, buildings, &c. Further particulars will be made known on day of the sale. Richmond, Fort Bend county, 27th Jan. 1841. Wm. LUSK, Surviving partner of Handy & Lusk; Mills M. BATTLE, Admr. of succession of R. E. HANDY.

County of Harris, Ophelia WILSON vs. David WILSON, Libel for Divorce. "In this case, it appearing to the satisfaction of the court that the said David WILSON is beyond the limits of the Republic & beyond the jurisdiction of this court, on motion of B. F. FRANKLIN, counsel for libelant, it is ordered that the said David WILSON be cited to appear at the next term of the District Ct., to be holden in the city of Houston, County of Harris, on the sxith Monday after the fourth Monday of March, A.D. 1841, and plead, answer or demur to the allegations contained in said libel. . .December 14th, A.D. 1841." James S. HOLMAN, District Clerk.

Sale of Lots in the Town of Swartout. A public sale of Lots in said Town will take place at Swartout on Monday the 1st of March. The town is situated on the Trinity river, 100 miles by land and 250 miles by water above Galveston Bay; the river is navigable by the Bay steamers up to this point at least 9 months out of the year; a steam mill is about to be built here, and we have two good houses of entertainment & several mercantile establishments. For further particulars, inquire of John S. SYDNOR, Galveston, or D. H. FITCH, Star Office, Houston. January 15th, 1841.

Thos. BAILEY named admr. of the est. of John MACKE, late of Harris co., decd.

Geo. W. POWELL named as admr. of est. of Elmira POWELL, decd.

Administrator's sale set for 1st Tuesday of March at courthouse door in Houston, all of the personal property belonging to the est. of John MACKE, decd., consisting of: one silver watch, 1 whip saw, a pair of cart wheels & the following real estate: lots 9, 10 & 11 in Block 24, city of Houston, with improvements; lots 5 & 6, Block 37, Frost Town; and lots 11 & 12, Frost Town. Thomas BAILEY, Admr. of J. MACKE, decd.

Notice. On or about the 11th Nov. 1840, I received from Sam. PATTERSON of Washington co., a bond for title to 640 acres of land, situated in Harrison co., on the Caddo trail and a few miles from Caddo lake, being a portion of the league granted to Hiram BLOSSOM. The above bond has been lost. This is to notify all persons that the same has been cancelled by said PATTERSON upon his becoming purchaser of said tract of land. A liberal reward will be given to the finder of the aforementioned bond, upon application to Sam. PATTERSON, Washington. James M. CRABTREE, Washington, Jan. 30th.

Property belonging to Robert WALKER in the city of Houston to be sold at sheriff's sale, Harris County, on 1st Tuesday in March, to satisfy a judgement obtained at the fall term of the District ct., in favor of Isaac CADE, admr. of C. B. FANOGR, decd., terms cash. Samuel G. POWELL, Sheriff, Harris Co.

Sale. By virtue of a special trust reposed in me by order of the Probate court of Austin co., I will expose to public Auction in the town of Houston on the first Tuesday in Feb. next, all that tract of land in Harris co., on the east side of Buffalo Bayou, adjoining the town of Houston, belonging to the succ. of Martin ALLEN, decd., containing 200 acres, more or less. James SUMERVILLE, Com. to sell, San Felipe, Dec. 1840.

Runaway Taken Up. Committed to the Jail of Fort Bend co., by Edward WALKER, a Negro man named JOE, 5'11" high, very black, says he belongs to a Mr. SPAN, of Brazoria co. The owner is requested to come forward, claim his property & pay all charges. John V. MORTON, Sheriff, Fort Bend co., Richmond, 11th Jan. 1841.

George R. MERCER named admr. of est. of John HODGSON, decd., by the December Term of Probate Court, Montgomery Co. Huntsville, Jan. 2nd.

E. S. CASLOR named admr. of the est. of Latt HUSTON, decd., Probate Ct., Washington Co.

Notice. Will be sold on the 1st Tuesday in March next, at Washington Court House, by order of the Probate Ct. of said county, all right, title & interest which Thos. GAY, late of said county, decd., had in two tracts of land situated on the Trinity river, in Montgomery Co., purchased by the said GAY and Edward BAILY, of the succession of Wm. H. CUMMINGS; one tract containing two thirds of a league, & the other tract consisting of a half league. Conditions, cash. Horatio CHRISMAN, Executor; Elma GAY, Executrix of Thos. GAY, decd. Washington, 14th Jan. 1841.

Petition for partition of John FOSTER Est. filed at December Term of Probate Ct., Fort Bend Co. Lists John FOSTER, Randolph FOSTER & John C. FOSTER as "heirs and distributees of the succession." It also notes that there are other "heirs residing beyond the limits of this Republic and one other heir, of the age of majority, residing within this Republic." Judge orders a notice of this petition to be published for 3 months, after which time he will act upon the petition. Dated at Richmond on 21st December 1840.

Wednesday, February 17, 1841

Congress approves an Act to incorporate the Harrisburg Rail Road Company. Board of directors consisting of: James B. MILLER & A. HODGE of Fort Bend co.; James LOVE & N. F. WILLIAMS, Galveston co.; Stephen RICHARDSON, DeWitt Clinton HARRIS, A. BRISCOE and Robert WILSON. Act approved by Congress on Jan. 9th, 1841.

Captions of the Acts and Joint Resolutions, passed by the Fifth Congress of the Republic of Texas. An act to change the name of Lydia Ann CHAPMAN to Mary Ann CHAPMAN WILSON; an act for the relief of John G. TOD; Jt. Res. for relief of Wm. AIKEN, Wm. DONOHO, Thos. D. ALLEN, L. B.

OUTLAW, Wm. H. MOSHER, David THOMAS, Margaret WRIGHT, Mrs. Sarah Ann WALKER, John R. WALSH, J. B. RANSOM, Maria Jesus De GARCIA, Ellen CASH, Wm. GAMBLE, Martha STANBACK, Henry H. EVANS, Wm. H. ALSBURY, Washington SEBEN, Jeremiah STRODE, A. McCLURE, A. C. HINTON & other persons, George W. DAVIS, Lorenzo de ZAVALA, Wm. SCURLOCK, Norman WOODS, Richard J. WOODS, B. M. CARR and Hail BARTON, James RILEY, M. B. SHACKLEFORD and W. ISSACS, E. R. KELLET, Edward WEST, Wm. K. SIMPSON, Rowland T. BRYARLY, Andrew Jackson DAVIS, Seth SHELDEN, Thomas ROSS, Thomas B. HULING, Mary MOFFIT, Cyrus CAMPBELL, M. HUNT and J. P. HENDERSON, W. S. WALLACE, Geo. OATMEAL, D. C. NEIL, Thomas Woods WARD, Arthur MERRILL, James W. SMITH, Louise GERDING and Frederick HOBEN, John WALL (decd.), George WHEELRIGHT, Bridgit FADDEN and Mary ARROUGH, Capt. James PENNOVER, John THOMAS & James PATTERSON, and the heirs of John HIBBITS. Other acts include: resolutions for the relief of David RUSK, Sheriff, Nacogdoches co.; R. J. CALDER, Sheriff, Brazoria co.; Wm. F. WILSON, Sheriff, Galveston co.; Jacob SNIVELY, Postmaster General; the heirs of G. W. SPICER, decd.; Joint Resolution for the relief of Mrs. Sarah ALWAY, admx. of Robt. ALWAY, decd.; Joint Res. for relief of Freeman GEORGE, late assessor for Colorado co.; an act declaring "Sam Houston DUCKWORTH, legit mate"; Joint Res. authorizing Ben. F. SMITH to adopt Ben. Josiah SMITH, son of Josiah C. SMITH; Joint Res. requiring the General Land Office to issue patents to Samuel JONES and Hugh McKEAN.

The troops under the command of Major CLENDENIN, which were lately stationed at the Waco village, have returned to the forts on Little River and the Falls of the Brazos. They remained at the Waco Village a month, but erected no block house.

We learn that Gen. MOREHOUSE, with about 100 volunteers, and a small party of Tonkewas, was at the Falls of the Brazos on the 1st inst. and was intending to march against the Indian village that his spies discovered high upon the water, said to be a "Towaccanies" & Waco village.

Wednesday, February 24, 1841

Congress on Jan. 19th, 1841, adopts a Joint Act to charter the Houston and Austin Turnpike Company, with the following individuals named as Commissioners: At Houston, John D. ANDREWS, G. ROBINSON and Wm. CARPER; at Galveston, Gail BORDEN Jr. and John S. SYDNOR; at San Felipe, John H. MONEY and N. H. MUNGER; at La Grange, Joseph SHAW & Dr. Wm. B. MERIWETHER; at Bastrop Theodore BISSELL, N. BOYCE and G. NOESSEL; and at Austin, Dr. Moses JOHNSON & Wm. S. THOMPSON.

Colorado Co., District Court. Heirs & Representatives at Law of Wm. ROBINSON, decd. vs. Martha BOSTICK, alias BRONSON, & Zeno BRONSON, Her Husband. Whereas in this case, at the fall term of said court, it was ordered that writs of seire facias be issued against the heirs at law of Martha BOSTICK, decd.; this is to notify the heirs, Mary & Ellen SHAW, and Betsy POGUE, who are absentees, to appear before said court on the 1st day of next term thereof, to begin on the fifth Monday after the fourth Monday in march next, then & there to answer, together with the other heirs of Martha BOSTICK, unto Susan Ann STEVESON, Robert STEVENSON, Sophenia E. ROBINSON, who sues by her guardian Robert STEVENSON, and Levi J. ROBINSON, who sues by his guardian W. H. SECREST; heirs at law of W. ROBINSON, decd, who sue for title to land, as set forth in their petition, now on file in my office. H. Montgomery SALLEE, District Clerk, Colorado County.

Notice. Taken up by the subscriber on 14th October last, a Negro boy about 20 years old, about 5'6" or 7" high, dark complexion, heavy built, down look, has a scar on his breast, calls his name BOB; says he belongs to Stephen LOW, now living on Trinity river, recently from Madison co., Mississippi. Said he was stolen by the Indians. The owner is requested to come forwad, claim his property, and take him away; or he will be dealt with according to the law. Skeaugh WALKER, Robertson co., TX, Feb. 13th.

Notice summons the heirs &c. of the vacant succession of Alexander DUNLAP, decd. to attend next term of the District court of Victoria Co. on third Monday of April, 1841, and answer the petition of Wm. P. MILLER or judgement will be taken against the effects belonging to the vacant possession of Alex. DUNLAP, decd. Order issued 30th Oct. 1840. John McCRABB, District Clerk, Victoria County.

Wednesday, March 3, 1841

An Act for Relief of Certain Free Persons of Color. "Be it enacted by the Senate & House of Representatives of the Republic of Texas, in Congress assembled, that Wm. ASHWORTH, Abner ASHWORTH, David ASHWORTH, Aaron ASHWORTH, Elisha THOMAS, and all free persons of color, together with their families who were residing in TX on the day of the declaration of independence, are, and shall be exempt from the operation & provisions of an Act of Congress, entitled "An Act concerning Free Persons of Color," approved 5th Feb. 1840, and that the above named persons, with their families, are hereby granted permission to remain in this republic; anything in the laws of the country notwithstanding." Approved 12th December 1840.

Advertisement. The New Orleans & Galveston Steam Packet "Neptune," Capt. Wm. ROLLINS, will sail from Galveston the 1st and 17th of every month, and from New Orleans on the 10th & 25th. This vessel is 750 tons burthen, 3 years old, 220 feet in length, has an engine of 250 horse power, and is considered the most magnificent ever built in the United States. McKINNEY, WILLIAMS & Co., Agents. Feb. 23.

Negroes & Plantation For Rent. For the present year, on Galveston bay, near to & adjoining New Washington, 100 acres of excellent Land under fence and ready for cultivation to which 100 or more acres can be easily added, together with 6 first rate field hands, homes, outhouses and farming utensils of all kinds, &c. Possession given immediately. For terms, apply to: D. H. FITCH, Star Office, Feb. 6.

Probate Notice. The undersigned having been appointed admr's. on the est. of Wm. NEWELL, decd., at the August Term, 1840, of the Probate court for the northern division of Liberty co., this is to notify all those with claims against said est. to present them within the time prescribed by law. Arthur GARNER, Alfred BRITTON, Admr's., Swartout, Dec. 31, 1840.

Probate Court, Fort Bend co., appoints Susan SUMMERS as admrx. on the est. of Wm. W. SUMMERS (decd.). Persons with claims should present them to her or her attorney and agent, C. V. BASSETT, Esq. at Richmond, Feb. 22, 1841.

County of Fort Bend. District Court, Fall Term, 1840. Washington H. SECREST vs. Samuel McILHANY, Action to Try Titles to Land. As it appears that the deft., Samuel McILHANY resides beyond the jurisdiction of this Republic, the Court orders publication of this notice, notifying the deft. of this suit and ordering him to appear in court in Richmond on the 2nd Monday after the 4th Monday in March next to show cause why the prayer of the petitioner should not be granted. Dated at Richmond on 23rd Feb. 1841. T. H. McMAHAN, Clerk pro tem, Dist. Ct.

Notice. The public is hereby notified not to purchase from Martin RUMPFF or from any person claiming under him, the following articles: a small wagon, a Mexican pony, 9 hogs, & 3 most excellent dogs---as the claim in which RUMPFF sets up to them is null & void, & was obtained through fraud. T. SCHRODER, March 3d.

To all Persons Interested. Before the hon. Chief Justice of Harris co., take notice, that on Saturday the 20th March next, I will apply for a discharge in bankruptcy. Samuel W. METCALFE, Houston, Feb. 24th. (R. C. CAMPBELL, Atty. for petitioner).

Before the Chief Justice of Harris co., on the 24th March, I will apply for a discharge in bankruptcy. John PALMES, March 3d.

Notice. All persons are hereby forewarned not to trade for a note of hand for $1,116, given by John D. HARVEY and Wm. KEASE, payable to Nicholas LAMPRORD or bearer, dated some time in Jan. 1841. Said note has been stolen & will not be paid unless by legal compulsion. John BROWNLEE, Feb. 24th.

Regular Packets. The "New York," Capt. J. T. WRIGHT, will leave Galveston on the 7th inst. The "Savannah," Capt. Jno. WADE, will leave Galveston on the 8th and 22nd, and New Orleans on the 1st and 15th of every month until further notice. McKINNEY, WILLIAMS & Co., Galveston.

Wednesday, March 10, 1841

Congress on Jan. 22nd approves an Act to organize part of Liberty co. for judicial & other purposes. Described as "all that portion of the county of Liberty comprised in the following limits, to wit: commencing on the west side of the Neches river, where the Houston county line strikes said river; thence west along said line of Houston, to the line of the northern division of Liberty county, thence south along said line 25 miles; thence due south to Village creek; thence down said creek with the line of Jefferson county, to the Neches river; thence up said creek to the place of beginning." The same is hereby constituted a separate district or territory for Judicial purposes. The Act also authorizes Robert BARCLAY, Josiah WHEAT, Addison SAPP and Benj. BERK to select two sites to be proposed to the people as the site for district and inferior courts.

Congress on Jan. 30th approves an Act to incorporate the Texas Trading, Mining & Immigrating Company with the following as directors: George W. BONNELL, Alex. McDONALD, John C. WATROUS, and Edwin MOREHOUSE of Texas, and Jonathon IKIN and Arthur IKIN of London.

Lost or Mislaid. Sometime in Oct. 1840, in or near the town of Bastrop, an original instrument of writing, of which the following is in substance a copy: Hired & received of Thomas P. HAWKINS, two negro men, TITUS & CHARLES, for which I promise to pay at the rate of $180 per annum, by the 1st day of Oct. 1840. Dated about 1st Feb. 1840 (Signed) A. KINCHELOE. As the above instrument is not negotiable and has never been signed by me to any person, the public is forwarned from trading for it, & finder is requested to forward it to the Bastrop post-

master. Thomas P. HAWKINS, 1st March 1841.
Henry F. FISHER, Notary Public, will execute Deeds, Powers of Attorney, &c., &c.; translate from the French, German & Spanish languages into English, or vice versa, & transact all business appertaining to his office at the shortest notice. Office at KESLER's Arcade, No. 4, upstairs, March 10 advertisement date.

Wednesday, March 17, 1841

An Act of Congress approved Dec. 24th, 1840, legalizes all official acts carried out by Samuel TODD, county clerk of Shelby Co., and his deputies.
An Act approved by Congress on February 4th, 1840, establishes and incorporates the "Austin Lyceum" with the following individuals as "body politic & corporate," all of Travis Co.: P. A. MORRIS, Thomas Gales FORSTER, Geo. W. BONNELL, Geo. K. TEULON, Richard F. BRENHAM, George J. DURHAM, James M. OGDEN, Henry J. JEWETT & M. P. WOODHOUSE.
An Act of Congress approved on Jan. 30th, authorizes Hancock SMITH, Samuel McCALL, Capt. COPELAND, William FITZGIBBONS, and James TIPPET as commissioners to select a site for the seat of justice of Harrison County.
An Act of Congress approved on February 5th, incorporates the "Galveston and Virginia Point Bridge Company" with the following men named as commissioners: James LOVE, Gail BORDEN Jr., Peter J. MENARD, Samuel M. WILLIAMS, Pizarra EDMONDS, John S. SYDNOR and E. L. UFFORD. All meetings to be held in Galveston.
An Act of Congress approved on Jan. 15th, authorizes Mariah L. ROUSSEAU to change her name to Mariah ROUSSEAU SMITH; and Margaret Ann ROUSSEAU to change hers to Margaret ROUSSEAU SMITH; the same act also declares the said Mariah & Margaret to be heirs at law of James SMITH of Bastrop co., and capable of inheriting his property in the same manner as if they were heirs by descent.
Killed by an Elephant. The united menageries of Messrs. HUMPHREY & LYNES, was to have

opened today, but as the elephant of Mr. LYNES killed a man yesterday, who travelled with the menagerie, and then broke off, the opening of the exhibition has been delayed until tomorrow. The name of the decd. was CRUMB, the keeper of Mr. HUMPHREY's elephant. Yesterday afternoon, when about 6 miles from this city, up the coast on the opposite side of the river, and as both elephants were walking along together, the deceased addressed some words to the elephant of which he had charge, when LYNES' elepant made a lunge of his trunk at him, then knocked him and his horse down. He then took him up, put him in his mouth & crushed him to death. The animal then escaped in the vicinity of Algiers.---From the New Orleans *Advertiser*.

    Information wanted on Samuel STRINGFELLOW, who emigrated to TX in 1827. He addressed a letter in 1833 to his friends, stating that he had joined an expedition against the Comanche Indians, since which time no tidings have been had of him. Any person who can give the undersigned information on said STRINGFELLOW will confer a favor on his relatives in Georgia; for more information: J. L. NICKELSON, *Telegraph* office.

    By virtue of an order from the hon. Probate Court of Harris co., I will sell on April 6th, at the residence of J. W. MOODY, decd., on Spring Creek, all the perishable property from said estate, consisting of 1 silver watch, one 4-horse wagon, a lot of cows & calves, & young cattle, household & kitchen furniture. M. B. GOHEEN, Admr. of the est. of J. W. MOODY, decd.

    Administrators Sale. To be sold at public outcry on 1st Tuesday in April next, at the city of Houston, all the personal property belonging to the est. of Albert FREDERICK, decd., consisting of 1 headright of 640 acres, one bounty claim of 1280 acres, 1 donation claim of 640 acres, and some personal property. Antone SCHOUTEN, Admr. of Dr. A. FREDERICK, decd.

    Sale of House & Lot at Auction. On Saturday the 17th April, will be sold at public auction, lot No. 10 in block 41, city of Houston, with the dwelling house & improvements thereon, to

satisfy & pay certain notes made by Wm. H. BURGESS to H. SANDERSON, atty. of A. J. YATES, dated Nov. 7, 1838, in accordance with the conditions of a contract of sale made between the parties on same date, & recorded in the clerk's office of Harris co.
Enoch KING and Jane HOWARD granted letters of adm. in the est. of C. B. HOWARD, decd., on 22nd Feb. 1841 by probate court of Washington County. Centre Hill, March 17.

Wednesday, March 24, 1841

Citizens of Crockett, Houston county, sign a letter dated March 5th to Col. James CARR, requesting publication of an address he delivered there on the 2nd inst. during a celebration of "our national independence." Names listed are: Steward A. MILLER, Geo. M. CASEY, J. A. BEESON, Eli MEAD, F. B. FAULKNER, Geo. ALDRICH, J. B. WALKER, Richard DUGLASS, John G. CALISON, J. P. BURNETT, H. W. BEESON, Cyrus H. RANDOLPH, J. H. STRAIN, L. E. DOWNES, J. H. ANDERSON, Wm. J. B. FORD, George LESTER M.D., J. P. SAUNDERS, Wm. REEVES, Jos. RICE, Elijah GOSSETT, John V. D. GOSSETT.

Wednesday, March 31, 1841

Congress approves an Act on Jan. 30th to incorporate the "Gaudalupe College" with the following to serve on the board of trustees: C. S. BROWN, Robert CARR, Thos. J. PILGRIM, Richard VEAL, Eli MITCHELL, D. B. FRIAR, Joseph O. CLEMENTS, B. D. McCLURE, Benjamin McCULLOCH, John L. WITTER, the County Judge of Gonzales Co. and the mayor of the City of Gonzales, in which the college is located.
Ranaway from my farm near Groce's Retreat, two boys, one by the name of MILES & the other by the name of BOB. MILES is aged about twenty years, with a large scar on his nose & is about 5'5" and a light black. BOB is about 16 or 17 years, very black, thick lips, and is known on the road as a wagoner. He is very free spoken. Reward of $25, par money. Caleb WALLIS.

A Card. The subscriber, late proprietor of the Tremont House at Galveston, has taken that well known stand, the Houston House, in this place. His Table and Bar will at all times be furnished with the best the market can afford. There is also a Stable and attentive Ostlers, attached to the House. Nathaniel NORWOOD.

Richmond Hotel. The subscriber having taken the hotel recently occupied by Messrs. HUGHES & LEVERING, informs the public that his table will be furnished with the best the country can afford. His stables will be attended by good & careful ostlers, & no pains spared to give general satisfaction. John HUGHES, March 21.

Wednesday, April 7, 1841

Congress on Jan. 30th adopts an Act to Incorporate Trinity College at Alabama in Houston co., with the following named as trustees: Geo. PRUITT, G. W. GRANT, Jacob ALLBRIGHT, Colin ALDRICK, Elisha CLAPP, John MORTHANS, Isaac PARKER, Ralph NELSON, Elijah GOSSETT, Wm. CLARK and James CARR.

The Hon. James WEBB, late Attorney General of the Republic, left the seat of govt. on the 31st ult., for Galveston, where he will sail in one of the govt. vessels to Vera Cruz, on his way to Mexico City as our fully accredited Envoy Extraordinary & Minister Plenipotentiary, to ascertain the results of the negotiations by the British Minister &, if possible, obtain the acknowledgement of our independence.

Capt. LEWIS & his 150 volunteers are rapidly collecting & will dash into the wild region of our red foe in a few days. He has the right sort of boys---real buckskin, hawkeyed fellows, who would as soon sleep in a creek as not.

Appointments. Mr. D. ROSS, supt. of armory; Mr. SEEGER, supt. of the naval bureau; & G. W. SINKS, supt. of the Post Office Dept.

The Hon. J. T. CRAWFORD, formerly English Consul of Tampico, has been appointed charge d'affaires of the British govt. for this Republic. He previously visited this country in 1836 & won the favor of many.

We received some weeks ago a prospectus for the Southern Quarterly Review, to be published shortly at New Orleans & simultaneously in the other principalities of the U.S. & TX by Mr. D. Kimball WHITAKER.

Notice. Frederick RANKIN, admr. of the est. of Solomon BROWN, decd., will attend the next term of Probate court, Austin co., on last Monday in April to make a final settlement of said estate, "so that I may be released from the further administration of the same."

Notice. The partnership heretofore existing between J. W. WHITE & J. L. POOL, doing business under the firm of White & Pool, is this day dissolved by mutual consent. J. W. WHITE is authorized to settle the business of above named firm, April 7.

Isaac BUNKER appointed admr. of the est. of Isaac BUNKER, Jr. at the March Term of Probate Court for Colorado co. Columbus, 30th March.

Lost or Stolen. The bounty claims of 640 acres each, granted me by B. E. BEE for survey. No. 178, dated 8 Nov. 1837; the other No. 3517, dated 13th May 1838. This is to notify that I have made diligent search for same & intend to seek duplicate copies. Thomas J. NICHOLS, Surveyor, Colorado, April 8.

Administrator's Sale for May 4th next, will be sold at court house door in Houston, Harris Co., by order of probate court, at public outcry, all the right, title and interest of Mary HAMILTON, decd., in & to a tract of land lying on the east side of White Oak Bayou, in this City, containing 6 acres more or less, with all of the improvements, consisting of a log house & cabin. Geo. FISHER, Admr. Houston, April 2.

Card. M. Heiskell SHYROCK, Attorney at Law, late of San Augustine co., TX, will attend to all business entrusted to him in the city of Houston. Office at the Auction Store of SHRYCOCK, JENKINS & Co., Main st., Houston, March 31st.

$50 Reward. Strayed or stolen from the home of the subscriber in City of Houston, a large American bay horse. Enquire at the office of the Telegraph. R. HUDSON, March 30th.

Wednesday, April 14, 1841

Indian Battle. The recent Indian engagement on the Perdinales found the Indians routed on the first brush. Only 18 minute men left Austin on March 29th, under Capt. DOLSON in pursuit of a small body of the enemy, who were reported to have left a trail near that place. After 30 hours of hard riding, they overtook the Indians (they were Towacconies, 34 in number), who immediately opened fire with their rifles. The gallant volunteers fired & charged, led by the determined Capt. DOLSON, who remained in the melee even after receiving severe wounds in the breast and thigh. The natives fled, taking the wounded with them. Seven Indians were slain. No other volunteers were injured, and we are happy to learn that DOLSON is in a fair way of recovery.

Alexander BLAIR named admr. of the est. of John BRISCOE, decd. at the Jan. Term of Probate Court of Austin Co. Notice dated April 6th at San Felipe.

Sale. I will as a commissioner appointed by the probate ct. of Austin co. sell for the purpose of closing the succession of Martin ALLEN, decd., & effecting final partition of the same, offer for sale at the courthouse door in Houston, Harris co., all right, title & interest in and to a tract of land containing 200 acres more or less, situate on the east side of Buffalo Bayou, nearly opposite the town of Harrisburg; on the 1st Tuesday of May next, on a credit of 12 months & approved security. James SOMERVELL, Commr., San Felipe, April 11th.

Regular Packet. The stanch & fast running Steamboat "Patrick Henry," J. R. HORD, Master, will ply during the present spring & summer, between Houston & Galveston, & stopping at all the intermediate landings, & carrying freight & passengers at the lowest rates.

Andrew G. HOLLAND---If he will make his residence known to the subscriber, will receive information greatly to his advantage. Any other person giving information relative to his whereabouts, will confer a lasting benefit on a poor old man & his helpless children. Address the subscriber at Houston. J. Davis GRAHAM, April 14.

Administrator's sale. By order of Probate Court, Harris Co., I will offer at public auction on May 14th, all the effects real & personal, belonging to the est. of Geo. W. HANCHETT, decd. G. S. BARNEYCASTLE, Admr., Houston, April 12.

Wednesday, April 21, 1841

Highly Important!! At a late hour last night, the "Patrick Henry" arrived with news by the steamer "New York." Gen. HARRISON is no more!! He died on 4th April, at 30 minutes before 1 o'clock A. M.

At a Meeting of the members of the Bar, on 19th April, at the office of B. F. TANKERSLY, R. C. CAMPBELL was called to the chair & F. R. LUBBOCK, District Clerk, appointed Secretary. The Bar adopts a resolution lamenting the death of their brother, Col. Wm. F. GRAY. As a tribute to the decd., the member of the Bar will wear the usual badge of mourning for 30 days, & send a copy of their resolution to the family of the deceased.

$500 reward will be given for the apprehension & delivery to the house of Thos. MARTIN, in Niaugua co., Mo., of a certain Alfred GIVENS who on the 16th inst., in town of Buffalo of said county, shot a young man by the name of Solomon JONES through his body. It is doubtful if he will recover. Said GIVENS is about 25 years old; 5'10" or 11"; stout built; rather fleshy with light hair, fair complexion; has a pleasant appearance when first spoken to; his right arm is broken, which prevents the face use of the same. He is supposedly riding a bay mare, 15½ or 16 hands high, blaze face, 2 white feet. We will give the above reward for his delivery as described. Given under our hands this 19th Feb. 1841. Lemuel JONES, James E. HOLLIS, J. W. SMITH.

Notice. The Chief Justice of Harris co., on 1st April 1841, committed to us the estate of

John PALMA, a bankrupt; therefore, after 3 and 6 months, at the sale days of the sheriff, our sales will be had. If claims against the trust estate be not presented to me within 1 year next after the above date, they will be barred. Geo. GAZLEY, J. S. STANSBURY, and Algernon P. THOMPSON, Trustees. April 21.

Thos. M. BAGBY named admr. of est. of Ewing H. CROCKETT, decd., April 21.

Massillon FARLEY & Henry J. JEWETT, Attys. & Counsellors at Law, City of Austin, offices on Congress Ave., opposite the Capitol.

Caroline JOHNSON named admrx. of the est. of AMES JOHNSON, decd., by the Probate Court of Montgomery Co. at the March term of court.

Wednesday, April 28, 1841

Spy Skirmish. A company of spies were lately sent out from Austin to look after the movements of the Mexicans upon the frontier. They came in collision with a marauding party of the enemy near Laredo. Paper publishes a report of Capt. John C. HAYS, leader of the little band, to the Hon. Branch T. ARCHER, Secretary of War, dated San Antonio, 14th April 1841. HAYS says he joined his forces with those of Capt. Antonio PAREZ, and after leaving Bexar, received reports of two bands of Mexican marauders robbing traders returning from Bexar. The two bands were led by AGATON, with 30 men, and Ignacio GARCIA, with 25 men. They enemy reached Laredo one day ahead of HAYS and his force. A battle ensued the next day, 10 miles this side of Laredo, in which 1 of GARCIA's men was killed and another wounded. The enemy later entrenched themselves on a slight eminence & another fight ensued, in which 25 of the enemy were killed, 19 wounded, and others fled. HAYS' forces, consisting of 13 Americans & 12 Mexicans, none of whom were injured. One of the prisoners, Eduardo FLORES, told us that Gen. ARISTA is at Matamoros or in that vicinity.

Married in the town of Victoria, on the 15th ult., James MOODY, Esq. and Miss Susan LINN, both of that place.

New Orleans & Galveston Steam Packet "Neptune," Capt. Wm. ROLLINS, will sail from Galveston on the 1st and 17th, & from New Orleans on the 10th and 25th of each month. The vessel is 750 tons burthen, 3 years old, 220 feet in length, has an engine of 220 horse power, & is considered the most magnificent ever built in the United States. McKINNEY, WILLIAMS & Co., Agents, Galveston; Geo. ALLEN & Co, Agents, Houston.

A Card. Mr. ANDREWS, portrait and minature painter, is leaving TX for a few months & expresses his gratitude to his fellow citizens for their liberal patronage. He has recently moved to the apartments over ANDREWS & SWAIN's Office, formerly the President's House, and having collected a considerable number of pictures that he has painted during the past three years residence in this City, he respectfully invites the ladies & gentlemen of Houston and its vicinity to call & view them, before they are returned to their respective owners. All persons indebted to Mr. ANDREWS are requested to make payment to Mr. SWAIN, who will act as his agent during this temporary absence.

Wednesday, May 5, 1841

M. DE SALIGNY, the French minister, intends spending the summer at Galveston. He will reach this city in a few days, in company with the American Minister, Mr. FLOOD, who will also remain some time at the Island. Mr. FLOOD, we are informed, sent in his resignation upon the inauguration of the lamented Gen. HARRISON. The son of David CROCKETT has been spoken of as the possible successor to FLOOD.

Probate sale scheduled for 1st Tuesday in June before the courthouse door in San Felipe, for 1 labor of land belonging to the succession of Robert ELDER, decd., said land situated on the east side of the Brazos, about 3 miles from San Felipe. By an order of Probate Court of Austin Co., at April Term. John W. HALL, Admr.

Public sale of lots in town of Liberty on 1st June next. Terms--notes with approved security (and mortgage on property), payble in 12 months, purchasers paying the expenses of conveyance. W. C. ABBOTT, Mayor, Liberty, Apr. 24.

Lost. A certificate of headright, No. 30, issued by the board of land commissioners of Liberty co., on 18th Jan., 1838, to William H. LOGAN, admr. of estate of Benj. FREEMAN, decd., for one third a league of land. Notice is given that I shall seek a duplicate copy in three months, unless intelligence is received otherwise. Joseph FREEMAN, legal representative, Liberty, April 24th.

Lost. A certificate for 320 acres, second class of headrights, issued by the board of Land Commissioners for county of Brazoria, to Alanson BAILEY, about Dec. 1838. Notice is hereby given that a duplicate will be sought in 3 months. Alanson BAILEY, Montgomery, Apr. 30.

A runaway Negro was committed to the Jail in Liberty co., about the 1st of Nov., who calls himself CHARLES, and says he belongs to Capt. OFFORD, formerly of Nacogdoches. Said negro is about 18, 5 feet high, spare built, very black. The owner is requested to come forward & claim his propety. B. W. HARDIN, Sheriff, Liberty county, May 5th.

Austin City Hotel & Travis House. The Subscriber having taken the Austin City Hotel, lately occupied by S. R. MILLER, and the Travis House, formerly kept by FESSENDEN & DENMAN, and also the House occupied by Messrs. WEBB & BEATY ---each of which, taken separately, is large & roomy, & collectively offers 25 large & commodious rooms, several of which will be kept for families; The Travis House, located on Congress avenue will be maintained as a Bar, & will be supplied with the choicest liquors from New Orleans. Charges will be not only reasonable, but low. Good stables, corn, fodder, hay and attentive Ostlers. G. B. HARRISON, Austin, April 28th.

Tin, Sheet, Iron & Copper Manufactory. Mr. A. McGOWEN carries on the above business in all its varieties, in the City of Houston, Nos. 8 & 9, Long Row, where he will fill all orders from the country on the shortest notice. His materials are all imported from England and of the best quality. He has now on hand a large assortment of wares from his own manufactory, which country merchants will do well to examine before they purchase abroad.

Wednesday, May 12, 1841

Probate Sale. By virtue of an order of the Probate Court, Austin co., made at the April term, I will sell on the 1st Tuesday in June next, before the courthouse door in the town of San Felipe, on a credit of 12 months, one labor of land belonging to the succession of Robert ELDER, decd., & situated on the east side of the Brazos, about 3 miles from the said town of San Felipe. John W. HALL, Admr., April 26.

Military Discharge & Draft Lost. This is to give notice that I have lost a soldier's discharge for 3 months service, No. 4018; also, a draft for $24.00, No. 5022, and shall apply for duplicates within 3 months time. Geo. BONDIES.

Wednesday, May 19, 1841

Noessel's Hotel at Bastrop. The subscriber respectfully informs the public that he has moved out of the Milam House & located 1 block above his former stand, where he has erected under his own name a house of public entertainment. His table will be supplied with the very choicest the market can offer. He has a hunter constantly employed to furnish him with wild game of every kind & a garden that will furnish his table with vegetables year round. He is conversant in English, Spanish, French & German and hope he make everyone feel at home. All charges will be moderate. G. NOESSEL, Bastrop, May 18th.

Ann L. FROST named admrx. of the estate of James C. FROST, decd., on 12th April 1841, by the Probate Ct., Montgomery co., May 13.

G. W. HALLMARK and Geo. W. HALLMARk named as admr's of the est. of John HALLMARK, decd., at the March term of Probate Court, Houston co., May 1st, 1841.

Lost or stolen sometime in September last, the headright claim of the undersigned, issued to him by the board of land commissioners of Harris co., for 640 acres, dated August 1838, No. 867. This is to give notice that I will seek a duplicate after 60 days time. John MORRISON, May 19th.

To all persons interested---Before the hon. chief justice of the county of Harris, Republic of TX, take notice, that on Friday, the 5th day of June next, I will apply for discharge in bankruptcy. Andrew BREWSTER, Houston, May 14.

For sale, a tract of land lying on Buffalo bayou, about 1 mile below Houston, nearly opposite the steam saw mill. On the above tract is about one half live oak & pine wood, the balance prairie land. It is also well calculated for a gardener. For particulars apply to: F. R. TAYLOR, May 18th.

Wednesday, May 26, 1841

From the <u>Morning Star</u>: Volunteers for Mexico. As fine a set of fellows as ever put foot in stirrup have formed themselves into a corps in this city, under the title of "Houston Pioneers," and this day they set off, with high hopes and buoyant hearts for the far-famed city of Santa Fe. Radcliffe HUDSON was elected as Captain; Thos, S. LUBBOCK, 1st Lieut. G. W. KENDALL, the editor of the N.O. <u>Picayune</u> will have representatives in this enterprise. The following correspondence was handed to us by the Chairman, & we are gratified in giving it an insertion:

G. W. KENDALL, Esq. Sir: The undersigned committee of the "Houston Pioneers," in compliance with a resolution of the company, take great pleasure in soliciting your company as a guest, & beg leave to assure you that an acceptance of this invitation will afford them great pleasure. A. Jackson DAVIS, Chairman of Comm.; Thos. S. LUBBOCK, R. HUDSON, G. L. GORDEN, and E. M. HAINES.

Letter follows, dated May 21st at Houston, in which Geo. Wilkins KENDALL regrets to say

he cannot give a direct answer until he has met with Cols. COOK & McLEOD in Austin.
Important Suit. A verdict has been given in favor of Sterling C. ROBERTSON, at the late term of the District Court, Austin, in the suit instituted by him against the Republic for his premium lands [Robertson's Colony]. An appeal has been taken by the Republic to the Supreme Court.
Colony for Texas. On the evenings of the 15th & 22nd of April last, a very large number of the citizens of Philadelphia, convened to consider the subject of forming a colony of emigrants to TX in the fall of the present year. Mr. John LOUD was called to the chair of the meeting, and Mr. James BROWN to the station of secretary. The Rev. W. B. McCALL & Mr. LOUD addressed the meeting & made many interesting remarks relative to the soil, climate & productions of the country. At the end of the meeting on the 22nd, a committee of seven was appointed to draft a Constitution & by-laws for the colony.
Died in this city on the 16th inst., Mrs. Sarah Ann Minerva CARPER, aged 19, consort of Dr. William M. CARPER.
Republic of TX, County of Harris. To I. N. MORELAND, Chief Justice of the county foresaid, and judge of probates: Your Petitioner would most respectfully represent unto your honor, that one Patrick McGEE, a citizen of your co., died some time in the fall of 1838. Said decd. was indebted to your petitioner as well as to sundry other citizens, & there has been no application for the administration of the decd., & the decd. having left property ample to satisfy his just debts, he therefore prays your honor to grant letters of administration to settle upsaid estate, & for all further & necessary relief, your petitioner will ever pray, &c. John SHAW. Sworn to & subscribed before me this 24th day of May 1841. James M. McGEE, Justice of the Peace, Harris co.
NOTICE---The chief justice of Fort Bend co., on 16th April 1841, committed to us the est. of Ezekiel GEORGE, a bankrupt; therefore, after 3,

and 6 months, at the sale days of the sheriff, our sale will be had; any claims presented after one year from this date will be barred from the trust estate. John H. HERNDON, Robert S. HERNDON, John V. MORTON, Trustees.

Wednesday, June 2, 1841

Alexander McGUFFEY has been appointed Texian Consul at Cincinnati, replacing B. DRAKE, decd.

Notice. Harriet CADE, Admrx., and Robert C. CAMPBELL have been granted letters of administration in the est. of said decd. at the April Term of Probate Court of Harris Co. [This notice does not list the name of the decd.] Advertisement is dated Houston, June 2.

Take Notice, that on the 26th day of June, I shall apply to the chief justice of Harris co., for a discharge in bankruptcy. Constant K. HALL, June 2 advertisement date.

Accommodation for Travellers. This Subscriber, Mail Contractor from Austin to Houston, has at considerable expense, established a line of Coaches for the benefit of the public between the two places. His carriages are neat and substantial, & teams are good and strong. A limited number of passengers only will be taken. M. F. JONES, June 2nd advertisement.

Capt. Mark LEWIS's Expedition. A company of about 180 volunteers & 10 or 12 Indian spies went out with Capt. LEWIS some 6 weeks since in pursuit of Comanches, & for sport generally; & a determination was expressed at the time to remian out during the whole summer, unless a respectable body of Indians could be found sooner. We learn by a gentleman lately from Austin, that a few of these men have returned to that city & report that the company, when they left, was at the head waters of the San Saba, that they had spent the whole time following trails of the Comanches, but could not overtake them.

Slaves Wanted. A number of good field hands wanted to hire or purchase for which a liberal price will be given. Enquire of F. GASSIOT.

Wednesday, June 9, 1841

Missouri Traders to Santa Fe. A late issue of the Missouri Republican states that the annual caravans that plod a weary way to reach this famous depot have already started. This dispatch from Independence, dated May 10th, was also published: "On yesterday, the few last wagons bound for Santa Fe left our village. . . In the company just started the most extensive traders were Messrs. HOUCK, McKNIGHT, MUZERVA, and MARTIN---there were many other individuals who attached themselves for self-protection to the company, & are going to Mexico. Some for pleasure, some for health, and others for the collection of curiosities and botanical plants. Today the Oregon & California Companies rendezvous at Sapling Grove to make arrangements for their departure. . .Mr. FITZPATRICK is expected to be elected Captain & take superintendence of both parties for some distance. A company is to arrive in a few days from Santa Fe. Messrs. GIDDINGS, from Fayette, McGUFFIN, GRAVIS & some Spanish gentlemen are in their number. They are bringing along with them 22 wagons and a large number of mules. . ."

KINNEY & AUBREY's Rancho. A gentleman just from the west states that KINNEY & AUBREY are doing an excellent business with the Mexican traders. It seems that KINNEY has lately been on to visit General ARISTA & has received some assurances from him that he will not be harmed.

Charlotte SECREST has been named admrx. of the est. of Mitchell SECREST by the probate ct. of the northern division of Liberty co., on the 28th December 1840. Swartout, May 24th.

Notice is hereby given that I have filed a final account of my administration on the est. of James HAUCK, decd., & will at the June term of the probate court, apply for a discharge from the same. H. R. ALLEN, June 3.

Administrator's Sale, by order of probate ct. of Harris co., will be held at courthouse door in Houston, on Saturday, 26th inst., to the highest bidder, at public auction, one certificate for 1/3 league of land, belonging to the est. of John FLANDERS, late of said county. Terms on the day. Allen VINCE, Admr., June 5.

Wednesday, June 23, 1841

Newspaper features an article from the <u>Edinburgh Review</u>, in which "The Rise, Progress, and Prospects of the Republic of Texas" by William KENNEDY, Esq. (London, 1841) is reviewed. The article states that "Mr. KENNEDY was one of the gentlemen who accompanied the late Lord DURHAM to Canada in 1838. After the abrupt termination of his Lordship's mission, he took the opportunity of visiting the United States; and was induced to extend his journey to Texas, by invitations from some of the leading persons of the new Republic. His residence there lasted several month. . ."

Another Indian Horde Routed. For about four years the citizens of Red River & Fannin co's. have been occasionally molested by a horde of Indians who have hitherto eluded all pursuit. General TORRENT of Bowie co., lately raised a company of about 70 men, & after traversing a large portion of the country west of the Cross Timber, about 400 miles from the settlements & finding no signs of the enemy, concluded to return. On the afternoon of the 24th ult., they discovered an Indian trail & following it, came directly upon an enemy village about 3 PM; they instantly rushed into it, driving the savages before them, who fled towards another village a few rods from the first. Gen. TORRENT and his gallant band charged through this in the same manner & through another, when they came upon a large town, where the savages had collected in such numbers that they did not consider it prudent to attack. They accordingly fell back, gathering up all the "plunder" they could find, consisting of some 35 horses, a few cattle, a large quantity of powder & lead, buffalo robes, saddles &c., which they sold in the settlements for $2000. Fifteen of the enemy were killed & a large number wounded. In the charge, Capt. J. B. DENTON was killed gallantly urging his steed into a thicket filled with savages. Capt. STOUT was slightly wounded.

The attack on this village took place at the same time that Capt. CHANDLER attacked another village on Richland Creek. The savages will doubtless imagine that combined movements have been made to attack them on every side.

It is with feelings of deepest sorrow that we announce the death of Mr. A. J. DAVIS, who was lately killed at Austin by the accidental discharge of a gun in his own hand, just as he was on the eve of departure with the Pioneers for Santa Fe. The Milam Guards met on the 21st an adopted a resolution of respect to his memory, as drafted by Lieut. SMITH, Corp. LUBBOCK, and Privates NICHOLS and CULP.

Notice. James COOPER, Esq. of Independence, is my authorized agent during my absence from the Republic. Jabez DEANE, Houston, June 21.

Goliad Out Lots For Sale. On Thursday, 9th Sept. next, will be offered for sale a portion of the Out Lots belonging to the town of Goliad & a liberal credit will be given to actual settlers. Goliad is a four league town & the lots will be laid off in 80-acre labors. Issac W. JOHNSON, Mayor; David R. SCOTT, Clerk, Corporation Goliad. 14th June 1841.

Houston Pioneers. This gallant company arrived at Austin on the 3rd inst. in fine health & spirits. The Austin *Gazette* says that "they marched through town to the camping ground about two miles distant, without stopping at any of the groceries to refresh themselves."

Santa Fe Pioneers. A stand of colors was presented to the Santa Fe Pioneers on Monday, the 7th inst., by Miss CAZNEAU. An introductory speech was made by Dr. BRANNUM, in behalf of the fair donor & responded to by Col. McLEOD who returned thanks in the name of the regiment & pledged the faith of the officers under his command that the trust should be preserved inviolate. An address was afterward made by the Hon. B. T. ARCHER, which was received with loud plaudits by the assembled soldiery.

Notice. Messrs. ANDREWS & SWAIN of Houston, are my only authorized attornies in fact, from this date, & I hereby revoke all powers heretofore given by me to any other persons. Jas. S.

WHITE, Admr. of the est. of W. H. WHITE, decd.
All persons indebted to the est. of Hiram TAYLOR, late of Fort Bend co., decd., will make immediate settlement with the undersigned, or C. N. BASSET, Richmond. Those having claims, will present them duly authenticated within the time prescribed by law. D. W. C. HARRIS, Admr.

Alabama House. The subscriber respectfully notifies the public that he has lately fitted up this spacious hotel, situated on the Court house square, corner of Congress & Fannin st's. & is prepared to accommodate boarders or travelers in the best possible manner. His rooms will be found neat & clean, and the Hotel to be connected with a convenient bathing room. Chas. MERLIN, Houston, June 15.

Wednesday, June 16, 1841

Bexar. By a letter fro Victoria of the 9th inst., we learn that the trade of Bexar continues dull. The market at that place is overstocked. It is reported that Col. SEGUIN has engaged the services of about 70 volunteers to join the standard of Gen. ARISTA, in the event of a quarrel with the Mexican government.

President LAMAR has appointed Samuel ROBERTS as Acting Secretary of State. It has been customary for the chief clerk of that department to perform the duties of that office during the absence of the Secretary of State.

Wednesday, June 30, 1841

Col. S. W. JORDAN, the hero of Saltillo, & well known as a leader of the Texians who fought last autumn in conjunction with the Federalists of the Rio Grande, died in New Orleans on the 22nd inst. It was supposed that he was sent to that City by ARISTA, to raise men & munitions to forward the operations of that General, with whom he had agreed upon terms of friendship.

Notice. At the next session of the Probate ct. of Harris co., I will apply to settle up & close the administration on the est. of Geo. B.

WILSON, decd., according to the accounts as now furnished & on file in this clerk's office. James O. SPILLMAN, Admr., June 30.

If Mr. Percy TYRWHITT, who came to Texas and brought letters of introduction to Barnard E. BEE, Esq., some 12 months ago, will communicate with me, he will hear of something to his advantage, or should any person know anything about the said Mr. TYRWHITT, I shall feel obliged by their giving me information. Charles POWER, June 30.

Wednesday, July 7, 1841

Census of San Augustine County --- According to the returns of Col. H. MABBIT, the Assessor of San Augustine co., the population of that county consists of whites over the age of 10 years, 1,012; under age 10, 555; slaves, 1200; total, 2,767.

M. GARCIA & H. MEUGENS, have this day formed a co-partnership under the name of M. Garcia & Co., for the purpose of transacting a General Commission business. M. GARCIA & Co., Strand, Galveston, July 7.

Probate Sale. By order of the probate court for Austin co., I will offer for sale to the highest bidder, before the court house door in Fort Bend co., on the 1st Tuesday in August next, all the right, title & interest of the succession of Martin ALLEN, decd., in and to 2 labors of land, being part of league number five, on the San Bernard, and sold for the purpose of effecting a partion & final settlement of said succession of Martin ALLEN. Terms of sale, 12 months credit. James SOMERVILLE, Special Commissioner.

Notice. On or about the 25th or 26th day of Sept., 1840, I, C. C. DYER, Admr. on the succ. of Wm. STAFFORD, gave Chisbey MADAMS of Shelby co., a power of attorney as agent for me in the counties of Shelby & Harrison; the said power of attorney is this day revoked, the 3rd day of July 1841. C. C. DYER, Admr. on the succ. of William STAFFORD.

James P. COLLINS of Shelby co., revokes and annuls all powers-of-attorney given by him to any persons, with the exception of one granted to Wm. PIERPONT, who is my only agent in Texas.

Notice. Public sale of lots in the town of Greenville, Spring Creek county, will commence on Monday, August 9th, at 10 a.m. & continue on day to day basis under the superintendence of the board of commissioners. "The town of Greenville is situated about one quarter of a mile south of Spring Creek, on a high, dry & elevated ridge. . .Travellers can be seen on the two great roads leading from the city of Houston to Washington & Austin, and to Red River by Montgomery, Cincinnati & Nacogdoches." Commissioners listed as: Abram ROBERTS, Wm. PIERPONT, James COOPER, Geo. W. CROPPER, Isaac DECKER and Arc'd. SMITH. Spring Creek County, July 3rd.

The Governor of Missouri proclaims that Wm. ROGERS, Wm. H. VERRY, Wm. JOHNSON, John CALLAGHAN, Thos. FINN, M. BODEN, Wm. MYERS and James FUGATE, after committing murder on Wm. BALLARD, one of the overseers of the penitentiary, have made their escape. A reward of $500 is offered for their apprehension.

Wednesday, July 14, 1841

A rumor has reached us that a party of several hundred Indians has lately been discovered on the Brazos. Col. COOKE, with the Santa Fe volunteers, has gone to attack it. He was to be joined by Capt. CHANDLER, with 200 men from Milam & Robertson counties. It is said these Indians have 1000 or 1500 acres of corn under cultivation & have about 60 Negroes.---From the Morning Star.

A Gang of Horse Thieves Discovered. A few weeks since the citizens of Clarksville, in Red River co., were alarmed by the cries of a man who came rushing into the village shouting Indians! Indians! Indians! Murder, murder! As this fellow had long been suspected as a horse thief, the citizens very coolly arrested him. Soon another man came in with the same alarm & was likewise arrested. Soon a party of citizens repaired to the spot where the Indians had committed such deeds & were alarmed to find a man named BROOKS weltering in his own blood; he had but lately left the village with his negro & a yoke of oxen & some articles for his farm. These had evidently been stolen. Suspicion fell on the two arrested men, one of whom was named FAULKNER. Both men denied it. The citizens tied FAULKNER to a black jack & after giving him a few hundred lashes, obtained the confession that the murderers were a gang that had long resided at the house of one named FURGURSON & had long been the rendevous point of these robbers. It is believed they were also associated with another gang in Arkansas. The individuals belonging to this gang are FAULKNER and his son Green, YOUNG, BOON, CRAIG, ROBERTSON, HILL, the last three of which were engaged in the murder. The citizens, after obtaining this confession, despatched a company to FAULKNER's house to secure the remainder of the gang. They had not returned to Clarksville when our informant left.

We regret to state that Gen. R. G. DUNLAP, formerly Secy. of Treasury of TX, died at New Orleans on the 24th of June.

Died in San Felipe, Austin co., TX, on the 6th of July, Mrs. Elizabeth C. McCREARY, late of Gallatin, Sumner co., TN, the wife of Dr. James K. McCREARY, in the 21st year of her age.

Cow Thieves. A party of 24 Cow Thieves, under the command of a Capt. OWENSBY, were lately surprised by Col. RUMAIRAS, commander of a Mexican regiment, and all killed. Another small party of cow thieves were captured on the Rio Colorado & all hung. Mr. HOPKINS, who lately made his escape from Matamoros, was overtaken & shot. It is said that troops of ARISTA killed about 47 cow thieves within a few weeks.

Administrators Notice. All persons indebted to or having claims against the est's. of Jacob KARCHER or Frederick PELTZER, will present them to the undersigned for adjustment. David P. PENN, Admr., Harris co., July 14th.

The following individuals are agents for the *Telegraph*: Joseph GRIGSBY, Beaumont, Jefferson co.; Geo. A. PATILLO, Patillo's & Mount Holland Post Office, Jefferson co.; R. C. DOOM, Jasper & Zavala, Jasper co.; Judge W. HART, Nacogdoches, Nacogdoches Co.; Col. J. H. BERRY, San Augustine, San Augustine co.; Edward SMITH, Elysium Fields, Panola co.; Judge J. M. HANSFORD, Wood's P.O., Panola co.; John H. WALKER, Port Caddo, Panola co.; Jacob McFARLIN, Epperson's Ferry, Bowie co.; R. H. GRAHAM, Clarksville, Red River co.; Col. J. H. JOHNSON, Jonesborough, Red River co.; Judge A. J. FOWLER, Paris, Lamar co.; and J. H. GEDDINGS, Washington.

Wednesday, July 21, 1841

The Hon. Benj. Fort SMITH testifies before a Committee of Congress: Question: "Were you with the army of TX commanded by Gen. Sam HOUSTON, on the Colorado, in March 1836, & what was your rank?" Answer: "I was with the army at Gonzales, & continued with it until August, 1836; and while the army was on the Colorado, I acted as Quarter-Master & Adjutant-General, in the absence of gentlemen who had been regularly appointed to these stations." Signed by Benj. Fort SMITH and notarized by James W. SMITH, Chief Justice, Travis co. on 24th Nov. 1840.

TX Congress adopts a bill to incorporate a company to be called the Franco Texienne Co. & recognizes J. P. H. BASTERICHE & P. F. de LASSAUIX as a body corporate. The company is authorized to introduce into the Republic 8,000 emigrants on or before 1st Jan. 1849. The said land is situated along the Rio Grande River, as follows: "A grant of 512,000 acres on the left bank of the Rio Grande, stretching from the San Antonio Road to the Presidio. . .upon which grant there shall be erected 3 military posts at the expense of the company; a grant of 192,000 acres on the river Nueces . . . a grant of 194,000 acres on the Rio Frio. . ." Numerous other grants described. This document does not include a date.

News from the West. We learn by a letter from Victoria, dated July 13th, that a party of Mexicans visited Corpus Christi lately and took

Mr. Phil DIMMIT, a Mr. SUTHERLAND, GRAHAM and some others with all the goods they had with them. They have been carried as prisoners to Matamoros. Messrs. AUBREY & KINNEY were not molested. It is currently reported that they claim protection under the Mexican government.

The steamer Savannah arrived at Galveston on the 13th inst., and among its passengers were the hon. Joseph EVE, Charge des Affairs from the U.S., and his lady.

Another Sign. Three Houston papers in succession have been discontinued at Galveston, within a few months, viz: the Courier, the Herald, and the People's Advocate. Lately a "Burnet" paper has started up in that place and has styled itself The Intelligencer. It is published by A. J. CODY & is evidently one of the best conducted periodicals in the Republic.

Administator's Notice. County of Milam. At its regular November term past the hon. Probate Court of the County aforesaid, appointed the undersigned admr. of the est. of Daniel McCOURT (decd.). Said McCOURT was a native of Temple, Patrick Co., Ireland (near Antrim), & was last a citizen of KY, one of the United States of the North. He was a traveller in this country, and died at my house in October. Alexander THOMSON, Nashville, July 1st.

Notice by Thos. BAILY, Admr. of the est. of John MACKE, late of Harris co., announces that property belonging to the estate, both real and personal, will be sold at public auction on 1st Tuesday in Sept., at the Court House door in Houston.

Wednesday, July 28, 1841

A number of counterfeiters of doublons have lately been arrested in New Orleans. Their names are: J. B. WILSON, Henry MILLER & Edward BLUMENTAL.

The remains of General [William Henry] HARRISON, were interred on his farm at North Bend, on the 7th inst. The Picayune says: "The hearse was attended by 26 pall-bearers, and the largest train of military & citizens from Ohio,

Kentucky & Indiana ever assembled in Cincinnati formed the procession. During the day the artillery of the city fired salutes, and every thing appropriate was done to give a solemn effect to the ceremonies."

Died at the residence of his brother, Shelby SMITH, in Montgomery co., on the 10th inst., Maj. Ben. Fort SMITH. Major SMITH was an old Texian; he emigrated to this country in 1833 & was one of that glorious band who on the plains of San Jacinto, achieved the liberty of Texas.

Republic of TX, County of Fannin. Wm. H. ANDERSON vs. Martha ANDERSON, petition for divorce. It appearing to the satisfaction of the Court that the said Martha ANDERSON resides beyond the limits of the Republic, it is therefore ordered that she be cited to appear at the next term of the district court to be holden in Fannin co., at court house thereof in the town of Warren, on the 8th Monday after the 1st Monday in Sept. 1841, & plead, answer or demur to the allegations contained in the original petition. A true extract from the Fannin County District Court Journal of April 26th, 1841. Test: Jefferson C. PARRISH, Clerk of the District Court, Fannin County.

Wednesday, August 4, 1841

Accident. We learn from the Austin Gazette, that Dr. CHALMERS & lady, while out riding on a pleasure excursion, were thrown from a bridge about 20 feet, upon the rocky bed of a creek below. Both were seriously hurt but are now recovering.

From the <u>Morning Star</u>: We have learned that Mr. P. DIMMIT & his 4 companions were arrested by the order of Gen. ARISTA, upon the charge that they were spies. It seems letters to this effect were sent to ARISTA by some settlers of the west. Capt. SANCHES, who captured them, according to the statement of Mr. R. CARILO (who was at Corpus Christi when the capture was made) treated all the prisoners with the greatest politeness.

The four Negroes, MADISON, WARWICK, SEWARD &

BROWN, convicted of the late murders in St. Louis, were hanged on the 9th inst., on an island in the Mississippi opposite that city.

Lost Subscribers. Some wiseacres have been lately circulating a report that we have lost upwards of 1,000 subscribers, owing to our opposing the election of Gen. HOUSTON. We have lost only 9 subscribers owing to this cause, viz: Thomas F. McKINNEY, Dr. HUNTER, Thomas TRIMMER, A. McFADDEN, J. BARTLETT, T. J. RUCKER, James WALKER, J. D. BURKS, and H. HIGGINS.

We learn by the Redlander that an affray occurred in that place [San Augustine] on the 16th ult., in which a Mr. PHIFER was severly wounded by a Mr. George MARTIN with a bowie knife. We had begun to indulge the hope that the villainous reign of the bowie knife in that place had ceased.

A meeting of the merchants of the city of Houston was held in the Counting House of J. M. ROBINSON on Monday, August 2nd. Merchants in attendance were: SHEPHERD & CRAWFORD, Wm. M. RICE, RANDALL & ROFF, ENNIS & KIMBALL, Joshua BURR, BAKER & JENKINS, BACHELDER & BAILEY, Geo. GAZLEY, J. SHACKELFORD & Co., Geo. ALLEN & Co., HEDENBERG, STANSBURY & Co., J. M. ROBINSON, F. GASSIOTT, and A. S. RUTHVEN. At the meeting, it was agreed to recognize Maj. T. S. HOWARD of Washington co., for bringing in the first 20 bales of cotton from this year's growth to our market in July. The article refers to HOWARD as a former resident of Mississippi.

Notice. Letters of administration have been granted to Mary Ann PRATT, of this city, on the est. of Albert PRATT, late of Harris county, July 31st.

Notice. A Camp Meeting will be held for Brazos Circuit, 8 miles above Columbia, on the road leading to the Mound and near the six mile Point, to commence on Thursday before the 3rd Sabbath in October, 1841. Ministers generally, are earnestly invited to attend. A. P. MANLEY, Preacher in Charge, Aug. 4.

Take Notice. I hereby announce that I absolutely revoke the power of attorney previouly granted to Jeremiah McCLOSKY, represented to be a citizen of Jefferson co., on the grounds that said power was obtained fraudulently and for fraudulent purposes. Benjamin PAGE, Harris county, July 23rd.

Lost or Mislaid. A discharge transferred to me by Wm. P. STICKNEY for his military services six months in Capt. Wm. GARRETT's Company of volunteers in 1839. Notice is hereby given that I will apply to the proper authorities for payment of same, as it was regularly transferred to the undersigned for a valuable consideration. John MORRISON, Houston, Aug. 4.

Lost of stolen some time in September last, the headright claim of the undersigned, issued to him by the board of land commissioners of Harris co. for 640 acres, dated Aug. 1838, No. 867. I will apply for a duplicate copy after 60 days time. John MORRISON, Houston, Aug. 4.

Sale. By virtue of an order of the Probate Ct. for Austin co., I will offer for sale to the highest bidder at the Courthouse door in Brazoria on the 1st Tuesday in Sept. next, on a credit of 12 months, 600 acres of land, taken off from the northwest corner of league number 43, on Cedar Lake in Brazoria co., and granted to Oliver JONES by the Mexican govt. Said property has been decreed to Lucretia ROACH, & is sold by me as guardian for the purpose of paying off all demands & handing the property over to the said Lucretia. Ira FISHER, Guardian &c. Brazoria, July 27th.

Administrators sale set for 1st Tuesday of Sept., at Courthouse door in San Felipe on the following Negroes: CURTIS, aged about 50; SARAH, aged about 25; MELISSA, aged about 15; TOM, aged about 10 years. For the purpose of paying the debts of the succession of Joseph THOMPSON, decd., said Negroes will be sold, as the property of said succession, or a credit of 12 months. Wiley HARRISON, Admr., San Felipe, July 27th.

From the Morning Star: The barque Marion from London, arrived at Galveston on Thursday last, with about 30 emigrants. We learn that these emigrants are well supplied with the necessaries of life.

Wednesday, August 11, 1841

News from the West. The late examination of Messrs. KINNEY & AUBREY, which resulted in their acquittal, elicited the important facts that the arrest of Mr. DIMMIT & his associates was not authorized by the Mexican govt. and was unknown to Gen. ARISTA. In consequence of this fact, Gen. LAMAR has ordered the Mexican traders lately captured to be released & their property restored. Messrs. SEGUIN & VAN NESS are in ARISTA's camp & it is expected they will make arrangements for the captives' release.

Montgomery Co., Libel for Divorce, Nancy B. IRON vs. Wm. H. IRON, District Court, Spring Term 1841. "It appearing to the Court that the deft. is not a resident of this Republic, it is ordered by the Court that publication . . . be made for 6 weeks of the pendency of said Libel, requiring the deft. to appear at the next term of this Court, to be holden in Montgomery Co., on the 7th Monday after the first Monday in Sept. next, to plead, answer or demur to the said Libel, or this will be tried ex parte. A true & full copy fo the minutes of Court, 30th July, A.D. 1841."

Valuable Real Estate for Sale. By virtue of an order of the hon. Probate ct. of Harris co., I will offer the following property for sale on the 1st Tuesday in Sept. at the Courthouse door in Houston, said property belonging to the est. of John W. MOODY, decd.: 392 acres, part of the headright of Wm. DUNN; 392 acres, part of the headright of Wm. MURRY; 160 acres, part of the headright of Joshua HUDSON; 1476 acres, being the headright of John CHRISTOPHER; 160 acres, part of the headright of Rich. HAGGARD; 160 acres, part of the headright of James FLETCHER; and 160 acres, part of the headright of Lawrence LONG. Said land, being regularly surveyed & situated on the waters of Spring Creek, in said Harris co. (now the county of Spring Creek), sold for the benefit of the succ. of said John W. MOODY, decd. Michael R. GOHEEN, Admr., August 7.

Information Wanted. My brother Thos. PEACE, a land surveyor, left England early last spring for Cincinnati. He left the latter place about one year since for St. Louis. I am anxious to gain information of his present residence and shall remain in Cincinnati in hopes of hearing from or meeting with him. Francis PEACE, August 11th.

Affidavit of Wm. THOMPSON, Victoria Co., in which he discusses the capture of DIMMIT & his party: "Wm. THOMPSON, of Corpus Christi Bay, in the county of San Patricio, maketh oath and saith, that he and James C. BOYD have been in the employment of Philip DIMMIT since May last, assisting him to erect a mercantile establishment on the Bay of Corpus Christi, about 15 miles below AUBREY & KINNEY's rancho, that there were also residing there Stephen W. FARO and a Mr. GRAHAM, that on the 4th inst. deponent was sent by Capt. DIMMIT to the Pass to purchase lumber from on board a vessel there, & on his return about 2 P.M. observed a number of Mexicans at their place, whom deponent supposed to be traders, but on landing was immediately seized & taken prisoner by them and removed a short distance inland, where he found DIMMIT, FARO & GRAHAM, also prisoners. Deponent further saith that the Mexican force consisted of 15 cavalry soldiers under the command of Capt. SANCHEZ, aid-de-camp to Gen. AMPUIDA, in command at Matamoros, together with Blas FALCON & Lieut. CHIPITA, well known as AUBREY & KINNEY's spy, travelling agent or courier. . ." This affidavit contains additional information on the incident. There is also a similar affidavit by James GOURLEY of Lamar, Refugio co., that supports the allegations of THOMPSON; & also there is an affidavit of J. E. L. SOLOMON, who was at the rancho when the DIMMIT party was captured. SOLOMON contends that KINNEY was not involved in the incident & was very upset by the arrests.

Administrators sale set for 7th Sept. at Zavala's Point, near Lynchburg, on one labor of land belonging to the succ. of Lorenzo de ZAVALA, decd. In addition to the land, there will be offered for sale 1 negro or griffe man slave named TOM, about 19 years old; also 13 head of cattle, 1 American horse, & some other property belonging to the succession. Terms of sale--- 12 months credit for notes satisfactorily endorsed & bearing special mortgage on said property until final payment. L. de ZAVALA, Admr., August 7th.

Wednesday, August 18, 1841

New Steamboats. A writer in the <u>Redlander</u> states that Mr. POMEROY, partner of P. F. KIMBALL, Esq. of Red river, has gone to Cincinnati to build a boat expressly for the Sabine trade. It is expected out this fall.
Col. Wm. ARNOLD has declined being a candidate to represent Nacogdoches county.

Wednesday, August 25, 1841

The newspaper publishes affidavits from Wm. H. CHESTER of Matagorda, Henry REDMOND of Victoria, and Hon. James WRIGHT of Victoria, dated Aug. 2, in which they know Mr. Wm. P. AUBREY & Mr. H. L. KINNEY to be upright individuals and that they have confined themselves to a "peaceable trade" with Mexico. Judge A. HUTCHINSON, 4th Judicial Dist., holds hearing in Austin on same date. As neither Wm. THOMPSON or any other person came forth to testify against AUBREY and KINNEY, the Judge releases them. (Both men came forward voluntarily on 31st. ult. to refute charges that they were participating in illegal operations with Mexico.)

Wednesday, September 1, 1841

On the 17th July, a party of 25 Comanches made a pass at attacking Fort Kingsboro, but were unable to intimidate the 10 or 12 men defending that place. The fort is situated on the east fork of the Trinity, some 50 miles above Fort Houston. It consists of four log cabins surrounded by pickets enclosing about three-quarters of an acre. These pickets are formed of poles only a few inches in diameter & 10 feet long. In this frail tenement a garrison of 10 to 12 men have bid defiance to the whole Indian force of that section.

From the <u>Morning Star</u>: Mr. McKEEVER or Mr. McIVER, who was arrainged & tried for the murder of Joseph SHANKS at Crockett, at the late term of the criminal court, was himself murdered recently at Kingsboro, by a man named James BURRUS. BURRUS was afterward killed while attempting to escape, by a man named BURTON.

NEGRO JAKE---This Negro, who was arrested at Nacogdoches some weeks since, for an attempt to poison the family of his master, was arraigned before Judge TERRELL on 17th Aug. in Nacogdoches. The jury returned a verdict of guilty and he was sentenced to be hanged on 20th of the same month.

The <u>Redlander</u> says, "Dr. E. VARNEY, respectable & worthy citizen of Sabine co., was way laid & seized a few days since while travelling in the public road, & forcibly dragged out of the county by a band of kidnappers from Louisiana, taken to Natchitoches, severely ironed and incarcerated in the Parish Jail." VARNEY was charged with running mortgaged slaves to TX; he was acquitted of the charges.

The troops under Generals SMITH & TORRANT, engaged in the expedition against the Indians supposed to be concentrated at the villages on the West Fork of the Trinity, reached those villages on July 24th, but found them all deserted. They learned from a trader from Red River that the whole Indian force had removed some days previous to the encampment on the Brazos, which they are fortifying; the soldiers destroyed all of the corn which the Indians had planted & broke up the old encampment.

Taken up and lodged in the Jail of this co., by a Mr. SMITH, on Caney, on Aug. 11th, a negro boy who says his name is ISAAC, about 15 years of age, and says he belongs to Judge BUCKNER of Houston. The owner is requested to claim his property, pay all charges, and taken him away.

Signed: R. Y. CALDER, Sheriff, Brazoria Co., August 22nd, Brazoria.

Estray Notice. County of Liberty. Taken up by Richard DAWZEY & estrayed before Jas. KNIGHT (a Justice of the Peace of said co.), on Aug. 4th, 1841, a certain mare. Said mare is a bright sorrell, about 12 years old, 14 hands high, with white fore feet & small star in the forehead, branded on the right shoulder with a Mexican brand, & appraised by Wm. W. MOORE and James ROBESON at $75. Wm. B. DUNCAN, County Clerk, Liberty co., Aug. 22nd.

Lost some time in the Fall of 1839, the head right claim of the undersigned, issued to him by the board of Land Commissioners of Harris co., for 640 acres, dated in year 1838. This is to give notice that I have made a diligent search for the same & will seek a duplicate in 60 days. James C. ERWIN, Houston, Aug. 25th.

Lost or mislaid the following certificates: headright cert. no. 218, issued by the board of land commissioners for Harris co., to Daniel TURNEY, for 1/3 of a league. Also my headright No. 254, issued by same board for 640 acres of bounty land, certificate No. 1194, issued by Secy. of War to John MURRAY for 640 acres. Also, bounty land warrant No. 7073, issued by Secy. of War to David WHISLER for 1280 acres. All of which are duly deeded to me, & if not found within 60 days I shall apply to the proper tribunals for duplicates. Robt. C. INGRAHAM, Sept. 1st.

Wednesday, September 8, 1841

An arrival from Tampa Bay brings the intelligence that WILD CAT & those who were captured with him, are still in irons there, awaiting the coming in of his Seminole tribesmen. Col. WORTH, whose headquarters are in his saddle, was at Tampa a few days past, & has left in pursuit of the Indians.

We learn from a gentleman from the West that some 300 Mexicans under the scoundrel SAVRIEGO, are now on this side of the Rio Grande, & are threatening to attack the Rancho of KINNEY and

AUBREY. We understand Messrs. KINNEY & AUBREY have a good field piece, well-mounted, & about 25 or 30 young men at their rancho & will probably be able to keep the cowardly miscreants at bay. SAVRIEGO formerly resided at Goliad & sided with SANTA ANNA in the Revolution. It is supposed that he headed the party that lately committed the robberies in the Bexar vicinity.

We learn from the <u>Galveston Intelligencer</u> that the body of Mr. LUSK, late of the firm of HANDY & LUSK, has been found in the Navidad, & buried by friends who went in search of him. The causes of his death are not known.

We learn from the <u>Sentinel</u> that one of Gen. TARRANT's soldiers has arrived in Robertson co. & stated that Gen. T. had to retrace his steps, for want of a sufficient force and provisions, before reaching the large Indian encampment on the Upper Brazos. Gen. BURLESON has received orders to raise a large force of volunteers and destroy it.

RIOT IN SHELBY. It will be recollected that last year the citizens of Shelby refused to pay taxes & were ridiculed by their neighbors as "The Independent Republic of Shelby." It seems they have not yet returned to the wholesome control of the law. A few weeks since, a party of the settlers of the county, headed by a Capt. JACKSON, styling themselves regulators, proceeded to the houses of 2 men who had long been regarded as outlaws, & not finding them at home, burned down their houses. This proceeding exasperated a large number of the neighbors of the 2 men, and a party of about 100 rose in arms, styling themselves moderators, & went in pursuit of JACKSON. They found him with a man named LOWER & shot down both. JACKSON died on the spot, while LOWER died later of his wounds. This occurred 18 miles from Shelbyville, near LEGUE's ferry on the Sabine.--<u>Morning Star</u>.

I wish to rent or sell my Centre Hill property, consisting of a large Store house, a Tavern House, a large & commodious dwelling House, several Log Cabins, Stables & Outhouses, three Gardens, & my Plantation; consisting of 12,000 acres, on which there are several Mill privileges, on durable streams of water, and a number of living springs of pure water. David AYRES, Centre Hill, Sept. 1.

Wednesday, September 15, 1841

Indian Defeat. We learn from the Austin City Gazette that several Shawnee traders reported to settlers on the Red River that a large body of white men had fought the Indians assembled on the upper Brazos for 3 successive days & defeated them. It is presumed this is the Santa Fe force. Gen. TARRANT in his late expedition to the Brazos struck the trail of these troops. Believing the force was sufficient to defeat the Indians, he concluded to return home.

Article on Burnet Co., refers to Fort Houston as county seat and states that a temperance society was organized there in the summer of 1840 with P. O. LUMPKIN as president. In the infancy of the settlement, a Presbyterian minister took up residence and preached there. His name was Rev. P. FULLENWIDER, who has since made a location in Montgomery Co.

Wednesday, September 22, 1841

Presbyterian Church. We have noticed, with pleasure, that work on this church is rapidly progressing under the superintendence of Mr. James BAILEY. It will be completed in a few weeks and opened for religious worship. We also understand that the Rev. W. Y. ALLEN, who has lately been married in Tennessee, will return with his lady in October & resume his pastoral duties at that time.

Public meeting held at Jasper on a series of land frauds there. The names of the guilty party is omitted. List of committee members selected on Aug. 31, include: M. B. LEWIS, chairman, T. B. HULING, Edward GOOD, John H. SMITH, Thos. H. ESPY, Hardy PACE, Wm. McMAHON, Josiah STEVENSON, E. W. HARPER, Britton HALL, James THOMASON, S. H. COCHRAN, Andrew J. ISAACS and Caleb BURNESTON.

Died at Dorchester, Mass., on 13th of Aug., Mrs. Sarah AMORY, 69, mother of Nathaniel AMORY (Secretary of TX Legation to United States).

P. P. BORDEN, admr. of est. of Moses LAPHAM, decd., takes this method of notifying those who may have had lands located by said LAPHAM, or other business entrusted to him, to come forward within 3 months & present claims to the est. Richmond, Sept. 14th.

$50 Reward. Stolen from Chambersia (formerly Anahuac) on the night of the 13th inst., two negroes, LEVICE and her child ADALIA; the former about 25 years old, black, her fore teenth out & quick spoken. Her child is about aged 14 months, has blue eyes, & very white. I will give the above reward to any person who will deliver said negroes to me at Chambersia or in any jail so I can get them. Or I will give one of the negroes for the apprehension & custody of the thief & negroes. Said negroes formerly belonged to Eli WILLIAMS, of Houston, and are probably harbored in that neighborhood. H. H. DAVIS, Chambersia, Sept. 15th.

The negroes described above by H. H. DAVIS, I have this day taken as my property and will hold onto them inasmuch as I have never received any consideration for them. Eli WILLIAMS, Houston, Sept. 22nd.

Wednesday, September 29, 1841

Attack on the Mission of Refugio - We have received a letter dated Victoria, Sept. 20th, containing the starting intelligence that the mission of Refugio was attacked on the morning of the 18th inst., just before daybreak, by a party of Mexicans, & after a short skirmish in which a Mexican was killed, the few inhabitants remainign in that place surrendered. Captain NEIL, Mr. McFARLANE, & a Mr. TALLY, made their escape to Victoria. The rest of the citizens were made prisoners, the women excepting. The ones who could speak Spanish were released, the remainder were taken to Matamoros. The names of the captives are Henry RYALS, John FOX, Jas. FOX, Israel CAMFIELD, B. ANNIBAL, James and Wm.

ST. JOHN, a Mexican boy, & a Negro boy. Most of the citizens were absent from the town at the time, having gone down the bay a day or two previous. The Mexicans left about 8 a.m. with their prisoners for Matamoros. One of these, Mr. H. RYALS, was treated with great rudeness & the Mexicans said they should kill him a short distance from town. He had fought desperately in the commencement of the attack & was responsible for killing the one Mexican & wounding 3 others. The party of Mexicans was probably a part of the gang of SAVRIEGO, who are reputed robbers by both Mexicans and Texans. We may expect to learn further particulars in the next mail.

Died at Prairie Bluff, Galveston Bay, on the 20th inst., Sally ALLEN, consort of Rowland ALLEN, age 54 years, lately a resident of Baldwinsville, NY, from whence the family emigrated. Article refers to the home as "Allenwood."

Notice. A Camp Meeting will be holden on the Centenary Camp ground, four miles south of Independence, commencing on Oct. 14th. Ample preparations are being made to accommodate visitors, therefore, preachers & people generally are invited to attend. Jesse HORD, Washington City, Sept. 11th.

Thomas McCONNELL named admr. of estate of Thomas F. PONGE, late of Victoria, at August Term of Probate Court, Victoria Co.

Elijah BENNETT named admr. of est. of F. W. SMITH, decd., at the August Term of Probate Ct. of Victoria County.

Thos. N. HAYNES named admr. of est. of James TOLEY, decd., at August Term of Probate Ct., Victoria County.

Constable's Sale. By virtue of an execution issued by Ezekiel T. FULGUM, a justice of the peace for Menard co., & to me directed and delivered in favor of Wm. FURGUSON and against Zackeriah HOPSON, I will offer for sale a tract of land, including 320 acres, being the north half of the section on which said HOPSON now is living. Sale scheduled for 25th Sept. at Court House door in Natches. John T. BEAN, Constable, September 21.

Wednesday, October 6, 1841

San Felipe Hotel. Having purchased this hotel, formerly kept by T. KINGSBURY & now occupied by John BOLLINGER, I will take possession of the said hotel on 1st Nov. Wm. P. HUFF, San Felipe de Austin, Oct. 1st 1841.

Expedition Against the Indians. We understand that the expedition under the command of Gen. BURLESON will start from Nashville, TX, on or about Nov. 1st. A large number of volunteers from Washington co. are expected to join him at Nashville under the command of Capt. COOK; 1 or 2 small pieces of Ordinance will be sent with the troops to be used in demolishing the fortifications of the Indians. It is hoped that Gen. BURLESON will improve his opportunity by surprising the Indians that may follow on his return trail. It will be recollected that a party of Indians followed on the return trail of Col. MOORE last winter, after he destroyed the Comanche village & recaptured 70 horses below Austin. A similar party followed on the return trail of Col. NEILL's expedition up the Brazos in 1839 & committed several depredations on the frontier just after the troops were disbanded. A large party also followed on the return trail of Captains LEWIS & CHANDLER; and it is almost certain that a party will follow on the return trail of this expedition.

Wednesday, October 13, 1841

Consul General. A gentleman of this city, received by the last mail, a letter from Glasgow, containing the intelligence that Charles ELLIOT, of the Royal Navy, has been appointed Consul General of TX by the British government.

Administrator's Sale. Agreeable to an order from the hon. G. W. MILLS, probate judge of Liberty co., I shall proceed to sell on the 2nd Nov. next, in the town of Liberty, 934 acres of land, lying on Middle creek in Harris co.; also 3,333 acres of land, located in Montgomery co., on the San Jacinto river. Terms of sale on a 12 months credit according to law. Sterling N.

DOBIE, Admr. of Wm. DOBIE, decd. Liberty, 6th October 1841.

John H. HERNDON & John V. MORTON appointed as admr's of the est. of Wm. LUSK, decd., at the Sept. term of Probate Ct. for Fort Bend co. Richmond, Oct. 5th.

A Card. The undersigned takes this method of informing the public that he has opened a public house on the corner of Travis & Prairie sts., near the old capitol; and he pledges himself that his Table & Bar will be furnished at all times with the best the Market can afford & to accommodate those who patronize him with good lodging & make the House truly the "Traveller's Rest." J. H. F. OLTMANN, Houston, October 9th.

Sale. By virtue of an order of the Probate Ct. for Austin co., I will offer for sale to the highest bidder, at the court house door in the town of Brazoria, on the 1st Tuesday in Nov. next, on a credit of 12 months, 600 acres of land, taken off from the NW corner of league no. 43, on Cedar Lake, in Brazoria co., & originally granted to Oliver JONES, by the Mexican authorities. Said property has been decreed to Lucretia ROACH, as heir of Geo. MADDISON, decd. & is now sold by me as guardian of said Lucretia, for the purpose of paying off all demands & handing over the property to her. Ira FISHER, Guardian &c. Brazoria, Oct. 1st.

An interesting letter from Swartout, dated Oct. 5th, Northern Division of Liberty county, contains the information that "our worthy & enterprising fellow citizen Moses L. CHOATE, road overseer, has succeeded in opening a road 30 ft in widith from Swartout to the County line, & caused mile posts to be placed at the end of every mile through its whole route." Letter is signed "T. H. J."

Harris Co., Libel for divorce. Robert C. INGRANAM vs. Elizabeth BOWLES, his wife. It appearing to the satisfaction of the court that said Elizabeth BOWLES is residing outside the Republic of TX, notices are to be published in various newspapers requiring her to be present on the 10th Monday after the 1st Monday in September 1841, and show cause why said petition should not be granted. Dated in Houston on 22d July 1841. F. R. LUBBOCK, Clerk.

John V. MORTON named admr. of est. of Wm. LITTLE at August Term of Probate Ct., for Fort Bend co., TX.

Notice is hereby given that John GRAY obtained letters of adm. of the est. of Thomas L. LOOKE, decd., at the August Term 1840 of the probate ct. of Victoria co. All persons are therefore required to exhibit claims to the same by the last Monday of Nov. next. Dated at Victoria, Sept. 27th.

Wednesday, October 20, 1841

From the Morning Star: "YOCUM.---The citizens of Jasper and Jefferson have lately been thrown into a state of excitement, owing to the "lynching" of a man named Thomas YOCUM. It seems this man had for several years excited the suspicions of his neighbors, in connection with a gang of villains who were constantly engaged in swindling, robbery or murder. He resided at a place styled the Pine Islands near the Neches river. Many negroes, fine horses & cattle stolen from different sections, have often been traced near to his house, & there the trails disappeared. Once a fine horse that was stolen at Liberty was tracked directly to his stable, but not found. A suit was brought against him & he was arraigned for stealing the horse, but by means of suborned witnesses, he proved that he was in a different part of the country when the horse was stolen, & was acquitted. The gang connected with him, it is supposed, were in the habit of taking the stolen property to Louisiana, where it was sold & the proceeds put in his hands. It has long been reported that several murders have been committed at his house. One of his negroes confessed that he committed seven murders; & it was currently reported that he had aided in the commission of 13 murders in LA. It is further stated that his father who lives on the Sabine, had been arraigned 7 times for murder, & each time was acquitted. The son seems to have followed his example. . . .A few years since a young man named WYLIE, with a large quantity of money, put up at his house overnight & was never heard of afterwards. His friends suspected that YOCUM had murdered him. For 20 years, he has been a constant subject of suspicion; but his crimes were perpetrated with impunity. A few weeks since he was detected in an attempt to swindle a man residing on Cedar bayou & it is believed, had laid plans to murder him. This roused the indignation of many respectable citizens, & they went to him, & notified him to leave the county. He promised to obey, but soon after, collected several of his gang and boasted that a large force of citizens would join in his defence. This conduct exasperated the party that had notified him to leave & they united to the number of 150, proceeded to his house, & not finding him, removed the women & children, & burnt the house to the ground. A part of the said company went in pursuit of YOCUM & found him at the house of one of his relatives on Cypress bayou. They immediately secured him & started with him towards the Trinity. A day or two afterwards he was found dead in a prairie near the San Jacinto, pierced with 5 rifle balls. It was reported that he attempted to make his escape & was shot while running away. Thus has perished one of most singular men to have disgraced our Republic, since the days of Lafitte."

A gentleman lately arrived from Jefferson co., states that a group of "Regulators" also have killed a man by the name of IRONS, in addition to YOCUM.

New Appointments in the Navy---W. F. MAURY & J. F. STEPHENS, Pursers; Messrs. SMITH, S. L. MILLER, G. PEYTON & Thos. HENDERSON, Midshipmen; and Messrs. SWISHER, ROBERTS & ARCHER, Lieutenants.

Settlement in the Cross Timbers -- We learn from *The Redlander* that 100 men (a part of whom have families) have lately removed from the vicinity of Fort English to the Indian villages, in the lower edge of the Cross Timber, lately discovered by Gen. TARRANT. They plan to occupy the villages from which the Indians have been driven. These villages are 60 or 70 miles NW of Fort Kingsborough, on the west fork of the Trinity. Several families have lately removed to Fort Kingsborough.

Died on the 8th inst., Mrs. LIPSCOMB, consort of Judge A. LIPSCOMB, at his residence on the Brazos. Also on the 12th inst., his daughter Ann Rebecca, aged 9 years.

Sally M. GRIGSBY has been named executrix of the est. of Joseph GRIGSBY, decd., by Probate Court of Jefferson co. on 11th Oct. 1841.

Daniel McDONALD named admr. of the est. of J. P. BLACK, decd., by the Probate Court for Victoria Co., March Term.

Wednesday, October 27, 1841

We learn from the Hon. G. A. PATILLO of Jefferson co., that the report that two men have been killed in that county by lynch law is incorrect. Mr. IRONS, one of those stated to have been killed, died of natural causes in a house near the residence of Mr. PATILLO. The other man, Mr. YOCUM, was killed in another county.

The Hon. H. K. MUSE arrived in town Monday, on his way to Austin. He confirms the reports published in the <u>Redlander</u> of the disgraceful proceedings in Shelby co. It seems a party of the "Regulators" from that county, pursued a few of the Teneha gang quite to Montgomery co., killed a man named BLEDSOE & dangerously wounded another by the name of STRICKLAND. Three others by the name of McFADDEN were taken back to Shelbyville & two of them were hanged on the 8th inst. The third, on account of his extreme youth, was released. BLEDSOE had wantomly and without provocation shot down an old man named PRUET a few days since. Although all of these men have merited their punishment, still their guilt cannot exculpate those who those executed them from the crime of murder.

J. L. P. MEREDITH has been named as admr. of

the est. of John T. PINCKNEY, late of the Northern Division of Liberty co., by the Probate Ct. of same on the last Monday in September, 1841.

[Several issues are missing here]

Wednesday, November 24, 1841

    Married in this city on the 17th inst., by the Rev. Mr. HUCKINS, Cornelius ENNIS, of the firm of ENNIS, KIMBALL & HOLT, to Miss Jennett, youngest daughter of P. KIMBALL of same place.
    Notice is hereby given that certificate No. 920, issued Sept. 6th 1838 by the Board of Land Commissioners of Harris co., to Edward O'HARE, for 640 acrs, is lost, & that at the expiration of 60 days from this date, I shall apply according to the law for a duplicate thereof. Isaiah CALL, Houston, Nov. 23d.
    James R. JENKINS & James WILLIE have connected themselves in the practice of Law, and will attend the courts of the Third Judicial Dist., and the Supreme Court of the Republic of Texas. Office: Independence, Washington co. Nov. 15.
    Information Wanted. Mrs. Mary WILSON writes us from Danville, KY, under date of 12th inst., requesting information about her 2 sons, Robert G. and John T. WILSON, In Texas. She states that John has been in this country for the last 6 years, & has reasons to believe that while he was battling for the liberties of the Republic of TX, was taken prisoner, but subsequently escaped with others. It seems that Robert left this city for Texas last Aug. 15th, on board the Kingston, in search of his brother. The distressed mother as yet has no information on either of her sons. She describes Robert as of rather dark complexion, dark eyes & black hair; rather spare built, about 5'8" or 10", & about 20 or 22 years of age.
    Sarah WEBB named admr. of the est. of Isom G. WEBB, decd., at the September term of the Probate Ct. of Montgomery Co. Cincinnati, Nov. 9th, 1841.

Wednesday, December 1, 1841

Notice. The undersigned has received from the Probate Ct. of Brazoria co., letters of administration upon the succ. of Wm. P. SCOTT, decd., dated Nov. 5th, 1841; all persons having claims are hereby notified to present them in the time prescribed by law. Robert J. CALDER, Brazoria, Nov. 26th.

Notice. I have lost my certificate of headright, issued by the Board of Land Commissioners, Jefferson co., on March 5th, 1838, for one league & one labor. After 60 days from this date, I shall apply for a duplicate of the same. John C. READ, Oct. 25th.

Wednesday, December 8, 1841

DIMMIT. Recent accounts from Mexico confirm the melancholy rumors of the death of this gallant man, although the reports of his suicide, we believe, are unfounded. The prisoners who have returned from Mexico generally confirm that he has been murdered by the Mexican authorities.

CAPTIVES OF REFUGIO. We are happy to report that all the prisoners captured lately at Refugio (with the exception of the unfortunate RYAL, who was massacred) have returned in safety. They were taken to "Lampacces beyond the Rio Grande," and released by order of Gen. VASQUEZ.

Martin D. HART named as admr. of the est. of John HART, decd., at the August term of Probate Court, Fannin Co.

Lost, by Matthew HURBERT, a certificate for 1 league & 1 labor, No. 14, & dated Jan. 6th, 1838, issued to the subscriber by the Board of Land Commissioners for Montgomery co. I will apply for duplicate after 60 days from this date. Thomas CHATHAM, Montgomery, Dec. 8th.

Wednesday, December 15, 1841

The undersigned have been appointed by the Probate Ct., Montgomery co., at the Sept. 1841

Term as Admr. of the est. of Wm. R. WILLIAMS, decd., all persons having claims against said est. are notified to present them within the time prescribed by law. Zarelda J. WILLIAMS, Admr. Oct. 25th 1841.
The undersigned has been appointed by the Hon. Chief Justice of Harris co. as Admr. on the est. of W. C. WALLACE, decd. N. W. TRAVIS, Admr. Elam STOCKBRIDGE, Agent. Houston, Dec. 12th, 1841.

Wednesday, December 22, 1841

Appointments by the President, by & with the consent of the Senate: Francis A. MORRIS, Attorney General of the Republic; Alexander McGUFFY, Consul for the Port of Cincinnati, Ohio; Samuel G. TAYLOR, Consul for the Port of Norfolk, VA; Ira M. FREEMAN, Notary Public, Houston co.; Chas. B. STEWART, Notary Public, Montgomery co.; John W. SMITH, Notary Public, Bexar co.; Thos. M. DUKE, Collector of Customs, Port of Calhoun; Peter McGREAL, District Attorney for the Second Judicial District.

Wednesday, December 29, 1841

Steam Boat Accident. (From the <u>Morning Star</u>) For the first time since the establishment of this newspaper . . . it becomes the editor's painful duty to record a loss of life from the explosion of a steam engine. The "Albert Gallatin," on her passage from Houston to Galveston, when within 8 miles of the latter place, burst one of her boilers, killing five persons. A rumor of this sad accident reached us as early as last Friday, but hoping the report might prove unfounded, and fearing to harass the feelings of the relatives and friends of those on board, we restrained our anxiety . . . until the arrival of the steamer "Dayton" on Sunday morning, confirmed the intelligence, and left no further room for hope or doubt. We copy from the <u>Civilian</u> a list of the persons killed and wounded: KILLED, Mr. John NELSON, Pilot; Mr. CHERRY from Alabama, passenger; Mr. HEATH, Bar-keeper; a negro man belonging to Mr. UGLOW; and one of the stewards. WOUNDED: Thos. GIBBONS of Somerset co., MD, dangerously scalded; Thos. CAREY, fireman, dangerously scalded; Captain LATHAM, from Cuba, slightly; Thos. CONNER, of Galveston, slightly; John NOYES, deckhand, ditto; John Carson COOK, ditto; Capt. WHILTBERRY, ditto; M. GIRAUD, ditto.

There is much to confirm the rumor of the capture of the Santa Fe Expedition. The letter which follows, was received by Mr. Alden A. M. JACKSON, Collector of Customs, Port of Galveston from W. T. BRANNUM, dated at New Orleans on 16th Dec. 1841: "By the city papers, taken over by the "Neptune," you will be put in possesion of the capture of the Santa Fe Expedition. I am enabled, however, this morning to give you the true version of this most unfortunate occurrence; that is if the accounts I get are correct & which were brought by the schooner "Sylph," just arrived here after a short passage from Yucatan, and which are as follows:

"The expedition was met about 60 miles from Santa Fe, by a force consisting of 1,200 volunteers, 300 regulars & 300 Rancheros, 1800 men in all. The action commenced in the morning and lasted until nearly night, when the ammunition of our brave troops giving entirely out, they were forced to surrender. The loss to the Mexicans was 320 killed; to the Texans only 2. The wounded on either side not stated..."

Members of the Bar of Harris Co. met on the 28th inst. and adopted a resolution honoring the memory of their decd. brother John R. REID.

Classical School. There will be a Select Classical School opened on Monday, Jan. 17th, 1842, by Rev. H. REID near Miss MORGAN's boarding house. Rates of tuition, $5.00 per month. Hours of instruction from 5 A.M. to 1 P.M. In this institution, youth will be prepared for entering any College or any active & useful business in life. All immorality and profane language strictly prohibited. 24th Dec. 1841.

Private Boarding, Commerce Street, Houston, for Transcient or Weekly Boarders. Daniel T. FITCHETT, Dec. 23d.

For sale or rent. Two small farms two miles below Houston on Buffalo Bayou with comfortable dwelling & out-houses, the above property can be had on reasonable terms, for further particulars inquire at the store of the subscriber second door in the Long Row. P. J. WILLESS, Dec. 25th.

Advertisement from Moses PARK, Independence, Washington co., announces he has a valuable new stock of fall and winter goods.

A

ABBOTT 174,248
ABERCROMBIE 3
ABORN 87
ABRAMS 53
ACKERMAN 146,147
ACOSTA 176
ADAMS 24,44,64,177,205
ADDICKS 121,212
ADKISSON 126
AEYTON 14
AGATON 246
AGUADO 9
AGUIRRE 9
AIKEN 233
ALBRIGHT 217
ALDERSON 126
ALDRETTE 113
ALDRICH 198,241,242
ALDRIDGE 81
ALEXANDER 18,21,54,82,
  92,100,103,118,126,
  133,192,205,224
ALLBRIGHT 201,217,242
ALLCORN 21,32,56,109
ALLEN 18,27,28,33,36,
  65,80,81,99,105,107,
  108,117,122,125,126,
  127,132,134,135,141,
  157,160,165,174,182,
  183,189,205,209,217,
  219,221,226,230,233,
  234,244,247,253,257,
  263,271,273
ALLENWOOD 30
ALLEY 26,62
ALLISON 104
ALLSBURY 110
ALRIDGE 57
ALSBROCKE 219
ALSBURY 105,234
ALSTON 107,143,184
ALWAY 234
AMMONS 169
AMORY 136,164,272
AMPUIDA 266
ANAYA 148,164,225
ANDERSON 6,15,35,68,
  99,125,126,130,134,
  153,187,201,241,262
ANDRESS 92
ANDREWS 1,2,7,21,22,
  24,26,39,42,89,113,
  116,126,198,210,235,
  247,255
ANDRUS 87
ANGIER 40
ANTHONY 53,74
APULIA 174
ARCHER 42,193,210,217,
  246,255,277
ARENAS 9
ARISTA 173,174,175,
  223,224,246,253,256,
  259,262,265
ARMINGS 149
ARMSTRONG 65,198
ARNOLD 60,169,225,267
ARRINGTON 65
ARROUGH 234
ASBERRY 199,203,204
ASHBAUGH 21
ASHBY 18,109
ASHWORTH 236
ATKINSON 82,192
ATORFF 83
ATTWELL 20
AUBREY 220,221,253,
  261,265,266,270
AUGHINBAUGH 82,117
AUGUSTINE 141,168
AULD 54
AUSTIN 1,3,18,20,21,
  22,25,38,67,82,97,
  104,106,107,152,
  197,228
AYERS 2,54,55,62,123
AYRES 12,13,14,85,
  197,271

B

BABCOCK 151,165
BACHE 33
BACHELDER 263
BACON 18
BAGBY 246
BAILEY 8,28,33,37,44,
  140,197,213,231,232,
  248,263,271
BAILY 146,183,233,261
BAKER 5,6,19,33,63,77,
  81,142,174,187,263
BALDRIDGE 76
BALIR 132,198
BALLARD 197,258
BALLENTINE 3
BALLEW 123
BALLINGER 135
BALLOU 8
BANCROFT 36,40,41,43
BANDILLO 176
BANISTER 41
BANKS 229
BANNISTER 1,27
BARBER 94
BARBOT 3
BARCLAY 4,101,176,238
BARKER 71,79,81,132,
  190
BARKLEY 30
BARNARD 73
BARNES 7,146
BARNETT 12,139,216,229
BARNEYCASTLE 245
BARNHART 126
BARR 47,51,153,155,
  176,184
BARRETT 105,111,118
BARRY 54,64
BARSTOW 10,118
BARTLETT 22,55,128,263
BARTON 126,162,234
BASQUES 176
BASSETT 237,256
BASTERICHE 260
BASTROP, DE 68,72,123
BATEL 208

BATTERSON 73,137
BATTLE 35,231
BAUGH 5
BAZLEY 153
BEALE 25
BEAM 102
BEAN 67,273
BEARD 142
BEASLY 114
BEASON 12
BEATY 248
BECKFORD 30
BECKHAM 219
BECKNELL 43
BEE 49,115,197,243,257
BEESON 24,241
BEGLEY 8
BELCHER 192
BELDEN 57,67,131
BELDIN 46
BELKNAP 117
BELL 125,131,141,191,
  196
BELLEPONT 5
BELT 109
BENAVIDES 3
BENBROOK 136
BENNET 58,72
BENNETT 34,85,126,128,
  133,142,169,273
BENSON 7,25
BENTON 75,100,169
BERK 238
BERNUTH 44
BERRA 9
BERRY 54,88,199,205,
  260
BERTRAND 38,152
BETT 30
BETTS 26,161
BEVIL 3
BEVILL 134
BICKNELL 117
BIERMAN 84
BIGELOW 115,165,203
BIGG 72

BIGHAM 69
BILLINGBERY 126
BILLINGSLY 103,126
BINGHAM 90,151
BIRCH 32
BIRD 102,217
BIRDSALL 46,141,151,
  195
BISHOP 40,72
BISSEL 66,71
BISSELL 87,235
BLACK 62,131,169,278
BLACKMAN 137
BLACKSTOCK 29
BLACKWELL 35
BLAIR 5,6,27,48,104,
  132?,198?,244
BLANCHET 78,79,148
BLANDIN 33
BLANERHASET 219
BLAZEBY 5
BLAZELY 58
BLEDSOE 278
BLOOD 5,219
BLOODGOOD 123,160
BLOSSOM 232
BLOUNT 58
BLUMENTAL 261
BODEN 258
BODHAM 158
BOLD 86
BOLLENGER 132
BOLLING 30
BOLLINGER 274
BOLTON 71
BONDIES 249
BONDS 65
BONELEE 105
BONELL 128
BONELY 105
BONHAM 3,6
BONNELL 166,238,239
BONZANO 58
BOOKER 30,11
BOOMER 12
BOON 259

BOONE 22
BOOTH 198
BORDEN 10,66,88,107,
  229,235,239,272
BORDLOW 39
BOSHER 114
BOSTWICK 20,48,235
BOSWELL 94
BOTTSFORD 58
BOUDINOT 149
BOURNE 6
BOWEN 40
BOWIE 1,5,15,23,162
BOWLES 22,83,140,144,
  165,167,181,275
BOWLS 21
BOWMAN 97,156,158
BOYCE 149,235
BOYD 67,115,126,203,
  266
BOYER 89
BOYINGTON 72
BOYLE 95
BOYLER 153
BOYLUM 102
BRACKEN 3,169
BRACKENRIDGE 142
BRACY 169
BRADLEY 10,11,86
BRANCH 96,144,184,201
BRANDON 191
BRANHAM 130
BRANNUM 255,282
BRASAIL 9
BRASHEAR 57,74,173
BRATT 219
BRATTON 21,139
BREEDIN 110
BREEDING 138
BREESE 96
BRENAN 14,92
BRENHAM 239
BRENNAN 121
BRENT 44,84,86,133
BREWER 159,167,168
BREWSTER 34,250

BRICKER 76
BRIDGEMAN 230
BRIGHAM 23,59,174
BRINSON 123
BRISCOE 43,44,54,91,97,
    117,121,122,132,135,
    151,185,188,195,221,
    233,244
BRISTER 1,100
BRITTAN 64
BRITTON 237
BROCK 58
BROCKWAY 30
BRONAUGH 124,221
BRONSON 235
BROOCKS 187
BROOKE 163
BROOKFIELD 115
BROOKS 14,81,103,122,
    193,198,259
BROTHERTON 145
BROWN 7,14,17,18,25,
    55,60,82,113,116,123,
    126,151,152,158,162,
    169,170,185,192,213,
    222,241,243,251
BROWNE 6
BROWNELL 202
BROWNLEE 237
BRUARBY 115
BRUME 30
BRYAN 19,56,106,188
BRYANT 25,104
BRYARLY 234
BRYNE 125
BUCHANAN 21,34,35,75
BUCKANON 46
BUCKLEY 39,72,84,132,
    138,146,153,172,195,
    202,227
BUCKNELL 40
BUCKNER 155,268
BULL 92,100,133
BULLOCK 4,14,60,169,
    217
BUNDICK 69,88

BUNKER 243
BUNTON 15,30,31,133
BURCH 44,131
BURCHARD 34
BURD 91
BURFORD 91
BURGESS 42,82,241
BURKE 14,134,216
BURKHAM 80
BURKITT 21
BURKS 263
BURLESON 3,125,126,
    165,167,181,191,270,
    274
BURNELL 6
BURNESTON 271
BURNET 10,11,87,216
BURNETT 185,223,241
BURNHAM 54
BURNS 6,21
BURR 263
BURRETT 87
BURRIT 64
BURROUGH 17
BURRUS 268
BURT 16,39
BURTON 268
BURUS 105
BUSHARE 58
BUSHEL 62
BUTLER 6,78,122,164
BUTTERFIELD 86
BYARS 89
BYERS 126
BYRNE 7,125?
BYROM 13,34,219

C

CADE 181,213,215,232,
   252
CAGE 95,98,118
CALDER 11,137,234,269,
   280
CALDERELL 3
CALDWELL 89,99,126,171,
   190,192,196,197
CALISON 241
CALL 158,279
CALLAGHAN 3,258
CALLAHAN 203
CALLIER 110
CALLIHAN 102
CALLIOTT 80
CALVIT 13
CAMFIELD 272
CAMPBELL 15,24,64,92,
   98,126,135,163,181,
   234,237,245,252
CANALES 173,174,175,
   218,219
CANALIZE 163
CANE 6
CANFIELD 51
CANNON 139
CANZE 126
CAPAL 21
CAPLE 32,56
CARBAJAL 55
CAREY 5,68,170,221,282
CARILL0 262
CARL 224
CARLOS 54,71,124,165
CARMELL 82
CARNES 92
CARNOLD 156
CAROTHERS 126
CARPENTER 138
CARPER 165,235,251
CARR 21,234,241,242
CARRAWAY 65
CARRERE 160
CARROLL 137

CARRON 146
CARSON 44,110,111,171
CARTER 18,24,86,104,
   106,126,127,131
CARTWELL 82
CARTWRIGHT 17,127
CARVAJAL 3
CASEMIRO 84
CASEY 171,241
CASH 17,21,234
CASLOR 233
CASPARI 77
CASTANIE 158
CASTLEMAN 182
CASTRILLON 9
CASTRO 9,165,189,212
CATE 22
CATLIN 209,215
CATO 26
CATS 19
CAVETT 21
CAYCE 16,19
CAZNEAU 255
CECIL 169
CERCHER 137
CHADWICK 3
CHAFFIN 20,35
CHALMERS 262
CHAMBERLIN 58,215
CHAMBERS 10,71,176,
   189,228,229
CHANCE 65,86
CHANDLER 255,258,274
CHAPLIN 66,163
CHAPMAN 122,233
CHASSAIGNE 76
CHASTINE 82
CHATHAM 280
CHAUMONT, DE 103
CHAVART 176
CHENOWETH 131
CHENY 199
CHERRY 281
CHESTER 267

CHILDERS 28
CHILDRESS 20,75,100,126
CHILDS 29
CHIPITA 266
CHIVERS 105
CHOAT 88,177
CHOATE 275
CHRISKO 86
CHRISMAN 192,233
CHRISTIAN 48,88
CLAPP 242
CLARE 76
CLARK 11,20,52,54,73,
  82,84,103,130,131,
  153,180,209,227,242
CLARKE 65
CLAUZEL 123
CLAY 131,150
CLEMENT 4
CLEMENTS 77,143,157,241
CLEMMON 166
CLEMMONS 81
CLENDENEN 147
CLENDENIN 146,187,218,
  224,234
CLOPPER 177
CLOPTON 126
CLOSSON 105
CLOUD 30,40
COALDRY 105
COCHRAN 16,20,21,68,
  130,197,271
COCHRANE 2,25,178,206
COCKE 163,165,192
COCKRUN 6
COCKS 138
CODET 124
CODY 261
COE 78,115
COFFEE 117
COFFMAN 60
COIT 157
COJART 4
COLE 71,76,79,86,103,
  118,201
COLEMAN 31,135

COLERICK 17
COLL 82
COLLARD 224
COLLINS 47,67,104,134,
  135,164,258
COLLINSWORTH 1,22,78
COLT 210
COLVER 126
COLVILLE 225
COMPFIELD 160
CONE 115
CONLEY 126
CONN 126
CONNER 282
CONRAD 105
CONREY 52
CONROY 147,156
COOK 12,43,76,81,104,
  107,154,194,224,251,
  274,282
COOKE 1,113,141,170,
  258
COONROD 95
COOPER 14,48,133,255,
  258
COPELAND 7,25,239
COPENDOLPHER 21
COPES 125,128
COPLAND 56
CORDA 176
CORDOVA 126,128
CORMICK 161
CORNICK 67
CORNWALL 87
CORRI 71,79
CORTES 25,60
CORZINE 117
COS 9
COTTER 162
COTTLE 6,51,107
COUGHLIN 33
COUNCILL 116
COUNSEL 17
COWAN 123
COWART 123
COWLES 96

COWN 3
COX 151,179,192,223
CRABTREE 232
CRAFT 45
CRAIG 25,259
CRAMP 4
CRANE 141,178
CRAWFORD 187,192,212,
  224,242,263
CRISIP 125
CRISP 142
CRIST 88
CRITTENDEN 44
CROCHERON 126
CROCKETT 5,23,24,35,
  246,247
CROMWELL 115
CRONICAN 72,127
CROPPER 258
CROSBY 44,47,54,62,
  168,196
CROSSMAN 6
CRUGER 82,144,166
CRUMB 240
CUDY 54
CULBERT 88
CULLEN 113,167
CULLENS 75
CULP 255
CUMMINGS 1,6,81,117,
  142,196,197,233
CUMMINS 48,100
CUNNINGHAM 6,21,126,
  148
CURTIS 7,22,54,55,74,
  96,129,233

D

DABBS 154
DACKMANN 131
DAGET 90
DAINGERFIELD 101,103,
  207
DANCER 126
DANCY 87,180
DANIEL 9
DANIELS 183,192,196
DART 137,181
DARWIN 25,46
DAUGHERTY 212
DAVENPORT 167
DAVIDSON 198
DAVIS 3,6,16,29,68,75,
  79,81,89,92,101,107,
  108,109,114,117,137,
  142,160,164,169,173,
  192,213,234,250,255,
  272
DAVY 215
DAWSON 169,212
DAWZEY 269
DAY 6
DE BASTROP 123
DE BROT 114
DE CHAUMONT 103
DE GARCIA 234
DE LA CORDA 176
DE LA GARZA 229
DE LASSAUIX 260
DE LEON 133,196
DE ORR 199
DE ROJAS 163
DE SALIGNY 158,165,
  182,188,207,247
DE ZAVALA 16,53,143,
  234,266,267
DEANE 255
DEARDUFF 6,75,124
DECHAUMS 64
DECKER 258
DECKROE 21
DECROW 157,195
DEES 39
DELANO 65
DELBOY 5
DELGADO 109,157
DELMOUR 145
DEMMIT 1

DEMOUSSENT 5
DEMPSEY 52
DENMAN 248
DENNISON 77
DENTON 254
DERRET 35
DESANQUE 6
DESPALIER 6
DEVAULT 6
DEVENNEY 103
DEVENPORT 85
DEWELL 6
DEWES 24
DEWEY 134
DEWITT 63,214
DEXTER 45,66,151,176
DEY 32
DIBBLE 72
DICK 135
DICKERSON 63
DICKINSON 3,6,15
DICKMANN 152
DICKSON 63,84
DIGGES 3
DILLEN 80
DIMITT 80
DIMMITT 261,262,265,
  266,280
DINKIN 6
DIROENS 71
DISNEY 168
DOBIE 63,75,105,139,
  162,173,213,275
DODD 197
DODGE 122
DODIMEAD 88
DOLSON 244
DONAHO 221
DONNELLY 4,219
DONOHO 221,233
DOOM 260
DORAN 188
DORSETT 104,169
DORSEY 73
DOSWELL 44,64
DOUGALL 30

DOUGLASS 23,83,87,92,
  137
DOWELL 132
DOWNES 241
DOWNING 4
DOYLE 86,221
DRAKE 3,252
DREW 198
DUCKWORTH 31,234
DUFFAU 223
DUFFY 88
DUGAN 220
DUGAT 132,133,148,156
DUGLASS 241
DUKE 16,281
DULONG 207
DUMPSEY 36
DUNBAR 185
DUNCAN 93,269
DUNLAP 18,95,103,105,
  152,159,235,236,259
DUNMAN 160,177
DUNN 28,32,68,86,88,
  116,197,265
DUNNINGHAM 171
DUNNINGTON 146
DURHAM 84,85,198,239,
  254
DURNET 194
DUROCHER 29
DURST 6,126,198
DUTCHER 88
DUTY 31,52,157
DUVAL 14,30,74
DUVALL 14
DWENNY 14
DWIGHT 198
DYER 96,112,208,213,
  257
DYKEMAN 80
DZSANSKI 12

E

EAGEN 70
EAKEN 126
EARLE 28,49,62,177,
  203,204
EARTHMAN 216
EAST 198
EASTON 33
EATON 16,20,133
EBERLY 14
ECHOLES 190
ECKEL 15,17
EDDY 33
EDEN 169,194
EDGAR 76
EDMONDS 239
EDMONDSON 155
EDSON 57,115
EDWARDS 3,26,37,38,109,
  137,181,209,226,231
EELES 73
EGBERT 60,88,227
EGG 144,165
EHRENBERG 14
EIGINAMER 81
ELAM 16
ELDER 247,249
ELDREDGE 192
ELDRIDGE 75,124
ELLIOTT 13,177,274
ELLIS 11,46
ELLISON 84
EMERY 73,86,88
ENGLEHART 126
ENGLISH 218
ENNIS 227,263,279
EPPERSON 197
ERWIN 269
ESPINO 9
ESPY 271
ESTES 29,142
EVANS 5,43,49,75,81,
  84,102,160,215,217,
  234
EVE 261
EVERITTE 72
EVERT 32
EVES 72,148
EWELL 146,156,177
EWING 6

F

FABER 202
FACETT 31
FADDEN 234
FANGER 156
FANNIN 1,4,14,73,74,
  109,123,138
FANOGR 232
FANTHORP 91,197,222
FARIS 81
FARLEY 246
FARNES 14
FARNEY 46
FARO 266
FARRELL 5
FARRIS 170
FAULKNER 241,259
FAWCETT 54
FEARIS 8
FELAN 118
FELTMAN 53
FENTRESS 126
FERGUSON 49,52,78,88,
  100,137
FERMID 21
FERNANDEZ 7,33
FESSENDEN 22,97,248
FIELDS 201
FIKE 127
FILLSHER 86
FINCKE 185
FINKE 154
FINN 258

FISHBACK 6
FISHER 33,88,89,131,
  147,173,185,186,188,
  216,239,243,264,275
FITCH 102,198,231,236
FITCHETT 82,83,282
FITSHUGH 10
FITZGERALD 172,205
FITZGIBBONS 239
FITZHUGH 76,169
FITZMORRIS 8
FITZPATRICK 253
FITZSIMMONS 51
FIZER 105
FLANDERS 6,37,254
FLEMING 5
FLESHER 126,153
FLEURY 16
FLICK 102
FLOOD 247
FLORES 12,246
FLOYD 6,34,45,67,68,72
FOGG 201
FOLEY 47,49
FONTAINE 148,149,213
FOOTE 119
FORBES 54,61,103,111
FORD 14,53,241
FORREST 88,126
FORSTER 239
FORSYTH 3,5
FOSTER 30,70,126,169,
  233
FOULHOUSE 213
FOWLER 56,62,123,224,260

FOX 272
FRAILEY 16
FRANCIS 7,25,69,172
FRANKLIN 14,17,131,
  136,146,231
FRANKS 73
FRAZIER 15,81,88,100,
  186
FREAM 21
FREDERICK 46,67,84,240
FREEMAN 248,281
FREESON 111
FRENCH 36,184
FREON 118
FRERET 183
FRIAR 241
FRIAS 9
FRIEND 13
FRISBY 181
FRO 22
FROST 39,44,51,61,166,
  249
FUGATE 258
FUGUN 6
FULCHER 99
FULGUM 273
FULLENWIDER 271
FULTON 197
FUQUA 81
FUQUEA 77
FUQUY 143
FURGURSON 259
FURGUSON 259

G

GADSON 115
GAFFIELD 198
GAGE 198
GAINES 129,181,198
GAITHER 33
GALE 219
GALENA 176
GALLAGHER 219

GALLARICK 219
GALLATIN 36,127
GAMBLE 206,234
GANETT 6
GANT 76,93,222
GARCIA 2,234,246,257
GARDINER 115,125,142
GARNER 237

GARRATY 107
GARRETT 14,109,264
GARVIN 6,92
GARZA 229
GASSIOT 252,263
GASTON 91,107
GATES 81
GATEWOOD 30
GAY 233
GAYLE 53,60
GAZLEY 46,56,96,133,
 185,246,263
GEACH 60
GEDDINGS 260
GEE 58
GENOIS 183
GEORGE 6,75,168,234,251
GERDING 234
GERLACH 97,156,165,201
GERLACK 91
GIBBONS 282
GIBBS 114
GIBSON 121,221
GIDDENS 56
GIDDINGS 33,253
GIDDREST 178
GIDRE 178
GILBERT 89
GILLAND 75
GILLET 126
GILMARTIN 71
GILMORE 126,153
GIRAUD 282
GIST 4
GIVENS 245
GLASS 121
GLASSCOCK 126
GOBBEN 148
GODDEN 53,78
GODFREY 115,187
GOHEEN 265
GOLDING 213
GONZALES 9,229
GOOD 271
GOODMAN 33,56

GOODRICH 3,31,36,41,
 81,226,227
GOODWIN 15
GORDEN 250
GORDON 15,22,91,184
GORMAN 126
GOSNEY 89
GOSSETT 241,242
GOULD 137,214
GOURLEY 266
GOURLY 116
GOWENS 201
GRAHAM 8,71,92,168,
 198,245,260,261,266
GRANDE 176
GRANDISON 151
GRANT 51,66,72,76,77,
 81,102,109,201,217,
 242
GRAVES 28,40,89,155
GRAVIS 253
GRAY 30,77,93,122,149,
 150,198,245,276
GRAYSON 80
GREEN 9,10,35,36,47,
 95,163,190,231
GRIEVES 29
GRIFFIN 2,52
GRIGG 46
GRIGGS 22,28
GRIGSBY 169,259,278
GRIMES 182
GROCE 17,37,76,119,
 129,157
GROOMS 180
GROSS 4
GRUNDY 225
GUBTILL 41
GUIDRY 178
GUILD 40,41,54,117
GUYMAN 77
GUZMAN 9
GWYNN 68

H

HACKODAY 104
HADLEY 14
HAFFORD 124
HAGGARD 81,265
HAINES 250
HAINEY 82
HALE 20,66,81
HALL 1,7,16,25,27,28,
  38,43,65,87,91,106,
  112,116,143,157,160,
  162,197,220,247,249,
  252,271
HALLMARK 249
HALSEY 56
HAMILTON 9,60,68,83,
  113,122,137,168,169,
  243
HAMLET 129
HANCHETT 115,245
HANDEY 25
HANDY 29,91,108,120,
  157,230,231,270
HANIE 197
HANKS 72,187
HANNA 49,60,120
HANNUM 16
HANSFORD 260
HANSONS 202,221
HARBERT 36
HARCOURT 9,13,73
HARDEMAN 12,70,126
HARDEN 59
HARDIN 28,118,122,137,
  148,157,158,191,193,
  225,248
HARDING 92,157
HARDMAN 198
HARGNIE 126
HARMAN 75
HARNETT 115
HARPER 271
HARRELL 169,211,216
HARRINGTON 130
HARRIS 6,15,17,22,25,

HARRIS (cont.) 26,27,
  36,49,51,52,64,98,
  122,127,137,146,151,
  177,195,203,209,213,
  233,256
HARRISON 5,26,46,115,
  149,201,245,248,261,
  264
HARRY 69,72,81,116
HART 81,102,137,200,
  260,280
HARTRIDGE 105,115,143
HARVEY 109,120,237
HARVY 190
HASKELL 104
HASKINS 18,24,86
HASLICK 54
HASSEL 19
HASSETT 155
HASTIE 89
HATCH 57
HATFIELD 157
HATHAWAY 30
HAUCK 253
HAVILAND 208
HAWKINS 6,13,21,28,32,
  36,47,73,86,108,163,
  238,239
HAWTHORN 205
HAYES 88,147
HAYNES 273
HAYNIE 169,216,224
HAYS 6,246
HAYSLETT 157
HAYWOOD 206,230
HAZEN 14,19
HEAD 20,49,173
HEADY 5
HEARD 2,26,29
HEARN 86
HEATH 281
HEDDENBERG 115,123,192
HEDENBERG 92,94,101,
  105,135,177,263

HEDRICK 109
HEERBRUGGER 204
HEFORD 159
HEISKELL 6
HELM 5,115
HEMPHILL 7,28,126,138,
  159,206,219
HENDERSHOT 92
HENDERSON 92,99,106,
  142,199,210,234,277
HENDRICK 100,117
HENNINGS 156
HENRY 69
HENSLEY 34,35,52
HERNDON 86,209,252
HERRARA 9
HERVEY 18
HEYDENFELT 65
HIBBETT 198
HIBBITS 234
HICKS 78,100,153
HIGGINBOTHAM 171,182
HIGGINS 263
HIGHSMITH 126
HILL 3,10,66,93,96,113,
  129,133,169,190,224,
  224,259
HILTON 156
HINDS 150
HINKSON 26
HINTON 234
HIRAM 109
HITCHCOCK 82,171
HITSELBERGER 53
HOBEN 234
HOCKETT 187
HOCKLEY 81,100
HODGE 9,37,60,70,165,
  198,204,233
HODGSON 233
HOES 137
HOFFLER 65
HOFFMAN 56,132,141,208
HOGAN 60
HOIT 5
HOLBROOK 33

HOLCOMB 9
HOLLAND 6,14,60,64,
  105,244
HOLLIDAY 14,194,217
HOLLIS 245
HOLLOWAY 6
HOLMAN 26,40,196,231
HOLMES 19,126,190,198
HOLSTEIN 142
HOLT 4,279
HOND 125
HOOD 71,72,171,224
HOPE 71,192
HOPKINS 115,201,259
HORD 114,244,273
HORDE 203
HORN 71
HORNSBY 126,153
HORTON 14,62,70,112,
  132,187
HOSKINS 17,81
HOTCHKISS 216,217
HOUCK 253
HOUSE 2,56,156,160,202
HOUSTON 18,20,33,67,
  69,101,144,167,260,
  263
HOUTH 118
HOWARD 25,56,65,146,
  170,171,173,194,230,
  241,263
HOWELL 6
HOWL 38
HOXIE 66,222
HUBBARD 21,39,65,71
HUBERT 137
HUCKINS 279
HUDSON 47,133,175,243,
  250,265
HUESER 133
HUFF 12,217,274
HUFFMAN 225
HUGHES 242
HULING 234,271
HULL 29,219
HULLING 199

HUMPHREY 239
HUMPHREYS 57,74,75,124,
  132,146,153,158,159,
  240
HUMPHRIES 31
HUNT 14,24,109,163,182,
  234
HUNTER 14,20,78,100,
  136,263
HUNTINGDON 62
HUNTINGTON 51

HURBERT 280
HURD 25,42,92,116,169,
  207,220,229
HURST 62,109
HUSTON 181,184,187,
  192,193,204,233
HUTCHINGSON 60
HUTCHINSON 6,21,267
HYATT 180
HYDE 197

I

IHAMS 87
IIAMES 26
IJAMS 26,35,43
IKIN 169,203,238
IMIN 115
INGLISH 198
INGRAHAM 269
INGRAM 5,6,41,118
INGRANAM 275
IRION 66
IRIS 178
IRISH 14

IRON 265
IRONS 216,277,278
IRVIN 104
IRVINE 15,77
ISAACS 234,271
ISAM 150
ISAMANI 84
ISBELL 200
ISAWACONY 73
IVES 5,130,202
IVISH 5

J

JACK 112
JACKSON 2,3,6,16,21,58,
  71,78,85,106,107,115,
  133,148,149,160,162,
  168,270,282
JACOBS 4
JAEGER 73
JAMES 1,34,62,65,88,
  187
JAMIESON 6,22,25
JANSEN 100
JANUARY 66
JAQUES 8,145
JARMON 56,177
JARVIS 60,145
JASPER 133
JAYNE 171

JEFFREYS 195,196
JEFFRIES 67
JENKINS 243,263,279
JENKS 22
JENNINGS 58
JEWETT 140,204,239,246
JOHNSON 6,32,33,36,58,
  63,66,68,72,73,81,
  104,120,126,133,144,
  169,180,187,198,220,
  235,246,255,258,260
JOHNSTON 44,54,72,77,
  141,156,194
JONES 4,8,14,24,25,28,
  37,38,39,45,46,55,
  56,58,59,62,65,66,
  74,78,79,82,83,90,

JONES (cont.) 95,104,
108,109,157,164,168,
169,180,184,197,198,
212,245,252,264,275

JORDAN 22,88,99,115,
173,218,219,256
JORDON 115,199
JOSDIN 48

K

KAMMAC 34
KANE 142
KARCHER 259
KARNES 84,98,128,169,
194,212
KAUFMAN 141,217
KAUFMANN 137
KEASE 237
KEATING 98
KEDESON 6
KEENER 62
KEESUCKER 8
KELCEY 14,60
KELCY 39
KELLERS 191
KELLET 234
KELLEY 18,29
KELLOGG 107,198
KELLUM 163
KELLY 34,35,36,40,171
KELSENGER 219
KEMP 14
KEMPTON 204
KENDALL 30,250
KENNEDY 131,254
KENNEY 32
KENNICOTT 80
KENNYMORE 89,160,194
KENT 6,76
KENYON 3
KER 25
KERR 7,52,115,169

KESCE 85
KESLER 44,58,152,155,
156,184,185,239
KICKER 167
KILGORE 28,53,230
KIMBALL 6,227,263,267,
279
KIMBELL 33,84
KINCAID 220
KINCHELOE 30,238
KING 6,60,77,82,87,95,
177,197,241
KINGSBERRY 199,215
KINGSBURY 81,274
KINGSLEY 69,72
KINNEY 6,220,221,253,
261,265,266,267,269,
270
KIRCHHOFFER 197
KIRK 101
KIRKHAM 150,220
KITCHEN 196,204
KLEBERG 54,179
KLESON 150
KNIGHT 23,30,101,269
KOEPF 84
KOKERNOT 9,13
KOOP 216
KOOPMAN 169
KRAIG 158
KUKENDALL 70
KUYKENDALL 34,201

L

LAMAR 142,256
LAMB 72
LAMPRORD 237
LANGAMAN 25

LANGFORD 33
LANGHUDGE 77
LANGTHORP 162
LAPHAM 95,272

LAPRELLE 197
LARISON 3
LARUMBO 9
LASSAUIX, DE 260
LATHAM 58,217,282
LAUGHBRIDGE 169
LAUGHEEN 7
LAUGHLIN 135
LAURENS 31,226,227
LAURTON 8
LAURY 88
LAW 81
LAWRENCE 43,45,57,81,
 148,200,204
LAWSON 69,160
LE GRAND 69,119
LEACH 77,82
LEAGUE 26,72,117,228
LeCLERC 207
LeCOMTE 130
LEE 2,79,81,95,96,98,
 124,147,158,160,208
LEEDS 4
LEFFEL 171
LEFTWICH 228
LeGRAND 69,119
LEMAN 72
LENTNER 7,26
LeRAY 101,103
LESSASSIER 19
LESSIAN 93
LESTER 54,126,192,241
LEUSHER 153
LEVENHAGEN 91,160,177,
 216
LEVERING 108,120,157,
 198,242
LEVEY 1
LEVINS 163
LEVY 32,42,66
LEWELLEN 108,115,199
LEWIS 6,7,33,54,62,80,
 160,165,229,252,271,
 274
LIGHTFOOT 49
LIGHTLE 151

LILLY 59
LINDLEY 6,79
LINN 6,169,246
LINSEY 64
LIPSCOMB 278
LITTING 221
LITTLE 276
LITTLEFIELD 183,187
LIVELY 150
LLEWELYN 3
LLOY 126
LOCKHART 74,77,89,106,
 142,170
LOCKRIDGE 192
LOGAN 9,27,56,58,122,
 158,172,248
LOGCOPE 83
LOLLER 3
LONG 4,45,90,109,127,
 152,265
LONG KING 152
LONGCOPE 83?,208
LOOKE 276
LOPEZ 29
LORD 208
LORORY 18
LOTHROP 142
LOUD 251
LOVE 33,107,176,208,
 233,239
LOVELAND 44
LOVING 199
LOW 235
LOWER 270
LOWERY 30
LOYERS 86
LUBBOCK 192,245,250,
 255,276
LUCAS 115,150
LUDLOW 168
LUDWICK 21
LUELMNO 9
LUM 83
LUMPKIN 271
LUNDT 34
LUSK 91,108,120,157,

LUSK (cont.) 230,231,
 270,275
LYNCH 23,126,148,180

LYNES 239,240
LYONS 12

M

MABBITT 257
MABRY 38,126
MacGREAL 111
MACKAY 4
MACKE 231,231,261
MACOMB 13
MADAMS 257
MADDEN 187
MADDISON 275
MADEIRA 79
MADERO 118
MAGEE 115
MAHAN 7
MAILLARD 226
MAIN 88,169
MALCOLM 33
MALDONADO 225
MALONE 81
MANCHACA 108,122,128,
 176,229
MANCHE 169
MANLEY 97,131,192,263
MANLY 224
MANN 81,90,208
MANNING 110,198
MANTON 180,197
MARK 109
MARKHAM 32
MARKS 90,106
MARLEY 33
MARLIN 111,169
MARSH 27,227
MARSHALL 74,88,100,
 107,122
MARTIN 6,14,33,42,119,
 131,154,155,157,169,
 230,245,253,263
MARTINDALE 14,114
MARTINEZ 9
MASON 63

MASTERSON 115
MATCHITT 11
MATHER 30,47
MATHIAS 48
MATOSSEY 204
MATTERN 102
MATTHEWS 27,63,160,
 179,180,198
MAUER 5
MAURAND 218
MAURY 277
MAXWELL 3
MAY 18,24,35
MAYS 73,81,197
McADAMS 41
McALISTER 33
McANELLY 124
McARTHUR 104
McCALL 199,239,251
McCAMPBELL 86,87
McCASKEY 29,52
McCASKILL 63,105,140
McCLANAHAN 47
McCLELLAND 209
McCLOSKY 263
McCLUNG 90
McCLURE 44,79,81,234,
 241
McCONNELL 273
McCORMIC 24
McCORMICK 5,12,160,
 167,177
McCOURT 261
McCOY 6,34,36,52,55,
 69,87,157
McCRABB 133,170,236
McCREARY 143,259
McCRORY 45,46
McCULLOCH 196,241
McDANIEL 197

McDERMITT 16
McDERMOTT 230
McDONALD 34,84,104,197,
    209,238,278
McDOUGAL 91
McELROY 31,111
McFADDEN 263,278
McFARLAND 17,35,44,49,
    65,102
McFARLANE 272
McFARLIN 260
McGABEY 131
McGAHEY 209
McGARY 28,72,128,169
McGEE 21,79,160,251
McGEHEE 201
McGLOIN 90
McGLOUN 133
McGOFFEU 199
McGOWEN 248
McGREAL 100,281
McGREGOR 6
McGUFFEY 252
McGUFFIN 180,253
McGUFFY 281
McHENRY 2
McILHANY 237
McINTYRE 81
McKARNAN 126
McKAY 3,52,92
McKEAN 234
McKEELY 180
McKEEVER 268
McKELVERE 88
McKENNEY 43
McKINLEY 7
McKINNEY 3,24,27,86,
    103,236,238,247,263
McKINSTRY 18,51
McKNIGHT 253
McLAUREN 89
McLELAND 68
McLELLAN 1
McLEOD 141,167,170,
    173,251,255
McLUNG 95

McMAHAN 237
McMAHON 54,271
McMILLEN 96
McNEALY 98
McNEEL 33,99,124,138
McNEILL 139,177,191
McNUNER 196
McNUTT 59,138,139,179
McPHERSON 75
McQUART 82
McRAE 163
McUNE 21
McVICOR 104
MEAD 241
MEANS 134
MELONE 107
MELTON 6
MENARD 239
MENDES 122
MENEFEE 26,216
MENIFEE 191,192
MERCER 197,233
MEREDITH 278
MERIGONCE 116
MERIWETHER 235
MERLIN 256
MERRILL 77,83,116,234
MERRY 32,44,208
MESHER 115
METCALFE 237
MEUGENS 257
MEXIA 147
MICHISON 5
MILAM 3,229
MILBURN 43
MILBY 24
MILES 48,109,183
MILLARD 26,101
MILLBROOKS 47
MILLER 3,6,57,62,67,
    75,81,94,121,126,
    134,136,141,143,151,
    154,196,216,233,241,
    248,261,277
MILLET 177
MILLICAN 39,47

MILLON 43,117
MILLS 76,97,112,124,
 126,175,274
MILLSAP 6
MILLSAPPS 74
MILON 85
MIMS 23
MINOR 86
MINTON 173
MITCHELL 4,6,7,69,80,
 81,119,132,146,156,
 169,172,199,241
MITCHUSSON 78
MIXON 100,152
MOCK 17
MOFFIT 234
MOLINA 9
MONEY 235
MONJARRA 9
MONK 65
MONROE 101
MONSOLA 122
MONTANA 9
MONTGOMERY 72
MONTOYA 218
MOODY 52,145,199,240,
 246,265
MOORE 6,16,30,35,41,
 49,60,61,62,64,105,
 117,118,126,129,132,
 142,144,145,146,149,
 151,155,165,166,190,
 203,204,208,209,210,
 212,213,216,217,218,
 221,223,269,274
MORA 9
MORDECAI 192,196
MOREHOUSE 77,227,234,
 238
MORELAND 38,52,87,184,
 186,251
MORGAN 44,47,62,64,78,
 81,82,85,93,108,115,
 126,127,160,171,202,
 282
MORISON 4

MOROU 122
MORRELL 27,161
MORRIS 1,5,67,75,81,
 105,123,131,133,135,
 154,160,239,281
MORRISON 98,250,264
MORROW 87,172
MORTHANS 242
MORTIMER 119
MORTON 3,101,153,220,
 230,232,252,275,276
MOSELY 15,24
MOSHER 234
MOSS 47,63,102
MOUNT 4
MUIRHARD 77
MUNCAS 103
MUNCUS 136
MUNGER 235
MUNROE 68
MUNSON 51,127,156
MURHARD 16
MURLINE 98
MURPHREA 21
MURPHREE 196,201
MURPHY 13,14,15,57,81,
 16,198
MURRAY 18,99,115,214,
 269
MURRY 265
MUSE 168,278
MUSELMAN 6
MUSQUES 176
MUSTARD 219
MUTCHINSON 169
MUZERVA 253
MYERS 115,258

N

NABERS 179
NAIL 192
NANCE 198
NASH 33
NAVAN 90
NAVARRO 9,68,87
NEAL 97,125
NEBLIN 71
NEGGAN 6
NEIBLING 66,76,77
NEIL 75,234
NEILL 57,79,81,132,
  136,148,274
NELSON 6,49,52,130,
  242,281
NERI 72
NESBETT 88
NEVILLE 194
NEWCOMB 126
NEWELL 84,236
NEWLAND 33,41,107
NEWLANDS 54,117,121,
  125,148,187

NEWMAN 8
NEWTON 63,71
NICHELSON 111
NICHOLLS 21
NICHOLS 215,243,255
NICHOLSON 48,146
NICKELSON 48,115,152,
  192,199,240
NIEBLING 28
NILES 160,165
NIXON 115,176,187,229
NOESSEL 235,249
NOLAN 30
NORGAN 94
NORRES 126
NORRIS 2
NORTH 107
NORTHINGTON 88
NORTHROP 149
NORTON 164,201
NORWOOD 150,242
NOYES 129,282
NUTTER 213

O

O'BRIAN 161
O'DONNOVAN 57
O'HARE 279
O'MALEY 205
O'NEIL 188,191,195,196
O'NEILL 54,145
O'ROURKE 137
O'STRANDER 30
OATMEAL 234
OBAR 213
OBERMEYER 124
OFFORD 248
OGDEN 146,239
OGSBURY 16
OKERMAN 41
OLAZARAN 9

OLDHAM 15,23
OLDMANN 34
OLTMANN 275
ORMOND 71
ORR 118
ORRICK 60
OSBORN 203
OSBORNE 165
OSTERMAN 208
OUTLAW 234
OWEN 24,36,89,191,212
OWENS 197
OWENSBY 259

P

PACE 271
PADILLA 143
PAGE 82,155,188,205, 264
PALACEAS 176
PALMA 246
PALMER 224
PALMES 237
PAQUIRT 33
PARAMORE 10
PAREZ 246
PARK 33,80,109,283
PARKER 6,21,25,34,72, 78,80,85,89,98,127, 131,185,186,187,225, 242
PARRIS 87
PARRISH 262
PARROT 48
PASSMORE 154
PATILLO 198,260,278
PATIS 115
PATRES 9
PATRICK 47,64,81,93
PATRIDGE 84
PATTERSON 187,220,232, 234
PAYNE 65,91,223,230
PEACE 266
PEARSON 197
PEASE 9,85
PECK 58,198
PEEK 16
PEGRAM 139
PELIE 116
PELTZER 259
PENA 176
PENADA 122
PENDLETON 39,81,126
PENN 147,259
PENNALL 115
PENNINGTON 17,86
PENNOVER 234
PENNY 208
PENROSE 48
PEOPLE 47
PEPIN 116,135
PERALTA 9
PERDEES 86
PERES 122
PERKINS 158,226
PERRY 3,19,23,25,36, 44,52,53,65,68,86, 97
PETERS 198
PETTERS 111
PETTINGER 215
PETTUCK 206
PETTUS 14,20,113
PETUS 100
PEWETT 56
PEYTON 176,277
PHELAN 87
PHELPS 68,198
PHIFER 263
PHILIPS 198,202
PHILLIPS 10,17,226
PICKERING 95
PICKETT 21
PICKUP 158
PIER 134
PIERCE 181
PIERPOINT 69
PIERPONT 107,116,167, 172,181,258
PILATE 200
PILGRIM 241
PILLIR 115
PINCKNEY 279
PINCKSTON 206
PIPER 33,122
PITKIN 185
PITTMAN 7,25
PITTUCK 64
PLACIDO 227
PLEASANTS 56
PLUMMER 51,55
POAGE 196

POCK 124
POGUE 235
POINDEXTER 123,135,154
POLLAN 186
POLLARD 5,14,38
POLLET 104
POLLEY 28,43
PONCHARD 180
PONGE 273
PONTON 77,81,109
POOL 68,155,243
PORTER 75,101,127,154,
 190,225
PORTIS 135,225
POSTELL 181
POSTLEWAITE 18
POTTER 94,228
POWELL 31,41,60,74,75,
 103,111,125,230,231,
 232

POWER 257
POWERS 28
PRATT 71,197,263
PRENTICE 122
PRENTISS 56,57,158
PRESTON 42
PREWITT 53,127
PRICE 14,27
PRIMM 198
PROCELLA 122
PROFFET 105
PRUET 278
PRUITT 242
PUELLES 9
PULSIFER 197
PUNCHARD 85
PUTNAM 106

Q

QUARLES 44
QUELIN 15
QUICK 59
QUIGLEY 8,33
QUIN 92,94

QUINDLEN 30
QUINN 98
QUIRK 98,100
QUITMAN 159

R

RABAGO 229
RABB 192,212
RAFFERTY 204
RAFFIN 83
RAGUET 104
RAINY 91
RAMESDALE 24,26
RAMSEY 128
RAMY 21
RANDALL 61,65,263
RANDOLPH 241
RANDON 21,154
RANKEN 78
RANKIN 243
RANSOM 181,234

RAQUET 104
RAWLETT 198
RAY 87
RAYMOND 138,184
READ 52,93,158,280
RECTOR 205
REDD 165,171
REDMOND 267
REED 9,24,33,62,69,88,
 202,213
REESE 14,141,153
REEVES 241
REID 47,149,183,282
REILY 152
RENAULT 85

RENDRANDO 131
REUX 148
REYNOLDS 8,20,25,54,
  149,176,179,213
RHOADES 38
RHODES 101
RHOTON 146
RIBEAU 151
RICE 126,153,241,263
RICHAMOND 146
RICHARD 121
RICHARDS 27,37
RICHARDSON 34,160,185,
  188,192,198,207,213,
  216,220,224,233
RICHERSON 81
RICHESON 169,196
RICHTER 73
RIDDELL 205
RIDDLE 22
RIDGE 149,150
RIDGWAY 141
RIGBY 180
RIGLEY 63
RIGON 176
RILEY 234
RIVES 104
RIVIER 114
ROACH 264,275
ROAME 119
ROARK 29,35
ROBB 225
ROBBINS 6,63,81,219
ROBERT 89
ROBERTS 21,82,83,93,99,
  107,110,157,159,160,
  169,192,256,258,277
ROBERTSON 22,23,36,39,
  41,95,117,229,251,259
ROBINSON 6,24,68,100,
  103,126,139,165,171,
  178,183,235,263
ROBISON 125,126,269
ROCHA 9
RODDY 192
RODERIGUES 221
RODGERS 57,81,89,91,
  135
RODRIGUEZ 9,221?
ROFF 263
ROGAN 26
ROGERS 4,45,141,183,
  258
ROJAS 163
ROLLINS 236,247
ROONEY 128
ROSAS 9
ROSE 6,18,57,122,127,
  164
ROSS 34,68,140,143,
  150,163,191,234,242
ROTH 104
ROULSTONE 34
ROUSSEAU 239
ROUTH 32,64,93
ROWE 75,124
ROXO 10
ROYAL 87
ROYALL 12,73,107
RUCKER 263
RUIS 175
RUMAIRAS 259
RUMPFF 237
RUSK 6,43,45,83,110,
  137,141,169,234
RUSSEL 82
RUSSELL 10,11,37,86,
  145
RUTER 69
RUTHVEN 263
RUTHERFORD 131,222
RUTLEDGE 169
RUTT 47
RYAL 280
RYALS 272,273
RYAN 6,75

S

SABATA 175
SACKET 80,111
SACKETT 115,134
SACKMAN 129,148
SAFFIN 188
SALAS 225
SALIGNY, DE 182,188,207
SALINAS 1
SALLEE 197,235
SALMON 44
SAMMARAT 225
SAMPLE 169,197
SANCHES 262
SANCHEZ 176,225,266
SANDERS 48,126
SANDERSON 42,68,241
SANGERMAN 201
SANOGDS 185
SANTA ANNA 48,165,270
SANTA CRUZ 9
SANTANGELO 128
SANTIESTABAN 9
SAPP 238
SARGENT 13,71,72
SARTUCHE 2
SAUL 169,209
SAUNDERS 241
SAVARIAGO 92
SAVRIEGO 269,270,273
SAWYER 89
SAYER 103,104
SCAGGS 14,15,24
SCALLELD 198
SCANNELI 69
SCARBOROUGH 186
SCATES 84,115
SCHEUSTER 48
SCHACHTENBERGER 155,185
SCHOOLFIELD 146
SCHOONHOVER 154
SCHOUTEN 240
SCHRODER 237
SCOBEY 13
SCOTT 3,10,11,30,36,41,55,59,60,78,93,105,111,117,126,138,143,149,201,210,213,222,255,280
SCURLOCK 81,234
SCURRY 227
SEBEN 234
SEBRING 77,115
SECREST 20,133,147,177,183,235,237,253
SEEGER 242
SEGMAN 230
SEGUIN 3,10,20,23,169,207,223,256,265
SEIBELS 182
SELIN 5
SELLERS 130
SERGEANT 9
SETTLE 105
SEVEY 60,112,227
SEWARD 100
SEWELL 6
SEYMORE 204
SEYMOUR 167
SHACKERLY 80
SHACKLEFORD 14,121,149,234,263
SHAINE 14
SHANKS 268
SHANNESSY 199
SHANNON 180
SHARP 30,42,126,128
SHARPE 13,14,63,73
SHAW 40,190,198,200,235,251
SHEA 58,117
SHEARN 202
SHELBY 111,203
SHELDEN 234
SHELDON 61
SHELLAN 68
SHELP 126
SHELTON 199

SHEPARD 71
SHEPHERD 76,82,84,130,
    134,200,263
SHEPPARD 133
SHEPPERD 198
SHERMAN 54,60
SHERROD 131
SHIELDS 129
SHIPMAN 75
SHIREY 99
SHOOK 224
SHORT 73
SHREVE 8
SHROCK 209
SHRUSTER 89
SHYROCK 243
SIBLEY 84
SLICRIGGS 169
SILVEY 90
SIMINGTON 214
SIMMONS 3,134,172,200
SIMON 87
SIMONS 102,201
SIMPSON 1,6,87,158,
    214,234
SIMPTON 91
SIMS 80,99,169
SINGLETON 87
SINKS 242
SKERITT 73
SKERRIT 218
SKINNER 118
SLACK 30
SLATTER 138,153
SLEEPER 87,96
SLEIGHT 58
SLOO 7
SMALL 138,169
SMEATHERS 34
SMEDIE 11
SMELSER 11
SMILEY 198
SMITH 1,3,6,9,12,14,17,
    18,24,25,27,32,37,39,
    41,44,46,47,49,51,54,
    55,60,66,68,72,78,81,

SMITH (cont.) 82,87,
    91,94,100,107,111,
    112,115,126,127,128,
    131,137,154,160,169,
    179,192,198,199,207,
    210,219,234,239,245,
    255,258,260,262,268,
    271,277,281
SMITHERS 73
SMOCK 22
SNEAD 224
SNELL 13,22,24
SNIDER 113
SNIVELY 234
SNOW 142
SNUD 136
SOLOMON 266
SOMERS 57
SOMERVELL 100
SOMERVILLE 13,257
SOULLARD 42
SOUTHMAYD 155
SOUZA 9
SPAN 232
SPARKS 63,137,169
SPEAKE 138
SPEIGHTS 139
SPICER 217,234
SPILLMAN 36,151,199,
    224,257
SPINKS 193
SPLANE 8,17
SPROAL 119
SPROWL 24,86
ST. CYR 5
ST. JOHN 273
STACK 164
STAFFORD 12,13,44,45,
    81,96,213,257
STANBACK 234
STANFORD 172
STANLEY 68,122,145,
    177,226,227
STANSBURRY 72
STANSBURY 155,207,246,
    263

STANSSBERRY 72
STAPP 3,29,62,65
STAR 130
STARK 169
STARR 6,65
STEEL 12,54
STEELE 111,228,229
STEPHENS 30,79,142,277
STEPHENSON 28,54,79,
  136,205
STERNE 81,198
STERRET 208
STEVENS 34,73,134,165,
  195,196,224
STEVENSON 15,24,59,77,
  87,178,226,231,235,
  271
STEWART 17,18,19,22,
  46,66,75,281
STICKNEY 264
STIFLER 109
STILL 219
STILLSBEY 153
STILLWELL 39,153
STILWELL 46
STIVERS 187
STOCKBRIDGE 281
STONE 130
STONUM 114
STOUFFER 8
STOUT 23,254
STOVAL 160
STRAIN 241

STRATTON 58,169
STRICKLAND 105,142,278
STRINGFELLOW 240
STRODE 234
STROM 133
STROTHER 13
STUART 4,6,183
STUBBLEFIELD 198,199
STULTZ 219
STURTEVANT 208
STYLES 4,27
SULLIVAN 224
SUMERVILLE 232
SUMMERAL 78
SUMMERS 224,237
SUTHERLAND 6,155,261
SUTTON 172
SWAIN 247,255
SWEITZER 119
SWETT 119
SWIFT 141,199
SWINNEY 193
SWISCHER 198
SWISHER 138,192,213,
  277
SWITZER 154,163
SWORD 104
SYDNOR 231,235,239
SYLVESTER 84
SYMONDS 209

T

TALBOT 74
TALLY 272
TANKERSLY 245
TARRANT 270,271,278
TASE 154,225
TATE 168
TATUM 87,207
TAYLOR 2,23,29,34,48,
  60,81,98,102,115,117,
  120,132,134,136,180,

TAYLOR (cont.) 199,
  215,223,250,256,281
TEAL 30,130
TEMPLIN 115
TERRELL 268
TERRY 39,115,184
TEULON 239
THACKSTER 8
THAXTER 15,16
THAYER 29,141

THIEL 160
THIELMAN 71,206
THOM 33,57,89
THOMAS 102,103,107,
    189,207,234,236
THOMASON 271
THOMPSON 6,14,20,31,41,
    42,43,52,104,122,136,
    140,171,198,202,207,
    214,221,223,235,246,
    264,266,267
THOMSON 261
THORN 14,137,176
THORNTON 55
THROCKMORTON 3
THURSTON 3,6
TIERWESTER 60
TIFFIN 13
TILESTON 60
TIMMINS 81
TINDALL 21
TINNIN 199
TINSLEY 48,92
TIPPET 239
TIVY 34
TOBY 17,91
TODD 13,233,239
TOLER 76,77,109
TOLEY 273
TOLLER 52

TOMKINS 33,72
TOMPKINS 71,78,149
TONY 152
TORRANT 268
TORRENT 254
TORRES 122
TORRICES 9
TOTEM 89
TOWNSEND 20,5,111,115,
    116,172
TRASK 105
TRAVIS 3,5,23,24,27,
    28,281
TREAT 219
TREMMIER 179
TREVINO 9
TRIMMER 263
TUDLOTH 65
TUMLINSON 6,20,92
TURNER 44,52,72,126,
    146,180
TURNEY 269
TUTTLE 55
TWIGS 117
TWISE 42
TWOMY 90
TYLEE 2
TYLER 49,131,193
TYNDELL 146
TYRWHITT 257

U

UFFORD 239
UGLOW 282
ULERY 144

UNDERWOOD 20,25,111,
    115,132,197
UPSHAW 56

V

VAIL 94
VALDEZ 9
VALENTINE 6
VALLEJO 9
VAN BENTHUYSEN 48
VAN BIBBER 14

VAN HORN 117
VAN HORNE 128
VAN NESS 113,173,265
VAN NORMAN 90
VAN PRADELLES 118
VANCALT 82

VANCE 214
VANCLEVE 7
VANDEVER 126
VANDEYENDER 225
VANVINEL 105
VARELA 176
VARNEY 268
VASQUEZ 280
VAUGHAN 22,122
VAUGHN 81
VEAL 241
VEDDER 94,101,105,
   115,123,135,160

VEGA 176
VELASQUEZ 9
VERAMENDI 68
VERGESS 79
VERRY 258
VICKERS 122
VIESCA 176
VINCE 73,204,254
VOLUNTINE 6
VON ROEDER 179
VOSE 11
VOST 71

W

WADDELL 26
WADE 238
WADHAM 133,149
WADSWORTH 4,14
WAGGONER 18,24
WAGNER 5
WAGONER 115
WAITE 142
WALCOTT 199
WALDEN 57,147
WALKER 7,31,53,76,78,
   117,126,162,172,185,
   213,232,234,235,241,
   260,263
WALL 234
WALLACE 3,5,14,33,77,
   154,225,234,281
WALLACH 167
WALLER 29,32,47,98,162
WALLEY 220
WALLINGFORD 123
WALLIS 118,241
WALSH 219,234
WAPLES 54
WARD 4,32,33,56,57,58,
   65,110,112,159,198,
   199,234
WARE 115
WARFIELD 158
WARNER 6,202

WATERS 10,210
WATKINS 21,208
WATROUS 105,152,184,
   238
WATSON 30,150,153
WATTS 191,192,193,194,
   195,196
WAUGH 224
WAY 119,165
WAYSHAM 208
WEAVER 54
WEBB 28,65,68,99,115,
   138,169,219,248,279
WEBSTER 30,153,160
WEEDEN 198
WEEDON 133,209
WEEKS 183
WEIGART 21
WEIR 197
WELCH 145,193
WELCHMYER 64
WELLS 6,86,92,95,171,
   199
WELSCHMEYER 21
WENDENBURG 41
WEST 12,107,198,234
WESTALL 23
WESTBROOK 61
WESTERN 133
WESTOVER 81,169

WETHERBY 174
WEYMOUTH 117
WHARTON 19,29,32,35,42,
  69,98,104,108,121,176
WHEAT 238
WHEELER 97,106,187
WHEELOCK 28
WHEELRIGHT 42,234
WHEELWRIGHT 29,31,32
WHILTBERRY 282
WHISKEY 10
WHISLER 269
WHITAKER 4,139,243
WHITE 3,6,15,17,18,19,
  21,23,34,45,60,116,
  122,164,168,177,178,
  189,205,243,256
WHITE PATH 106
WHITESIDE(S) 157,164
WHITFIELD 59
WHITING 51,122,126,127,
  158,166
WHITLEY 177
WHITNEY 171
WICKSON 157
WIER 119
WIGEN 40
WIGGINGTON 138
WIGGINS 219
WIGGINTON 52,151
WILBARGER 189,190,200
WILBOURNE 73
WILCOX 119
WILD CAT 269
WILKINS 58,74
WILKINSON 26
WILKS 209
WILLCOX 118
WILLESS 283
WILLIAM 32
WILLIAMS 12,14,43,44,57,
  60,77,83,86,87,105,
  106,135,143,148,157,
  176,197,198,199,215,
  224,228,230,233,236,
  238,239,247,272,281

WILLIAMSON 5,26,91
WILLIE 279
WILLIS 198
WILSON 3,6,7,18,53,60,
  74,84,104,115,122,
  126,151,153,160,187,
  203,213,219,224,231,
  233,234,257,261,279
WINBURN 3
WINCHELL 184
WINFIELD 36,85,155,156
WINGATE 51
WINSHIP 43
WINSTON 2,26
WINTER 87
WINTERSMITH 72
WISEMAN 118
WITLERMANN 225
WITTER 241
WOLFE 3
WOLSEY 115
WOOD 1,3,36,45,199,
  221,225
WOODARD 186
WOODHOUSE 239
WOODLIEF 8,25,135
WOODRUFF 33,72,131,219
WOODS 59,60,126,129,
  203,225,234
WOODWARD 18,21,42,83,
  143,151,168,191,195,
  197
WOOSTER 29,203
WOOTEN 199
WORK 200
WORNEL 6
WORTH 269
WORTHINGTON 13,105
WRAY 28,53
WRENTMORE 1
WRIGHT 6,45,46,49,54,
  82,86,97,103,115,
  146,169,177,234,238,
  267
WYATT 70,122
WYBRANTS 168

WYERS 25
WYLIE 225,277
WYNGATE 81

WYNN 4,32,45
WYNNS 43,57,81,204

Y

YARBOROUGH 88
YATES 51,230,241
YEAGER 86
YERBY 21

YOCUM 198,276,277,278
YORK 3,20,30
YOUNG 17,18,19,34,54,
    259

Z

ZAMBRANO 113,114
ZANCO 6
ZAVALA 16,53,234,266,267

ZAVALLA 143,177
ZUMWALT 65,69

PLACE INDEX

ALABAMA, TX 201,242
ALGIERS, LA 240
ALLEY'S CROSSING 20
ANAHUAC 58,76,189,207, 272
ANGELINA RIVER 83,109
ARROYO SECO 84,98
ATTUSCACITO 20,26
AUSTIN 130,134,153,159, 160,163,165,166,170, 173,181,182,184,187, 188,189,190,191,197, 200,205,210,216,218, 224,228,229,235,239, 244,246,248,251,252, 255,262,267,271,274, 278
AUSTIN COUNTY 20,25,26, 34,39,65,66,82,85,88, 103,111,118,123,178, 180,181,182,185,196, 197,199,200,201,209, 215,221,230,232,243, 244,247,249,257,259, 264,275
AUSTIN'S COLONY 70,98
AYISH BAYOU 109
BAILEY'S PRAIRIE 13,27, 28,46
BASTROP 68,128,134,147, 159,171,191,197,206, 207,230,231,238,249
BASTROP COUNTY 52,89, 103,109,125,132,133, 157,165,198,200,239
BATIST VILLAGE 79
BAY PRAIRIE 1
BEAUMONT 27,79,197,259
BERNARD 118
BEXAR COUNTY 35,65,66, 67,68,72,87,90,101, 103,107,113,132,145, 207,281
BIDAIS VILLAGE 221

BIG CREEK 142,157,230
BOIS D'ARC 188,217,218
BOLIVAR 173
BOSQUE RIVER 188
BOWIE COUNTY 254,260
BRAY'S BAYOU 49,61, 150,164
BRAZORIA 3,7,8,10,11, 12,13,15,17,19,22, 28,30,31,32,33,37, 38,41,42,44,45,51, 85,93,97,99,101,105, 116,117,118,119,124, 138,181,275
BRAZORIA COUNTY 17,18, 20,22,23,24,26,27, 30,35,36,37,39,44, 47,49,56,61,62,66, 67,68,73,75,82,85, 86,90,102,104,105, 106,109,111,113,116, 118,124,125,130,133, 137,138,151,152,197, 199,220,232,234,248, 264,268,269,275,280
BRAZOS DE SANTIAGO 29
BRAZOS RIVER 7,11,12, 14,18,35,38,39,48, 53,69,76,96,97,103, 104,108,111,112,119, 129,154,157,176,184, 188,189,190,214,217, 222,229,258,263,270, 271,278
BRAZOS SANTIAGO 163
BRAZOS TIMBER 127
BRUSHY CREEK 165
BUFFALO BAYOU 30,32, 203,208,213,232,250, 283
BURNET'S COLONY 88
CALHOUN 202,281
CAMP ARNOLD 110
CAMP HARRIS 146

CAMP INDEPENDENCE 22
CAMP JOHNSON 12,13,14,
  16,18,19
CAMP LaBACCA 12
CAMP RABB 211
CANEY 21,118,157
CANEY CREEK 12,16,70,
  178,268
CAROLINA 147,172
CASA BLANCA 196
CAYCE'S FERRY 16
CEDAR BAYOU 37,122,123,
  210,277
CEDAR LAKE 157
CENTRE HILL 54,62,82,
  123,179,200,270,271
CHAMBERS' CREEK 217
CHAMBERSIA 189,207,272
CHEROKEE NATION 140,
  141,144,146,149,150
CHEROKEE VILLAGE 83
CHIHUAHUA 34
CHOCOLATE BAYOU 17,27,
  40
CIBOLO 34,35,132
CINCINNATI, TX 58,93,
  205,258,266,267,279
CLARKSVILLE 106,258,
  259,260
CLEAR CREEK 162
COAHUILA 109
COLE'S SETTLEMENT 15,24
COLETO 9,186
COLORADO CITY 99,180
COLORADO COUNTY 8,26,
  46,51,66,96,109,149,
  197,198,212,215,234,
  235,243
COLORADO RIVER 15,16,
  20,26,45,76,89,118,
  125,147,157,161,162,
  178,188,190,192,211,
  212
COLUMBIA 8,9,10,11,12,
  13,14,15,16,17,18,19,
  20,21,22,23,24,25,27,

COLUMBIA (cont.) 31,
  34,37,43,49,61,73,
  74,75,82,103,104,
  111,142,263
COLUMBUS 51,54,133,
  147,178
COMANCHE VILLAGE 211,
  212,274
CONCHO RIVER 211
COPANO BAY 86
CORPUS CHRISTI 161,
  221,260,262,266
COUSHATTA VILLAGES 56
CROCKETT 224,241,268
CROSS TIMBERS 254,277,
  278
CUMMINGS CREEK 1,46,
  129,177
CYPRESS BAYOU 277
CYPRESS CREEK 223
DIMMIT'S LANDING 12,
  14,66,190
DOUBLE BAYOU 207
DUNCAN'S FERRY 93
EAGLE ISLAND 121
EAST COLUMBIA 87,128
EGYPT 215
ELYSIUM FIELDS 260
FALLS-OF-THE-BRAZOS
  108,111,224,229,234
FANNIN COUNTY 65,106,
  140,148,197,198,214,
  254,262,280
FARMINGTON 91
FAYETTE COUNTY 34,97,
  129,177,178,179,180,
  188,197,198,211,212,
  213,216
FAYETTEVILLE 127
FORT BEND 21,46
FORT BEND COUNTY 62,
  65,68,78,90,96,101,
  108,119,127,136,138,
  144,145,157,184,185,
  197,213,220,221,225,
  230,231,232,233,237,

FORT BEND (cont.) 251,
  252,256,275,276
FORT ENGLISH 277
FORT HOUSTON 88,146,
  267,268
FORT JESSUP 182
FORT KINGSBORO 267,268
FORT KINGSBOROUGH 278
FORT LAMAR 145
FORT OLDHAM 69,76
FRANKLIN 139,176,208
FROST TOWN 232
GALVESTON 18,19,29,30,
  33,49,58,60,72,78,80,
  80,82,84,91,101,102,
  107,115,130,134,136,
  142,145,146,150,151,
  159,160,162,164,170,
  187,191,199,200,202,
  206,213,215,217,219,
  221,224,227,231,236,
  238,239,242,244,247,
  257,261,264,281,282
GALVESTON BAY 37,38,41,
  42,51,58,93,102,189,
  201,210,214,236,273
GALVESTON COUNTY 88,89,
  94,128,137,198,234
GALVESTON ISLAND 40,45,
  62,74
GOLIAD 1,14,34,59,73,
  74,92,102,255,270
GOLIAD COUNTY 67,87,
  198,230,231
GONZALES 3,6,12,62,89,
  106,107,136,147,192,
  260
GONZALES COUNTY 63,65,
  75,76,77,79,84,87,92,
  124,143,154,157,165,
  191,198,199,241
GREEN'S BAYOU 197
GREENVILLE 258
GROCE'S RETREAT 17,46,
  76,121,154,182,225,
  241

GUADALUPE RIVER 12,68,
  101,103,126,192
GULF PRAIRIE 23
HARRIS COUNTY 171,177,
  183,185,186,193,195,
  197,198,199,201,203,
  204,209,210,213,221,
  223,227,230,231,232,
  237,240,241,244,245,
  250,252,252,253,254,
  256,257,259.261,263,
  264,265,269,274,275,
  279,281,282
HARRISBURG 10,11,28,
  32,33,39,46,49,52,
  53,57,59,66,74,88,
  102,120,135,141,166,
  188,233
HARRISBURG COUNTY 26,
  35,36,37,40,43,54,
  59,61,64,67,69,72,
  74,75,77,80,81,82,
  84,85,88,89,91,92,
  102,103,105,111,113,
  115,116,117,119,121,
  122,125,127,130,131,
  132,136,138,140,146,
  148,149,150,151,152,
  153,154,155,156,159,
  160,162,164,167,201,
  204,215,219
HARRISON COUNTY 198,
  199,232,239,257
HODGE'S BEND 127
HOUSTON 25-36,38-49,
  51-58,60,61,63,66,
  67-69,71,72,74,76,
  77,78-80,82-85,87,
  88,90,91,93,94,96,
  97-99,101,103-111,
  113-117,119,121-125,
  127,129-132,134,136,
  137,139-141,143,144,
  147,150-152,154,155,
  159,160,162,163,166,
  167,172-174,182-189,

HOUSTON (cont.) 197,
  199,200,202-204,206,
  207,208,210,214,216,
  217,219,221,224-227,
  230-232,235,237,239,
  240,243-248,250-252,
  255,256,261,263,264,
  268,271,275,276,281,
  282,283
HOUSTON COUNTY 65,88,
  194,197,198,205,241,
  249,281
HUNTSVILLE 72,93
INDEPENDENCE 139,179,
  222,255,273,279
INDIAN VILLAGES 268,
  277,278
JACKSON COUNTY 24,52,55,
  56,57,65,66,77,78,86,
  88,89,109,114,115,
  155,198,199
JASPER 224,260,271
JASPER COUNTY 65,134,
  135,197-199,260,276
JEFFERSON COUNTY 65,79,
  183,198,199,205,259,
  260,264,276-278,280
JONESBOROUGH 260
KINGSBORO 268
KRONKEWAY BAYOU 164
LA BACA, PORT OF 119
LA BACCA RIVER 8,12,13,
  14,18,19,76,147
LA BAHIA 9
LaGRANGE 97,99,129,147,
  157,161,179,189,190,
  192,213,230
LAKE CREEK 17
LAMAR 266
LAMAR COUNTY 260
LAREDO 100,218,219,246
LAVACA RIVER 147,192
LEPANTILAN 2
LIBERTY 22,27,57,58,66,
  118,122,137,148,150,
  151,156,158,172,183,

LIBERTY (cont.) 224,
  225,247,248,274-276
LIBERTY COUNTY 27,79,
  94,118,122,127,130,
  132,133,134,137,148,
  156,157,158,183,191,
  193,198,199,201,221,
  225,231,237,238,248,
  253,269,275,279
LINNVILLE 147,190,191,
  192-196,209
LITTLE RIVER 2,194,
  217,229,234
LYNCHBURG 13,120,181,
  209,266
MARION 16,23,24,25,35,
  43,46,54,62
MATAGORDA 15,16,19,23,
  24,32,41,99,101,104,
  118,151,167,191,192,
  202,203,267
MATAGORDA COUNTY 21,
  30,66,142,149,171,
  197,198
MATAMOROS 25,29,35,42,
  92,109,117,121,163,
  164,206,259,261,265,
  272,273
MEDINA RIVER 184
MELON CREEK 86
MENARD COUNTY 273
MENARD'S CREEK 156
MEXICO 46,148,151,163,
  154,166,167,174,175
MEXICO CITY 22,242
MILAM 27,41,85
MILAM COUNTY 28,65,66,
  75,78,100,127,139,
  166,190,198,199,214,
  228,261
MILAM'S COLONY 20,157
MINA 1,31,32,45
MISSION SAN JOSE 173
MONTGOMERY 80,93,125,
  128,130,133,139,160,
  179,180,209,224,248

MONTGOMERY COUNTY 63,
    65,72,75,76,91,93,98,
    99,125,128,139,143,
    151,163,165,177,178,
    180,182,197,198,205,
    215,217,222,223,233,
    246,249,262,265,271,
    274,278,279,280,281
MONTVILLE 2
MORALES 174
NACAMCHE RANCH 129
NACOGDOCHES 6,8,10,26,
    45,63,64,66,67,76,80,
    83,93,100,101,104,
    123,126,129,130,132,
    137,141,168,177,200,
    224,248,258,260,268
NACOGDOCHES COUNTY 65,
    78,167,197,198,199,
    234,267
NASHVILLE, TX 184,224,
    229,261,274
NASHVILLE COLONY 228
NAVASOTA 231
NAVASOTA RIVER 110,176
NAVIDAD RIVER 55,62,155
NECHES RIVER 109,141,
    238,276
NECHES SALINE 145
NEW ORLEANS 1,2,3,4,5,
    6,7,9,13,17,19,21,24,
    25,29,30,39,41,42,54,
    63,71,74,75,76,77,80,
    84,86,91,92,93,106,
    121,125,146,161,183,
    187,188,206,206,225,
    236,240,247,256,259,
    261,282
NEW WASHINGTON 47,62,
    64,81,93,94,202,214,
    236
NEW YEAR'S CREEK 22,85,
    91,157,230
NUECES RIVER 1,34,100,
    161,185,260
OCEOLA 205

OLD RIVER 94,118
ORANGE GROVE 42,44
OROZIMBO 10
OYSTER CREEK 29,32,37
PANOLA COUNTY 260
PARIS, TX 260
PASEO DE NORTE 167
PEACH CREEK 157,163,
    230
PEACH POINT 18,23,44
PECAN BAYOU 167
PEDERNALES RIVER 160,244
PIN OAK CREEK 157
PINA CREEK 82
PINE ISLAND BAYOU 276
PINE POINT 68
PINEY POINT 51
PLEASANT HILL 76
PLUM CREEK 191,192,
    193,196
POINT BOLIVAR 14
PORT CADDO 260
POWHATAN 231
PRAIRIE BAY 273
PRESIDIO DE RIO GRANDE
    175
QUINTANA 9,10,37,105,
    114
RED LANDS, THE 25,96
RED RIVER 27,141,148,
    188,214,218,258,267
RED RIVER COUNTY 66,
    97,105,106,107,114,
    117,197,198,199,254,
    258,259
REFUGIO 272,280
REFUGIO COUNTY 66,85,
    86,140,197,198,266
RICHLAND CREEK 255
RICHMOND 25,29,49,56,
    66,73,77,82,91,96,
    101,109,112,120,127,
    129,139,145,152,157,
    174,220,226,230,231,
    232,237,242,256,271,
    272,275

RIO BLANCO 73,157,230
RIO COLORADO 259
RIO FRIO 260
RIO GRANDE 100,140,189,
 256,260,269,280
RIO NOSA 191
RIVER DEL NORTE 166,167
ROBERTSON COUNTY 66,77,
 106,113,166,175,176,
 197,208,214,228,229,
 235,270
ROBERTSON'S COLONY 18,
 20,33,51,228,229,251
ROBINSON COUNTY 136,139
RUTERSVILLE 172,187,
 188,224
SABINE CITY 164
SABINE COUNTY 41,65,78,
 85,134,198,199,227,
 268
SABINE RIVER 44,54,218,
 267,270
SAINT MARKS 190
SALT CREEK 205
SALTILLO 218,219,256
SAN ANTONIO 7,40,43,67,
 73,84,133,147
SAN ANTONIO DE BEXAR
 1,2,3,4,5,6,12,17,20,
 23,33,35,36,48,69,72,
 76,77,80,92,95,96,98,
 100,103,106,108,135,
 148,170,171,173,174,
 181,184,187,189,194,
 199,206,212,230,246,
 256
SAN ANTONIO PRAIRIE
 76,77
SAN ANTONIO RIVER 101,
 111,184
SAN ANTONIO ROAD 111
SAN AUGUSTINE 30,45,89,
 108,109,113,116,117,
 122,136,187,200,224,
 260,263,267
SAN AUGUSTINE COUNTY
 27,65,108,163,167,
 198,199,243,257
SAN BERNARD 38,70,149,
 181,257
SAN BERNARD RIVER 19,
 38,76,181
SAN FELIPE 47,54,127,
 141,150,157,159,232,
 273
SAN FELIPE DE AUSTIN
 1,2,5,12,14,16,30,
 68,100,180,182,185,
 197,215,228,244,247,
 249,259,264,274
SAN GABRIEL 153,160,
 210
SAN JACINTO 8,9,104,
 105,119,174,182,224
SAN JACINTO BAY 13,16
SAN JACINTO RIVER 93,
 130,163,274
SAN LEON 95
SAN LUIS 194,207,221,
 222
SAN MARCOS RIVER 143
SAN PATRICIO 2,25,44,
 121,206
SAN PATRICIO COUNTY
 66,67,140,185,266
SAN SABA 162,252
SAN SABA RIVER 210
SANTA FE 34,207,250,
 253,255,258,282
SEGUIN 181
SEVILLA 34
SHELBY COUNTY 106,110,
 123,191,198,199,213,
 239,257,258,270,278
SHELBYVILLE 123,270,
 278
SHREVEPORT 90,209
SPILLMAN'S ISLAND 224
SPRING CREEK 2,31,144,
 154

SLAVE NAME INDEX

ABRAM 97,195,188
ADALIA 272
ADILEGNA 37
ADO 37
AGGA 93
AMANDA 221
ANDREW 93
ANN 137
ANTHONY 37
ARCH 33
ARTHUR 38
BARCOLA 37
BARKER 120
BEN 36,54,105
BETSY 105
BILL 64,220
BOB 70,172,220,235, 241
BROWN 263
BUCK 99
CAIN 152
CALEB 139
CAREY 169
CAROLINE 93
CATO 37, 136
CATY 143
CHARLES 238,248
CHARLOTTE 93,152
CORNELIUS 214
CUDJO 37
CURTIS 264
DANIEL 37
DAVID 191
DICK 37,137
DOC 120
DOCTOR 51
DOO 124
DUDLEY 62,85
EDWARD 105
ELI 37
ELIZA 82
ELLEN 177
EMILA 93
EPHRAIM 136
EVELINA 133
FRANK 143,221

FRED 183
FREDERICK 183
GABRIEL 79,152
GEORGE 37,38
GUMBY 29
HARRIET 64
HARRY 37
HENRY 51,93,105,178
HET 86
IONA 33
ISAAC 132,221,268
ITALIA 31,37
JACOB 121,136
JAKE 268
JANE 44,64
JEFFERSON 90
JERRY 223
JESSE 36,186
JIM 16,148
JINNEY 64
JOE 27,28,51,158,177, 232
JOHN 6
JUDA 105
JUDGE 105
JULIA 52
LAVINIA 158
LEM 167
LEMUEL 67
LEVI 162
LEVICE 272
LEWIS 6,64
LUFA 124
LUFFER 120
LUKE 39
LUTHER 124
MADISON 262
MARANDA 101
MARIA 64
MARK 85
MARLA 105
MARY 105
MELISSA 264
MILES 241
MILLY 156
MINTA 147

MOSES 156
NANCY 139
NELSON 8,215
NIECE 105
PATSY 183
PEN 172
PENNY 172
PETER 37,121,169
PLANNER 57,173
PRISCILLA 105
QUACCO 37
RALPH 143
RAPHAEL 125
REUBEN 82
RICHARD 137
SACKEY 62
SAM 180,209
SANCO 124
SANDY 209
SARAH 143,222,264

SEWARD 262
SHELBY 51
SIMON 37
SYRUS 121
THORNTON 94
TITUS 238
TOM 29,135,137,264, 267
TONEY 37
VIOLET 121
WARWICK 262
WASH 72,114
WASHINGTON 72
WILL 31
WILLARD 152
WILLIAM 93
WILLOWE 37
WINNY 93
WINTER 90

www.ingramcontent.com/pod-product-compliance
Lightning Source LLC
Chambersburg PA
CBHW070230230426
43664CB00014B/2262